S0-BNK-069

The Other Minorities

Nonethnic Collectivities
Conceptualized as
Minority Groups

Edited by
Edward Sagarin
City College of New York

The Other
Minorities

XEROX COLLEGE PUBLISHING

Waltham, Massachusetts   Toronto

CONSULTING EDITORS

Gladys E. Lang
Center for Urban Education, New York City

Kurt Lang
State University of New York at Stony Brook

To Esther Gertrude Sagarin
who understands the meaning of compassion

Preface

The idea for this work grew out of many classroom discussions with students in my minority groups classes, and was sharpened during my own studies of deviant behavior (and then, specifically, organizations of deviant people), in which I could not help but be struck by the similarities of the rhetoric used by the ethnic minorities and by deviant people, and by the forces opposing both of these types of groups. Over a period of time, I discussed this theme on many occasions with Milton Barron of City College of New York, who offered many helpful suggestions.

The articles by Hacker (homosexuals), Goldstein, Kuehn, Kameny and Howard are original for this book. Jordan has added new material to his article. The introductory chapter, written by myself, was read by several of my colleagues and friends, and I benefited from numerous suggestions that they made. I want to thank all of them: Joseph Bensman, Robert Bierstedt, Arnold Birenbaum, Robert J. Kelly, and Kurt Lang. Finally, Kurt Lang went over the plan for the book before it really got under way, and the entire book after it was completed (or at least I thought it was, until he sent me a couple of suggestions).

My thanks to all.

EDWARD SAGARIN

Spring, 1971

Contents

1

From the Ethnic Minorities to the Other Minorities 1

EDWARD SAGARIN

2

Gender and Sex 21

Women as a Minority Group
HELEN MAYER HACKER 23

A Parallel to the Negro Problem
GUNNAR MYRDAL 42

Homosexuals as a Minority Group
FRANKLIN E. KAMENY 50

Homosexuals: Deviant or Minority Group?
HELEN MAYER HACKER 65

3

Young and Old 93

The Image of the Adolescent Minority
EDGAR Z. FRIEDENBERG 95

The Condemnation and Persecution of Hippies
MICHAEL E. BROWN 107

Adolescents as a Minority Group in Era of Social Change
EUGENE B. BRODY   133

The Aged as a Quasi-Minority Group
MILTON L. BARRON   148

4

Disabled and Disadvantaged   163

Uncle Tom and Tiny Tim:
  Some Reflections on the Cripple as Negro
LEONARD KRIEGEL   165

Lilliputians in Gulliver's Land: The Social Role of the Dwarf
MARCELLO TRUZZI   183

Physical Disability as a Social Psychological Problem
LEE MEYERSON   205

The Social Psychology of Physical Disability
ROGER G. BARKER   210

Social Changes, Minorities, and the Mentally Retarded
LOUIS H. ORZACK   224

Clumsiness and Stupidity: An Analogy
LEWIS ANTHONY DEXTER   236

Status, Ideology, and Adaptation to Stigmatized Illness:
  A Study of Leprosy
ZACHARY GUSSOW AND GEORGE S. TRACY   242

The Disadvantaged Group:
  A Concept Applicable to the Physically Handicapped
SIDNEY JORDAN   262

5

Transgressors and Enforcers   275

Ex-Convicts Conceptualized as a Minority Group
WILLIAM C. KUEHN   277

The Radical Right as a Minority Group
JOHN HOWARD   288

Crisis in Blue: The Police as a Minority Group
JEFFREY GOLDSTEIN   306

6

Intellectuals and Stereotypes   319

The Intellectual and the Language of Minorities
MELVIN SEEMAN   320

Sociology and the Intellectuals: An Analysis of a Stereotype
BENNETT M. BERGER   339

From the Ethnic Minorities to the Other Minorities

1

Edward Sagarin

Social scientists have for many years delved into the phenomenon by which some groups of people are hereditarily assigned to a subordinate position in societies by virtue of their race, religion, caste, country of origin, ancestry, language community, and, perhaps, class. Excepting for the moment class, one can combine the variety of hereditary or ascribed groups under the single heading of ethnicity (although sometimes *ethnic* is used in a narrower sense, referring only to societal identification and not racial or religious). In a pluralistic society, when an ethnic group, or several of them, is kept in a subordinate position and its members are judged collectively rather than individually, the subordinate ethnic collectivity is called a minority group. The superordinate is generally called the dominant or majority group, for which the former terminology is preferable because it expresses power relationships and avoids placing the minority into a numerical framework.

I

American sociology at an early period became deeply interested in minority groups in the effort to understand and to explain (in some instances, to explain away) the nature of a pluralistic society in which there was inequality of opportunity or, to use Weber's expression, "of life chances," built not only along social class lines but much more obviously and immutably along ethnic lines. Thus, the sociology of minority groups began to concentrate almost exclusively on the study of ethnic groups in a subordinate position. The concept of minorities (but not the word) was discussed in the proceedings of the German Sociological Society as early as 1910 or 1911.[1] In 1932, Donald Young coined the term *minority* in his text on intergroup

1

relations, *The American Minority Peoples*,[2] taking the word from the phrase *national minorities*, which had been in use for some time.

As the sociology of intergroup relations grew, Young's *minority peoples* became *minority groups*. At the same time, other writers, such as the European, Ernst Gruenfeld, were describing marginal men or peripherals: for example, the maimed, the blind, the old, and the lepers.[3] One might describe such persons, both the ethnic minorities and the peripherals, as being not quite in a society but on the outskirts of it; perhaps in it but not of it; a part of it, yet apart from it.

Despite some apparent similarity, marginals and peripherals began to be differentiated from ethnic minorities in sociological description and analysis. For one thing, marginals were often individuals—not entire families sharing their marginality with large numbers of other families, not living together as a cohesive interacting subunit of a society, and not passing on the marginality by self-perpetuating heredity. Some marginals would lose their marginality in due time. For example, the immigrant would have American-born children who would not speak with the accent of a foreigner. Other peripherals could not aspire to the same blamelessness for their subordinate position in society as did the ethnic minorities. This was the case with habitual drunkards, skid row derelicts, and prostitutes.

The two themes were developing side by side; it remained for some writers to see that the aspects of minority groups mentioned by Young and developed entirely around racial and ethnic examples were in a limited way applicable to the nonethnic marginals and peripherals.

II

Some sociologists have objected, and still do, that the word "minority" has a clear-cut numerical connotation. Perhaps it was an unfortunate choice. Bierstedt wrote:

> . . . in recent years problems of prejudice have been identified with—and labeled as—minority-group problems. The relationship of majorities is indeed relevant to prejudice, but it is incorrect to conclude that the victims of prejudice are always members of minority groups. Many minority groups are not discriminated against at all and some majority groups have attracted vicious persecution. Doctors of philos-

ophy, millionaires, and residents of the city of St. Louis, Missouri, for example, are all minorities in the American population, but they hardly suffer discrimination on that account.[4]

Where in retrospect Young may be criticized for coining this phrase and using it in the form that he did, Bierstedt was here fighting a losing battle. Language has changed to the point where one can speak of the black people of Rhodesia as a minority group in the sociological meaning of the term, and of the white people of that country as a minority (the idiom of the language restrains me from writing, *as a minority group*) in the numerical sense of the word. Bierstedt's objection might prove helpful, however, in focusing attention on the neglected question of majority groups, that is, numerical majorities, on which he has himself written one of the few pieces in a very sparse literature.[5]

One of the first efforts to define the concept of minority, after it had been in use for several years, was made by Louis Wirth:

> We may define a minority as a group of people who, because of their physical or cultural characteristics, are singled out from the others in the society in which they live for differential and unequal treatment and who therefore regard themselves as objects of collective discrimination.[6]

Implicit in this definition is that the minority singled out for differential and unequal treatment is accorded inferior treatment. Quite obviously, the whites of Mississippi (or for that matter of America generally) have been singled out from others "for differential and unequal treatment," and the white schools have been separate and unequal just as have the black. But the whites were on the upper end of the inequality continuum, and from that point of view, a minority existed, but the whites were not such.

Although it is seen in his definition, and in other aspects of Wirth's discussion of this relationship, that many groups other than ethnics might fit into the minority group framework that he had built, nowhere is this lead followed by Wirth himself. When Wirth speaks of physical or cultural characteristics, he refers not to gender or age, disability or stigmatized behavior pattern, but specifically to race, religion, and other ethnic-identification qualities. Thus, his explicit examples center around Negroes and Jews, around racial and ethnic groups.

Wirth's definition that the singled out groups "regard themselves as objects of collective discrimination" is a subjective criterion similar to the famed Thomas dictum: "If men define situations as real, they are real in their consequences." But Wirth goes a step further, for he seems to be saying here that if men define a situation as real (that is, that they are singled out for unequal treatment), then it is real (that is, they are a minority group).

One turns to another definition, whose simplicity would tend to conceal its sociological origin. From Arnold and Caroline Rose: "The mere fact of being generally hated because of religious, racial or nationality background is what defines a minority group."[7]

Later, I shall return to the question of being hated, and first wish to focus on Wirth's collective discrimination.

III

What is collective discrimination? It can be likened, as by Peter Berger,[8] to "bad faith," *la mauvaise foi* of Jean-Paul Sartre. The bad faith consists in perceiving an individual as a member of a group and fitting him into a mental framework for prejudging him accordingly. In the colorful expression of Libby Benedict, what a minority group seeks is "the right to have fools and scoundrels—without being condemned as a group. Every group has about the same proportion of wrongdoers. But when wrongdoers belong to a minority their number is magnified in the minds of other people. . . . Minorities would gladly give up the reflected glory of their great men, if only the world didn't burden them with the ignominy of their scoundrels."[9] Such is a theme that runs through the Simple stories of Langston Hughes, and the best textbooks on prejudice and minority group relations. It is expressed by those who dissociate from wrongdoers in their ethnic group, as an Italian-American lawmaker who was asked by an accused racketeer why it is always one of his own kind who turns on him, and the lawmaker replied:

> I am not your kind and you're not my kind. My manner, morals and mores are not yours. The only thing we have in common is that we both spring from an Italian heritage and culture—and you are the traitor to that heritage and culture which I am proud to be part of.[10]

"Give us the right to have scoundrels among us!" suggests Benedict as a rational slogan for minority groups.[11] When the theme of collective discrimination, of being judged collectively and at the same time negatively as a member of a group rather than as an individual, is studied, it becomes clear that it is applicable to many other than the ethnics. Several writers were to see this, sometimes quite sharply, often quite controversially, but usually drawing an analogy not between the marginal, peripheral, stigmatized generally and the ethnic minorities, but between one such group and minorities, or between one subordinate or disadvantaged nonethnic and another that was ethnic. Early in American history, the feminist and the Abolitionist movements were linked, most of those in one movement lending support to the other, and Frederick Douglass, in fact, ardently supported woman suffrage as part of his struggle for total human suffrage and human equality.

Everett Hughes, in an article on the marginal man which appeared, significantly, in *Phylon,* repeatedly showed similarities between the status of women in American society and the status of Negroes. "People are accustomed to act toward women in certain ways. Likewise, the Negro has a traditional role."[12] And again, discussing the possibility that marginality might be reduced, Hughes points out that a given status might disappear *as a status:* "The word 'woman' could cease to have social meaning, and become merely a biological designation without any status or role connotations. . . . The word Negro would disappear, as it has tended to do in certain times and countries—in favor of a series of terms which would describe complexion and feature." Here, Hughes emphasizes that people would still have dissimilarity (the physiological differences), and would still be grouped according to that similarity, but there would no longer be role expectations specifically assigned to a given person by virtue of the fact that she is a woman or that he or she is a Negro.

But the convergence of the two themes—marginality defined as a result of ethnic-minority status and as a result of some other characteristic—is made most explicit by Hughes in another passage:

> Up to this point, I have kept women and Negroes before you as illustrations of people with a status dilemma. American Negroes, products of migration and of the mixing of races and cultures that

they are, are the kind of case to which the term marginal man has been conventionally applied. I have used the case of women to show that the phenomenon is not, in essence, one of racial and cultural mixing.[13]

The perceptive literary critic and social thinker, Kenneth Burke, likewise linked an ethnic minority theme with peripheral-marginality. Speaking of André Gide's *Travels in the Congo,* "with its protests against the systematic injustice meted out to the Negroes at the hands of the concessionaires," Burke went on to comment:

> It is doubtful, I grant, whether Gide arrived at his useful position through wholly untrammeled motives. The Olympian result shows traces of troubled, Orphic beginnings. It seems likely that his concern with homosexuality, and his struggle for its "recognition," early gave him a sense of divergence from the social norms among which he lived, and in time this sense of divergence was trained upon other issues. In seeking, let us say, to defend a practice which society generally considered reprehensible, he came to defend practices which society considered more reprehensible.[14]

Among those who found a link of similarity between the minorities (particularly the American Negroes) and women was Gunnar Myrdal. As he makes explicit in the appendix devoted to this subject in *An American Dilemma,*[15] the treatment of the Negro has some points of similarity with treatment of women and children in Europe (in fact, in every society), but in the development of his argument, he completely drops the children from sight. Simone de Beauvoir, French existentialist and modern-day feminist, expands the analogy in *The Second Sex.*

> The central thesis of Mlle de Beauvoir's book [writes the translator in a preface] is that since patriarchal times women have in general been forced to occupy a secondary place in the world in relation to men, a position comparable in many respects with that of racial minorities in spite of the fact that women constitute at least half of the human race, and further that this secondary standing is not imposed of necessity by natural "feminine" characteristics but rather by strong environmental forces of educational and social tradition under the purposeful control of men.[16]

What de Beauvoir maintained was that men were (in their own eyes) people, women were members of the female sex, the second sex, the other sex:

> A man never begins by presenting himself as an individual of a certain sex; it goes without saying that he is a man. The terms *masculine* and *feminine* are used symmetrically only as a matter of form, as on legal papers. . . .
> The category of the *Other* is as primordial as consciousness itself.[17]

When Simone de Beauvoir writes that the sphere to which woman belongs "is everywhere enclosed, limited, dominated, by the male universe," she is writing also of the sphere in which American Negroes are enclosed, Ulster Catholics and Spanish Protestants, Jews in many lands and Arabs in Israel, and homosexuals, cripples, and others. Two themes, the ethnics and the peripherals, including the stigmatized and the deviant, here converge.

IV

While several writers looking at women, homosexuals, aged, teenagers, physically handicapped, and others, drew the comparison and began to think of the group under study as a minority group, with few exceptions general studies of minority groups and of dominant-majority/subordinate-minority relations tended to continue to emphasize only the ethnics. Even the civil rights struggle, with its slogans that had origins in the racial situation and which were then taken over by other groups for their own advancement and purposes, did not succeed in broadening the minority group concept.

In the sociological literature, Simpson and Yinger entitle their work *Racial and Cultural Minorities*[18] (probably the longest and most comprehensive of the texts) but do not define cultural to be able to encompass other than the hereditary, family-linked ethnic groups within the rubric. There is little in Allport's *The Nature of Prejudice*[19] that deals specifically with prejudice other than against ethnics. Although most of his broad conceptual formations and insights are readily applicable to wide numbers of stigmatized peoples, Allport stops short of calling such to the reader's attention. Barron has written an essay on the aged as a minority (or to use his term, a "quasi-minority"),[20] but in his work devoted to minorities there is nothing on the aged, women, teenagers, or any other non-ethnic,[21] an indication of the manner in which sociologists have tended to compartmentalize their substantive areas of interest. In the more psychologically oriented studies of prejudice, particularly *The Authoritarian Personality*,[22] negative attitudes toward homosexuals are linked with those against Negroes and Jews, but, although this suggests that the victims or targets of this prejudice might be in the same social situation, nowhere do Adorno and his colleagues draw this conclusion (which is not to criticize a major work for what it failed to do, because their focus was on the personality of the prejudiced person, not on the group identification, defenses, and retaliation of the victims). Even in a paper whose title, "Minority Groups—A Revision of Concepts," gave promise that the minority theme might properly be extended to encompass some nonhereditary groups, one finds the author concerned rather with the problem of what constitutes a people, a nation, a race, an ethnic group, or a nationality.[23]

V

There is another expression or phrase that might have been used to describe oppressed sections of a society; it is a phrase that was used by Weber: "pariah people." Essentially, the concept of pariah has been applied to caste societies, as, for example, in this passage from Berreman:

> Pariah status or "untouchability" is another special variety of caste organization; in this case structurally rather than regionally or culturally specific. It refers to the intrinsically polluted, stigmatized, denigrated and excluded caste status found in many societies. . . . Pariah castes and the relations between pariah and nonpariah castes are recurrent and interesting phenomena within the category of caste organization.[24]

Berreman proceeds to compare the pariah-nonpariah relations in India with those of other national and ethnic groups, but nowhere does he suggest a similarity between the caste pariahs and, for example, lepers (who have been and for that matter still are defined by members of societies as untouchables, intrinsically polluted, denigrated, and excluded).

But if one were to shift one's label and the connotations thereof from minority to pariah, the definition given by Arnold and Caroline Rose (a definition of minority group) begins to make more sense: "the mere fact of being generally hated." One does not have to add the rest of their statement: "because of religious, racial or nationality background [or caste]." What defines the pariah group is that just being a member induces hate. The factor of collective discrimination is there, of course, but it serves only to buttress hatred which already exists. True, one cannot afford to have scoundrels, as Benedict has stated, but in the pariah group it does not matter, because one will be hated, excluded, and seen as polluted, whether one has the scoundrels or not.

The Indian untouchables are (or were, for there is sign that in India this is relenting) such a group. In a different manner, with entirely different symbols, reasoning, and with less religious overtones, the American Negroes have been a pariah people (likewise, from my view, diminishing, albeit far too slowly to suit many in the society). But what of the nonhereditary? The lepers have already been mentioned; in medieval society there were the physically disabled and mentally unbalanced. The homosexuals have been a pariah group and perhaps also ex-convicts (although there were notable exceptions, for example, if one had been convicted and served a prison term for a white collar crime). But this stronger concept of pariah, rather than the weaker one of minority, would not have permitted the development of the analogy with women, the aged, teenagers, and others. Even under conditions of the greatest collective discrimination, where the errors or shortcomings of one is something for which all must suffer, women cannot be pariahs. Biological, sexual, and familial considerations would make it impossible that they be collectively hated, seen as polluted, and stigmatized. They can be the second sex, the other sex, but this is the minority group status, not the pariah status. However, the pariah group concept would never have enabled a dilution of the nature and severity of inequality, as has been done by those who, properly or improperly noting discrimination but without any element of exclusion or oppression, have applied the minority label to clinical psychologists,[25] educated women,[26] Catholic sociologists,[27] and even American businessmen![28]

VI

There are several problems that should be thought through before the minority group is redefined to include the collectivities, other than ethnics, that are stigmatized, stereotyped, and subjected to irrelevant collective discrimination. The first consists of an objection that one may encounter from the self-righteous ethnic victims, who instead of seeing themselves with new allies, will find their struggle vitiated by inclusion of people who are sick, denigrated (in the eyes of some ethnics, perhaps justly), whose subjection to discrimination may not be entirely irrelevant, and whose struggle does not carry the intellectual respectability that has become part of those fighting anti-Negro racism and anti-Semitism, for example. "Why link us with them?" a black student, unwilling to be tarnished from guilt by association, will ask with some indignation, when he is shown some similarities between the treatment of Negroes, Jews, homosexuals, and epileptics, and one can only imagine the heightened indignation had the professor included (as indeed he should have) the lepers among these groups of people. Why link "us" (the good guys) with "them" (the bad guys)?

It is an important question from the viewpoint of strategy. One always picks allies to strengthen one's own cause. But social science is involved here with description, analysis, concept-sharpening and concept-broadening. To compare two things because they are alike in some respect is not a normative process, unless the area of likeness is one that involves being "good" or "bad"—that is, unless the concept itself has normative boundaries, or ethical ones, or unless the category is based on valuations, such as would be the case if one were to create a group called "great works of art" or "profound literature." Donald Cressey, for example, draws useful comparisons between the organizational structure of organized criminals in America and Phi Beta Kappa,[29] but in so doing he is not suggesting that the two groups are equally good, desirable, or useful.

To return to a matter mentioned earlier, when the Abolitionists and feminists were struggling for universal franchise following the Civil War, the feminists were prevailed upon to postpone their demands because those of the Negroes would be weakened, the white American male being unready to endow people with the vote, regardless of sex or color. This, however, involved strategy, and historically many would say that it turned out to be unfortunate; but the similarity of the position in society of these two important groups of disfranchised people is a matter of study and scrutiny, unaffected by the extent to which the struggles of either or both of them may be aided or hindered by the results of such examination. The same is true today, as a century ago: if sociologists and social psychologists are to understand the nature of prejudice, minority group membership and relationships, they must be willing to see similarities where they exist, and differences as well, between Jews and homosexuals, Negroes and epileptics, Italian-Americans and lepers, regardless of the consequences. Seeing these conceptual likenesses and unlikenesses, they can then be forewarned of the consequences, and place their findings before the world in such way, not to distort the truth as they see it, but to encourage the use of this truth in the manner that they would most thoroughly endorse.

This theme, of the value-free nature of definitions and of the conceptual frameworks surrounding them, runs through the works of Max Weber, but is specifically explicated in Max Rheinstein's introduction to an English translation of some of Weber's writings:

In legal philosophy we find time and again definitions of law which imply some ethical or political value as a necessary element of the very concept of law and which thus excludes from the concept of law every phenomenon which does not live up to the particular value postulated. . . . The sociologist has to deal equally with the social order of primitive cannibals, the ancient Babylonians, Greeks or Romans, Angevin England, or the contemporary United States, the Soviet Union, or National-Socialist Germany of the recent past. Nothing in the nature of things prevents him from reserving the term "law" to those orders which happen to please him. . . . The only question is whether or not . . . a variation of terms is helpful within the framework of a scientific inquiry. . . . Weber would see no practical use in making a terminological distinction between those orders which happen to please and those which would displease his ethical, political, or esthetic sensitivities.[30]

It must be made clear, axiomatic as it may sound, that to say that two things are similar in some respects (hence belong to the same category and are described by the same label), never implies that they are identical, nor even that they are alike in any way other than that expressed by virtue of inclusion under the given rubric.

There is, however, another problem, in some respects the reverse of the first. Namely, that some disadvantaged groups might seek to use the "minority group" umbrella in order to receive the fallout of respectability and in order to be seen as victims of injustice. It might seem, at first glance, that no group of people wants to be or to become a minority, with all the stigmatization and subjugation that this implies; but it is very possible that some groups might want to emphasize that they are minorities (whether they are or not), because they find this useful as an ideological weapon, particularly if they do not have to have the unpleasant consequences of being minorities. The police come to mind; for many would say that they are the dominant group, they have the power or at least the authority,[31] they are free of stigma (which depends on who does the stigmatizing),[32] and are only slightly subject to negative collective judgment; and at the same time they seek to obtain the advantages of displaying themselves as the disadvantaged.

An interesting example of an effort being made to display a group as a minority, in order to arouse sympathy or, more exactly, anger among those victimized, is found in the oft-reprinted article by Jerry Farber, "The Student as Nigger."[33] Here Farber writes:

> Students are niggers. When you get that straight, our schools begin to make sense. It's more important, though, to understand why they're niggers.

So Farber takes a look at what's happening where he was teaching, California State L.A., where students have separate and inferior dining facilities, and where there is an unwritten law barring student-faculty lovemaking. The students at the school are politically disfranchised, although given a toy government, "run for the most part by Uncle Toms and concerned principally with trivia." Students, furthermore, are expected to know their place; the student calls a faculty member "Sir" or "Professor"—and "he smiles and shuffles some as he stands outside the professor's office waiting for permission to enter. The faculty tell him what courses to take . . . what to read, what to write, and, frequently, where to set margins on his typewriter."

So what school amounts to is a twelve-year course in how to be slaves:

> As do black slaves, students vary in their awareness of what's going on. Some recognize their own put-on for what it is and even let their rebellion break through to the surface now and then. Others— including most of the "good students"—have been more deeply brainwashed. . . .
> Students, like black people, have immense and unused power. They could, theoretically, insist on participation in their own education. They could make academic freedom bilateral. They could teach their teachers to thrive on love and admiration, rather than fear and respect, and to lay down their weapons. Students could discover community. And they could learn to dance by dancing on IBM cards. They could make coloring books . . .

And on and on, so they could.

There is much that can be discussed and perhaps disputed in the trenchant remarks of Farber, and it would warrant serious discussion to determine the point of differentiation between rational and functional superordination and irrational domination. At least one area of criticism (and of conceptual differentiation between students and blacks) is made by Hoult, Hudson and Mayer in a publication of the American Association of University Professors (oh, *them!*, one can hear the Farberites saying, as they shriek with laughter):

> The knowledge and campus privilege differential between faculty and students does not, of course, imply that faculty are "better" than students; it implies only that members of the two groups temporarily have different tasks in the division of labor. Thus, there is no

master-slave relationship between students and faculty, as claimed in Jerry Farber's "The Student as Nigger." Students become teachers, but slaves never become masters.[34]

Perhaps, however, Farber (despite the quotations above to the contrary) never made the assertion that students are slaves. Perhaps it was rhetoric; they are, in Farber's view, slaves in a metaphorical sense—with a touch of hyperbole added. Then we are back at the minority group concept: there is, he would be saying, a meaningful analogy between the two groups; but he is saying this, not because it is so (which it might very well be) but because it is ideologically helpful to his aims to say it.

There is inequality in the society, unequal starting points, unequal biological givens, and unequal opportunities. Sometimes the inequality is temporary, sometimes at least a portion of it is rational. Children become adults, and while they are children they cannot be given, probably not in any society but certainly not in the urbanized and industrial one of the twentieth century, all the rights and privileges accorded to adults. But that this can become an excuse for the oppression of certain children, and for the irrational exclusion of them from some rights to which they ought to be entitled, is demonstrated by child labor exploitation and by the history of juvenile courts in America.[35]

VII

There are few areas of sociological study that have become so completely outdated by fast-moving events and a fast-changing society to the extent that has marked the study of racial and ethnic relations. History itself, in a manner that sociologists cannot claim to have foreseen, has made the texts, the conceptual frameworks, and the approaches of the 1950's and even later largely irrelevant. Black protest, militancy, and confrontation tactics have imbued the ethnic scene with a sense of urgency; but more than that, the new racial struggles brought home to Americans an awareness that they had hitherto lacked of oppression, injustice, and victimization on the one hand, and of the power of the oppressed to change their condition by group identification, organization, and solidarity, on the other.

What happens in one portion of society cannot help but affect all others, and so it was that black militancy brought new efforts at organization not only to Indians, Mexican-Americans, and other ethnics, but to women, homosexuals, and even ex-convicts.[36]

If during this time, that subsection of sociology as a discipline or field of specialization centered around intergroup relations had largely ignored this phenomenon, if it was unaware that the old-fashioned perimeters of the minority group concept was a thing of the ancient past buried all of a decade ago, the same cannot be said for the sociologists who were turning their attention to deviance. Deviant behavior, long linked with criminal behavior (the two can be said to be overlapping but by no means identical concepts), was being examined, particularly by Lemert, Becker, and their colleagues in what has come to be called the labeling school, from the vantage-point of the victims of the process by which some people are labeled deviant and are reacted to, not as whole human beings, but as in-capacitated persons, with damaged identity and spoiled self-image.[37] In the manner in which many of these sociologists described the plight of the physically and mentally handicapped, the homosexual, and others, one can find striking similarities to the social condition of the ethnic minorities. What some but not all of the deviants lacked, however, was a sense of collective membership in the deviant group; while others sought to escape from such membership, or at least to conceal it.

Many of the problems that beset the student of ethnic minorities will be found when one studies deviants and other nonethnic minorities. Under what conditions do people who are victimized form subcultures of their own? Do these subcultures look to assimilation into the larger culture of the society, or to equal treatment as a separate group without assimilation? Will ethnic minority status take precedence over other minority status in a clash for loyalties? How does one stop a cycle in which discrimination results in inferior training and ability, and the latter results in discrimination?[38] And, from a sociological viewpoint the most important question, how does a society plan for social differentiation without inequality?

As an example of the welding together into a single conceptual framework the study of deviant people and minority groups, one turns particularly to the work of Goffman. In a brief and most relevant piece entitled "Normal Deviants," Goffman writes:

> Our society appears to have several basic types of stigma. There are "tribal" stigmas, arising from unapproved racial, national, and religious affiliations. There are the stigmas attached to physical handicap, including—to stretch the term—those associated with the undesirable characteristics of female sex and old age. And there are stigmas pertaining to what is somehow seen as a decay of moral responsibility, including those persons who are unemployed or who have a known record of alcoholism, addiction, sexual deviation, penal servitude, or who have been committed to a mental hospital.[39]

Goffman then proceeds to examine the social processes common to normal deviants under four headings: intrapersonal, interpersonal responses within the deviant groupings, interpersonal responses between members of the deviant grouping and the wider society, and collective responses. In each of these four categories, the "normal deviants" and the "tribally stigmatized" not only have similar responses, but have indubitably influenced each other.

VIII

If sociologists are to understand the nature of prejudice, of the self-fulfilling prophecy in which peoples treated as if they were inferior develop some of the traits of that inferiority, of the social movements that develop in defense of those denied privileges granted to others, of the conditions under which minorities arise and the conditions under which they cease to be minorities, then it would seem that the concept of the minority group must be broadened to include nonethnics and nonhereditary persons who fit the other aspects of Wirth's definition: a sense of group identification, a subjective view of themselves as being the victims of collective discrimination and unequal treatment (always, I repeat, on the short end of the inequality continuum) at the hands of a dominant group. Not all the groups described in these articles fit into this model, even in the view of the authors. Some are nonethnics subjected to ethnic-type stereotyping; some are minority groups that have been given, to use the Hacker phrase (adapted, as she states, from Marx and Marcuse) surplus discrimination.[40]

Two major concepts in sociology come together, yet must be kept separate, in order to understand the process by which the theme of the minority group has come to be broadened. These are the concepts of social differentiation and social inequality. All human beings are like all others in some respects, sociology has taught us; they are like some and unlike others in many respects; and each human is unlike all others in still other respects. It is in the second of these statements that social differentiation takes place: when people are like others in certain respects and unlike others in certain respects. What, then, are the social conditions, or the nature of the similarity or dissimilarity, that results in a meaningful differentiation taking place in society? And, derived therefrom, is the next problem: under what conditions do such differentiations result in social inequality? For it is when the social differentiation takes place, followed by the social inequality, and resulting in collective and irrelevant discrimination, that the minority group emerges.

In the final analysis, some are more minority groups than others, just as some countries are democracies, dictatorships, or colonial powers more than others. We will profit by conceptualizing as minority groups those people who are subjected to irrelevant and unwarranted collective discrimination, provided we do not allow this to be used as an ideological weapon that muddies rather than clarifies, and provided we do not end up with a general and broadened view of the sociology of inequality, in which we lose sight of the very real differences among class, caste, pariah people, ethnic minorities, and what I am here calling, with indebtedness to Michael Harrington, the other minorities.

REFERENCES

1. Everett C. Hughes, private communication.
2. Peter I. Rose, *The Subject Is Race* (New York: Oxford University Press, 1968). Rose offers an historical account of the minority group concept in American sociology, including the contribution of Young.
3. Ernst Gruenfeld, *Die Peripheren* (Amsterdam: N. v. Nord Hollandsche Uitgevers Mij, 1939). Gruenfeld's book was called to my attention by Everett C. Hughes (private communication) who reviewed the book upon its appearance, in *American Journal of Sociology,* 46:4 (1941).

18 ■ *From the Ethnic Minorities to the Other Minorities*

4. Robert Bierstedt, *The Social Order* (New York: McGraw-Hill, 2nd ed., 1963), p. 479. Social scientists were commenting on the special use of the word *minority* long before Bierstedt's objection. In the first edition of *Encyclopedia of Social Sciences* (10, p. 518), Max Hildebert Boehm, writing the article entitled, "Minorities, National," stated: "Although there are national minorities which actually constitute the ruling and privileged groups within a state, current usage has restricted the application of the term national minority to those which are in a defensive position."
5. Robert Bierstedt, "The Sociology of Majorities," *American Sociological Review*, 13 (1948), pp. 700–10.
6. Louis Wirth, "The Problem of Minority Groups," in Ralph Linton, ed., *The Science of Man in the World Crisis* (New York: Columbia University Press, 1945), p. 347. Note how frequently this article, and even this specific passage, is cited by the authors in the present volume.
7. Arnold and Caroline Rose, *America Divided: Minority Group Relations in the United States* (New York: Knopf, 1948), p. 3.
8. Peter Berger, *Invitation to Sociology* (Garden City, N.Y.: Doubleday, 1963), p. 142ff.
9. Libby Benedict, "The Right to Have Scoundrels," *Saturday Review of Literature*, Oct. 6, 1945.
10. Quoted in Donald R. Cressey, *Theft of the Nation: The Structure and Operations of Organized Crime in America* (New York: Harper & Row, 1969), p. 12.
11. Benedict, *op. cit.*
12. Everett C. Hughes, "Social Change and Status Protest: An Essay on the Marginal Man," *Phylon*, 10 (1949), pp. 58–65.
13. *Ibid.*, p. 63.
14. Kenneth Burke, *Counter-Statement* (Chicago: University of Chicago Press, 2nd ed., 1957), pp. 104–5.
15. Gunnar Myrdal, *An American Dilemma* (New York: Harper, 1944); appendix reprinted in this volume.
16. H. M. Parshley, "Translator's Preface" in Simone de Beauvoir, *The Second Sex* (New York: Knopf, 1957), p. vii.
17. De Beauvoir, *op. cit.*, pp. xv, xvi.
18. George Eaton Simpson and J. Milton Yinger, *Racial and Cultural Minorities: An Analysis of Prejudice and Discrimination* (New York: Harper, rev. ed., 1958).
19. Gordon W. Allport, *The Nature of Prejudice* (Garden City, N.Y.: Doubleday, rev. ed., 1958).
20. Milton L. Barron, "The Aged as a Quasi-Minority Group," from *The Aging Americans* (New York: Thomas Y. Crowell, 1961); reprinted in this volume.
21. Milton L. Barron, *Minorities in a Changing World* (New York: Knopf, 1967).
22. T. W. Adorno, Else Frenkel-Brunswik, Daniel J. Levinson, and R. Nevitt Sanford, *The Authoritarian Personality* (New York: Harper, 1950).
23. E. K. Francis, "Minority Groups—A Revision of Concepts," *British Journal of Sociology*, 2 (1951), pp. 219–30.

24. Gerald D. Berreman, "The Concept of Caste," *International Encyclopedia of the Social Sciences* (New York: Macmillan, 2, 1968), p. 337.
25. John O. Noll, "The Clinical Psychologist—A Member of a Minority Group," *Wisconsin Sociologist*, 3 (1964), pp. 13–17.
26. Ellen E. McDonald, "Educated Women: The Last Minority?" *Columbia University Forum* (Summer, 1967), pp. 30–34.
27. John J. Kane, "Are Catholic Sociologists a Minority Group?" *American Catholic Sociological Review*, 14 (1953), pp. 2–12.
28. The suggestion that businessmen should be viewed as a minority group was made by Ayn Rand, in a talk at New York University.
29. Cressey, *op. cit.*, p. 158.
30. Max Rheinstein, "Introduction" to *Max Weber on Law in Economy and Society* (New York: Simon and Schuster, 1967), pp. lvi–lvii.
31. For a discussion of the concepts of power and authority, see Robert Bierstedt, "The Problem of Authority," in Morroe Berger, Theodore Abel, and Charles H. Page, eds., *Freedom and Control in Modern Society* (Princeton, N.J.: Van Nostrand, 1954); also Bierstedt, "An Analysis of Social Power," *American Sociological Review*, 15 (1950), pp. 730–38.
32. An objection may be made that the police are stigmatized, when they are called pigs, for instance; but the stigmatizing group is not the dominant one in society.
33. Jerry Farber, "The Student as Nigger," *Los Angeles Free Press*, March 3, 1967; widely reprinted, including in Jerry Hopkins, ed., *The Hippie Papers: Notes from the Underground Press* (New York: New American Library, 1968).
34. Thomas Ford Hoult, John W. Hudson, and Albert J. Mayer, "On Keeping Our Cool in the Halls of Ivy," *A.A.U.P. Bulletin*, 55 (June, 1969), p. 187.
35. See majority decision of the United States Supreme Court, Re Gault, 387 U.S. *1* (1967).
36. For further elaboration of this theme, see Edward Sagarin, *Odd Man In: Societies of Deviants in America* (Chicago: Quadrangle Books, 1969).
37. For this literature, see the writings on deviance by Edwin M. Lemert, Howard S. Becker, Kai T. Erikson, John I. Kitsuse, among others, the writings on stigma of Erving Goffman, and the work on mental health of Goffman, Thomas S. Szasz, Thomas J. Scheff, and Ronald D. Laing.
38. Robert K. Merton, "The Self-Fulfilling Prophecy," in Merton's *Social Theory and Social Structure* (New York: Free Press of Glencoe, 1957), pp. 421–36.
39. Erving Goffman, "Normal Deviants," in Thomas J. Scheff, ed., *Mental Illness and Social Process* (New York: Harper & Row, 1967), pp. 267–71. See also, for a fuller treatment, Goffman's *Stigma: Notes on the Management of Spoiled Identity* (Englewood Cliffs, N.J.: Prentice-Hall, 1963).
40. Helen Mayer Hacker, "Homosexuals: Deviant or Minority Group?" in this volume.

Gender and Sex 2

It has been said that social inequality is ubiquitous, and certainly this can be said of social differentiation. It would be difficult to find a category of human beings to serve as an example of these two statements as universal as women.

With the advent of Women's Liberation a new word has come into the language. It is the pejorative term, "sexist," the analogue of racist for "those who would show their prejudice against people because of gender or sex," and to this is added, "because of sexual preference or tendency." Nevertheless, women as a minority group, and homosexuals seen in that category, illustrate somewhat different aspects of sociological thinking. Women, treated unequally, in a subordinate position in almost all societies, granted token equality of opportunity, constitute a completely visible group, with ascribed status, certainly not pariahs, and free from stigma. Homosexuals, on the contrary, are often "invisible" insofar as their homosexuality is concerned; highly stigmatized (because of concealment, theirs is what Goffman has called a discreditable rather than a discredited stigma), and the group itself lacks legitimacy in the society.

The four articles in this chapter illustrate several facets of the problems encountered as one draws an analogy between the ethnic and nonethnic minorities: institutionalized versus noninstitutionalized roles, extremely high versus relatively low visibility, the ascribed status (common to ethnics and women) as contrasted with the moral issues of the achieved status (if it is achieved) of homosexuals. In two of these articles, we are seeing the world of the minority from within (Hacker on women and Kameny on homosexuals), and the problems that arise as one examines whether the insider brings to the study greater insight, or greater ideological bias, or both.

In another article, Myrdal draws an historical analogy between the position of women and that of Negroes, an analogy born out of his classic study of race in America. The black slave was a chattel, and wives too have been chattels, pieces of property that belonged to their men, and who had few rights outside of those conferred on them by their owners. That this is neither a caricature nor a parody when one examines other times and other places should be apparent; I hope that my belief that this is hardly an accurate description of America in the latter decades of the twentieth century is not the delusion of a male sociologist, viewing the world as a male rather than as a sociologist.

The study of women and of homosexuals leads to an examination of the problem of the self-fulfilling prophecy: to what extent does the belief in inferiority and the treatment of these groups as inferior result in just such inferiority? Finally, both groups, and many of the others in this volume, can profitably be examined with Hacker's theme of surplus discrimination in mind.

Women as a Minority Group

Helen Mayer Hacker

Although sociological literature reveals scattered references to women as a minority group, comparable in certain respects to racial, ethnic and national minorities, no systematic investigation has been undertaken as to what extent the term "minority group" is applicable to women. That there has been little serious consideration of women as a minority group among sociologists is manifested in the recently issued index to *The American Journal of Sociology* wherein under the heading of "Minority Groups" there appears: "See Jews; Morale; Negro; Races and Nationalities; Religious Groups; Sects." There is no cross-reference to women, but such reference is found under the heading "Family."

Yet it may well be that regarding women as a minority group may be productive of fresh insights and suggest leads for further research. The purpose of this paper is to apply to women some portion of that body of sociological theory and methodology customarily used for investigating such minority groups as Negroes, Jews, immigrants, etc. It may be anticipated that not only will principles already established in the field of intergroup relations contribute to our understanding of women, but that in the process of modifying traditional concepts and theories to fit the special case of women new viewpoints for the fruitful reexamination of other minority groups will emerge.

In defining the term "minority group," the presence of discrimination is the identifying factor. As Louis Wirth[1] has pointed out, "minority group" is not a statistical concept, nor need it denote an alien group. Indeed for the present discussion I have adopted his definition: "A minority group is any group of people who because of their physical or cultural characteristics, are singled out from the others in the society in which they live for differential and unequal treatment, and who therefore regard themselves as objects of collec-

Source: *Social Forces*, 30 (1951), pp. 60–69. Reprinted by permission of University of North Carolina Press and the author.

tive discrimination." It is apparent that this definition includes both objective and subjective characteristics of a minority group: the fact of discrimination and the awareness of discrimination, with attendant reactions to that awareness. A person who on the basis of his group affiliation is denied full participation in those opportunities which the value system of his culture extends to all members of the society satisfies the objective criterion, but there are various circumstances which may prevent him from fulfilling the subjective criterion.

In the first place, a person may be unaware of the extent to which his group membership influences the way others treat him. He may have formally dissolved all ties with the group in question and fondly imagine his identity is different from what others hold it to be. Consequently, he interprets their behavior toward him solely in terms of his individual characteristics. Or, less likely, he may be conscious of his membership in a certain group but not be aware of the general disesteem with which the group is regarded. A final possibility is that he may belong in a category which he does not realize has group significance. An example here might be a speech peculiarity which has come to have unpleasant connotations in the minds of others. Or a lower class child with no conception of "class as culture" may not understand how his manners act as cues in eliciting the dislike of his middle class teacher. The foregoing cases all assume that the person believes in equal opportunities for all in the sense that one's group affiliation should not affect his role in the larger society. We turn now to a consideration of situations in which this assumption is not made.

It is frequently the case that a person knows that because of his group affiliation he receives differential treatment, but feels that this treatment is warranted by the distinctive characteristics of his group. A Negro may believe that there are significant differences between whites and Negroes which justify a different role in life for the Negro. A child may accept the fact that physical differences between him and an adult require his going to bed earlier than they do. A Sudra knows that his lot in life has been cast by divine fiat, and he does not expect the perquisites of a Brahmin. A woman does not wish for the rights and duties of men. In all these situations, clearly, the person does not regard himself as an "object of collective discrimination."

For the two types presented above: (1) those who do not know that they are being discriminated against on a group basis; and (2) those who acknowledge the propriety of differential treatment on a group basis, the subjective attributes of a minority group member are lacking. They feel no minority group consciousness, harbor no resentment, and, hence, cannot properly be said to belong to a minority group. Although the term "minority group" is inapplicable to both types, the term "minority group status" may be substituted. This term is used to categorize persons who are denied rights to which they are entitled according to the value system of the observer. An observer, who is a firm adherent of the democratic ideology, will often consider persons to occupy a minority group status who are well accommodated to their subordinate roles.

No empirical study of the frequency of minority group feelings among women has yet been made, but common observation would suggest that consciously at least, few women believe themselves to be members of a minority group in the way in which some Negroes, Jews, Italians, etc., may so conceive themselves. There are, of course, many sex-conscious women, known to a past generation as feminists, who are filled with resentment at the discriminations they fancy are directed against their sex. Today some of these may be found in the National Woman's Party which since 1923 has been carrying on a campaign for the passage of the Equal Rights Amendment. This amendment, in contrast to the compromise bill recently passed by Congress, would at one stroke wipe out all existing legislation which differentiates in any way between men and women, even when such legislation is designed for the special protection of women. The proponents of the Equal Rights Amendment hold the position that women will never achieve equal rights until they abjure all privileges based on what they consider to be only presumptive sex differences.

Then there are women enrolled in women's clubs, women's auxiliaries of men's organizations, women's professional and educational associations who seemingly believe that women have special interests to follow or unique contributions to make. These latter might reject the appellation of minority group, but their behavior testifies to their awareness of women as a distinct group in our society, either overriding differences of class, occupation, religion, or ethnic identification, or specialized within these categories. Yet the number of women who participate in "women's affairs" even in the United States, the classic land of associations, is so small that one cannot easily say that the majority of women display minority group consciousness. However, documentation, as well as a measuring instrument, is likewise lacking for minority consciousness in other groups.

Still women often manifest many of the psychological characteristics which have been imputed to self-conscious minority groups. Kurt Lewin[2] has pointed to group self-hatred as a frequent reaction of the minority group member to his group affiliation. This feeling is exhibited in the person's tendency to denigrate other members of the group, to accept the dominant group's stereotyped conception of them, and to indulge in "mea culpa" breast-beating. He may seek to exclude himself from the average of his group, or he may point the finger of scorn at himself. Since a person's conception of himself is based on the defining gestures of others, it is unlikely that members of a minority group can wholly escape personality distortion. Constant reiteration of one's inferiority must often lead to its acceptance as a fact.

Certainly women have not been immune to the formulations of the "female character" throughout the ages. From those, to us, deluded creatures who confessed to witchcraft to modern sophisticates who speak disparagingly of the cattiness and disloyalty of women, women reveal their introjection of prevailing attitudes toward them. Like those minority groups whose self-castigation outdoes dominant group derision of them, women frequently exceed men in the violence of their vituperations of their sex. They are more severe in moral judgments, especially in sexual matters. A line of self-criticism may be traced from Hannah More, a blue-stocking herself, to Dr. Marynia Farnham, who lays most of the world's ills at women's door. Women express themselves as disliking other women, as preferring to work under men, and as finding exclusively female gatherings repugnant. The *Fortune* polls conducted in 1946 show that women, more than men, have misgivings concerning women's participation in industry, the professions, and civic life. And more than one-fourth of women wish they had been born in the opposite sex![3]

Militating against a feeling of group identification on the part of women is a differential factor in their socialization. Members of a minority group are frequently socialized within their own group. Personality development is more largely a resultant of intra- than inter-group interaction. The conception of his role formed by a Negro or a Jew or a second-generation immigrant is greatly dependent upon the definitions offered by members of his own group, on their attitudes and behavior toward him. Ignoring for the moment class differences within the group, the minority group person does not suffer discrimination from members of his own group. But only rarely does a woman experience this type of group belongingness. Her interactions with members of the opposite sex may be as frequent as her relationships with members of her own sex. Women's conceptions of themselves, therefore, spring as much from their intimate relationships with men as with women. Although this consideration might seem to limit the applicability to women of research findings on minority groups, conversely, it may suggest investigation to seek out useful parallels in the socialization of women, on the one hand, and the socialization of ethnics living in neighborhoods of heterogeneous population, on the other.

Even though the sense of group identification is not so conspicuous in women as in racial and ethnic minorities, they, like these others, tend to develop a separate subculture. Women have their own language, comparable to the argot of the underworld and professional groups. It may not extend to a completely separate dialect as has been discovered in some preliterate groups, but there are words and idioms employed chiefly by women. Only the acculturated male can enter into the conversation of the beauty parlor, the exclusive shop, the bridge table, or the kitchen. In contrast to men's interest in physical health, safety, money, and sex, women attach greater importance to attractiveness, personality, home, family, and other people.[4] How much of the "woman's world" is predicated on their relationship to men is too difficult a question to discuss here. It is still a controversial point whether the values and behavior patterns of other minority groups, such as the Negroes, represent an immanent development, or are oriented chiefly toward the rejecting world. A content analysis contrasting the speech of "housewives" and "career women," for example, or a comparative analysis of the speech of men and women of similar occupational status might be one test of this hypothesis.

We must return now to the original question of the aptness of the designation of minority group for women. It has been indicated that women fail to present in full force the subjective attributes commonly associated with minority groups. That is, they lack a sense of group identification and do not harbor feelings of being treated unfairly because of their sex membership. Can it then be said that women have a minority group status in our society? The answer to this question depends upon the values of the observer whether within or outside the group—just as is true in the case of any group of persons who, on the basis of putative differential characteristics, are denied access to some statuses in the social system of their society. If we assume that there are no differences attributable to sex membership as such that would justify casting men and women in different social roles, it can readily be shown that women do occupy a minority group status in our society.

Minority Group Status of Women

Formal discriminations against women are too well known for any but the most summary description. In general they take the form of being barred from certain activities or, if admitted, being treated unequally. Discriminations against women may be viewed as arising from the generally ascribed status "female" and from the specially ascribed statuses of "wife," "mother," and "sister." (To meet the possible objection that "wife" and "mother" represent assumed, rather than ascribed statuses, may I point out that what is important here is that these statuses carry ascribed expectations which are only ancillary in the minds of those who assume them.)

As female, in the economic sphere, women are largely confined to sedentary, monotonous work under the supervision of men, and are treated unequally with regard to pay, promotion, and responsibility. With the exceptions of teaching, nursing, social service, and library work, in which they do not hold a proportionate number of supervisory positions and are often occupationally segregated from men, they make a poor showing in the professions. Although they own 80 percent of the nation's wealth, they do not sit on the boards of directors of great corporations. Educational opportunities are likewise unequal. Professional schools, such as architecture and medicine, apply quotas. Women's colleges are frequently inferior to men's. In co-educational schools women's participation in campus activities is limited. As citizens, women are often barred from jury service and public office. Even when they are admitted to the apparatus of political parties, they are subordinated to men. Socially, women have less freedom of movement, and are permitted fewer deviations in the proprieties of dress, speech, manners. In social intercourse they are confined to a narrower range of personality expression.

In the specially ascribed status of wife, a woman—in several States —has no exclusive rights to her earnings, is discriminated against in employment, must take the domicile of her husband, and in general must meet the social expectation of subordination to her husband's interests. As a mother, she may not have the guardianship of her children, bears the chief stigma in the case of an illegitimate child, is rarely given leave of absence for pregnancy. As a sister, she frequently suffers unequal distribution of domestic duties between herself and her brother, must yield preference to him in obtaining an education, and in such other psychic and material gratifications as cars, trips, and living away from home.

If it is conceded that women have a minority group status, what may be learned from applying to women various theoretical constructs in the field of intergroup relations?

Social Distance Between Men and Women

One instrument of diagnostic value is the measure of social distance between dominant and minority group. But we have seen that one important difference between women and other minorities is that women's attitudes and self-conceptions are conditioned more largely by interaction with both minority and dominant group members. Before measuring social distance, therefore, a continuum might be constructed of the frequency and extent of women's interaction with men, with the poles conceptualized as ideal types. One extreme would represent a complete "ghetto" status, the woman whose contacts with men were of the most secondary kind. At the other extreme shall we put the woman who has prolonged and repeated associations with men, but only in those situations in which sex-awareness plays a prominent role or the woman who enters into a variety of relationships with men in which her sex identity is to a large extent irrelevant? The decision would depend on the type of scale used.

This question raises the problem of the criterion of social distance to be employed in such a scale. Is it more profitable to use we-feeling, felt interdependence, degree of communication, or degrees of separation in status? Social distance tests as applied to relationships between other dominant and minority groups have for the most part adopted prestige criteria as their basis. The assumption is that the type of situation into which one is willing to enter with average members of another group reflects one's estimate of the status of the group relative to one's own. When the tested group is a sex-group rather than a racial, national, religious, or economic one, several important differences in the use and interpretation of the scale must be noted:

1. Only two groups are involved: men and women. Thus, the test indicates the amount of homogeneity or we-feeling only according to the attribute of sex. If men are a primary group, there are not many groups to be ranked secondary, tertiary, etc., with respect to them, but only one group, women, whose social distance cannot be calculated relative to other groups.

2. Lundberg[5] suggests the possibility of a group of Catholics registering a smaller social distance to Moslems than to Catholics. In such an event the group of Catholics, from any sociological viewpoint, would be classified as Moslems. If women expressed less social distance to men than to women, should they then be classified sociologically as men? Perhaps no more so than the legendary Negro who, when requested to move to the colored section of the train, replied, "Boss, I'se done resigned from the colored race," should be classified as white. It is likely, however, that the group identification of many women in our society is with men. The feminists were charged with wanting to be men, since they associated male physical character-

istics with masculine social privileges.) A similar statement can be made about men who show greater social distance to other men than to women.

Social distance may be measured from the standpoint of the minority group or the dominant group with different results. In point of fact, tension often arises when one group feels less social distance than the other. A type case here is the persistent suitor who underestimates his desired sweetheart's feeling of social distance toward him.

3. In social distance tests the assumption is made of an orderly progression—although not necessarily by equal intervals—in the scale. That is, it is not likely that a person would express willingness to have members of a given group as his neighbors, while simultaneously voicing the desire to have them excluded from his country. On all scales marriage represents the minimum social distance, and implies willingness for associations on all levels of lesser intimacy. May the customary scale be applied to men and women? If we take the expressed attitude of many men and women not to marry, we may say that they have feelings of social distance toward the opposite sex, and in this situation the usual order of the scale may be preserved.

In our culture, however, men who wish to marry, must perforce marry women, and even if they accept this relationship, they may still wish to limit their association with women in other situations. The male physician may not care for the addition of female physicians to his hospital staff. The male poker player may be thrown off his game if women participate. A damper may be put upon the hunting expedition if women come along. The average man may not wish to consult a woman lawyer. And so on. In these cases it seems apparent that the steps in the social distance scale must be reversed. Men will accept women at the supposed level of greatest intimacy while rejecting them at lower levels.

But before concluding that a different scale must be constructed when the dominant group attitude toward a minority group which is being tested is that of men toward women, the question may be raised as to whether marriage in fact represents the point of minimum social distance. It may not imply anything but physical intimacy and work accommodation, as was frequently true in nonindividuated societies, such as preliterate groups and the household economy of the Middle Ages, or marriages of convenience in the European upper class. Even in our own democratic society where marriage is sup-posedly based on romantic love there may be little communication between the partners in marriage. The Lynds[6] report the absence of real companionship between husband and wife in Middletown. Women have been known to say that although they have been mar-ried for twenty years, their husband is still a stranger to them. There is a quatrain of Thoreau's that goes:

> Each moment as we drew nearer to each
> A stern respect withheld us farther yet
> So that we seemed beyond each other's reach
> And less acquainted than when first we met.

Part of the explanation may be found in the subordination of wives to husbands in our culture, which is expressed in the separate spheres of activity for men and women. A recent advertisement in a maga-zine of national circulation depicts a pensive husband seated by his knitting wife, with the caption, "Sometimes a man has moods his wife cannot understand." In this case the husband is worried about a pen-sion plan for his employees. The assumption is that the wife, know-ing nothing of the business world, cannot take the role of her hus-band in this matter.

The presence of love does not in itself argue for either equality of status nor fullness of communication. We may love those who are either inferior or superior to us, and we may love persons whom we do not understand. The supreme literary examples of passion without communication are found in Proust's portrayal of Swann's obsession with Odette, the narrator's infatuation with the elusive Albertine, and, of course, Dante's longing for Beatrice.

In the light of these considerations concerning the relationships between men and women, some doubt may be cast on the propriety of placing marriage on the positive extreme of the social distance scale with respect to ethnic and religious minority groups. Since in-equalities of status are preserved in marriage, a dominant group member may be willing to marry a member of the group which, in general, he would not wish admitted to his club. The social distance scale which uses marriage as a sign of an extreme degree of acceptance is inadequate for appreciating the position of women, and perhaps for other minority groups as well. The relationships among similarity of status, communication as a measure of intimacy, and love must be clarified before social distance tests can be applied usefully to attitudes between men and women.

Caste-Class Conflict

Is the separation between males and females in our society a caste line? Folsom[7] suggests that it is, and Myrdal[8] in his well-known Appendix 5 considers the parallel between the position of and feelings toward women and Negroes in our society. The relation between women and Negroes is historical, as well as analogical. In the seventeenth century the legal status of Negro servants was borrowed from that of women and children, who were under the *patria potestas*, and until the Civil War there was considerable cooperation between the Abolitionist and woman suffrage movements. According to Myrdal, the problems of both groups are resultants of the transition from a pre-industrial, paternalistic scheme of life to individualistic, industrial capitalism. Obvious similarities in the status of women and Negroes are indicated in Table 1.

While these similarities in the situation of women and Negroes may lead to increased understanding of their social roles, account must also be taken of differences which impose qualifications on the comparison of the two groups. Most importantly, the influence of marriage as a social elevator for women, but not for Negroes, must be considered. Obvious, too, is the greater importance of women to the dominant group, despite the economic, sexual, and prestige gains which Negroes afford the white South. Ambivalence is probably more marked in the attitude of white males toward women than toward Negroes. The "war of the sexes" is only an expression of men's and women's vital need of each other. Again, there is greater polarization in the relationship between men and women. Negroes, although they have borne the brunt of anti-minority group feeling in this country, do not constitute the only racial or ethnic minority, but there are only two sexes. And, although we have seen that social

TABLE 1. Castelike Status of Women and Negroes

NEGROES	WOMEN

1. High Social Visibility

a. Skin color, other "racial" characteristics	a. Secondary sex characteristics
b. (Sometimes) distinctive dress —bandana, flashy clothes	b. Distinctive dress, skirts, etc.

2. Ascribed Attributes

a. Inferior intelligence, smaller brain, less convoluted, scarcity of geniuses	a. ditto
b. More free in instinctual gratifications. More emotional, "primitive" and childlike. Imagined sexual prowess envied.	b. Irresponsible, inconsistent, emotionally unstable Lack strong super-ego Women as "temptresses"
c. Common stereotype "inferior"	c. "Weaker"

3. Rationalization of Status

a. Thought all right in his place	a. Woman's place is in the home
b. Myth of contented Negro	b. Myth of contented woman— "feminine" woman is happy in subordinate role

4. Accommodation Attitudes

a. Supplicatory whining intonation of voice	a. Rising inflection, smiles, laughs, downward glances
b. Deferential manner	b. Flattering manner
c. Concealment of real feelings	c. "Feminine wiles"
d. Outwit "white folks"	d. Outwit "menfolk"
e. Careful study of points at which dominant group is susceptible to influence	e. ditto
f. Fake appeals for directives; show of ignorance	f. Appearance of helplessness

5. Discriminations

a. Limitations on education— should fit "place" in society	a. ditto

Table 1 (*Cont.*)

NEGROES	WOMEN
b. Confined to traditional jobs—barred from supervisory positions Their competition feared No family precedents for new aspirations	b. ditto
c. Deprived of political importance	c. ditto
d. Social and professional segregation	d. ditto
e. More vulnerable to criticism	e. e.g. conduct in bars

6. *Similar Problems*

a. Roles not clearly defined, but in flux as result of social change
   Conflict between achieved status and ascribed status

distance exists between men and women, it is not to be compared with the social segregation of Negroes.

At the present time, of course, Negroes suffer far greater discrimination than women, but since the latter's problems are rooted in a biological reality less susceptible to cultural manipulation, they prove more lasting. Women's privileges exceed those of Negroes. Protective attitudes toward Negroes have faded into abeyance, even in the South, but most boys are still taught to take care of girls, and many evidences of male chivalry remain. The factor of class introduces variations here. The middle class Negro endures frustrations largely without the rewards of his white class peer, but the lower class Negro is still absolved from many responsibilities. The reverse holds true for women. Notwithstanding these and other differences between the position of women and Negroes, the similarities are sufficient to render research on either group applicable in some fashion to the other.

Exemplary of the possible usefulness of applying the caste principle to women is viewing some of the confusion surrounding women's roles as reflecting a conflict between class and caste status. Such a conflict is present in the thinking and feeling of both dominant and minority groups toward upper class Negroes and educated women. Should a woman judge be treated with the respect due a judge or the gallantry accorded a woman? The extent to which the rights and duties of one role permeate other roles so as to cause a role conflict has been treated elsewhere by the writer.[9] Lower class Negroes who have acquired dominant group attitudes toward the Negro resent upper class Negro pretensions to superiority. Similarly, domestic women may feel the career woman is neglecting the duties of her proper station.

Parallels in adjustment of women and Negroes to the class-caste conflict may also be noted. Point 4 "Accommodation Attitudes" of the foregoing chart indicates the kinds of behavior displayed by members of both groups who accept their caste status. Many "sophisticated" women are retreating from emancipation with the support of psychoanalytic derivations.[10] David Riesman has recently provided an interesting discussion of changes "in the denigration by American women of their own sex" in which he explains their new submissiveness as in part a reaction to the weakness of men in the contemporary world.[11] "Parallelism" and "Negroidism" which accept a racially-restricted economy reflect allied tendencies in the Negro group.

Role segmentation as a mode of adjustment is illustrated by Negroes who indulge in occasional passing and women who vary their behavior according to their definition of the situation. An example of the latter is the case of the woman lawyer who, after losing a case before a judge who was also her husband, said she would appeal the case, and added, "The judge can lay down the law at home, but I'll argue with him in court."

A third type of reaction is to fight for recognition of class status. Negro race leaders seek greater prerogatives for Negroes. Feminist women, acting either through organizations or as individuals, push for public disavowal of any differential treatment of men and women.

Race Relations Cycle

The "race relations cycle," as defined by Robert E. Park,[12] describes the social processes of reduction in tension and increase in communication in the relations between two or more groups who are living in a common territory under a single political or economic system. The sequence of competition, conflict, accommodation, and assimilation may also occur when social change introduces dissociative forces into an assimilated group or causes accommodated groups to seek new definitions of the situation.[13] The ethnic or nationality characteristics of the groups involved are not essential to the cycle. In a complex industrialized society groups are constantly forming and re-forming on the basis of new interests and new identities. Women, of course, have always possessed a sex-identification though perhaps not a group awareness. Today they represent a previously accommodated group which is endeavoring to modify the relationships between the sexes in the home, in work, and in the community.

The sex relations cycle bears important similarities to the race relations cycle. In the wake of the Industrial Revolution, as women acquired industrial, business, and professional skills, they increasingly sought employment in competition with men. Men were quick to perceive them as a rival group and made use of economic, legal, and ideological weapons to eliminate or reduce their competition. They excluded women from the trade unions, made contracts with employers to prevent their hiring women, passed laws restricting the employment of married women, caricatured the working woman, and carried on ceaseless propaganda to return women to the home or keep them there. Since the days of the suffragettes there has been no overt conflict between men and women on a group basis. Rather than conflict, the dissociative process between the sexes is that of contravention,[14] a type of opposition intermediate between competition and conflict. According to Wiese and Becker, it includes rebuffing, repulsing, working against, hindering, protesting, obstructing, restraining, and upsetting another's plans.

The present contravention of the sexes, arising from women's competition with men, is manifested in the discriminations against women, as well as in the doubts and uncertainties expressed concerning women's character, abilities, motives. The processes of competition and contravention are continually giving way to accommodation in the relationships between men and women. Like other minority groups, women have sought a protected position, a niche in the economy which they could occupy, and, like other minority groups, they have found these positions in new occupations in which dominant group members had not yet established themselves and in old occupations which they no longer wanted. When women entered fields which represented an extension of services in the home (except medicine!), they encountered least opposition. Evidence is accumulating, however, that women are becoming dissatisfied with the employment conditions of the great women-employing occupations and present accommodations are threatened.

What would assimilation of men and women mean? Park and Burgess in their classic text define assimilation as a "process of interpenetration and fusion in which persons and groups acquire the memories, sentiments, and attitudes of other persons or groups, and, by sharing their experiences and history, are incorporated with them in a cultural life." If accommodation is characterized by secondary contacts, assimilation holds the promise of primary contacts. If men and women were truly assimilated, we would find no cleavages of interest along sex lines. The special provinces of men and women would be abolished. Women's pages would disappear from the newspaper and women's magazines from the stands. All special women's organizations would pass into limbo. The sports page and racing news would be read indifferently by men and women. Interest in cookery and interior decoration would follow individual rather than sex lines. Women's talk would be no different from men's talk, and frank and full communication would obtain between the sexes.

The Marginal Woman

Group relationships are reflected in personal adjustments. Arising out of the present contravention of the sexes is the marginal woman, torn between rejection and acceptance of traditional roles and attributes. Uncertain of the ground on which she stands, subjected to conflicting cultural expectations, the marginal woman suffers the psychological ravages of instability, conflict, self-hate, anxiety, and resentment.

In applying the concept of marginality to women, the term "role" must be substituted for that of "group."[15] Many of the traditional devices for creating role differentiation among boys and girls, such as dress, manners, activities, have been de-emphasized in modern urban middle class homes. The small girl who wears a play suit, plays games with boys and girls together, attends a co-educational school, may have little awareness of sexual differentiation until the approach of adolescence. Parental expectations in the matters of scholarship, conduct toward others, duties in the home may have differed little for herself and her brother. But in high school or perhaps not until college she finds herself called upon to play a new role. Benedict[16] has called attention to discontinuities in the life cycle, and the fact that these continuities in cultural conditioning take a greater toll of girls than of boys is revealed in test scores showing neuroticism and introversion.[17] In adolescence girls find the frank, spontaneous behavior toward the neighboring sex no longer rewarding. High grades are more likely to elicit anxiety than praise from parents, especially mothers, who seem more pleased if male callers are frequent. There are subtle indications that to remain home with a good book on a Saturday night is a fate worse than death. But even if the die is successfully cast for popularity, all problems are not solved. Girls are encouraged to heighten their sexual attractiveness, but to abjure sexual expression.

Assuming new roles in adolescence does not mean the complete relinquishing of old ones. Scholarship, while not so vital as for the boy, is still important, but must be maintained discreetly and without obvious effort. Mirra Komarovsky[18] has supplied statements of Barnard College girls of the conflicting expectations of their elders. Even more than to the boy is the "all-round" ideal held up to girls, and it is not always possible to integrate the roles of good date, good daughter, good sorority sister, good student, good friend, and good citizen. The superior achievements of college men over college women bear witness to the crippling division of energies among women. Part of the explanation may lie in women's having interiorized cultural notions of feminine inferiority in certain fields, and even the most self-confident or most defensive woman may be filled with doubt as to whether she can do productive work.

It may be expected that as differences in privileges between men and women decrease, the frequency of marginal women will increase. Widening opportunities for women will call forth a growing number of women capable of performing roles formerly reserved for men, but whose acceptance in these new roles may well remain uncertain and problematic. This hypothesis is in accord with Arnold Green's[19] recent critical reexamination of the marginal man concept in which he points out that it is those Negroes and second-generation immigrants whose values and behavior most approximate those of the dominant majority who experience the most severe personal crises. He believes that the classical marginal man symptoms appear only when a person striving to leave the racial or ethnic group into which he was born is deeply identified with the family of orientation and is met with grudging, uncertain, and unpredictable acceptance, rather than with absolute rejection, by the group he is attempting to join, and also that he is committed to success-careerism. Analogically, one would expect to find that women who display marginal symptoms are psychologically bound to the family of orientation in which they experienced the imperatives of both the traditional and new feminine roles, and are seeking to expand the occupational (or other) areas open to women rather than those who content themselves with established fields. Concretely, one might suppose women engineers to have greater personality problems than women librarians.

Other avenues of investigation suggested by the minority group approach can only be mentioned. What social types arise as personal adjustments to sex status? What can be done in the way of experimental modification of the attitudes of men and women toward each other and themselves? What hypotheses of intergroup relations may be tested in regard to men and women? For example, is it true that as women approach the cultural standards of men, they are perceived as a threat and tensions increase? Of what significance are regional and community variations in the treatment of and degree of participation permitted women, mindful here that women share responsibility with men for the perpetuation of attitudes toward women? This paper is exploratory in suggesting the enhanced possibilities of fruitful analysis, if women are included in the minority group corpus, particularly with reference to such concepts and techniques as group belongingness, socialization of the minority group child, cultural differences, social distance tests, conflict between class and caste status, race relations cycle, and marginality. I believe that the concept of the marginal woman should be especially productive, and am now engaged in an empirical study of role conflicts in professional women.

REFERENCES

1. Louis Wirth, "The Problem of Minority Groups," in Ralph Linton, ed., *The Science of Man in the World Crisis* (New York: Columbia University Press, 1945), p. 347.
2. Kurt Lewin, "Self-Hatred Among Jews," *Contemporary Jewish Record,* 4 (1941), pp. 219–32.
3. *Fortune* (September, 1946), p. 5.
4. P. M. Symonds, "Changes in Sex Differences in Problems and Interests of Adolescents with Increasing Age," *Journal of Genetic Psychology, 50* (1937), pp. 83–89, as referred to by Georgene H. Seward, *Sex and the Social Order* (New York: McGraw-Hill, 1946), pp. 237–38.
5. George A. Lundberg, *Foundations of Sociology* (New York: Macmillan, 1939), p. 319.
6. Robert S. and Helen Merrell Lynd, *Middletown* (New York: Harcourt, Brace, 1929), p. 120, and *Middletown in Transition* (New York: Harcourt, Brace, 1937), p. 176.
7. Joseph Kirk Folsom, *The Family and Democratic Society* (New York: John Wiley, 1943), pp. 623–24.
8. Gunnar Myrdal, *An American Dilemma* (New York: Harper, 1944), pp. 1073–78, reprinted in this volume.
9. Helen M. Hacker, "Verso una Definizione dei Conflitti di Ruolo nelle Donne Moderne," *Studi di Sociologica,* 6 (1965), pp. 332–41.
10. As furnished by such books as Helene Deutsch, *The Psychology of Women* (New York: Grune & Stratton, 1944–45), and Ferdinand Lundberg and Marynia F. Farnham, *Modern Woman: The Lost Sex* (New York: Harper, 1947).
11. David Riesman, "The Saving Remnant: An Examination of Character Structure," in John W. Chase, ed., *Years of the Modern: An American Appraisal* (New York: Longmans, Green, 1945), pp. 139–40.
12. Robert E. Park, "Our Racial Frontier on the Pacific," *Survey Graphic, 56* (May 1, 1926), pp. 192–96.
13. William Ogburn and Meyer Nimkoff, *Sociology* (Boston: Houghton Mifflin, 2d ed., 1950), p. 187.
14. Howard Becker, *Systematic Sociology on the Basis of the "Beziehungslehre" and "Gebildlehre" of Leopold von Wiese* (New York: John Wiley, 1932), pp. 263–68.
15. Kurt Lewin, *Resolving Social Conflicts* (New York: Harper, 1948), p. 181.
16. Ruth Benedict, "Continuities and Discontinuities in Cultural Conditioning," *Psychiatry, 1* (1938), pp. 161–67.
17. Georgene H. Seward, *op. cit.,* pp. 239–40.
18. Mirra Komarovsky, "Cultural Contradictions and Sex Roles," *American Journal of Sociology, 52* (November, 1946), pp. 184–89.

19. Arnold Green, "A Re-Examination of the Marginal Man Concept," *Social Forces,* 26 (December, 1947), pp. 167–71.

A Parallel to
the Negro Problem

Gunnar Myrdal

In every society there are at least two groups of people, besides the Negroes, who are characterized by high social visibility expressed in physical appearance, dress, and patterns of behavior, and who have been "suppressed." We refer to women and children. Their present status, as well as their history and their problems in society, reveal striking similarities to those of the Negroes. In studying a special problem like the Negro problem, there is always a danger that one will develop a quite incorrect idea of its uniqueness. It will, therefore, give perspective to the Negro problem and prevent faulty interpretations to sketch some of the important similarities between the Negro problem and the women's problem.

In the historical development of these problem groups in America there have been much closer relations than is now ordinarily recorded. In the earlier common law, women and children were placed under the jurisdiction of the paternal power. When a legal status had to be found for the imported Negro servants in the seventeenth century, the nearest and most natural analogy was the status of women and children. The ninth commandment—linking together women, servants, mules, and other property—could be invoked, as well as a great number of other passages of Holy Scripture. We do not intend to follow here the interesting developments of the institution of slavery in America through the centuries, but merely wish to point out the paternalistic idea which held the slave to be a sort of family member and in some way—in spite of all differences—placed him beside women and children under the power of the *paterfamilias.*

Source: *An American Dilemma,* pp. 1073–78, copyright © 1944, 1962 by Harper & Row, Publishers, Incorporated. Reprinted by permission of the publishers.

There was, of course, even in the beginning, a tremendous difference both in actual status of these different groups and in the tone of sentiment in the respective relations. In the decades before the Civil War, in the conservative and increasingly antiquarian ideology of the American South, woman was elevated as an ornament and looked upon with pride, while the Negro slave became increasingly a chattel and a ward. The paternalistic construction came, however, to good service when the South had to build up a moral defense for slavery, and it is found everywhere in the apologetic literature up to the beginning of the Civil War. For illustration, some passages from George Fitzhugh's *Sociology for the South,* published in 1854, may be quoted as typical:

> The kind of slavery is adapted to the men enslaved. Wives and apprentices are slaves; not in theory only, but often in fact. Children are slaves to their parents, guardians and teachers. Imprisoned culprits are slaves. Lunatics and idiots are slaves also.[1]
> A beautiful example and illustration of this kind of communism, is found in the instance of the Patriarch Abraham. His wives and his children, his men servants and his maid servants, his camels and his cattle, were all equally his property. He could sacrifice Isaac or a ram, just as he pleased. He loved and protected all, and all shared, if not equally, at least fairly, in the products of their light labour. Who would not desire to have been a slave of that old Patriarch, stern and despotic as he was? . . . Pride, affection, self-interest, moved Abraham to protect, love and take care of his slaves. The same motives operate on all masters, and secure comfort, competency and protection to the slave. A man's wife and children are his slaves, and do they not enjoy, in common with himself, his property?[2]

Other protagonists of slavery resort to the same argument:

> In this country we believe that the general good requires us to deprive the whole female sex of the right of self-government. They have no voice in the formation of the laws which dispose of their persons and property. . . . We treat all minors much in the same way. . . . Our plea for all this is that the good of the whole is thereby most effectually promoted. . . .[3]

Significant manifestations of the result of this disposition [on the part of the Abolitionists] to consider their own light a surer guide than the word of God, are visible in the anarchical opinions about human governments, civil and ecclesiastical, and on the rights of women, which have found appropriate advocates in the abolition publications. . . . If our women are to be emancipated from subjection to the law which God has imposed upon them, if they are to quit the retirement of domestic life, where they preside in stillness over the character and destiny of society; . . . if, in studied insult to the authority of God, we are to renounce in the marriage contract all claim to obedience, we shall soon have a country over which the genius of Mary Wolstonecraft would delight to preside, but from which all order and all virtue would speedily be banished. There is no form of human excellence before which we bow with profounder deference than that which appears in a delicate woman, . . . and there is no deformity of human character from which we turn with deeper loathing than from a woman forgetful of her nature, and clamorous for the vocation and rights of men.[4]

. . . Hence her [Miss Martineau's] wild chapter about the "Rights of Women," her groans and invectives because of their exclusion from the offices of the state, the right of suffrage, the exercise of political authority. In all this, the error of the declaimer consists in the very first movement of the mind. "The Rights of *Women*" may all be conceded to the sex, yet the rights of *men* withheld from them.[5]

The parallel goes, however, considerably deeper than being only a structural part in the defense ideology built up around slavery. Women at that time lacked a number of rights otherwise belonging to all free white citizens of full age.

So chivalrous, indeed, was the ante-bellum South that its women were granted scarcely any rights at all. Everywhere they were subjected to political, legal, educational, and social and economic restrictions. They took no part in governmental affairs, were without legal rights over their property or the guardianship of their children, were denied adequate educational facilities, and were excluded from business and the professions.[6]

The same was very much true of the rest of the country and of the rest of the world. But there was an especially close relation in the South between the subordination of women and that of Negroes. This is perhaps best expressed in a comment attributed to Dolly

Madison, that the Southern wife was "the chief slave of the harem."[7]

From the very beginning, the fight in America for the liberation of the Negro slaves was, therefore, closely coordinated with the fight for women's emancipation. It is interesting to note that the Southern states, in the early beginning of the political emancipation of women during the first decades of the nineteenth century, had led in the granting of legal rights to women. This was the time when the South was still the stronghold of liberal thinking in the period leading up to and following the Revolution. During the same period the South was also the region where Abolitionist societies flourished, while the North was uninterested in the Negro problem. Thereafter the two movements developed in close interrelation and were both gradually driven out of the South.

The women suffragists received their political education from the Abolitionist movement. Women like Angelina Grimke, Sarah Grimke, and Abby Kelly began their public careers by speaking for Negro emancipation and only gradually came to fight for women's rights. The three great suffragists of the nineteenth century—Lucretia Mott, Elizabeth Cady Stanton, and Susan B. Anthony—first attracted attention as ardent campaigners for the emancipation of the Negro and the prohibition of liquor. The women's movement got much of its public support by reason of its affiliation with the Abolitionist movement: the leading male advocates of woman suffrage before the Civil War were such Abolitionists as William Lloyd Garrison, Henry Ward Beecher, Wendell Phillips, Horace Greeley, and Frederick Douglass. The women had nearly achieved their aims, when the Civil War induced them to suppress all tendencies distracting the federal government from the prosecution of the War. They were apparently fully convinced that victory would bring the suffrage to them as well as to the Negroes.[8]

The Union's victory, however, brought disappointment to the women suffragists. The arguments "the Negro's hour" and "a political necessity" met and swept aside all their arguments for leaving the word "male" out of the 14th Amendment and putting "sex" alongside "race" and "color" in the 15th Amendment.[9] Even their Abolitionist friends turned on them, and the Republican party shied away from them. A few Democrats, really not in favor of the extension of the suffrage to anyone, sought to make political capital out of the women's demands, and said with Senator Cowan of Pennsylvania, "If I have no reason to offer why a Negro man shall not vote, I have no reason why a white woman shall not vote." Charges of being Democrats and traitors were heaped on the women leaders. Even a few Negroes, invited to the women's convention of January, 1869, denounced the women for jeopardizing the black man's chances for the vote. The War and Reconstruction Amendments had thus sharply divided the women's problem from the Negro problem in actual politics.[10] The deeper relation between the two will, however, be recognized up till this day. Du Bois' famous ideological manifesto *The Souls of Black Folk*[11] is, to mention only one example, an ardent appeal on behalf of women's interests as well as those of the Negro.

This close relation is no accident. The ideological and economic forces behind the two movements—the emancipation of women and children and the emancipation of Negroes—have much in common and are closely interrelated. Paternalism was a pre-industrial scheme of life, and was gradually becoming broken in the nineteenth century. Negroes and women, both of whom had been under the yoke of the paternalistic system, were both strongly and fatefully influenced by the Industrial Revolution. For neither group is the readjustment process yet consummated. Both are still problem groups. The women's problem is the center of the whole complex of problems of how to reorganize the institution of the family to fit the new economic and ideological basis, a problem which is not solved in any part of the Western world unless it be in the Soviet Union or Palestine. The family problem in the Negro group, as we find when analyzing the Negro family, has its special complications, centering in the tension and conflict between the external patriarchal system in which the Negro was confined as a slave and his own family structure.

As in the Negro problem, most men have accepted as self-evident, until recently, the doctrine that women had inferior endowments in most of those respects which carry prestige, power, and advantages in society, but that they were, at the same time, superior in some other respects. The arguments, when arguments were used, have been about the same: smaller brains, scarcity of geniuses and so on.

The study of women's intelligence and personality has had broadly the same history as the one we record for Negroes. As in the case of the Negro, women themselves have often been brought to believe in their inferiority of endowment. As the Negro was awarded his "place" in society, so there was a "woman's place." In both cases the rationalization was strongly believed that men, in confining them to this place, did not act against the true interest of the subordinate groups. The myth of the "contented women," who did not want to have suffrage or other civil rights and equal opportunities, had the same social function as the myth of the "contented Negro." In both cases there was probably—in a static sense—often some truth behind the myth.

As to the character of the deprivations, upheld by law or by social conventions and the pressure of public opinion, no elaboration will here be made. As important and illustrative in the comparison, we shall, however, stress the conventions governing woman's education. There was a time when the most common idea was that she was better off with little education. Later the doctrine developed that she should not be denied education, but that her education should be of a special type, fitting her for her "place" in society and usually directed more on training her hands than her brains.

Political franchise was not granted to women until recently. Even now there are, in all countries, great difficulties for a woman to attain public office. The most important disabilities still affecting her status are those barring her attempt to earn a living and to attain promotion in her work. As in the Negro's case, there are certain "women's jobs," traditionally monopolized by women. They are regularly in the low salary bracket and do not offer much of a career. All over the world men have used the trade unions to keep women out of competition. Woman's competition has, like the Negro's, been particularly obnoxious and dreaded by men because of the low wages women, with their few earning outlets, are prepared to work for. Men often dislike the very idea of having women on an equal plane as co-workers and competitors, and usually they find it even more "unnatural" to work under women. White people generally hold similar attitudes toward Negroes. On the other hand, it is said about women that they prefer men as bosses and do not want to work under another woman. Negroes often feel the same way about working under other Negroes.

In personal relations with both women and Negroes, white men generally prefer a less professional and more human relation, actually a more paternalistic and protective position—somewhat in the nature of patron to client in Roman times, and like the corresponding strongly paternalistic relation of later feudalism. As in Germany it is said that every gentile has his pet Jew, so it is said in the South that every white has his "pet nigger," or—in the upper strata—several of them. We sometimes marry the pet woman, carrying out the paternalistic scheme. But even if we do not, we tend to deal kindly with her as a client and a ward, not as a competitor and an equal.

In drawing a parallel between the position of, and feeling toward, women and Negroes we are uncovering a fundamental basis of our culture. Although it is changing, atavistic elements sometimes unexpectedly break through even in the most emancipated individuals. The similarities in the women's and the Negroes' problems are not accidental. They were, as we have pointed out, originally determined in a paternalistic order of society. The problems remain, even though paternalism is gradually declining as an ideal and is losing its economic basis. In the final analysis, women are still hindered in their competition by the function of procreation; Negroes are laboring under the yoke of the doctrine of unassimilability which has remained although slavery is abolished. The second barrier is actually much stronger than the first in America today. But the first is more eternally inexorable.[12]

REFERENCES

1. George Fitzhugh, *Sociology for the South* (Richmond: A. Morris, 1854), p. 86.
2. *Ibid.,* p. 297.
3. Charles Hodge, "The Bible Argument on Slavery," in E. N. Elliott, ed., *Cotton is King, and Pro-Slavery Arguments* (Augusta, Ga.: Pritchard, Abbott and Loomis, 1860), pp. 859–60.
4. Albert T. Bledsoe, *An Essay on Liberty and Slavery* (Philadelphia: Lippincott, 1856).
5. W. Gilmore Simms, "The Morals of Slavery," in *The Pro-Slavery Argument as Maintained by the Most Distinguished Writers of the Southern*

States (Philadelphia: Lippincott, Grambo, 1853). See also Simms' "Address on the Occasion of the Inauguration of the Spartanburg Female College," August 12, 1855 (Spartanburg: Published by the Trustees, 1855).

6. Virginius Dabney, *Liberalism in the South* (Chapel Hill: University of North Carolina Press, 1932), p. 361.

7. Cited in Harriet Martineau, *Society in America* (New York: Saunders and Otley, 1837), 1842 ed., 2, p. 81.

8. Carrie Chapman Catt and Nettie Rogers Shuler, *Woman Suffrage and Politics* (New York: Scribner's, 1923), p. 32ff.

9. The relevant sections of the 14th and 15th Amendments of the Constitution are (italics ours):

    14th Amendment
    Section 2. Representatives shall be apportioned among the several States according to their respective numbers, counting the whole number of persons in each State, excluding Indians not taxed. But when the right to vote at any election for the choice of Electors for President and Vice President of the United States, Representatives in Congress, the executive and judicial officers of a State, or the members of the Legislature thereof, is denied to any of the *male* inhabitants of such State, being twenty-one years of age, and citizens of the United States, or in any way abridged, except for participation in rebellion, or other crime, the basis of representation therein shall be reduced in the proportion which the number of such *male* citizens shall bear to the whole number of *male* citizens twenty-one years of age in such State.
    15th Amendment
    Section 1. The right of citizens of the United States to vote shall not be denied or abridged by the United States or by any State on account of *race, color or previous condition of servitude.*

10. While there was a definite affinity between the Abolitionist movement and the woman suffrage movement, there was also competition and, perhaps, antipathy, between them that widened with the years. As early as 1833, when Oberlin College opened its doors to women—the first college to do so—the Negro men students joined other men students in protesting (Catt and Shuler, *op. cit.*, p. 13). The Anti-Slavery Convention held in London in 1840 refused to seat the women delegates from America, and it was on this instigation that the first women's rights convention was called (*ibid.*, p. 17). After the passage of the 13th, 14th, and 15th Amendments, which gave legal rights to Negroes but not to women, the women's movement split off completely from the Negroes' movement, except for such a thing as the support of both movements by the rare old liberal, Frederick Douglass. An expression of how far the two movements had separated by 1903 was given by one of the leaders of the women's movement at that time, Anna Howard Shaw, in answer to a question posed to her at a convention in New Orleans:
    " 'What is your purpose in bringing your convention to the South? Is it the desire of suffragists to force upon us the social equality of

black and white women? Political equality lays the foundation for social equality. If you give the ballot to women, won't you make the black and white woman equal politically and therefore lay the foundation for a future claim of social equality?' . . .

"I read the question aloud. Then the audience called for the answer, and I gave it in these words, quoted as accurately as I can remember them:

" 'If political equality is the basis of social equality, and if by granting political equality you lay the foundation for a claim of social equality, I can only answer that you have already laid that claim. You did not wait for woman suffrage, but disfranchised both your black and white women, thus making them politically equal. But you have done more than that. You have put the ballot into the hands of your black men, thus making them the political superiors of your white women. Never before in the history of the world have men made former slaves the political masters of their former mistresses!' " (*The Story of a Pioneer*, 1915, pp. 311–12).

11. W. E. Burghardt Du Bois, *The Souls of Black Folk* (Chicago: McClurg, 1903).
12. Alva Myrdal, *Nation and Family* (New York: Harper, 1941).

Homosexuals as a Minority Group

Franklin E. Kameny

The concept of the homosexual as a member of a minority group was introduced into modern thinking by Donald Webster Cory, in 1951, in his book *The Homosexual in America,* and has been one of the underlying themes of what has come to be known as the homophile movement (the movement to improve the status of the homosexual and to create better lives for homosexuals as homosexuals) which had its immediate origin in that book. It has only been since the early and middle 1960's, however, with the beginning of the almost explosive growth of that movement, and the development by it of a widely publicized, extensive, detailed, and positive philosophy and ideology in support of its claim to full equality of the homosexual with the heterosexual and (distinct, but equally important) of homosexuality with heterosexuality, that the minority concept has been strongly pushed and solutions actively sought for

ffect—a "snowballing"—which results in reinforcement or ex-
n of the stereotyping and other aspects of the negative re-
es of the majority.

will easily be seen, every group which is considered a socio-
l minority group meets the four criteria for as long as it re-
a minority group (the minority condition, being a function
onsequence of majority attitudes toward the minority, and of
ity–majority interaction, is not a permanent state).

ile for those at all familiar with the position of the homosexual
society, it will be reasonably self-evident that he comes well
the definition just set up, it might be worthwhile, neverthe-
explore briefly but in somewhat greater detail, the manner in
the homosexual meets the four points or criteria of the minor-
inition.

definition of homosexual, given earlier, provides the basis
int 1. The defining characteristic is, of course, a dominant or
ry preference for entering into close and intimate affectional
xual relationships with persons of the same gender, rather than
hose of the opposite gender (note that, frequent misconcep-
o the contrary notwithstanding, homosexuality is far more a
of love and affection than it is commonly considered to be;
sexuality is less so than it is rationalized into being; and, in
of fact, love and lust enter in about the same proportions
oth).

ubstantiation of Point 2, one need only cite the fact that had
mosexual the visibility of the Negro, there would be close to
,000 unemployed homosexuals in this country; that homo-
s are excluded from Federal employment totally without regard
npetence and ability; from eligibility for security clearances,
vhen publicly acknowledged (and, therefore, not subject to
ail—in itself a consequence of the prejudice and discrimina-
issue); and from service in the military and from many vet-
benefits available to others with identical discharges; that a
homosexual will find his educational opportunities severely
; various provisions of the criminal law, nominally applicable
to both homosexuals and heterosexuals are, in actual fact,

the problems afflicting homosexuals in terms derived from classification of these problems as minority group ones.

However, if the problems of the homosexual are to be classed as
minority group problems, a demonstration must be made that homosexuals are indeed a minority group. This categorization of homosexuals is resisted by many.

If the concept of a minority group applied to the homosexual is
to be discussed intelligently and conclusions drawn therefrom, both
terms, *homosexual* and *minority*, must be defined. Both—particularly the latter—are rather loosely used. In addition, a certain amount
of intellectual underbrush and clutter—particularly the characterization of homosexuality as pathological—must be cleared out of the
way.

Let us start with the definition of *homosexual*. When we examine
the large mass of people, we find that for whatever the reasons (and
those reasons are not relevant here) most people have a dominant
preference in respect to the gender of the persons with whom they
enter into close and intimate affectional and sexual relationships.
Either they prefer to enter into such relationships with those of the
opposite gender, or with those of the same gender. Relatively few
feel even approximately equally attracted toward both. Thus we find
a bimodal distribution with a lightly populated continuum between
the two unequal peaks. One might put the matter somewhat more
lightly and note that most men have an "erotic eye"; that, traditionally, most are—potentially or actually—"girl watchers"; most of
the remainder are "boy watchers" (using the term "boy" in precise
parallel with the usage of the term "girl" to mean an attractive
woman and, of course, not, in either case, to mean a juvenile), while
a few are both; and fewer are neither. One has there in a nutshell,
the heterosexuals, the homosexuals, the bisexuals, and the asexuals,
which includes just about everybody.

Behavior, of course, does not always concord with inclinations and
preferences. Not all heterosexuals can indulge their preference (for
example, those unfortunate enough to be in prison) nor can all
homosexuals (for example, those unfortunate enough to be hetero-
sexually married), and so the definition must remain in terms of
what people *would* do, not what they *do* do.

As stated, the term *minority* is loosely and promiscuously used, with little effort made to define it. Obviously it refers to something more than a mere mathematical entity; women—in the numerical majority in this country—are properly considered to be a minority group.

Looking at those to whom the term is applied, one finds a broad and disparate group of groups indeed, seemingly having no unifying rationale or basis: religion, country of ancestral origin, skin color, gender, etc. Some of these, such as skin color (that is, so-called *race*) are genetic and inherited; some, such as country of ancestral origin, are little more than historical facts; some, such as religion, are environmentally determined. In order to apply the term *minority* to the homosexual, one must, therefore, define the term as it is applied to others where the usage is incontrovertible, find the unifying factors, and then see if the definition and unifying factors so derived do, in fact, apply to the homosexual.

When one examines the concept, as it is applied to all of the varied groups regularly and uncontroversially included within it, it is seen that all groups considered as minorities meet four basic criteria, which together can be taken as a definition of the minority condition or of a *sociological minority*. These are:

1. *The minority characteristic:* This is a characteristic, or group of closely related characteristics, serving to define the minority group. This can be skin color, mode of religious worship, etc.

2. *Prejudice and discrimination:* Because of the minority characteristic, but not in logical consequence of it, the minority group member is subjected to adverse prejudice and discrimination (usually severe). There are few features of lesser significance in judging any aspect of a person than the color of his skin. Yet, because of the color of a Negro's skin, but not in logical consequence of it, he is subjected to severe adverse prejudice and discrimination.

3. *Depersonalization:* The member of the minority group is not considered and judged upon his own merits and demerits, strengths and weaknesses, but is considered and judged upon the basis of an impersonal—and almost invariably derogatory—characterization of the

entire group, and relegated, thereby, to second ⋯ to be a member of the minority group is consid⋯ a basis for contempt, derision, and scorn. Ster⋯ which are actually representative of at most a mi⋯ ity, or of none at all. Let a white, Anglo-Saxon⋯ estant commit a crime, make himself ridiculou⋯ offensive, and he alone bears the consequences⋯ member of a minority group do likewise, and ⋯ reinforce existing low performance expectations⋯ stereotypes applied to all members of the minorit⋯ own individual conduct or demeanor. A minor⋯ not considered for a job upon the basis of hi⋯ and competence, but upon a usually adverse pr⋯ of his entire group. Thus there is a profound ⋯ deindividualization.

4. *Internalization:* In response to the attitud⋯ him, the minority group and its members deve⋯ and "they." Group cohesiveness, subcultures, ⋯ and withdrawal from the larger society, and ofte⋯ an inward looking tendency (all built around th⋯ istic) develop in varying degrees. The minorit⋯ ally of secondary importance at best (logicall⋯ minority group member, the primary basis for ⋯ self-identification (that is, he becomes, first, a N⋯ sexual, and only second a physicist, an artist, ⋯ man being). Depending in a complex way u⋯ kind of psychological support which the min⋯ culture supply to its individual members, and ⋯ of the individual member at which such sup⋯ significant role, the minority group member ⋯ cepts a significant amount of society's negative ⋯ with the resulting lowered self-esteem, damag⋯ self-confidence and self-respect. All of these⋯ themselves in the incidental features of the s⋯ its literature, its amusements, for example), as ⋯ of its individual members, often resulting in ⋯

applied selectively against homosexuals. This brief listing of manifestations of prejudice and discrimination, logically unrelated to affectional and sexual preference, could be augmented considerably. There seems to be little point; criterion 2 is obviously well met by the homosexual.

The basis for Point 3 is also well established. The stereotype of the effeminate homosexual is too well known to warrant further discussion, aside from noting explicitly that it applies to but a small minority of the minority. The generalized contempt, scorn, derision, and ridicule directed at homosexuality and at the homosexual per se, totally without regard for him as an individual human being, are also too well known to warrant lengthy discussion here. The type of job discrimination alluded to above, in which applicants are excluded not upon the basis of their own relevant qualifications or the lack thereof, but upon the basis of irrelevant characteristics of their private lives, is also evidence of the Point 3 depersonalization in question.

Finally, in respect to Point 4, there has long existed a homosexual subculture, with its own jargon or argot, gathering places, special customs, group humor, lines of communication, a rudimentary (but growing) sense of unity, and a stronger sense of community. Although one's affectional and sexual preferences, and the portion of one's life built around them, is not unimportant, they do not logically define a person. Nevertheless, the homosexual, in response to society's attitudes toward him, and in common with the members of other minority groups, does have a strong Point 4 tendency to think of himself as a homosexual first, and anything else second. The concept of a homosexual community is being put forth and is being accepted by both the homosexual minority itself, and by the majority.

As discussed below, the community is formally organized, both in terms of inner directed group interests, and in terms of action directed toward altering the attitudes and actions of the majority which create the minority state. In the sense of Point 4, the homosexual minority exists as a well-defined entity, although perhaps (and in no sense detracting from the reality of its existence) with somewhat fuzzy outer edges.

Thus consideration shows that the homosexual in modern America also meets all of the criteria set forth, and meets them well. It follows that one may, and properly should, consider the homosexuals as constituting a sociological minority group.

With how large a minority is one dealing? While accurate figures are extremely difficult to obtain, it would seem, upon the basis of the Kinsey data examined and interpreted in the light of the definition given above, plus knowledgeable observation of the homosexual community, both its visible and hidden sectors, that as a somewhat conservative estimate, probably not too far from the truth, and a convenient figure to use, one can assume that about 10 percent of the nonjuvenile population, men and women both, are homosexual. This amounts to some 15,000,000 Americans—the nation's largest minority after women and Negroes—and, as a minority group, having problems different in detail but not different in essence from those of all other minority groups, and raising problems for a nominally pluralistic society different in detail but not different in essence from those raised by all other minority groups.

Because of the unfortunate hold which psychiatry has upon the current American outlook, there is a tendency for many troublesome social problems to be categorized and dealt with in psychiatric and psychological terms. This is, at times, a useful approach. All too often, however, it has the double effect of throwing burdens of responsibility, blame, and culpability upon undeserving individuals or groups victimized by societal prejudice, while tacitly exculpating an often highly culpable society and, more important, diverting efforts at solution of the problem into intrinsically unproductive channels. One would get nowhere, for example, by directing efforts to cure anti-Semitism at individual Jews or at all Jews, instead of at anti-Semites, singly or *en masse,* and their anti-Semitism conceptually.

The handling of homosexuality is, perhaps, as superb an example of this process as can be found. In past years, homosexuals were condemned as sinful. Sin is no longer very fashionable, and the high priests and religions of old have been replaced, as authorities in our society, by the high priests and religions of the new—the psychiatrists and the psychoanalysts, and their dogmas and revealed "truths." So (with a detour via "criminal," the consequences of which are still with us) homosexuals are now "sick." The attribution of sickness stands up to examination as poorly as did that of sinfulness.

By approaching homosexuality as a problem in emotional or psychological disorder, rather than as a problem in prejudice against a minority group, society very effectively shrugs off the major portion, if, indeed, not all of the burden of responsibility and guilt for its persecution of, maltreatment of, and prejudice and discrimination against its homosexual members, and very effectively throws onto the homosexual himself the onus of correcting a situation which not only is not his to correct (not, be it noted, because he may not be able to change, but because he himself needs no change, even were it possible) but of which he is the victim.

It can be argued, of course, that to be ill, sick, defective, or otherwise "less than whole" is not only not inconsistent with minority status, but, in fact, may be the basis for minority status. This is a weak argument, at best. Part of the essence of minority status, as the term is usually used, is a placing of persons into a second class status who are, in actuality, full, first class individuals, on par with others in *all* respects. More important, perhaps, in a pragmatic sense, is the profound sense of inferiority, diminished self-esteem, and damaged self-image, which is frequently (not always) part of the minority condition. A misconception that the particular minority condition is a sickness, disturbance, or other defect or disorder (particularly a mental or emotional one, given our society's very real reaction, rightly or wrongly, to "mental illness") with the aura of second rateness which goes with that, is extremely effective both in preventing the establishment of the minority group member's self-esteem and in reinforcing society's efforts to derogate and denigrate him and, therefore, in aborting efforts to create better lives for the members of the minority.

When an attribution of sickness is accepted, one finds that instead of efforts by enlightened members of the majority to raise the minority members to a full and meaningful equality, there is a kind of condescendingly patronizing compassion for "these poor, (physically or emotionally) maimed or crippled individuals who really shouldn't be looked down upon" (but who are, anyway). While enormously satisfying to many members of the majority (who sometimes gain a great deal of their own self-respect from efforts to help the disadvantaged and who, therefore—often quite unintentionally and without conscious malice—tend to try to keep the underdog down, so that they will continue to have someone to whom to feel superior), this is degrading to the minority group member, and utterly destructive of his self-respect. He does not want crumbs of sympathy thrown at him from the table of the self-satisfied "whole" majority group members. Further, a considerable amount of effort is diverted, as a result of the attribution of illness, to the "cure" and prevention of the condition, and diverted from the cure and prevention of the prejudice against the condition. In the case of some conditions, of course, the facts support an appellation of pathology of one kind or another, and those facts must then be lived with realistically. In the case of homosexuality, this is explicitly not so, and the attribution of pathology merely adds unnecessarily to the burdens borne by the homosexual as a result of majority attitudes toward this minority.

Before constructive solutions can be sought for the problems of a particular minority, these problems must obviously be examined from the proper perspective. Because the parallel is a good one, it will bear repetition to say that one will get nowhere, for example, in solving the problems accompanying anti-Semitism by studying Judaism, and by efforts to "reform" Jews or to convert them from their "heresies" and to Christianity; the problem lies not with the Jews, but with the anti-Semites. The Jew does not want sympathy for his "poor inferior religious state." He wants a cure for anti-Semitism, so that he can practice a Judaism which is objectively on a par with Christianity, as homosexuality is with heterosexuality.

In the case of the homosexual, of course, as stated and despite widespread misimpressions to the contrary, his condition is in no way a sickness or disorder. Clearly, for many this will need demonstration.

One must commence by noting that psychologically based deviance is not properly equated, *a priori,* with sickness, disturbance, or disorder. Therefore when such deviance is made the basis for an allegation of sickness, the total burden of proof and demonstration rests with those asserting sickness, not with those refuting the assertion. Those claiming that homosexuality is a sickness or disorder have clearly not only not shouldered their burden, but they have failed abysmally to do so.

A study of the psychiatric literature on homosexuality shows that in attempting to shoulder this burden, it fails upon three counts:

1. *Poor definition:* When any effort is made at all to define terms such as sickness, disturbance, pathology, etc., in this context (and in a large number of instances, not even an attempt at such effort is made), the definition amounts to little if at all anything more than mere nonconformity.

When the homosexual persists in his nonconformity, despite the punitive disadvantages imposed upon him by society—when (as religious minorities have been doing through history) he chooses to follow the path of *his* choice or preference, rather than society's choice, and chooses to remain true to himself instead of submitting to society—then he is termed unrealistic, masochistic, or (the psychiatrists' ultimate "dirty word," used for the final condemnation of those who do not submit to their "human engineering" or to the dicta of society), *compulsive.*

2. *Poor scientific technique:* The bulk of the existing literature on homosexuality is based upon studies of patients coming to a psychiatrist's office—a sampling obviously pre-selected for an almost 100 percent incidence of emotional problems, disturbance, and disorder. Generalization to an entire group from such a sampling is clearly invalid and intellectually dangerous. There are eminent proponents of the "sickness" theory of homosexuality, who are on formal record as having never seen a homosexual, meaningfully, outside a clinical or therapeutic setting. And yet they generalize from this obviously biased sampling to all homosexuals.

This generalization constitutes a total disregard for basic scientific investigative technique. Allegations, for example, that certain types of family background produce homosexuality are made with no attempt to investigate heterosexual control groups to discover whether or not such patterns are not simply characteristic of late twentieth century American families in general.

From the viewpoint of a scientist, the literature on homosexuality presents an unparalleled and depressing example of shabby, shoddy, slovenly, slipshod, just plain bad science.

3. *Poor logic:* Over and over, in reading the literature on homosexuality, one encounters *a priori* assumptions fed in at the beginning of an investigation, only to be plucked out, intact, at the end, as conclusions.

One eminent "authority" states, for example: "All psychoanalytic theories *assume* that adult homosexuality is psychopathologic . . . ." (Emphasis added.) No effort is made to prove the assumption. This same "authority" then goes on to say: "We *assume* that heterosexuality is the biologic norm and that unless interfered with all individuals are heterosexual." (Emphasis added.) Questions aside as to the connotations with which the word *norm* is possibly being imbued here, no effort is ever made to prove this assumption (either half of it, or as a whole). Obviously, given two such "revealed truths" it is small wonder that this "researcher" "finds" homosexuality to be pathological. Disprove his assumptions, and the entire ornate intellectual edifice which he has erected collapses. He is typical of his colleagues.

Another prominent "authority" tells us, in one breath, with an utterly irrational and almost Puritan indignation, that homosexuals are taking the easy way out (because homosexual sex, allegedly, is so much more easily available than heterosexual sex) and are therefore sick; and, in the next breath, that anyone who would persist in homosexuality despite the harsh, savage, and punitively applied strictures of society is masochistically choosing the hard way, and is therefore sick. Inconsistency, thy name is Psychiatry.

Poor logic also characterizes discussions of the nature, causes, and origins of homosexuality. Obviously, if the only alternatives considered are pathological in some way, homosexuality will be "found" to have pathological causes and to be pathological. The process goes farther. Unconventional but nonpathological backgrounds (such as a family with a dominant mother) which are alleged (falsely) to produce homosexuality, are considered pathological, in part, because the homosexuality supposedly arising from them is looked upon as pathological. This last serves as an excellent, highly sophisticated device for supporting the traditional patriarchal family, departures from which seem to leave many psychiatrists and, especially, psychoanalysts, extremely uneasy, because (heaven forfend!) the old, sacred gender roles are being successfully brought into question, and much of classical psychiatry might crumble if this should succeed.

Those few psychiatric studies which have successfully avoided these three pitfalls have consistently found no pathology in homosexuality, per se, or in homosexuals, per se.

The use of the sickness designation serves much the same purpose in keeping homosexuals subordinate, as did the older anthropological studies purporting to show that, in one way or another, the Negro was intellectually and otherwise inferior.

In short, homosexuals have, in effect, been *defined* into sickness by a mixture of moral, cultural, social, and theological value judgments, cloaked and camouflaged in the language of science.

To sum up, the total lack of valid scientific evidence to the contrary, homosexuality cannot correctly be considered as a sickness, illness, disturbance, disorder, neurosis, or other pathology of any kind, nor as a symptom of any of these, but must be considered as a preference, orientation, or propensity, not different in kind from heterosexuality, and fully on par with it.

Having disposed of the sickness fallacy, as a bit of intellectual clutter, and having, thereby, cleared the underbrush, one can proceed to get consideration of homosexuality off the psychoanalyst's couch and out of the psychiatrist's office, and approach it realistically, constructively, and productively as the problem in prejudice and discrimination against a minority group that it actually is. As is well known in the homosexual community, the majority of homosexuals are reasonably well adjusted to their homosexuality and have found an acceptable *modus vivendi* if, perhaps, through no fault of their own, not an ideal one, in which that minority who have any specific difficulties with their homosexuality (beyond coping with the generalized societal contempt and nonacceptance) are far more likely to have employment problems not of their own making, than they are to have emotional problems.

As with other minority groups, the problems of the homosexual as such, in their entirety, either are or stem directly from problems of prejudice and discrimination directed against their minority by the hostile majority around them.

It has well and correctly been said that there is no Negro problem, there is a white problem. It can equally correctly be said that
with this minority, too, there is no homosexual problem, there is a
heterosexual problem.

It seems obvious that to the extent that any minority group has
organized itself or is capable of group feeling and expression, or has
developed any extensive sense of self-identity, in line with Point 4
above, its aim, in sum, will be its removal from minority status.[1]
Many American groups, to a greater or lesser degree, have succeeded
in this—sometimes by a process of passive evolution, and in other
instances through action directed at the elimination of the minority
defining prejudice. Among these are the Irish and the Italians and,
more recently, the generalized group of Catholics (of whom the
Irish and Italians make up the two major white sectors). Well advanced, but with some way yet to go, are the Jews and women.
Advancing, but with a rather long way yet to go, are the Negroes.
American homosexuals have just begun their effort. It is an increasingly well organized, increasingly extensive effort, gradually gaining
support from outside the minority.

Upon analysis, within the framework of the minority definition
set up above, this effort is seen to be two pronged. One prong is a
multifaceted attempt to eliminate the prejudice and discrimination
by changing the attitudes of the majority, eliminating stereotypes,
changing laws and governmental policies. In short, it is an attack
upon Points 2 and 3 of the definition.

The other prong is an attack upon the attitudes toward and conceptions of self which go with Point 4. A systematic effort is being
made to instill into the homosexual a sense of his own worth; of
pride in his homosexuality; of confidence in homosexuality as a way
of life as rewarding and satisfying to the homosexual as heterosexuality is to the heterosexual, and not only harmless to society but
one in which the homosexual can potentially live a life useful and
productive to society if society will allow him to do so; of the full
equality of homosexuality with heterosexuality; of his moral right
to be homosexual and to live his homosexuality, fully, freely, openly,
and with dignity, free of arrogant and insolent pressures upon him
to convert to the prevailing heterosexuality. A major aspect of that

effort is an attempt to counter the insidious conception of homosexuality as a sickness or disorder, or as the effect of a flawed background, since, aside from their factual incorrectness, these concepts serve to rob the homosexual of dignity and are degrading and demeaning. One result of all of these efforts is a rapidly growing militancy upon the part of the homosexual community—particularly younger homosexuals. The homosexual is no longer willing to look upon his homosexuality as an affliction, to be put up with at worst, and to be prevented, discouraged, or changed, at best. He would not change if he could, nor has any valid reason been supplied to him for making such a change even if he could, or for prevention of his condition.

In parallel with the slogan *Black is Beautiful,* so wisely adopted by the Negro community, and serving precisely the same psychologically supportive and reparative functions, the homophile movement has adopted the slogan *Gay is Good.*[2] It is not impossible that as an intermediate step, the separation of Point 4 may, perhaps, be exacerbated, as it is for the Negro at present, but if that should occur for the homosexual minority, it is likely to be an unfortunate temporary stage on the road to the acceptance which marks the vanishing of minority status.

The effort is directed then (and properly so) at eliminating minority status *not* by eliminating or preventing occurrence of the Point 1 characteristic, but by elimination of the Point 2 and 3 abuses, and those of their Point 4 effects which may be less desirable—by modifying the society, and not, in any fundamental sense, by modifying or eliminating the homosexual.

The homosexual minority, like other minorities, is organizing, in order to achieve its goals. Some forty or fifty organizations have sprung up across the country, most of them united into a loose superstructure called the North American Conference of Homophile Organizations. By working through the communications media, by direct public appearances in large and growing number of homosexuals as homosexuals, by court test cases and negotiations with public officials, by meetings with the clergy and religious groups, by use of the ballot box and other effective forms of political action, and by other externally directed methods, and by working, as well, with the homosexual community and with individual homosexuals, these organizations attempt to create better lives for homosexuals as homosexuals. This is to be achieved through acceptance, by society and himself, of the homosexual and his homosexuality as equal to and on par with the heterosexual and his heterosexuality. All of this can readily be seen as parallel with the efforts by other minorities to achieve the acceptance as equals which marks the end of their status as sociological minorities.

One immediate manifestation of all this is the increasing doffing by homosexuals of the "masks" and "camouflage" which they have traditionally worn. They have had enough of furtivity, with the distortions of life and psyche which go with it, and in "coming out of the closet" in ever greater numbers, are finding the fresh air and sunshine of public disclosure refreshing, relaxing, and to their liking.

In consequence, homosexuals are finding that, one by one, and gradually, the rights, freedoms, and amenities of life, routinely accepted by the heterosexual majority, are opening up to them *as homosexuals*—running the gamut from (as examples) changing laws, declining restrictions upon employment, and diminishing assaults upon their dignity and their status as first class human beings and first class citizens, to an increasingly open social life for homosexuals comparable to that which heterosexuals have always enjoyed, including, illustratively, open public dances for homosexual college students similar to those long considered an integral part of heterosexual college life.

In summary, then, the homosexual meets the criteria met by all other groups commonly accepted as sociological minorities and must, therefore, be considered as a minority group not different, as such, from other American minorities. His minority status is one based upon an objectively neutral condition, manifested by a mere non-pejorative mathematical deviance from the statistical norm and a resulting adverse societal reaction arising from unsubstantiated prejudice. Neither the minority status, the deviance, nor the prejudice arise from nor are they based upon pathology, misfortune, defect, or inferiority of any kind, either of the homosexual or of his condition. Like many other minority groups, but later than most, the homosexual is following closely in the American tradition of refusal to accept his disadvantaged status, and of organization to better his lot, with the ultimate goal of transforming himself from the status of a sociological minority to that of a mere numerical minority, and is meeting with significant success in that endeavor, although the road ahead is likely to be a long, difficult, and often discouraging one.

REFERENCES

1. This does not necessarily imply loss of group identity, although it may. Elimination of the abuses of criteria 2 and 3 does not necessarily eliminate the existence of the characteristic of criterion 1 (and is not likely to do so in the case of the homosexual) and may significantly alter, without at all eliminating, the manifestations of criterion 4.
2. In common with many other minority groups, as a part of the Point 4 development of a subculture, the homosexual community has developed its own jargon. For many years, this was confined to the in-group, but within the past half decade, certain portions of it have become very widely known and accepted. One of the most basic terms in that jargon, the one now most widely known in the heterosexual community, and accepted by Webster's dictionary as a noncolloquial, nonsubstandard usage, is *gay,* a synonym for *homosexual* or *homosexuality.*

Homosexuals: Deviant or Minority Group?

Helen Mayer Hacker

At no time since the Civil War has American society been so conscious of the problem of minority groups. Not only has social action acquired a new impetus in the implementation of rights for the traditionally recognized minority groups, but ever widening social categories are being proposed as candidates for minority group status. The essence of the minority group concept is that persons with some socially defined characteristic or syndrome of characteristics are denied full participation in certain social roles for which these attributes are deemed irrelevant.

The question arises, though: In whose scheme of values does this irrelevance obtain? Only when there is some cleavage of values can we speak of minority group status, because obviously if everyone agreed on the criteria for entrance into a social status, there would be equal consensus on when exclusion was warranted or when it represented discrimination.

The relevance or irrelevance of a given characteristic for a given status can be viewed both objectively and subjectively. Skin color, for example, is objectively irrelevant to performance as a physician, but subjectively, a white patient may lack confidence in a black doctor, or a black student for similar psychological reasons may learn more readily from a black teacher. Usually, the group which sees itself as having minority status stresses the functional or objective irrelevance of the trait which members possess in common, and it is the dominant group which insists on the subjective relevance of the minority attribute.

A further distinction must be made in this matter of relevance. It may not be an all-or-nothing situation. That is, some degree, for example, of physical strength or intelligence may be required for a particular job, but not as much as the job definition specifies or which would prevent mentally or physically handicapped persons from performing adequately. In this instance, following the lead of Marx and Marcuse, one might speak of surplus-discrimination.

Thus we see that the minority group problem, as Myrdal pointed out so long ago in *An American Dilemma*,[1] lies in the conflict between social values which push toward the increasing implementation of the democratic creed and those which make for the persistence and creation of groups defined by some common and negatively evaluated characteristic. The issue centers around the relevance of this characteristic to various kinds of social participation. Relevance may represent a continuum, and minority group status consists in being assigned to an erroneous and unwarranted place on this continuum. The error can arise from an unrealistic inflation of the requirements of the status which bars otherwise capable individuals from entering that status, or from an unrealistic and erroneous perception of the capabilities of a person or group seeking entrance to it. An example of the first kind of error might be the recent case of a Negro policeman who protested that the command of fine grammatical points tested in a promotional examination would not be required in the position to which he aspired. The second kind of error is seen, for example, in an inadequate appreciation of the extent to which a physically handicapped person may be able to compensate for his defect. Those making these two kinds of errors make some pretense at least of an objective assessment of the relationship between qualification and admittance. Overriding both of these is a simple dislike or rejection of the group in question on the basis of a negative evaluation of its defining characteristic.

This view of the minority group problem permits us to apply the concept to many social categories which in the past have been considered in terms of some other organizing principle, such as the family in the case of women, and deviance for homosexuals. The practical and theoretical importance of employing the minority group designation is to identify the locus of the problem presented by the differential treatment of a socially defined group or category of persons, whether it is to be found within the group itself or in the attitudes of the environing society. Thus, homosexuals and their sympathizers are quick to refer to that category as a minority group, whereas supposedly more neutral observers, including psychiatrists and sociologists, refer to its members as deviants. Reflective of social attitudes indeed is the fact that until quite recent years, the empirical study of homosexuals, both individually and collectively, was neglected by sociologists, presumably as either too difficult or too stigmatizing. ("If you can or want to study them, you must be one," was the unexpressed slogan.)

The studies and analyses of homosexuals which have begun to emerge in the past decade, however, are to be found under the fashionable title of "deviance," as in "deviant behavior" or "deviant group" or "deviant subculture." In the professional sociological literature, one finds no reference to homosexuals as a minority group. One influential text on social problems[2] underscores this approach. It distinguishes between problems stemming from deficiencies in the functioning of social systems or "social disorganization," and those arising from the failure of individuals to conform to social norms. Homosexuality is discussed in the first portion of the book, the one devoted to deviant behavior, while race and ethnic relations find their place in the part on social disorganization. In the first case the problem is seen as inducing the individual or group to conform, and in the second as persuading the society to accept.

Differences between the "minority group" and "deviant group" terminology, however, should not be exaggerated, since the convergence between them appears to be growing, as approaches to deviance recapitulate developments in the study of minority groups. First, it can be noted that in the nineteenth century attempts to explain prejudice against minority groups were often couched in terms of their biological and/or cultural differences from dominant groups; that is, the traits of the minority constituted an adequate theory of the dislike they encountered. Modern theories, on the other hand, are more concerned with how prejudice and discrimination serve personal, social, and economic needs of dominant groups.

Similarly, sociologists of deviance, such as Becker, Lemert, and Kitsuse,[3] focus more on the social processes by which individuals and groups come to be labelled as deviant, the range of reactions to the perception of deviance, and the effects of "normal" reactions in crystallizing deviance in persons who are so labelled, than on the causes of deviance, defined in some absolute way, even when these causes are ascribed to "society as the patient."

Secondly, both minority group and deviance theorists lay stress on the question of social definitions and who has the power to make them. The earlier definition of deviant behavior as conduct that objectively appears to violate a social norm is being superseded by one which calls it conduct that is perceived by others as contrary to a norm. This relativistic point of view obtains also in the case of minority groups. There may be discrepancies in the judgments of members and nonmembers as to whether the group experiences discrimination. This distinction between the objective and subjective dimensions of the minority group problem is elaborated by the writer elsewhere.[4] In like manner, a person may define himself as deviant, when others do not, or vice versa. For example, Albert J. Reiss[5] points out that delinquent peers (another label!) who engage in sexual transactions with male homosexuals do not define themselves as homosexuals, for which they deem elements other than homosexual behavior, in and of itself, as more crucial. In his words, they have not converted deviant acts into a deviant role. By not defining themselves as homosexuals, which to these young people is the pejorative and stigmatizing status, they in effect escape self-definition as deviant.

In the third place, a bridge can be built between the deviant and minority group concepts by viewing them as possible successive stages in the life history of individuals and groups. Merton's differentiation between aberrant and nonconforming behavior points the way.[6] The nonconformist, in contrast to the aberrant, challenges the legitimacy of the social norms he rejects, and appeals to values which he hopes will one day be embodied in these norms. One does not, however, think of the nonconformist as joining with his fellows in an organized effort for social change. It may well be that many persons in their own self-definitions move through the statuses of deviant to nonconformist to minority group members in that they progressively legitimize their own departures from accepted norms and reject the propriety of societal sanctions for their behavior. Does this process describe the development of homosexuals in American society today?

Schofield suggests that it does.[7] He sketches a four stage progression in the homosexual career: (1) discovery of sexual persuasion; (2) fears and misgivings leading to social isolation; (3) learning to lead two lives, passing back and forth between the gay and straight worlds; and (4) moving exclusively in a homosexual group, with attendant feelings of hostility to outsiders. To this, a fifth stage might be added, that of active and sometimes open participation in the homophile movement. Obviously, individuals halt at various stages in this cycle, and a minority group consciousness need not be reserved for the later stages.

What basis can be found in the social attitudes surrounding homosexuals for considering them as a minority group? Note that a homosexual may be defined as a person who is perceived by himself and/or others as being primarily sexually responsive to members of his own sex.

Mutability of the Minority Group Characteristic

The immediate stimulus for differential treatment of members of a minority group is a characteristic or cluster of characteristics im-

puted to them, either validly or invalidly, which are evaluated negatively. Apart from the question of the justifiability of such evaluation is the matter of the involuntary nature of the characteristic.
Obviously, Negroes cannot become white (although some do pass
as white, always with the fear that they may be discovered); women
cannot be transformed into men (again, a few pass, but many more
retain female identification while gaining male privileges); nor can
Jews be reborn as non-Jews (but a few do convert, not changing
their original status). However, it may be noted that all three groups
can, in a favorable social climate, modify some of the traits which
have been ascribed to them. In a forceful statement contending that
homosexuals do constitute a minority group, Kameny does not even
consider the possibility of homosexuals changing into heterosexuals,
nor does he raise the question of whether homosexuals are born or
made.[8] Homophile organizations and many homosexuals, however,
claim that homosexual inclinations either are genetic or result from
irreversible childhood experiences, and in either case they are powerless with therapeutic intervention, efforts of the will or by any other
means, to change them. In this respect they feel that they can no
more be held responsible for their minority characteristic than can
those groups whose minority status rests on a biological factor. Theoretically, Catholics could change their religion, but it is unrealistic
to expect people on any large scale basis to overthrow their earliest
emotional learnings. Like other socially disapproved groups, such as
the KKK or the Communist Party in the United States, homosexuals for the most part are constrained to secrecy about their intentions and actions, but unlike these groups, in their own minds, they
are not able to change their affiliation, which in their case is a sexual
one.[9] As a sociologist sympathetic to the symbolic interactionist
approach, I tend to believe that homosexuality can be unlearned, but
that the definitive answer must be left to other disciplines.

Relevance of Homosexuality to Social Participation

Further, the homophile movement and many homosexuals emphatically reject any negative evaluation of their sexual preference.
They consider homosexuality to be as normal, good, and healthy as
heterosexuality. To them homosexuality is not a vice, a crime, nor

a disease. It is simply a preference, and, as such, should no more be made the basis of social definitions nor differential treatment than should taste in food or furniture. They would be distinguished from age groups, the physically handicapped, and the mentally retarded on the grounds that these latter groups do raise the problem of the relevance of their physical characteristics to the opportunities from which they are excluded.

Let us grant for the moment the equal desirability of heterosexuality and homosexuality, and still inquire whether any justification can be found for placing social restrictions on homosexuals. First, it must be conceded that apart from its intrinsic worth, at the present time the majority of Americans favor heterosexuality and want their children to be heterosexual, just as they would like them to remain in the faith of their fathers. To protect this latter parental right, religious instruction has been barred from the public schools, and for those who wish it, parochial schools may be substituted. In positions which call for interaction with children, it is possible for sexual orientation to be relevant. The issue for the moment is not whether homosexuals are any more likely to seduce children and adolescents than are heterosexuals, but the kind of role model which they provide and emotional nuances which they may convey. Those who have this reservation in regard to the employment of homosexuals in "sensitive" occupations do not subscribe to "diaper determinism" in the formation of the sexual self, but rather regard sexual socialization as a lifelong process marked by crucial stages or turning points, particularly in early adolescence. What is being asserted, however, is not the inevitability but the possibility of the relevance of homosexual inclinations for a limited range of jobs. Still two qualifications must be made. First, the influence of any one person on a child should not be exaggerated. Secondly, it should not be assumed that every homosexual cannot guard himself, if he wishes to do so, against exerting any sway on the psychosexual development of vulnerable persons in a close or subordinate relationship to him. Reference must be made again to the concept of surplus-discrimination. When homosexuals are barred from jobs which do not involve counseling, teaching, or supervision of the young or if they are automatically excluded even from such positions on a categorical rather than an individual basis, then support is given to their claim of unwarranted discrimination.

What can be said about the allegation that homosexuals are more prone to seduce young persons, either physically or emotionally, than are heterosexuals? Both psychological and social explanations have been given of this supposed fact. On the psychological side it is sometimes stated that the sexual impulses of homosexuals are less susceptible to postponement in the demand for immediate gratification than those of heterosexuals and indeed are of a more imperious nature, and that homosexuals are prepared to take greater risks to gain that gratification. From a social or structural point of view, it is asserted that since homosexuals have access to a much smaller pool of eligibles than do heterosexuals, they are constrained to make the most of every opportunity. It may be just as plausibly argued, however, that this very circumstance would cause the homosexual to "go slow" under the fear of rejection, that the incentive to approach would be more than counterbalanced by the wish to avoid social sanctions.

Indeed, according to Simon and Gagnon, "Homosexuals vary profoundly in the degree to which their homosexual commitment and its facilitation becomes the organizing principle of their lives."[10] Further, some writers, such as Hoffman,[11] contend that if the social obstacles to homosexual intimacy between consenting adults were removed, any need to exploit the young would be diminished in like measure. Exception could also then be taken to the notion of the paucity of available partners. Many minority groups of smaller size, such as Jews, are largely endogamous without suffering severe sexual frustration.

So far we have been concerned with the relevance of a homosexual propensity per se for certain kinds of employment. It is often assumed, however, that homosexuality is symptomatic or expressive of personality disorders which are not directly sexual. As Becker says, "Possession of one deviant trait may have a generalized symbolic value, so that people automatically assume that its bearer possesses other undesirable traits allegedly associated with it."[12] Thus, homosexuals may have been accused of being immature, irresponsible, overly impulsive, narcissistic, hedonistic, dependent, negativistic, and so on through a catalogue of traits in keeping with the "arrested development" theory of homosexuality.[13] Whether homosexuality in and of itself constitutes a personality disorder is irrelevant to the consideration of homosexuals as a minority group, unless one can specify relevant behavioral manifestations of this so-called disorder. There is no evidence, however, to suggest that homosexuality as such prevents anyone from performing adequately in social and non-sexual roles. To date, psychological tests have not revealed any conclusive differences in the overall patterns of adjustment of comparable groups of homosexual and heterosexual males and females. That the homosexual career is fraught with such difficulties in our society as to cause some personality distortion cannot be denied and does not serve to distinguish homosexuals from other minority groups. A compromise position would be that a homosexual outcome may or may not be indicative of neurosis, and that any judgment on this point must be predicated on deep insight into individual cases. Certainly no blanket indictment of homosexuals as a group or pre-judgment of individual homosexuals is warranted. So the upshot of this inquiry into the relevance of homosexual preference as a minority characteristic is that, given the prevailing sentiment endorsing heterosexuality in our society, a person's homosexual proclivities are relevant only when there is some reason to believe in individual cases that he will exert an undesired influence on impressionable youth.

Homosexuals Yes, Homosexualism No

Representatives of the homophile movement assert that homosexuals are not accorded equal rights until homosexuality gains equal status with heterosexuality. As long as social values give preference to heterosexuality, homosexuals will suffer damaged self-esteem from being regarded at best as objects of compassion and conde-scension. Kameny[14] makes an explicit parallel between anti-homo-sexualism and anti-Semitism, arguing that both represent ideological outlooks which must be overcome before individual homosexuals and Jews can feel secure in their equal humanity with others. This comparison seems to be a false analogy. In the twentieth century and in the United States at least, prejudice against Jews is not based on any adherence to Judaism as a religion, but on personality traits attributed to Jews on a biological basis. If some Jews adopt other religions to avoid discrimination, it is for the purpose of concealing their Jewish birth, not their religious beliefs. American Jews are not and have no need of propagandizing to place Judaism on a par with Christianity. Rather their problem is to counter a negative stereotype which has nothing to do with religion. In contrast, the minority characteristic which defines the homosexual is his very homosexuality. To the extent that the homosexual image has accretions which do not inhere in homosexuality per se, the problems of Jews and homosexuals are similar. Both must fight the ascription of *false* attributes.

A closer parallel to the homosexual situation is found in the relationship between the Roman Catholic Church and individual Catholics. In the recent past, opposition to certain doctrines, especially the social teachings, of the Catholic Church tended to increase the prejudice and discrimination manifested against Catholic individuals, even though these two aspects of anti-Catholic feelings are logically distinct. As the Roses state, "It should be possible for people to oppose each other's doctrines much as do the adherents of two political parties without hating them personally and trying to hurt them materially."[15] In like manner, it should be possible to defend the rights of homosexual individuals without endorsing homosexuality. Granting equal opportunity to homosexuals need not be viewed as giving aid and comfort to homosexuality. Nor should homosexuals be asked to change their sexual persuasion any more than Catholics need change their religious persuasion. Homosexual organizations, like the Catholic Church, can be left free to proselytize, but social acceptance of homosexuality as being "just as good" as heterosexuality need not be a precondition of social acceptance of homosexuals as fully equal human beings.

There is one sense, however, in which the lower evaluation of homosexuality vis-à-vis heterosexuality does lend credence to the neurotic label so frequently attached to homosexuals. It has often been noted that homosexual unions are frequently of a transient and superficial character, exacting few of the responsibilities and obligations of heterosexual marriage. Hoffman believes that the withholding of community support provides an adequate explanation.[16] To some observers the neurotic aspect of homosexuality lies in the lack of deep monogamous commitment rather than in the choice of sexual partner; and, in their eyes, part of the appeal of the homosexual way of life arises from this fact. One might suppose that the homosexual community substitutes for the larger society in providing regulatory norms, but studies of such communities in San Francisco and other areas reveal that it acts rather to legitimize instability.

It is not to be assumed that marriage and parenthood represent the achievement of psychological maturity for every individual, even if he be heterosexual. The criteria for mental health vary according to the aspirations and potentialities of the individual, but most psychologists agree that the ability to love someone other than the self is one of the characteristics of the mature personality. Whether the denial to homosexuals of a "normal" family life constitutes an important discrimination against them or an escape from the tasks of adulthood depends on the evaluation made of family institutions and their relationship to other important social structures. At the present time societal pressures confront the homosexual, especially the male, with a difficult dilemma. Patterns of sustained living together may testify to his psychological adjustment, but at the same time remove him from the possibility of fulfilling the culturally valued role of husband and father. This dilemma could be overcome if a system governing homosexual relationships, parallel to that governing heterosexual relations, were evolved.[17] This institutionalization of homosexuality would involve such matters as marriage and divorce, age of consent, and the rights, duties, and role differentiation of homosexual partners. Further, children might be made available to homosexual couples either through adoption in the case of males or also through artificial (or natural, if so desired) insemination in the case of females. An alternative possibility is bigamy or a *ménage à trois,* permitting a man to have both a man-wife and a woman-wife, and similarly for a woman; or the man could be the husband to a woman and the "wife" to a man, even in the manner of Caesar. Of course homosexual marriage need not exclude the possibility of homosexual or heterosexual affairs, anymore than heterosexual marriage does. Indeed occasional homosexual "lapses" might enable bisexuals to perform in heterosexual marital and parental roles.

Theories of Anti-Homosexualism

Since a radical change in public attitudes is prerequisite to any institutionalization of homosexuality, it becomes pertinent to inquire into the social and psychological factors which enter into contemporary negative feelings. Conscious rejection of homosexuality is so strong and deep that few persons feel called upon to rationalize or justify their sentiments as they do in the case of racial and religious minorities.

The most prevalent explanation in modern sociology stems from the structural-functional approach to social institutions, and is best exemplified by Kingsley Davis.[18] He holds that every society, in the interest of social order, must develop some set of social norms to regulate the powerful libidinal drive to prevent sexual exploitation and a sexual war of each against all, and to channel sexuality into socially useful ends. Davis writes:

> In evolving an orderly system of sexual rights and obligations, societies have linked this system with the rest of the social structure, particularly with the family. They have also tended to economize by having only one such system, which has the advantage of giving each person only one role to worry about in his sex life—namely, a male or female role—which can thus be ascribed and will vary only with age. Homosexuality in itself cannot lead to reproduction and the formation of normal family life; it also involves, for one partner or the other, a reversal of sex role, though sex is one of the most fundamental bases for status ascription. A male who assumes the feminine role, or a woman who assumes the masculine role, is looked down upon—interestingly enough, even by homosexuals themselves.[19]

Davis does not think that a society can at the same time equally foster durable sexual unions between men and women and between persons of the same sex. Agricultural, handicraft societies had to protect the family in order to achieve a birth rate which was higher than the death rate, and so children were imbued with the notion of a complementary division of functions between the two sexes and the attitudes and behaviors appropriate to their own sex. These early emotional learnings about sex and gender form the core of the personality, and are strongly resistant to change. Thus, negative attitudes toward homosexuality are the expectable consequences of the socialization process which itself fulfilled a functional prerequisite of this type of society.

The industrial revolution, however, with concomitant advances in medicine and public sanitation, has lowered the death rate, modified the sexual division of labor, separated recreation from procreation, and in general altered the circumstances of life from which the traditional sex mores, with their proscription of homosexuality, grew. Does continued disapproval of homosexuality then represent a cultural lag? No, says Davis; it now serves another function: ". . . in urbanized, mobile industrial societies, familial relationships seem to be particularly valued because they are virtually the only ones that are both personal and enduring; marital and parental ties therefore receive strong sentimental support . . . . Homosexual relations are notoriously ephemeral by comparison."[20] True, withdrawal of social disapproval and the normative regulation of homosexual relations, it has been claimed by some, might render homosexual unions more durable and a viable alternative to the heterosexual family,[21] but the complications of such a dual system, even greater than those of the present single system, make it a doubtful prospect.

At the opposite end of ideology from Davis, Marcuse[22] too has a functional explanation, a kind of synthesis of Freud and Marx, of the interdiction of homosexuality. He puts forward the thesis that contemporary industrial societies are characterized by a "suprarepressive organization of societal relationships under a principle which is the negation of the pleasure principle," and which harnesses sexuality in alienated labor under an irrational authority. Homosexuality, symbolized by Orpheus, represents a protest "against the repressive order of procreative sexuality." Orpheus, according to Marcuse, stands for a "fuller Eros" and the liberation of the world. In this view, the privileged group which exercises domination opposes sexual pleasure which is not a means for an end.

Homosexuals, for Marcuse, serve as a revolutionary vanguard in freeing society from genital tyranny and leading the way to a resexualization of the whole body of man. Only such a polymorphously perverse body, he believes, can resist being deformed into an instrument of labor. Those readers who may think that homosexuality partakes more of the "perverse" than of the "polymorphous" in Freud's phrase may turn to another representative of the "Freudian left,"[23] Norman O. Brown, for a more consistent interpretation. Brown believes that any form of sexual organization, including homosexuality, is repressive and that the full measure of human happiness must be sought in the anarchic eroticism of early infancy.

Both views postulate a societal need to limit sexual gratification in the interest of social order, though differing in their evaluation of contemporary social organization, but from either standpoint one can understand how deviations from strongly internalized sexual norms arouse defensive, rejecting attitudes. The strength and irrationality of majority reactions stem also from an important difference between homosexuals and the more traditional minority groups. Such traits as skin color, hair form, and dress, for example, are used by the dominant group mainly to identify a minority which may then be disliked in terms of the stereotype ascribed to it. Repressed desires of the dominant group may be projected onto the minority group in a symbolic way, but in this two-step process there is no real fear on the part of a white, for instance, that he will turn into a black, or that a Christian will become a Jew. Feelings about homosexuals, however, are not symbolic. The imputation of homosexuality to others presents a real threat to the self-conceived heterosexual. His conscious feelings of contempt, disgust, repugnance, pity, scorn, amusement, or even boredom and indifference may serve as insulation against contact with an ego-alien part of himself. The homosexual opens old wounds concerning feelings about parents, establishment of sexual identity, and unresolved negative oedipal feelings, among others. And by the same token, homosexuals' conscious hostility toward heterosexuals may represent not only a response to their negative attitudes and discriminatory treatment, but also a defense against their own heterosexual components, unresolved positive oedipal feelings, and so on. There is more tension in the reciprocal attitudes of heterosexuals and homosexuals than in most minority group–dominant group relationships, because of the ambivalence centering in the power of the sex drive. Also, as mentioned above, in the absence of institutionalization of homosexual relationships, the heterosexual may envy the homosexual's freedom from the responsibilities of sexual expression which are foisted upon the heterosexual, while the homosexual may envy the stability, security, and affection in the other group. To the extent that segregation of masculine and feminine social roles persists, the male homosexual is free from the burden of family support and the female homosexual from the maintenance of a home and the rearing of children. But since these activities imply privileges as well as obligations, one might equally say that the homosexual is shut out from them. In short, the plight of the homosexual in American society must be seen as a result of a complex interplay of psychological and social forces.

In the case of any large minority group, its own members constitute an important segment of the social environment. Further, the nature of the minority characteristic serves to define the kinds of social categories to be placed in juxtaposition or in opposition to the minority group. Thus, there are many religious, occupational, and racial groups in this country, but only, with minor exceptions, two sexes. If for the purpose of analytic simplicity, one ignores bisexuals and asexuals, the relevant categories, defined by sex and preferred sexual object, emerge as: male heterosexual, female heterosexual, male homosexual, and female homosexual. Table 1 suggests in the form of an imaginative reconstruction, both negative and positive, conscious and unconscious, reciprocal attitudes among these four groups, with the exception of heterosexual reactions to heterosexuals, which would be irrelevant in this context.

Objective Evidence of Prejudice Against Homosexuals

There is little need to dwell on discriminations against homosexuals. In the words of Kitsuse, "Individuals who are publicly identified as homosexuals are frequently denied the social, economic, and legal rights of 'normal' males. Socially they may be treated as objects of amusement, ridicule, scorn, and often fear; economically

TABLE 1. Reciprocal Attitudes of Heterosexuals and Homosexuals.

MALE HETEROSEXUAL

1. Toward male homosexual

a. Conscious contempt, distrust.
b. Fear of seduction attempts.
c. Secret and unacceptable attraction.
d. Envy of "bachelor" life.
e. Seen as vicarious expression of own hostility to females, especially own mother.
f. Seen as vicarious expression of repressed love and contempt for own father.
g. Serves to reinforce own feelings of masculinity.

2. Toward female homosexual

a. Seen as embodiment of aggression because she rejects his masculinity, the power of his difference; source of humiliation.
b. Presents threat of castration, competitor in nonsexual areas, out to get his balls.
c. Seen as competitor for females.
d. Serves as challenge to conquest.
e. Expression of identification with female role so as to be passive and protected.
f. Feeling of relief at not having sexual and other demands made upon him.

FEMALE HETEROSEXUAL

1. Toward male homosexual

a. Resentment of denial of her femininity.
b. Rival in competition for men.
c. Supposition of hostility toward her.
d. Passive, so less threatening, can relax and be friendly.
e. Regret at diminution of male market.
f. Fears insight into "feminine wiles."
g. Personal disappointment, if attracted.

2. Toward female homosexual

a. Fear of being seduced.
b. Pique, if no passes.
c. Strain of managing friendship while avoiding overt rebuff.
d. Envy of her aggression and freedom to act like a male.

TABLE 1 (*Cont.*)

e. No worry about her as a sexual rival.
f. Fears her competition in business and professions.
g. Some promise of maternal warmth and protection.
h. Reinforcement of own feelings of femininity.

MALE HOMOSEXUAL

1. *Toward male homosexual*

a. Bond of sympathy, in-group complicity.
b. Sexual and social competitor.
c. Sees conflict of friend and lover roles.
d. Hostility in intimate relationship, arising from competition in playing masculine role, who will be the boss.
e. Fear of exposure by association or actual betrayal.
f. Feels contempt, if too effeminate, and fears contempt as symbol of self-hatred.
g. Opportunity for sexual gratification.
h. Relief from social pretence, opportunity to express feminine interests and identifications.

2. *Toward female homosexual*

a. Seen as embodiment of everything hateful in women, the arch-usurper of masculinity.
b. Contempt for self is projected onto her.
c. Potential accomplice in heterosexual masquerade.
d. Comrade in protest movement.
e. Trustworthy confidante.
f. Party and bar associate.

3. *Toward male heterosexual*

a. Feelings of inferiority and impotence vis-à-vis him.
b. Envy arising from self-hatred.
c. Desire for friendship and acceptance.
d. Symbol of sexual climbing.
e. Feelings of attraction to "trade."
f. Feelings of own superiority from presumed greater self-insight.

4. *Toward female heterosexual*

a. Fear of excessive demands on her part.
b. Wish for sisterly or motherly affection.
c. Seen as rival for men.

Table 1 (*Cont.*)

d. Fear of her exploitation of him.
e. Wish for "understanding" and support in masculine role.

FEMALE HOMOSEXUAL

1. *Toward male homosexual*

a. Projected self-disdain; justification of contempt for men: "*You* are a man?"
b. Hostility for presumed anti-feminism.
c. Maternal compassion.
d. Seen as potential friend and confidante.
e. No danger of masculine demands.
f. No threat nor rival.

2. *Toward female homosexual*

a. Same as items a, b, c, e, g, and h in attitudes of male homosexual toward male homosexual.
b. Embarrassment, if too masculinized.
c. Hostility in intimate relationships arising from competition as to who will play feminine, protected role.
d. Opportunity to alternate mother and child roles.
e. Jealousy of her in regard to both sexes.

3. *Toward male heterosexual*

a. Deep-seated, intense feelings of competition, rival both in business and in love.
b. Pride in ability to "lead him on," mixed with contempt for him as an insensitive simpleton.
c. Desire for a brotherly good friend and pal.
d. Desire for affectionate, protective father.
e. Fear of derision as not a "real woman."
f. Narcissistic wish to be desired.

4. *Toward female heterosexual*

a. Strong attraction, coupled with fear of rejection.
b. Fear of loss of friendship.
c. Mixed envy and contempt for her presumed feminine identification.
d. Maternal more than competitive feeling; a projected identification like that of a proud mother for a good representative of the female sex.
e. Jealousy toward and hatred of frustrating object.

they may be summarily dismissed from employment; legally they are frequently subject to interrogation and harassment by police."[24] While fewer disabilities are visited upon female homosexuals, they too may feel forced by public attitudes either to a humiliating concealment with concomitant fear of exposure or to a renunciation of many high status jobs, gratifying social contacts, and ordinary human respect.

Homosexuals feel that the root of their problem lies in social attitudes toward them. The question may be raised of the extent of this social prejudice. Is it true, as Cory states, that homosexuals "live in an atmosphere of universal rejection . . . of a social world that jokes and sneers at every turn?"[25]

To my knowledge, no survey data on a national scale exist on the attitudes of a representative sample of Americans toward homosexuals. Several small studies and my own informal interviewing on the subject, however, indicate that the present social climate is more favorable than many homosexuals may believe. Kitsuse, for example, interviewed seven hundred college undergraduates in regard primarily to how they came to think certain individuals they had encountered were homosexual and how they reacted to this definition of them. He found that a "live and let live" response was fairly common, and in no case was moral indignation or revulsion communicated to the putative homosexual:

> . . . the interview materials suggest that while reactions toward persons defined as homosexuals tend to be negatively toned, they are far from homogeneous as to the forms or intensity of the sanctions invoked and applied. Indeed, reactions which may appear to the sociological observer or to the deviant himself as negative sanctions, such as withdrawal or avoidance, may be expressions of embarrassment, a reluctance to share the burden of the deviant's problems. . . . In view of the extreme negative sanctions against homosexuality which are posited on theoretical grounds, the generally mild reactions of our subjects are striking.[26]

Some limitations on the usefulness of this study must be noted. First, as the investigator himself acknowledges, college students may have more liberal views than less educated segments of the population, but the study does indicate that reactions to homosexuals are not uniform. This very unpredictability of response, as in the case of the marginal man, may contribute to the psychological tension of the homosexual in his perpetual conflict between the wish to reveal and the need to conceal.

Secondly, the respondents told of their experiences with homosexuals who were in varying kinds of relationships and degrees of closeness to them, ranging from a stranger to a roommate. But except for the ever-present danger of arrest if caught in some blatant behavior, the homosexual is most concerned about the reactions of persons of long acquaintanceship or in important relationships to him. His problem is to keep his heterosexual and homosexual audiences separate. In view of this situation, it would be most interesting to administer social distance tests to see how a broad spectrum of Americans feel about homosexuals in a variety of relationships. Social distance tests, however, may provide information as much on the respondent's estimation of the social standing of homosexuals as on his own attitudes. Persons who are themselves free of prejudice toward homosexuals may nevertheless feel impelled to act in accordance with their perception of the social climate in a manner reminiscent of Merton's distinction between fair-weather and all-weather liberals.[27] A white mother, for example, may frown on her daughter's dating blacks, not because she personally objects, but because she anticipates social difficulties in an interracial marriage; or complicating this matter, may give one of these as the reason (both to herself and/or to others) when the other is the genuine motivation for the objection. Similarly, a homosexual may not be employed or retained in certain positions because the employer anticipates adverse reaction from his clients and other employees or, if only the employer is aware of the applicant's homosexuality, he fears that the homosexual may be constrained to acts of disloyalty or malfeasance under the threat of disclosure.

While social attitudes toward homosexuals may be less punitive than formerly, it is probable that few Americans consider homosexuals to be "normal." According to a 1965 study of a fairly representative sample of 180 persons, homosexuals were mentioned most frequently in answer to a question asking the respondent to name "deviants."[28] Other terms applied to homosexuals were, in rank order: "sexually abnormal," "perverted," "mentally ill," "maladjusted," and "effeminate." Undoubtedly, considerable modification of prevailing attitudes must occur before the status of the homosexual in the popular mind can be changed from that of deviant to nonconformist, let alone member of an unjustly treated minority group.

Frequency of Minority Group Feelings Among Homosexuals

Do homosexuals have a minority group consciousness? Again, systematic data are largely lacking. We do not know what percentage of homosexuals accept the "sick" or "deviant" label, with accompanying self-depreciation; nor how many regard homosexuality as a psychological and social adjustment commensurate with heterosexuality, and react to a hostile environment with resentment. The development of a homophile movement attests to a self-definition of minority status on the part of some homosexuals, but the proportion of the total homosexual population which participates in or is even aware of such organizations has been estimated at less than one per cent.[29]

How homosexuals feel about being homosexual appears to be a matter of controversy. It is popularly supposed that they are ridden with feelings of guilt, inferiority, and self-hatred, as well as a defensive converse of these feelings. Indeed, current literary and dramatic productions by or about homosexuals seem to indicate these classic minority group symptoms. Thus, one of the characters in Mart Crowley's play, "The Boys in the Band," exclaims, "Show me a happy homosexual and I'll show you a gay corpse." Writing in the *New York Times,* Donn Teal,[30] however, questions whether homosexuals are really anguished and protests the distorted way homosexuals are portrayed in this play, objecting particularly to the sadistic games and self-degrading confessions. He claims that the wail, "If we could just learn not to HATE ourselves so much!" represents only a minority of homosexuals. Without multiplying instances, it can be said that in the majority of novels, plays, and films dealing with homosexuals, even when authored by homosexuals, no happy outcome is given to the homosexual way of life and the homosexual characters rarely emerge as human beings with whom the average person can identify.

Letters to *New York Times* and discussions on radio and tele-vision programs testify to the wish of many homosexuals to change the public image from a self-demeaning to a self-respecting one. One recent television program, with Aline Saarinen as hostess, had two homosexuals disavowing any wish to be "cured."[31]

> Female homosexual: "Well, most of us do not want to be cured because we don't regard our activities as disease. If I enjoy going to bed with another woman, and this is pleasurable, and does not de-bilitate me in any way, if I can fulfill my functions on the job, and enjoy myself, and subjectively feel that I am having a good time, I don't see where the disease is. . . ."
>
> Male homosexual: "I have a nice relationship with another man, which has been going on for some time. I have a very nice group of friends. I function well. I make a living, and I do the things I want to do. I'm not very unhappy. I don't feel like I'm sick. . . ."

However, Sagarin found that many homosexuals described them-selves or others as neurotic, sick, or disturbed.[32]

Regardless of psychological or moral self-evaluations or commit-ment to organized forms of social protest, many homosexuals mani-fest a feeling of group belongingness by their participation in a homosexual community. Such a community serves, in varying de-grees, the following functions for individual homosexuals:[33]

1. It provides a source of social support and validation of a posi-tive self-image.

2. It offers a shared set of norms and practices to overcome anomie.

3. It confers a sense of identity in a world in which traditional group identifications are crumbling.

4. It serves as a sexual market place.

5. It affords opportunities for friendship, recreation, and other social gratifications which are not directly sexual.

6. It permits the enjoyment of "camp" behavior in self or in others.

7. It acts as an agency of social control in protecting individual homosexuals from impulsive sexual "acting out."

8. It represents a new kind of opportunity structure for upward social mobility.

9. It reduces anxiety and conflicts, thus freeing the individual to perform more productively outside the community, particularly by

relieving the tensions of concealment and fear of exposure by those who pass back and forth in two worlds.

10. It dispenses social services to meet individual problems and crises.

The homosexual community, however, differs in important ways from other communities. Among the more traditional minority groups of race and ethnicity, a subculture is perpetuated by residential segregation and family inheritance. The homosexual community, based only on a similarity of sexual interest—though residential clusters of homosexuals exist—has very limited content. A shared sexual commitment is not sufficient to transcend larger social and cultural differences. For very few participants can this community be anything approximating a "total society." In fact, immersion in the homosexual community often entails the sacrifice of family and friends in the larger community. Considering the cultural impoverishment of the homosexual community, the price of dropping the sexual mask may be too high.

Summary

This discussion should conclude with tentative answers to two questions. First, to what extent do homosexuals fit the definition of a minority group? Secondly, does viewing homosexuals as a minority rather than as a deviant group bring out sociologically important aspects of their situation which previously may have been obscured?

In regard to the first question, it may be said that homosexuals are the object of collective discrimination in that they are barred from social opportunities for which their sexual preference is functionally and objectively irrelevant. Further, they do possess in large measure many of the attributes of the more traditional racial, religious, and ethnic minorities: they resent the discrimination and pejorative attitudes directed against them; they have a sense of group identification and have developed a separate subculture with a distinctive argot, meeting places, leadership, and protective organizations; they often experience a conflict between their class status and their "caste" status; they are actively seeking to modify the present accommodation between them and heterosexuals which tends to segregate them occupationally and to drive them underground; they are subject to the psychological ravages of marginality since they can neither fully accept nor completely disavow adverse social judgments of their sexual inclinations and activities; they have developed a double consciousness which can fix on the hypocrisy and sham of a sexually-repressive society, as well as a defensive ideology which legitimizes their claim to equal moral and psychological worth.

They differ from other minority groups in the following ways: the continuing involuntary nature of their minority characteristic is a controversial matter; they seek rather than are born into a minority subculture; their minority status is not based on birth or family inheritance, and the characteristic which gives them this status is direct rather than symbolic; their way of life rarely has religious sanction; differential treatment of them does not arouse as much guilt in the dominant group and indeed there is less value consensus regarding them; measurement of social distance toward them, as in the case of women but for a different reason, cannot specify marriage as the level of greatest intimacy; reciprocal minority-dominant group attitudes involve more complex cultural and psychological factors; the shared interest which unites the homosexual community is more specific and limited and thus less capable of superseding class and cultural divergences than the more diffuse bond which unites some ethnic and racial groups; and, finally, one of the strategies suggested to overcome social opposition, namely, the institutionalization of homosexual relationships, is unique to this group.

Turning to the second question, the tradition has been to treat homosexuals under the sociology of deviance, in which *they* were considered the social problem, similar to prostitutes, drug addicts, alcoholics, and the mentally ill. They constituted a social problem in the sense that their existence threatened strong social values. This definition of the problem posed by homosexuals suggested a two-pronged attack of societal prevention and individual cure: on the one side to determine what kind of social engineering would prevent persons from becoming homosexual, such as allowing greater freedom of heterosexual expression in early years, fostering less rigid social sex-role differentiation, diverting the energies of "close-binding" mothers into outside employment, and encouraging fatherhood, and, on the other hand, to seek therapeutic approaches which would transform homosexuals into heterosexuals.

Conceptualizing homosexuals as a minority group shifts the focus of attention from their libidinal drives to their social interaction with their own egos, other homosexuals, and heterosexuals, and to the various life styles they have adopted in reaction to their sexual proclivities and dominant group attitudes toward them. In this manner the minority group concept has greater explanatory power than the deviance concept. It sheds light on the problems of managing a homosexual career, on the characteristic features of homosexual unions, on the attraction and avoidance aspects of the homosexual community, on the tension between "secret" and "overt" homosexuals, and on a host of social phenomena which flow from the minority status of homosexuals. It also redefines the social problem as residing mainly in prejudicial attitudes toward homosexuals.

Consideration of homosexuals as a minority group opens the way for a fruitful reexamination of the minority group concept, suggesting extensions and refinements. Under what social conditions do new minority groups emerge? What kinds of societies are characterized by a continual process of the establishment and disestablishment of minority groups? Do findings with respect to one group stimulate new insights in regard to other groups? It would seem that in a pluralistic society, criss-crossed with conflict, with a variety of value standpoints, the relativism and the subjectivism connoted by the minority group approach represents a closer approximation to social facts than the assumption of an absolute and objective standard of values implicit in the notion of deviance.

REFERENCES

1. Gunnar Myrdal, *An American Dilemma* (New York: Harper, 1944).
2. Robert K. Merton and Robert A. Nisbet, eds., *Contemporary Social Problems* (New York: Harcourt, Brace & World, 1966).
3. See Howard S. Becker, *Outsiders: Studies in the Sociology of Deviance* (New York: Free Press of Glencoe, 1963); Becker, ed., *The Other Side: Perspectives on Deviance* (New York: Free Press, 1964); Edwin M. Lemert, *Social Pathology* (New York: McGraw-Hill, 1951); Lemert, *Human Deviance, Social Problems and Social Control* (Englewood Cliffs,

N.J.: Prentice-Hall, 1967); John I. Kitsuse, "Societal Reaction to Deviant Behavior," *Social Problems,* 9 (Winter, 1962), pp. 247–56.

4. Helen Mayer Hacker, "Women as a Minority Group," *Social Forces,* 30 (October, 1951), pp. 60–69; reprinted in this volume.

5. Albert J. Reiss, Jr., "The Social Integration of Queers and Peers," *Social Problems,* 9 (Winter, 1962), pp. 247–56.

6. Robert K. Merton, "Social Problems and Sociological Theory," in Merton and Nisbet, eds., *op. cit.,* pp. 808–11.

7. M. Schofield, *Sociological Aspects of Homosexuality: A Comparative Study of Three Types of Homosexuals* (Boston: Little, Brown, 1965).

8. Franklin E. Kameny, "Homosexuals as a Minority Group," in this volume.

9. This theme and the analogy are developed by Edward Sagarin, *Structure and Ideology in an Association of Deviants,* unpublished doctoral dissertation, New York University, 1966.

10. William Simon and John H. Gagnon, "Homosexuality: The Formulation of a Sociological Perspective," *Journal of Health & Social Behavior,* 8 (September, 1967), p. 180.

11. Martin Hoffman, *The Gay World* (New York: Basic Books, 1968).

12. Becker, *Outsiders, op. cit.,* p. 33.

13. The view that homosexuality is symptomatic of personality disorder is well put in a letter by Dr. Morton Friedman of the New Jersey College of Medicine, published in the *New York Times* on January 28, 1968:

> While we can agree with the view recently expressed in "Homosexuals and Civil Rights" that the arbitrary abridgement of the civil rights of homosexuals is a wrong long practiced by our society, we must be careful not to be seduced into accepting the idea that the only difference between the homosexual and the heterosexual is the choice of sexual object.
>
> One of the problems revealed by a study of the psychological dynamics in the development of the homosexual is his (or her) poor identification with parental figures and therefore with the moral values of adult society. This poor identification leads to an arrest of psychosexual development, "immaturity," evidenced in many aspects of both thought and behavior. In general, the homosexual tends to have poor impulse control and his values tend to be both narcissistic and hedonistic.
>
> His tolerance for frustration, for delay of gratification, is much less than that of the average heterosexual, and this frequently leads to a compulsive quality in his sexual drive which is seldom seen in adult heterosexuals. Because of this, contrary to the anonymous opinion expressed in letters recently, the homosexual teacher is much more likely to become involved with his male students than the heterosexual teacher is with female students. The same likelihood has also been noted with female homosexual teachers.
>
> The backlash of society's persecution of homosexuals is being expressed today by our being too ready to declare all values as being equal in worth to humanity, even in the instance in which one set of

values represents the infantile needs of individuals and is therefore harmful to a mature society. Much of the display of narcissism and the tendency toward irresponsible hedonism in contemporary society is rooted in and sustained by the homosexual "value system."

14. Kameny, *op. cit.*
15. Arnold and Caroline Rose, *America Divided: Minority Group Relations in the United States* (New York: Knopf, 1948), p. 60.
16. See Hoffman, *op. cit.* This psychiatrist believes that "the social prohibition against homosexuality" is largely responsible for the impermanence of male homosexual relations. "To put the matter in its most simple form, the reason that males who are homosexually inclined cannot form stable relations with each other is that society does not want them to" (p. 176).
17. This discussion is based, though with a different bias, on Kingsley Davis, "Sexual Behavior," in Merton and Nisbet, eds., *op. cit.*, pp. 341–42.
18. Davis, *ibid.*, pp. 323–25. Davis's statement that even homosexuals look down upon the homosexual partner who assumes the role of the opposite sex is open to question. Given the dominance of masculine values in our society, it is probable that a man is exposed to greater social opprobrium than a woman.
19. *Ibid.*, p. 339.
20. *Ibid.*, p. 341.
21. Hoffman, *op. cit.*
22. Herbert Marcuse, *Eros and Civilization: A Philosophical Inquiry into Freud* (New York: Vintage Books, 1961). See particularly Chapter 8, "The Images of Orpheus and Narcissus," pp. 144–56.
23. See Paul A. Robinson, *The Freudian Left: Wilhelm Reich, Geza Roheim, Herbert Marcuse* (New York: Harper & Row, 1969), esp. pp. 207, 208, 228.
24. Kitsuse, *op. cit.*, p. 250.
25. Donald Webster Cory, *The Homosexual in America* (New York: Greenberg, 1951), p. 12.
26. Kitsuse, *op. cit.*, p. 255.
27. Robert K. Merton, "Discrimination and the American Creed," in Robert M. MacIver, ed., *Discrimination and National Welfare* (New York: Harper, 1949), pp. 99–126.
28. J. L. Simmons, "Public Stereotypes of Deviants," *Social Problems, 13* (1965), pp. 223–32.
29. For a discussion of the homophile movement, and of the extent of support that it has in homosexual circles, see Edward Sagarin, *Odd Man In: Societies of Deviants in America* (Chicago: Quadrangle, 1969).
30. *New York Times,* June 1, 1969.
31. *New York Times,* March 30, 1969, p. 21 of Section 2, Arts and Leisure.
32. Sagarin, *Odd Man In, op. cit.*, and in greater detail, Sagarin, *Structure and Ideology in an Association of Deviants, op. cit.*
33. This list has been culled from the following sources: Maurice Leznoff and William A. Westley, "The Homosexual Community," *Social Problems, 3* (April, 1956), pp. 257–63; Simon and Gagnon, *op. cit.;* Evelyn

Hooker, "The Homosexual Community," in John H. Gagnon and William Simon, eds., *Sexual Deviance* (New York: Harper & Row, 1967), pp. 167–84; Nancy Achilles, "The Development of the Homosexual Bar as an Institution," in *idem*, pp. 228–44; Simon and Gagnon, "The Lesbians: A Preliminary Overview," in *idem*, pp. 247–82; Edwin M. Schur, *Crimes Without Victims* (Englewood Cliffs, N.J.: Prentice-Hall, 1965), pp. 85–88; and Hoffman, *op. cit.*, pp. 43–63.

Young and Old 3

The young will always be with us, but they will not always be young. This self-evident statement, trivial as it may sound at first reading, illustrates an unusual aspect of this minority group, perhaps even a unique aspect: the transitory minority. For whatever else one may find in the youth that is analogous to blacks, to Jews, or to such social minorities as are examined in this volume (women, homosexuals, cripples), no other group is in their minority status for such a finite period of time. There will be an adolescent or teenager or youthful category in the next decade and the one following, but all of its present members will, if they have survived, be in their middle years, and many of them may be part of the oppressive group of parents and the older generation. To paraphrase Nicholas Von Hoffman, they will be the parents that their peers had warned them against.

Transitory though it may be, the youth, and some subsections of it (as the hippies, the dissidents, and others) are subject to treatment that many have seen as a minority. The young and the old superbly exemplify the statement that a social category can exist with meaningful role differentiations, but which do not have to carry with them inequality and collective discrimination. Whereas the ethnic minorities strive for continuation of separate status without role differentiation, the age minorities, young and old, could accept such role differentiations without implication of unequal treatment.

The four articles in this chapter illustrate the labeling theory of deviance, as applied to minorities. That is, the minority status is not seen in the group itself, but rather in the way the group is labeled, treated, and reacted to by dominant others in the society. That these others are parents and children of those maltreated only serves to illustrate points of difference between various subordinate groups in society; for lower social classes and lower ethnic groups (lower in the sense of the distribution of power and other desiderata) are groupings of family units. Here, the minority member is differentiated from others *within* the family; the ethnic minorities, on the contrary, consist of a collectivity of families.

Friedenberg differentiates between the "hot-blooded" and the "long-suffering" minorities, and in the former group he places the youth, in the latter, women. It is a matter of militancy and blatancy, and the blacks seem to have passed from the second to the first category. Perhaps what characterizes our era is that there has been an avalanche toward the first and away from the second; even his example of women is not quite the typical long-suffering of just a few years ago. For Brown, not youth, but a sector of it, the hippies, are the minority, and another aspect of minority group relations comes into play: the scapegoat. For Brody, with a Parsonian frame of reference, the adolescent as a minority is a creation of a society in the throes of fast social change. And finally we have Barron, coining the term "quasi-minority," speaking of a group that, unlike the ethnics, is not hated, but nevertheless subject to discrimination and prejudice, to exclusion rather than to hostility. It is a group consisting of people who cannot even look forward to surviving a transitory status.

The Image of the
Adolescent Minority

Edgar Z. Friedenberg

In our society there are two kinds of minority status. One of these I will call the "hot-blooded" minorities, whose archetypical image is that of the Negro or Latin. *In the United States, "teen-agers" are treated as a "hot-blooded" minority.* Then there are the "long-suffering minorities," whose archetype is the Jew, but which also, I should say, includes women. Try, for a second, to picture a Jewish "teen-ager," and you may sense a tendency for the image to grate. "Teen-agers" err on the hot side; they talk jive, drive hot-rods and become juvenile delinquents. Young Jews talk volubly, play the violin, and go to medical school, though never on Saturday.

The minority group is a special American institution, created by the interaction between a history and an ideology which are not to be duplicated elsewhere. Minority status has little to do with size or proportion. In a democracy, a dominant social group is called a majority and a part of its dominance consists in the power to arrange appropriate manifestations of public support; while a subordinate group is, by the logic of political morality, a minority. The minority stereotype, though affected by the actual characteristics of the minority group, develops to fit the purposes and expresses the anxieties of the dominant social group. It serves as a slimy coating over the sharp realities of cultural difference, protecting the social organism until the irritant can be absorbed.

Now, when one is dealing with a group that actually is genetically or culturally different from the dominant social group, this is perhaps to be expected. It is neither desirable nor inevitable, for xenophobia is neither desirable nor inevitable; but it is not surprising.

What is surprising is that the sons and daughters of the *dominant* adult group should be treated as a minority group merely because of their age. Their papers are in order and they speak the language

Source: *The Dignity of Youth and Other Atavisms*, copyright © 1965 by Edgar Z. Friedenberg. Reprinted by permission of the Beacon Press.

adequately. In any society, to be sure, the young occupy a subordinate or probationary status while under tutelage for adult life. But a minority group is not merely subordinate; it is not under tutelage. It is in the process of being denatured; of becoming, under social stress, something more acceptable to the dominant society, but essentially different from what its own growth and experience would lead to. Most beasts recognize their own kind. Primitive peoples may initiate their youth; we insist that ours be naturalized, though it is what is most natural about them that disturbs adults most.

The court of naturalization is the public school. A high school diploma is a certificate of legitimacy, not of competence. A youth needs one today in order to hold a job that will permit even minimal participation in the dominant society. Yet our laws governing school attendance do not deal with education. They are not *licensing* laws, requiring attendance until a certain defined minimum competence, presumed essential for adult life, has been demonstrated. They are not *contractual;* they offer no remedy for failure of the school to provide services of a minimum quality. A juvenile may not legally withdraw from school even if he can establish that it is substandard or that he is being ill-treated there. If he does, as many do, for just these reasons, he becomes *prima facie* an offender; for, in cold fact, the compulsory attendance law guarantees him nothing, not even the services of qualified teachers. It merely defines, in terms of age alone, a particular group as subject to legal restrictions not applicable to other persons.

Second-Class Citizen

Legally, the adolescent comes pretty close to having no basic rights at all. The state generally retains the final right even to strip him of his minority status. He has no right to *demand* the particular protection of *either* due process or the juvenile administrative procedure—the state decides. We have had several cases in the past few years of boys eighteen and under being sentenced to death by the full apparatus of formal criminal law, who would not have been permitted to claim its protection had they been accused of theft or disorderly conduct. Each of these executions has so far been forestalled by various legal procedures,[1] but none in such a way as to establish the right of a juvenile to be tried as a juvenile; though he long ago lost his claim to be treated as an adult.

In the most formal sense, then, the adolescent is one of our second-class citizens. But the informal aspects of minority status are also imputed to him. The "teen-ager," like the Latin or Negro, is seen as joyous, playful, lazy, and irresponsible, with brutality lurking just below the surface and ready to break out into violence.[2] All these groups are seen as childish and excitable, imprudent and improvident, sexually aggressive, and dangerous, but possessed of superb and sustained power to satisfy sexual demands. *West Side Story* is not much like *Romeo and Juliet;* but it is a great deal like *Porgy and Bess.*

The fantasy underlying this stereotype, then, is erotic; and its subject is male. The "hot-blooded" minorities are always represented by a masculine stereotype; nobody asks "Would you want your *son* to marry a Negro?" In each case, also, little counter-stereotypes, repulsively pallid in contrast to the alluring violence and conflict of the central scene, are held out enticingly by the dominant culture; the conscientious "teen-ager" sold by Pat Boone to soothe adults while the kids themselves buy *Mad* and *Catcher;* the boy whose Italian immigrant mother sees to it that he wears a clean shirt to school every day on his way to the Governor's mansion; *Uncle Tom.* In the rectilinear planning of Jonesville these are set aside conspicuously as Public Squares, but at dusk they are little frequented.

One need hardly labor the point that what the dominant society seeks to control by imposing "hot-blooded" minority status is not the actual aggressiveness and sexuality of the Negro, the Latin, or the JD, but its own wish for what the British working classes used to call "a nice game of slap and tickle," on the unimpeachable assumption that a little of what you fancy does you good. This, the well-lighted Public Squares cannot afford; the community is proud of them, but they are such stuff as only the driest dreams are made of. These are not the dreams that are wanted. In my experience, it is just not possible to discuss adolescence with a group of American adults without being forced onto the topic of juvenile delinquency. Partly this is an expression of legitimate concern, but partly it is because only the JD has any emotional vividness for them.

I would ascribe the success of *West Side Story* to the functional equivalence in the minds of adults between adolescence, delinquency, and aggressive sexuality. Many who saw the show must have wondered, as I did, why there were no Negroes in it—one of the best things about Juvenile Delinquency is that, at least, it is integrated. Hollywood, doubtless, was as usual reluctant to show a member of an enfranchised minority group in an unfavorable light. But there was also a rather sound artistic reason. Putting a real Negro boy in *West Side Story* would have been like scoring the second movement of the *Pastorale* for an eagle rather than flute. The provocative, surly, sexy dancing kids who come to a bad end are not meant realistically. Efforts to use real street-adolescents in *West Side Story* had to be abandoned; they didn't know how to act. What was depicted here was neither Negro nor white nor really delinquent, but a comfortably vulgar middle-class dream of a "hot-blooded" minority. In dreams a single symbolic boy can represent them all; let the symbol turn real and the dreamer wakes up screaming.

Adolescents are treated as a "hot-blooded" minority, then, because they seem so good at slap-and-tickle. But a number of interesting implications flow from this. Slap-and-tickle implies sexual vigor and attractiveness, warmth and aggression, salted with enough conventional perversity to lend spice to a long dull existence. Such perversity is a kind of exuberant overflow from the mainstream of sexuality, not a diversion of it. It is joyous excess and bounty; extravagant foreplay in the well-worn marriage bed; the generosity of impulse that leads the champion lover of the high school to prance around the shower-room snapping a towel on the buttocks of his teammates three hours before a hot date, just to remind them that life can be beautiful.

Experience Repressed

When a society sees impulsiveness and sexual exuberance as minority characteristics which unsuit the individual for membership until he is successfully naturalized, it is in pretty bad shape. Adolescents, loved, respected, taught to accept, enjoy, and discipline their feelings, grow up. "Teen-agers" don't; they pass. Then, in middle-age, they have the same trouble with their former self that many ethnics do. They hate and fear the kinds of spontaneity that remind them of what they have abandoned, and they hate themselves for having joined forces with and having come to resemble their oppressors.[3] This is the vicious spiral by which "hot-blooded" minority status maintains itself. I am convinced that it is also the source of the specific hostility—and sometimes sentimentality—that adolescents arouse in adults. The processes involved have been dealt with in detail by Daniel Boorstin, Leslie Fiedler, Paul Goodman, and especially Ernest Schachtel.[4] Their effect is to starve out, through silence and misrepresentation, the capacity to have genuine and strongly felt experience, and to replace it by the conventional symbols that serve as the common currency of daily life.

Experience repressed in adolescence does not, of course, result in amnesia, as does the repression of childhood experience; it leaves no temporal gaps in the memory. This makes it more dangerous, because the adult is then quite unaware that his memory is incomplete, that the most significant components of feeling have been lost or driven out. We at least know that we no longer know what we felt as children. But an adolescent boy who asks his father how he felt on the first night he spent in barracks or with a woman will be told what the father now thinks he felt because he ought to have; and this is very dangerous nonsense indeed.

Whether in childhood or in adolescence, the same quality of experience is starved out or repressed. It is still the spontaneous, vivid, and immediate that is most feared, and feared the more because so much desired. But there is a difference in focus and emphasis because in adolescence spontaneity can lead to much more serious consequences.

This, perhaps, is the crux of the matter, since it begins to explain why our kind of society should be so easily plunged into conflict by "hot-blooded" minorities in general and adolescent boys in particular. We are consequence-oriented and future-oriented. Among us, to prefer present delights is a sign of either low or high status, and both are feared. Schachtel makes it clear how we go about building this kind of character in the child—by making it difficult for him to notice his delights when he has them, and obliterating the language in which he might recall them joyfully later. This prepares the ground against the subsequent assault of adolescence. But it is a strong assault, and if adolescence wins, the future hangs in the balance.

The Adolescent Girl

In this assault, adolescent boys play a very different role from adolescent girls and are dealt with unconsciously by totally different dynamics. Adolescent girls are not seen as members of a "hot-blooded" minority, and to this fact may be traced some interesting paradoxes in our perception of the total phenomenon of adolescence.

Many critics of the current literature on adolescence—Bruno Bettleheim[5] perhaps most cogently—have pointed out that most contemporary writing about adolescents ignores the adolescent girl almost completely. Bettelheim specifically mentions Goodman and myself; the best novels about adolescents of the past decade or so have been, I think there would be fair agreement, Salinger's *The Catcher in the Rye,* John Knowles' *A Separate Peace,* and Colin MacInnes' less well known but superb *Absolute Beginners.* All these have adolescent boys as heroes. Yet, as Bettelheim points out, the adolescent girl is as important as the adolescent boy, and her actual plight in society is just as severe; her opportunities are even more limited and her growth into a mature woman as effectively discouraged. Why has she not aroused more interest?

There are demonstrable reasons for the prominence of the adolescent boy in our culture. Conventionally, it is he who threatens the virtue of our daughters and the integrity of our automobiles. There are so many more ways to get hung up on a boy. "Teenagers," too, may be all right; but would you want your daughter to marry one? When she doesn't know anything about him except how she feels—and what does that matter when they are both too young to know what they are doing; when he may never have the makings of an executive, or she of an executive's wife?

For this last consideration, paradoxically, also makes the *boy,* rather than the girl, the focus of anxiety. He alone bears the terrible burden of parental aspirations; it is his capacity for spontaneous commitment that endangers the opportunity of adults to live vicariously the life they never manage to live personally.

Holden, Finny, and the unnamed narrator of *Absolute Beginners*, are adolescent boys who do not pass; who retain their minority status, their spontaneous feelings, their power to act out and act up. They go prancing to their destinies. But what destiny can we imagine for them? We leave Holden in a mental hospital, being adjusted to reality; and Finny dead of the horror of learning that his best friend, Gene, had unconsciously contrived the accident that broke up his beautifully articulated body. The Absolute Beginner, a happier boy in a less tense society, fares better; he has had more real contact with other human beings, including a very satisfactory father, and by his time there is such a thing as a "teen-ager," little as it is, for him to be. On this basis the Beginner can identify himself; the marvelous book ends as he rushes out onto the tarmac at London Airport, bursting through the customs barrier, to stand at the foot of the gangway and greet a planeload of astonished immigrants by crying, "Here I am! Meet your first teen-ager."

Political Disinterest

There are still enough Finnys and Holdens running around free to give me much joy and some hope, and they are flexible enough to come to their own terms with reality. But the system is against them, and they know it well. Why then, do they not try to change it? Why are none of these novels of adolescence political novels? Why have their heroes no political interests at all? In this respect, fiction is true to American life; American adolescents are notably free from political interests. I must maintain this despite the recent advances of SANE kids and Freedom Riders; for, though I love and honor them for their courage and devotion, the causes they fight for are not what I would call political. No controversy over basic policy is involved, because nobody advocates atomic disaster or racial persecution. The kids' opponents are merely in favor of the kind of American society that these evils flourish in, and the youngsters do not challenge the system itself, though they are appalled by its consequences.

Yet could they, as adolescents, be political? I don't think so; and I don't know that I would be pleased if they were. American politics is a cold-blooded business indeed. Personal clarity and commitment are not wanted in it and not furthered by it. I do not think this is necessarily true of all politics; but it becomes true when the basic economic and social assumptions are as irrational as ours.

Political effectiveness in our time requires just the right kind of caginess, pseudo-realism, and stereotyping of thought and feeling; the same submergence of spontaneity to the exigencies of collective action, that mark the ruin of adolescence. Adolescents are, inherently, anti-mass; they take things personally. Sexuality, itself, has this power to resolve relationships into the immediate and interpersonal. As a symbol the cocky adolescent boy stands, a little like Luther, an obstacle to compromise and accommodation. Such symbols stick in the mind, though the reality can usually be handled. With occasional spectacular failures we do manage to assimilate the "teen-age" minority; the kids learn not to get fresh; they get smart, they dry up. We are left then, like the Macbeths, with the memory of an earlier fidelity. But Lady Macbeth was less resourceful than ourselves; she knew next to nothing about industrial solvents. Where she had only perfume we have oil.

The Girl as Woman

This is how we use the boy, but what about the girl? I have already asserted that, since she is not perceived as a member of the "hot-blooded" minority she cannot take his place in the unconscious, which is apt to turn very nasty if it is fobbed off with the wrong sex. Is she then simply not much involved by our psychodynamics, or is she actively repressed? Is she omitted from our fantasies or excluded from them?

It may seem very strange that I should find her so inconspicuous. Her image gets so much publicity. Drum-majorettes and cheerleaders are ubiquitous; *Playboy* provides businessmen with a new *playmate* each month. Nymphets are a public institution.

Exactly, and they serve a useful public function. American males are certainly anxious to project a heterosexual public image, and even more anxious to believe in it themselves. None of us, surely, wishes to feel obligated to hang himself out of respect for the United States Senate; it is, as Yum-Yum remarked to Nanki-Poo, such a stuffy death. I am not questioning our sincerity; the essence of my point is that in what we call maturity we feel what we are supposed to feel, and nothing else. But I am questioning the depth and significance of our interest in the cover or pin-up girl. Her patrons are concerned to experience their own masculinity; they are not much interested in her: I reject the celebration of "babes" in song and story as evidence that we have adolescent girls much on our minds; if we did we wouldn't think of them as "babes." I think, indeed, that in contrast to the boy, of whom we are hyperaware, we repress our awareness of the girl. She is not just omitted, she is excluded.

The adolescent heroine in current fiction is not interpreted in the same way as the adolescent hero, even when the parallel is quite close. Her adolescence is treated as less crucial; she is off-handedly accepted as a woman already. This is true even when the author struggles against it. *Lolita,* for example, is every bit as much a tragic heroine of adolescence as Holden is a hero—she isn't as nice a girl as he is a boy, but they are both victims of the same kind of corruption in adult society and the same absence of any real opportunity to grow up to be themselves. Lolita's failure is the classic failure of identity in adolescence; and Humbert knows this and accepts responsibility for it; this is the crime he expiates. But this is not the way Lolita—the character, not the book—is generally received. Unlike Holden, she has no cult and is not vouchsafed any dignity. It is thought to be comical that, at fourteen, she is already a whore.

A parallel example is to be found in Rumer Godden's *The Green-gage Summer.* Here the story is explicitly about Joss's growing up. The author's emphasis is on the way her angry betrayal of her lover marks the end of her childhood; her feelings are now too strong and confused, and too serious in their consequences, to be handled with childish irresponsibility; she can no longer claim the exemptions of childhood. But what the movie presented, it seemed to me, was almost entirely an account of her rise to sexual power; Joss had become a Babe at last.

One reason that we do not take adolescent growth seriously in girls is that we do not much care what happens to people unless it has economic consequences: what would Holden ever be, since he never even graduates from high school; who would hire him? He has a problem; Lolita could always be a waitress or something; what more could she expect? Since we define adulthood almost exclusively in economic terms, we obviously cannot concern ourselves as much about the growth of those members of society who are subject from birth to restricted economic opportunity. But so, of course, are the members of the "hot-blooded" minorities; though we find their hot-bloodedness so exciting that we remain aware of them anyway.

But girls, like Jews, are not supposed to fight back; we expect them, instead, to insinuate themselves coyly into the roles available. In our society, there are such lovely things for them to be. They can take care of other people and clean up after them. Women can become wives and mothers; Jews can become kindly old Rabbis and philosophers and even psychoanalysts and lovable comic essayists. They can become powers behind the power; a fine old law firm runs on the brains of its anonymous young Jews just as a husband's best asset is his loyal and unobtrusive wife. A Jewish girl can become a Jewish Mother, and this is a role which even Plato would have called essential.

Effects of Discrimination

Clearly, this kind of discrimination is quite different from that experienced by the "hot-blooded" minorities and must be based on a very different image in the minds of those who practice it and must have a different impact upon them. Particularly, in the case of the adolescent, the effect on the adult of practicing these two kinds of discrimination will be different. The adolescent boy must be altered to fit middle-class adult roles, and when he has been he becomes a much less vital creature. But the girl is merely squandered, and this wastage will continue all her life. Since adolescence is, for boy and girl alike, the time of life in which the self must be established, the girl suffers as much from being wasted as the boy does from being cut down; there has recently been, for example, a number of tragic suicides reported among adolescent girls, though suicide generally is far less common among females. But from the point of view of the dominant society nothing special is done to the female in adolescence—the same squeeze continues throughout life, even though this is when it hurts most.

The guilts we retain for our treatments of "hot-blooded" and "long-suffering" minorities therefore affect us in contrasting ways. For the boy we suffer angry, paranoid remorse, as if he were Billy the Kid, or Budd. We had to do our duty, but how can we ever forget him? But we do not attack the girl; we only neglect her and leave her to wither gradually through an unfulfilled life; and the best defense against this sort of guilt is selective inattention. We just don't see her; instead, we see a caricature, not brutalized as in the case of the boy, to justify our own brutality, but sentimentalized, roseate, to reassure us that we have done her no harm, and that she is well contented. Look: she even has her own telephone, with what is left of the boy dangling from the other end of the line.

A Lonely Ride

This is the fantasy; the reality is very different, but it is bad enough to be a "teen-ager." The adolescent is now the only totally disfranchised minority group in the country. In America, no minority has ever gotten any respect or consistently decent treatment until it began to acquire political power. The vote comes before anything else. This is obviously true of the Negro at the present time; his recent advances have all been made under—sometimes reluctant— Federal auspices because, nationally, Negroes vote, and Northern Negroes are able to cast a ballot on which their buffeted Southern rural fellows may be pulled to firmer political ground. This is what makes it possible to stop Freedom Rides; just as the comparable militance of the Catholic Church in proceeding toward integration in Louisiana may have less to do with Louisiana than Nigeria, which is in grave danger of falling into the hands of Black Muslims. People generally sympathetic with adolescents sometimes say, "Well, it really isn't fair; if they're old enough to be drafted, they're old enough to vote," which is about as naive as it is possible to get.

Can the status of the "teen-ager" be improved? Only, presumably, through increased political effectiveness. Yet, it is precisely here that a crucial dilemma arises. For the aspirations of the adolescent minority are completely different from those of other minorities. All the others are struggling to obtain what the adolescent is struggling to avoid. They seek and welcome the conventional American middle-class status that has been partially or totally barred to them. But this is what the adolescent is left with if he gives in and goes along.

In the recent and very moving CORE film, *Freedom Ride,* one of the heroic group who suffered beatings and imprisonment for their efforts to end segregation says, as nearly as I can recall, "If the road to freedom leads through the jails of the South, then that's the road I'll take." It may be the road to freedom; but it is the road to suburbia too. You can't tell which the people are headed for until they are nearly there; but all our past ethnic groups have settled for suburbia, and the people who live there bear witness that freedom is somewhere else.

I am not sure that there *is* a road to freedom in America. Not enough people want to go there; the last I can recall was H. D. Thoreau, and he went on foot, through the woods, alone. This still may be the only way to get there. For those with plenty of guts, compassion, and dedication to social justice, who nevertheless dislike walking alone through the woods, or feel it to be a Quixotic extravagance, a freedom ride is a noble enterprise. Compared to them, the individual boy or girl on a solitary journey must seem an anachronism. Such a youngster has very little place in our way of life. And of all the criticisms that might be directed against that way of life, this is the harshest.

REFERENCES

1. Two were finally hanged this past June, five years later.
2. A very bad—indeed, vicious—but remarkably ambivalent reenactment of the entire fantasy on which the minority-status of the teenager is based can be seen in the recent movie *13 West St.* Here, the legal impotence of the "teen-ager" is taken absolutely for granted, and sadistic hostility of adults against him, though deplored, is condoned and accepted as natural. Occasional efforts are made to counterbalance the, in my judgment, pornographic picture of a brutal teen-age gang by presenting "good" teen-agers unjustly suspected, and decent police trying to resist sadistic pressure from the gang's victim, who drives one of its members to suicide. But despite this, the picture ends with a scene of the gang's victim—a virile-type rocket scientist—

beating the leader of the gang with his cane and attempting to drown the boy in a swimming pool—which the police dismiss as excusable under the circumstances. A Honolulu paper, at least, described this scene of attempted murder as "an old-fashioned caning that had the audience cheering in its seats."

3. Cf. Abraham Kardiner and Lionel Ovesey's classic, *The Mark of Oppression* (New York: Norton, 1951), for a fascinating study of these dynamics among American Negroes.

4. Daniel Boorstin, *The Image* (New York: Atheneum, 1962); Leslie Fiedler, "The Fear of the Impulsive Life," *WFMT Perspective* (October, 1961), pp. 4–9; Paul Goodman, *Growing Up Absurd* (New York: Random House, 1960), p. 38; Ernest Schachtel, "On Memory and Childhood Amnesia," widely anthologized, see the author's *Metamorphosis* (New York: Basic Books, 1959), pp. 279–322. A more systematic and profound treatment, I have since learned, is to be found in Norman Brown, *Life Against Death* (Middletown, Conn.: Wesleyan University Press, 1959).

5. In Bruno Bettleheim, "Adolescence and the Conflict of Generations," *Daedalus* (Winter, 1962), p. 68.

The Condemnation and Persecution of Hippies

Michael E. Brown

This article is about persecution and terror. It speaks of the Hippie and the temptations of intimacy that the myth of Hippie has made poignant, and it does this to discuss the institutionalization of repression in the United States.

When people are attacked as a group, they change. Individuals in the group may or may not change, but the organization and expression of their collective life will be transformed. When the members of a gathering believe that there is a grave danger imminent and that opportunities for escape are rapidly diminishing, the group loses its organizational quality. It becomes transformed in panic. This type of change can also occur outside a situation of strict urgency: When opportunities for mobility or access to needed resources are cut off, people may engage in desperate collective actions. In both

Source: *TRANS-action Magazine*, 6:10 (September 1969), pp. 33–46; copyright © by *TRANS-action Magazine*, New Brunswick, N.J. Reprinted by permission of publisher and author.

cases, the conversion of social form occurs when members of a collectivity are about to be hopelessly locked into undesired and undesirable positions.

The process is not, however, automatic. The essential ingredient for conversion is social control exercised by external agents on the collectivity itself. The result can be benign, as a panic mob can be converted into a crowd that makes an orderly exit from danger. Or it can be cruel.

The transformation of groups under pressure is of general interest; but there are special cases that are morally critical to any epoch. Such critical cases occur when pressure is persecution, and transformation is destruction. The growth of repressive mechanisms and institutions is a key concern in this time of administrative cruelty. Such is the justification for the present study.

Social Control as Terror

Four aspects of repressive social control such as that experienced by Hippies are important. First, the administration of control is suspicious. It projects a dangerous future and guards against it. It also refuses the risk of inadequate coverage by enlarging the controlled population to include all who might be active in any capacity. Control may or may not be administered with a heavy hand, but it is always a generalization applied to specific instances. It is a rule and thus ends by pulling many fringe innocents into its bailiwick; it creates as it destroys.

Second, the administration of control is a technical problem which, depending on its site and object, requires the bringing together of many different agencies that are ordinarily dissociated or mutually hostile. A conglomerate of educational, legal, social welfare, and police organizations is highly efficient. The German case demonstrates that. Even more important, it is virtually impossible to oppose control administered under the auspices of such a conglomerate since it includes the countervailing institutions ordinarily available. When this happens control is not only efficient and widespread, but also legitimate, commanding a practical, moral and ideological realm that is truly "one-dimensional."

Third, as time passes, control is applied to a wider and wider range of details, ultimately blanketing its objects' lives. At that point, as Hilberg suggests in his *The Destruction of the European Jews,* the extermination of the forms of lives leads easily to the extermination of the lives themselves. The line between persecution and terror is thin. For the oppressed, life is purged of personal style as every act becomes inexpressive, part of the struggle for survival. The options of a life-style are eliminated at the same time that its proponents are locked into it.

Fourth, control is relentless. It develops momentum as organization accumulates, as audiences develop, and as unofficial collaborators assume the definition of tasks, expression and ideology. This, according to W. A. Westley's "The Escalation of Violence Through Legitimation," is the culture of control. It not only limits the behaviors, styles, individuals and groups toward whom it is directed, it suppresses all unsanctioned efforts. As struggle itself is destroyed, motivation vanishes or is turned inward.

These are the effects of repressive control. We may contrast them with the criminal law, which merely prohibits the performance of specific acts (with the exception, of course, of the "crime without victims"—homosexuality, abortion, and drug use). Repression converts or destroys an entire social form, whether that form is embodied in a group, a style or an idea. In this sense, it is terror.

These general principles are especially relevant to our understanding of tendencies that are ripening in the United States day by day. Stated in terms that magnify it so that it can be seen despite ourselves, this is the persecution of the Hippies, a particularly vulnerable group of people who are the cultural wing of a way of life recently emerged from its quiet and individualistic quarters. Theodore Roszak, describing the Hippies in terms of their relationship to the culture and politics of dissent, notes that "the underlying unity of youthful dissent consists . . . in the effort of beat-hip bohemianism to work out the personality structure, the total life-style that follows from New Left social criticism." This life style is currently bearing the brunt of the assault on what Roszak calls a "counter-culture"; it is an assault that is becoming more concentrated and savage every day. There are lessons for the American future to be drawn from this story.

Persecution

Near Boulder, Colorado, a restaurant sign says: "Hippies not served here." Large billboards in upstate New York carry slogans like "Keep America Clean: Take a Bath" and "Keep America Clean: Get a Haircut." These would be as amusing as ethnic jokes if they did not represent a more systematic repression.

The street sweeps so common in San Francisco and Berkeley in 1968 and 1969 were one of the first lines of attack. People were brutally scattered by club-wielding policemen who first closed exits from the assaulted area and then began systematically to beat and arrest those who were trapped. This form of place terror, like surveillance in Negro areas and defoliation in Vietnam, curbs freedom and forces people to fight or submit to minute inspection by hostile forces. There have also been one-shot neighborhood pogroms, such as the police assault on the Tompkins Square Park gathering in New York's Lower East Side on Memorial Day, 1967: "Sadistic glee was written on the faces of several officers," wrote the *East Village Other*. Some women became hysterical. The police slugged Frank Wise, and dragged him off, handcuffed and bloody, crying, "My God, my God, where is this happening? Is this America?" The police also plowed into a group of Hippies, Yippies, and straights at the April, 1968, "Yip-in" at Grand Central Station. The brutality was as clear in this action as it had been in the Tompkins Square bust. In both cases, the major newspapers editorialized against the police tactics, and in the first the Mayor apologized for the "free wielding of nightsticks." But by the summer of 1968, street sweeps and busts and the continuous presence of New York's Tactical Police Force had given the Lower East Side an ominous atmosphere. Arrests were regularly accompanied by beatings and charges of "resistance to arrest." It became clear that arrests rather than subsequent procedures were the way in which control was to be exercised. The summer lost its street theaters, the relaxed circulation of people in the neighborhood and the easy park gatherings.

Official action legitimizes nonofficial action. Private citizens take up the cudgel of law and order newly freed from the boundaries of due process and respect. After Tompkins Square, rapes and assaults became common as local toughs assumed the role, with the police, of defender of the faith. In Cambridge, Massachusetts, following a virulent attack on Hippies by the Mayor, *Newsweek* reported that vigilantes attacked Hippie neighborhoods in force.

Ultimately more damaging are the attacks on centers of security. Police raids on "Hippie pads," crash pads, churches and movement centers have become daily occurrences in New York and California over the past two and a half years. The usual excuses for raids are drugs, runaways and housing violations, but many incidents of unlawful entry by police and the expressions of a more generalized hostility by the responsible officials suggest that something deeper is involved. The Chief of Police in San Francisco put it bluntly; quoted in *The New York Times Magazine* in May 1967, he said:

> Hippies are no asset to the community. These people do not have the courage to face the reality of life. They are trying to escape. Nobody should let their young children take part in this hippy thing.

The Director of Health for San Francisco gave teeth to this counsel when he sent a task force of inspectors on a door-to-door sweep of the Haight-Ashbury—"a two-day blitz" that ended with a strange result, again according to *The Times:* Very few of the Hippies were guilty of housing violations.

Harassment arrests and calculated degradation have been two of the most effective devices for introducing uncertainty to the day-to-day lives of the Hippies. Cambridge's Mayor's attack on the "hipbos" (the suffix stands for body odor) included, said *Newsweek* of October 30, 1967, a raid on a "hippie pad" by the Mayor and "a platoon of television cameramen." They "seized a pile of diaries and personal letters and flushed a partially clad girl from the closet." In Wyoming, *The Times* reported that two "pacifists" were "jailed and shaved" for hitchhiking. This is a fairly common hazard, though Wyoming officials are perhaps more sadistic than most. A young couple whom I interviewed were also arrested in Wyoming during the summer of 1968. They were placed in solitary confinement for a week during which they were not permitted to place phone calls and were not told when or whether they would be charged or released. These are not exceptional cases. During the summer of 1968, I interviewed young hitchhikers throughout the country; most of them had similar stories to tell.

In the East Village of New York, one hears countless stories of apartment destruction by police (occasionally reported in the newspapers), insults from the police when rapes or robberies are reported, and cruel speeches and even crueler bails set by judges for arrested Hippies.

In the light of this, San Francisco writer Mark Harris' indictment of the Hippies as paranoid seems peculiar. In the September 1967 issue of *The Atlantic,* he wrote,

> The most obvious failure of perception was the hippies' failure to discriminate among elements of the Establishment, whether in the Haight-Ashbury or in San Francisco in general. Their paranoia was the paranoia of all youthful heretics. . . .

This is like the demand of some white liberals that Negroes acknowledge that they (the liberals) are not the power structure, or that black people must distinguish between the good and the bad whites despite the fact that the black experience of white people in the United States has been, as the President's Commission on Civil Disorder suggested, fairly monolithic and racist.

Most journalists reviewing the "Hippie scene" with any sympathy at all seem to agree with *Newsweek* that "the hippies do seem natural prey for publicity-hungry politicians—if not overzealous police," and that they have been subjected to varieties of cruelty that ought to be intolerable. This tactic was later elaborated in the massive para-military assault on Berkeley residents and students during a demonstration in support of Telegraph Avenue's street people and their People's Park. The terror of police violence, a constant in the lives of street people everywhere, in California carries the additional threat of martial law under a still-active state of extreme emergency. The whole structure of repression was given legitimacy and reluctant support by University of California officials. Step by step, they became allies of Reagan's "dogs of war." Roger W. Heyns, chancellor of the Berkeley campus, found himself belatedly re-asserting the university's property in the lot. It was the law and the rights of university that trapped the chancellor in the network of control and performed the vital function of providing justification and legitimacy for Sheriff Madigan and the National Guard. Heyns said: "We will have to put up a fence to re-establish the conveniently forgotten fact that this field is indeed the university's, and to exclude unauthorized personnel from the site. . . . The fence will give us time to plan and consult. We tried to get this time some other way and failed—hence the fence." And hence "Bloody Thursday" and the new regime.

And what of the Hippies? They have come far since those balmy days of 1966–67, days of flowers, street-cleaning, free stores, decoration and love. Many have fled to the hills of Northern California to join their brethren who had set up camps there several years ago. Others have fled to communes outside the large cities and in the Middle West. After the Tompkins Square assault, many of the East Village Hippies refused to follow the lead of those who were more political. They refused to develop organizations of defense and to accept a hostile relationship with the police and neighborhood. Instead, they discussed at meeting after meeting how they could show their attackers love. Many of those spirits have fled; others have been beaten or jailed too many times; and still others have modified their outlook in ways that reflect the struggle. Guerrilla theater, Up Against the Wall Mother Fucker, the Yippies, the urban communes; these are some of the more recent manifestations of the alternative culture. One could see these trends growing in the demonstrations mounted by Hippies against arrests of runaways or pot smokers, the community organizations, such as grew in Berkeley for self-defense and politics, and the beginnings of the will to fight back when trapped in street sweeps.

It is my impression that the Hippie culture is growing as it recedes from the eye of the media. As a consequence of the destruction of their urban places, there has been a redistribution of types. The flower people have left for the hills and become more communal; those who remained in the city were better adapted to terror, secre-

tive or confrontative. The Hippie culture is one of the forms radicalism can take in this society. The youngsters, 5,000 of them, who
came to Washington to counter-demonstrate against the Nixon in-
augural showed the growing amalgamation of the New Left and its
cultural wing. The Yippies who went to Chicago for guerrilla theater and learned about "pigs" were the multi-generational expression
of the new wave. A UAWMF (Up Against the Wall Mother
Fucker) drama, played at Lincoln Center during the New York City
garbage strike—they carted garbage from the neglected Lower East
Side and dumped it at the spic 'n' span cultural center—reflected
another interpretation of the struggle, one that could include the
politically militant as well as the culturally defiant. Many Hippies
have gone underground—in an older sense of the word. They have
shaved their beards, cut their hair, and taken straight jobs, like the
secret Jews of Spain; but unlike those Jews, they are consciously an
underground, a resistance.

What is most interesting and, I believe, a direct effect of the persecution, is the enormous divergence of forms that are still recog-
nizable by the outsider as Hippie and are still experienced as a shared
identity. "The Yippies," says Abbie Hoffman, "are like Hippies, only
fiercer and more fun." The "hippie types" described in newspaper
accounts of drug raids on colleges turn out, in many cases, to be
New Leftists.

The dimensions by which these various forms are classified are
quite conventional: religious-political, visible-secret, urban-hill, com-
munal-individualistic. As their struggle intensifies, there will be
more efforts for unity and more militant approaches to the society
that gave birth to a real alternative only to turn against it with a
mindless savagery. Yippie leader Jerry Rubin, in an "emergency letter to my brothers and sisters in the movement" summed up:

> Huey Newton is in prison.
> Eldridge Cleaver is in exile.
> Oakland Seven are accused of conspiracy.
> Tim Leary is up for 30 years and how many of our brothers are in
> court and jail for getting high?
> . . .
> Camp activists are expelled and arrested.

War resisters are behind bars.
Add it up!

Rubin preambles his summary with:

> From the Bay Area to New York, we are suffering the greatest depression in our history. People are taking bitterness in their coffee instead of sugar. The hippie-yippie-SDS movement is a "white nigger" movement. The American economy no longer needs young whites and blacks. We are waste material. We fulfill our destiny by rejecting a system which rejects us.

He advocates organizing "massive mobilizations for the spring, nationally coordinated and very theatrical, taking place near courts, jails, and military stockades."

An article published in a Black Panther magazine is entitled "The Hippies Are Not Our Enemies." White radicals have also overcome their initial rejection of cultural radicals. Something clearly is happening, and it is being fed, finally, by youth, the artists, the politicos and the realization, through struggle, that America is not beautiful.

Some Historical Analogies

The persecution of the Jews destroyed both a particular social form and the individuals who qualified for the Jewish fate by reason of birth. Looking at the process in the aggregate, Hilberg describes it as a gradual coming together of a multitude of loose laws, institutions, and intentions, rather than a program born mature. The control conglomerate that resulted was a refined engine "whose devices," Hilberg writes, "not only trap a larger number of victims; they also require a greater degree of specialization, and with that division of labor, the moral burden too is fragmented among the participants. The perpetrator can now kill his victims without touching them, without hearing them, without seeing them. . . . This ever growing capacity for destruction cannot be arrested anywhere." Ultimately, the persecution of the Jews was a mixture of piety, repression and mobilization directed against those who were in the society but suddenly not of it.

The early Christians were also faced with a refined and elaborate administrative structure whose harsh measures were ultimately directed at their ways of life: their social forms and their spiritual claims. The rationale was, and is, that certain deviant behaviors endanger society. Therefore, officials are obligated to use whatever means of control or persuasion they consider necessary to strike these forms from the list of human possibilities. This is the classical administrative rationale for the suppression of alternative values and world views.

As options closed and Christians found the opportunities to lead and explore Christian lives rapidly struck down, Christian life itself had to become rigid, prematurely closed and obsessed with survival.

The persecution of the early Christians presents analogies to the persecution of European Jews. The German assault affected the quality of Jewish organizations no less than it affected the lives of individual Jews, distorting communities long before it destroyed them. Hilberg documents some of the ways in which efforts to escape the oppression led on occasion to a subordination of energies to the problem of simply staying alive—of finding some social options within the racial castle. The escapist mentality that dominated the response to oppression and distorted relationships can be seen in some Jewish leaders in Vienna. They exchanged individuals for promises. This is what persecution and terror do. As options close and all parts of the life of the oppressed are touched by procedure, surveillance and control, behavior is transformed. The oppressed rarely retaliate (especially where they have internalized the very ethic that rejects them), simply because nothing is left untouched by the persecution. No energy is available for hostility, and, in any case, it is impossible to know where to begin. Bravery is stoicism. One sings to the cell or gas chamber.

The persecution of Hippies in the United States involves, regardless of the original intentions of the agencies concerned, an assault on a way of life, an assault no less concentrated for its immaturity and occasional ambivalence. Social, cultural and political resources have been mobilized to bring a group of individuals into line and to prevent others from refusing to toe the line.

The attractiveness of the Hippie forms and the pathos of their persecution have together brought into being an impressive array of defenders. Nevertheless theirs has been a defense of gestures, outside the realm of politics and social action essential to any real protection. It has been verbal, scholarly and appreciative, with occasional expressions of horror at official actions and attitudes. But unfortunately the arena of conflict within which the Hippies, willynilly, must try to survive is dominated not by the likes of Susan Sontag, but by the likes of Daniel Patrick Moynihan whose apparent compassion for the Hippies will probably never be translated into action. For even as he writes in the *American Scholar* (Autumn, 1967) that these youths are "trying to tell us something" and that they are one test of our "ability to survive," he rejects them firmly, and not a little ex cathedra, as a "truth gone astray." The Hippie remains helpless and more affected by the repressive forces (who will probably quote Moynihan) than by his own creative capacity or the sympathizers who support him in the journals. As John Kifner reported in *The Times*, " 'This scene is not the same anymore,' said the tall, thin Negro called Gypsy. '. . . There are some very bad vibrations.' "

Social Form and Cultural Heresy

But it's just another murder. A hippie being killed is just like a housewife being killed or a career girl being killed or a hoodlum being killed. None of these people, notice, are persons; they're labels. Who cares who Groovy was; if you know he was a 'hippie,' then already you know more about him than he did about himself.

See, it's hard to explain to a lot of you what a hippie is because a lot of you really think a hippie IS something. You don't realize that the word is just a convenience picked up by the press to personify a social change thing beginning to happen to young people. (*Paul William, in an article entitled "Label Dies—But Not Philosophy," Open City, Los Angeles, November 17-23, 1967.*)

Because the mass media have publicized the growth of a fairly well-articulated Hippie culture, it now bears the status of a social form. Variously identified as "counter-culture," "Hippie-dom,"

"Youth" or "Underground," the phenomenon centers on a philosophy of the present and takes the personal and public forms appropriate to that philosophy. Its values constitute a heresy in a society
that consecrates the values of competition, social manipulation and
functionalism, a society that defines ethical quality by long-range
and general consequences, and that honors only those attitudes and
institutions that affirm the primacy of the future and large-scale over
the local and immediately present. It is a heresy in a society that es-
chews the primary value of intimacy for the sake of impersonal service to large and enduring organizations, a society that is essentialist
rather than existentialist, a society that prizes biography over interactive quality. It is a heresy in a country whose President could be
praised for crying, "Ask not what your country can do for you, but
what you can do for your country!" Most important, however, it is
heresy in a society whose official values, principles of operation and
officials themselves are threatened domestically and abroad.

For these reasons the Hippie is available for persecution. When
official authority is threatened, social and political deviants are readily
conjured up as demons requiring collective exorcism and thus a
reaffirmation of that authority. Where exorcism is the exclusive
province of government, the government's power is reinforced by the
adoption of a scapegoat. Deviant style and ideals make a group vulnerable to exploitation as a scapegoat, but it is official action which
translates vulnerability into actionable heresy.

By contrast, recent political developments within black communities and the accommodations reached through bargaining with various official agencies have placed the blacks alongside the Viet Cong
as an official enemy, but not as a scapegoat. As an enemy, the black
is not a symbol but a source of society's troubles. It is a preferable
position. The Hippie's threat lies in the lure of his way of life
rather than in his political potential. His vulnerability as well as
his proven capacity to develop a real alternative life permits his selection as scapegoat. A threatened officialdom is all too likely to take
the final step that "brings on the judge." At the same time, by defining its attack as moderate, it reaffirms its moral superiority in the
very field of hate it cultivates.

A Plausible Force

We are speaking of that which claims the lives, totally or in part, of perhaps hundreds of thousands of people of all ages throughout the United States and elsewhere. The number is not inconsiderable.

The plausibility of the Hippie culture and its charisma can be argued on several grounds. Their outlook derives from a profound mobilizing idea: Quality resides in the present. Therefore, one seeks the local in all its social detail—not indulgently and alone, but openly and creatively. Vulnerability and improvisation are principles of action, repudiating the "rational" hierarchy of plans and stages that defines, for the grounded culture, all events as incidents of passage and means to an indefinitely postponable end—as transition. The allocation of reality to the past and the future is rejected in favor of the present, and a present that is known and felt immediately, not judged by external standards. The long run is the result rather than the goal of the present. "Psychical distance," the orientation of the insulated tourist to whom the environment is something forever foreign or of the administrator for whom the world is an object of administration, is repudiated as a relational principle. It is replaced by a principle of absorption. In this, relationships are more like play, dance or jazz. Intimacy derives from absorption, from spontaneous involvement, to use Erving Goffman's phrase, rather than from frequent contact or attraction, as social psychologists have long argued.

This vision of social reality makes assumptions about human nature. It sees man as only a part of a present that depends on all its parts. To be a "part" is not to play a stereotyped role or to plan one's behavior prior to entering the scene. It is to be of a momentum. Collaboration, the overt manifestation of absorption, is critical to any social arrangement because the present, as experience, is essentially social. Love and charisma are the reflected properties of the plausible whole that results from mutual absorption. "To swing" or "to groove" is to be of the scene rather than simply at or in the scene. "Rapping," an improvised, expansive, and collaborative conversational form, is an active embodiment of the more general ethos. Its craft is humor, devotion, trust, openness to events in the process of formation, and the capacity to be relevant. Identity is neither strictly personal nor something to be maintained, but something always to be discovered. The individual body is the origin of sounds and motions, but behavior, ideas, images, and reflective thought stem from interaction itself. Development is not of personalities but of situations that include many bodies but, in effect, one mind. Various activities, such as smoking marijuana, are disciplines that serve the function of bringing people together and making them deeply interesting to each other.

The development of an authentic "counter-culture," or, better, "alternative culture," has some striking implications. For one, information and stress are processed through what amounts to a new conceptual system—a culture that replaces, in the committed, the intrapersonal structures that Western personality theories have assumed to account for intrapersonal order. For example, in 1966, young Hippies often turned against their friends and their experience after a bad acid trip. But that was the year during which "the Hippie thing" was merely one constructive expression of dissent. It was not, at that point, an alternative culture. As a result, the imagery cued in by the trauma was the imagery of the superego, the distant and punitive authority of the Western family and its macrocosmic social system. Guilt, self-hatred and the rejection of experience was the result. Many youngsters returned home filled with a humiliation that could be forgotten, or converted to a seedy and defensive hatred of the dangerously deviant. By 1968 the bad trip, while still an occasion for reconversion for some, had for others become something to be guarded against and coped with in a context of care and experienced guidance. The atmosphere of trust and new language of stress inspired dependence rather than recoil as the initial stage of cure. One could "get high with a little help from my friends." Conscience was purged of "authority."

Although the ethos depends on personal contact, it is carried by underground media (hundreds of newspapers claiming hundreds of thousands of readers), rock music, and collective activities, artistic and political, which deliver and duplicate the message; and it is processed through a generational flow. It is no longer simply a constructive expression of dissent and thus attractive because it is a vital answer to a system that destroys vitality; it is culture, and the young are growing up under the wisdom of its older generations. The ethos is realized most fully in the small communes that dot the American urbscape and constitute an important counter-institution of the Hippies.

This complex of population, culture, social form, and ideology is both a reinforcing environment for individuals and a context for the growth and elaboration of the complex itself. In it, life not only begins, it goes on; and, indeed, it must go on for those who are committed to it. Abbie Hoffman's *Revolution for the Hell of It* assumes the autonomy of this cultural frame of reference. It assumes that the individual has entered and has burned his bridges.

As the heresy takes an official definition and as the institutions of persecution form, a they-mentality emerges in the language which expresses the relationship between the oppressor and the oppressed. For the oppressed, it distinguishes life from nonlife so that living can go on. The they-mentality of the oppressed temporarily relieves them of the struggle by acknowledging the threat, identifying its agent, and compressing both into a quasi-poetic image, a cliché that can accommodate absurdity. One young man said, while coming down from an amphetamine high: "I'm simply going to continue to do what I want until they stop me."

But persecution is also structured by the they-mentality of the persecutors. This mentality draws lines around its objects as it fits them conceptually for full-scale social action. The particular uses of the term "hippie" in the mass media—like "Jew," "Communist," "Black Muslim," or "Black Panther"—cultivates not only disapproval and rejection but a climate of opinion capable of excluding Hippies from the moral order altogether. This is one phase of a subtle process that begins by locating and isolating a group, tying it to the criminal, sinful or obscene, developing and displaying referential symbols at a high level of abstraction which depersonalize and objectify the group, defining the stigmata by which members are to be known and placing the symbols in the context of ideology and readiness for action.

At this point, the symbols come to define public issues and are, consequently, sources of strength. The maintenance of power—the next phase of the story—depends less on the instruction of reading and viewing publics than on the elaboration of the persecutory institutions which demonstrate and justify power. The relationship between institution and public ceases to be one of expression or extension (of a public to an institution) and becomes one of transaction or dominance (of a public with or by an institution). The total dynamic is similar to advertising or the growth of the military as domestic powers in America.

An explosion of Hippie stories appeared in the mass media during the summer of 1967. Almost every large-circulation magazine featured articles on the Hippie "fad" or "subculture." *Life's* "The Other Culture" set the tone. The theme was repeated in *The New York Times Magazine* (May 14, 1967), where Hunter Thompson wrote that "The 'Hashbury (Haight-Ashbury in San Francisco) is the new capital of what is rapidly becoming a drug culture." *Time's* "wholly new subculture" was "a cult whose mystique derives essentially from the influences of hallucinogenic drugs." By fall, while maintaining the emphasis on drugs as the cornerstone of the culture, the articles had shifted from the culturological to a "national character" approach, reminiscent of the World War II anti-Japanese propaganda, as personal traits were piled into the body of the symbol and objectification began. The Hippies were "acid heads," "generally dirty," and "visible, audible and sometimes smellable young rebels."

As "hippie" and its associated terms ("long-haired," "bearded") accumulated pejorative connotation, they began to be useful concepts and were featured regularly in news headlines: for example, "Hippie Mother Held in Slaying of Son, 2" (*The New York Times,* November 22, 1967); "S Squad Hits Four Pads" (*San Francisco Chronicle,* July 27, 1967). The articles themselves solidified usage by dwelling on "hippie types," "wild drug parties" and "long-haired, bearded" youths (see, for example, *The New York Times* of February 13, 1968, September 16, 1968 and November 3, 1967).

This is a phenomenon that R. H. Turner and S. J. Surace described in 1956 in order to account for the role of media in the development of hostile consciousness toward Mexicans. The presentation of certain symbols can remove their referents from the constraints of the conventional moral order so that extralegal and extramoral action can be used against them. Political cartoonists have used the same device with less powerful results. To call Mexican-Americans "zootsuiters" in Los Angeles, in 1943, was to free hostility from the limits of the conventional, though fragile, antiracism required by liberal ideology. The result was a wave of brutal anti-Mexican assaults. Turner and Surace hypothesized that:

> To the degree, then, to which any symbol evokes only one consistent set of connotations throughout the community, only one general course of action with respect to that object will be indicated, and the union of diverse members of the community into an acting crowd will be facilitated . . . or it will be an audience prepared to accept novel forms of official action.

First the symbol, then the accumulation of hostile connotations, and finally the action-issue: Such a sequence appears in the news coverage of Hippies from the beginning of 1967 to the present. The amount of coverage has decreased in the past year, but this seems less a result of sympathy or sophistication and more one of certainty: The issue is decided and certain truths can be taken for granted. As this public consciousness finds official representation in the formation of a control conglomerate, it heralds the final and institutional stage in the growth of repressive force, persecution and terror.

The growth of this control conglomerate, the mark of any repressive system, depends on the development of new techniques and organizations. But its momentum requires an ideological head of steam. In the case of the Hippie life the ideological condemnation is based on several counts: that it is dangerous and irresponsible, subversive to authority, immoral, and psychopathological.

Commenting on the relationship between beliefs and the development of the persecutory institutions for witch-control in the sixteenth century, Trevor-Roper, in an essay on "Witches and Witchcraft," states:

> In a climate of fear, it is easy to see how this process could happen: how individual deviations could be associated with a central pattern. We have seen it happen in our own time. The "McCarthyite"

experience of the United States in the 1950's was exactly comparable: Social fear, the fear of an incompatible system of society, was
given intellectual form as a heretical ideology and suspect individuals
were persecuted by reference to that heresy.

The same fear finds its ideological expression against the Hippies in
the statement of Dr. Stanley F. Yolles, director of the National In-
stitute of Mental Health, that "alienation," which he called a major
underlying cause of drug abuse, "was wider, deeper and more diffuse now than it has been in any other period in American history."
The rejection of dissent in the name of mental health rather than
moral values or social or political interest is a modern characteristic.
Dr. Yolles suggested that if urgent attention is not given the problem:

> there are serious dangers that large proportions of current and future
> generations will reach adulthood embittered towards the larger soci-
> ety, unequipped to take on parental, vocational and other citizen
> roles, and involved in some form of socially deviant behavior. . . .

Dr. Seymour L. Halleck, director of student psychiatry at the University of Wisconsin, also tied the heresy to various sources of sin:
affluence, lack of contact with adults, and an excess of freedom. Dr.
Henry Brill, director of Pilgrim State Hospital on Long Island and
a consultant on drug use to federal and state agencies, is quoted in
The New York Times, September 26, 1967:

> It is my opinion that the unrestricted use of marijuana type sub-
> stances produces a significant amount of vagabondage, dependency,
> and psychiatric disability.

Drs. Yolles, Halleck, and Brill are probably fairly representative
of psychiatric opinion. Psychiatry has long defined normality and
health in terms of each other in a "scientific" avoidance of serious
value questions. Psychiatrists agree in principle on several related
points which could constitute a medical rational foundation for the
persecution of Hippies: They define the normal and healthy individual as patient and instrumental. He plans for the long range and
pursues his goals temperately and economically. He is an individual
with a need for privacy and his contacts are moderate and respectful.
He is stable in style and identity, reasonably competitive and opti-

mistic. Finally, he accepts reality and participates in the social forms which constitutes the givens of his life. Drug use, sexual pleasure, a repudiation of clear long-range goals, the insistence on intimacy and self-affirmation, distrust of official authority and radical dissent are all part of the abnormality that colors the Hippies "alienated" or "disturbed" or "neurotic."

This ideology characterizes the heresy in technical terms. Mental illness is a scientific and medical problem, and isolation and treatment are recommended. Youth, alienation and drug use are the discrediting characteristics of those who are unqualified for due process, discussion or conflict. The genius of the ideology has been to separate the phenomenon under review from consideration of law and value. In this way the mutual hostilities that ordinarily divide the various agencies of control are bypassed and the issue endowed with ethical and political neutrality. Haurek and Clark, in their "Variants of Integration of Social Control Agencies," described two opposing orientations among social control agencies, the authoritarian-punitive (the police, the courts) and the humanitarian-welfare (private agencies, social workers), with the latter holding the former in low esteem. The Hippies have brought them together.

The designation of the Hippie impulse as heresy on the grounds of psychopathology not only bypasses traditional enmity among various agencies of social control, but its corollaries activate each agency. It is the eventual coordination of their efforts that constitutes the control conglomerate. We will briefly discuss several of these corollaries before examining the impact of the conglomerate. Youth, danger, and disobedience are the major themes.

Dominating the study of adolescence is a general theory which holds that the adolescent is a psychosexual type. Due to an awakening of the instincts after a time of relative quiescence, he is readily overwhelmed by them. Consequently, his behavior may be viewed as the working out of intense intrapsychic conflict—it is symptomatic or expressive rather than rational and realistic. He is idealistic, easily influenced, and magical. The idealism is the expression of a threatened superego; the susceptibility to influence is an attempt to find support for an identity in danger of diffusion; the magic, reflected in adolescent romance and its rituals, is an attempt to get a grip on a reality that shifts and turns too much for comfort. By virtue of his entrance into the youth culture, he joins in the collective expression of emotional immaturity. At heart, he is the youth of Golding's *Lord of the Flies,* a fledgling adult living out a transitional status. His idealism may be sentimentally touching, but in truth he is morally irresponsible and dangerous.

Youth

As the idealism of the young is processed through the youth culture, it becomes radical ideology, and even radical practice. The attempts by parents and educators to break the youth culture by rejecting its symbols and limiting the opportunities for its expression (ranging from dress regulations in school to the censorship of youth music on the air) are justified as a response to the dangerous political implications of the ideology of developed and ingrown immaturity. That these same parents and educators find their efforts to conventionalize the youth culture (through moderate imitations of youthful dress and attempts to "get together with the kids") rejected encourages them further to see the young as hostile, unreasonable and intransigent. The danger of extremism (the New Left and the Hippies) animates their criticism, and all intrusions on the normal are read as pointing in that direction. The ensuing conflict between the wise and the unreasonable is called (largely by the wise) the "generation gap."

From this it follows that radicalism is the peculiar propensity of the young and, as Christopher Jencks and David Riesman have pointed out in *The Academic Revolution,* of those who identify with the young. At its best it is not considered serious; at its worst it is the "counter-culture." The myth of the generation gap, a myth that is all the more strongly held as we find less and less evidence for it, reinforces this view by holding that radicalism ends, or should end, when the gap is bridged—when the young grow older and wiser. While this lays the groundwork for tolerance or more likely, forbearance, it is a tolerance limited to youthful radicalism. It also lays the groundwork for a more thorough rejection of the radicalism of the not-so-young and the "extreme."

Thus, the theory of youth classifies radicalism as immature and, when cultivated, dangerous or pathological. Alienation is the explanation used to account for the extension of youthful idealism and paranoia into the realm of the politically and culturally adult. Its wrongness is temporary and trivial. If it persists, it becomes a structural defect requiring capture and treatment rather than due process and argument.

Danger

Once a life-style and its practices are declared illegal, its proponents are by definition criminal and subversive. On the one hand, the very dangers presupposed by the legal proscriptions immediately become clear and present. The illegal life-style becomes the living demonstration of its alleged dangers. The ragged vagabondage of the Hippie is proof that drugs and promiscuity are alienating, and the attempts to sleep in parks, gather and roam are the new "violence" of which we have been reading. Crime certainly is crime, and the Hippies commit crime by their very existence. The dangers are: (1) crime and the temptation to commit crime; (2) alienation and the temptation to drop out. The behaviors that, if unchecked, become imbedded in the personality of the susceptible are, among others, drug use (in particular marijuana), apparel deviance, dropping out (usually of school), sexual promiscuity, communal living, nudity, hair deviance, draft resistance, demonstrating against the feudal oligarchies in cities and colleges, gathering, roaming, doing strange art and being psychedelic. Many of these are defused by campaigns of definition; they become topical and in fashion. To wear bell-bottom pants, long side-burns, flowers on your car and beads, is, if done with taste and among the right people, stylish and eccentric rather than another step toward the brink or a way of lending aid and comfort to the enemy. The disintegration of a form by co-opting only its parts is a familiar phenomenon. It is tearing an argument apart by confronting each proposition as if it had no context, treating a message like an intellectual game.

Drugs, communalism, gathering, roaming, resisting and demonstrating, and certain styles of hair have not been defused. In fact, the drug scene is the site of the greatest concentration of justificatory energy and the banner under which the agencies of the control conglomerate unite. That their use is so widespread through the straight society indicates the role of drugs as temptation. That drugs have been pinned so clearly (despite the fact that many Hippies are non-users) and so gladly to the Hippies, engages the institutions of persecution in the task of destroying the Hippie thing.

The antimarijuana lobby has postulated a complex of violence, mental illness, genetic damage, apathy and alienation, all arising out of the ashes of smoked pot. The hypothesis justifies a set of laws and practices of great harshness and discrimination, and the President recently recommended that they be made even more so. The number of arrests for use, possession or sale of marijuana has soared in recent years: Between 1964 and 1966 yearly arrests doubled, from 7,000 to 15,000. The United States Narcotics Commissioner attributed the problem to "certain groups" which give marijuana to young people, and to "false information" about the danger of the drug.

Drug raids ordinarily net "hippie-type" youths although lately news reports refer to "youths from good homes." The use of spies on campuses, one of the bases for the original protest demonstrations at Nanterre prior to the May revolution, has become common, with all its socially destructive implications. Extensive spy operations were behind many of the police raids of college campuses during 1967, 1968, and 1969. Among those hit were Long Island University's Southampton College (twice), State University College at Oswego, New York, the Hun School of Princeton, Bard College, Syracuse University, Stony Brook College, and Franconia College in New Hampshire; the list could go on.

It is the "certain groups" that the Commissioner spoke of who bear the brunt of the condemnation and the harshest penalties. The laws themselves are peculiar enough, having been strengthened largely since the Hippies became visible, but they are enforced with obvious discrimination. Teenagers arrested in a "good residential section" of Naugatuck, Connecticut, were treated gently by the circuit court judge:

I suspect that many of these youngsters should not have been arrested. . . . I'm not going to have these youngsters bouncing around with these charges hanging over them.

They were later released and the charges dismissed. In contrast, after a "mass arrest" in which 15 of the 25 arrested were charged with being in a place where they knew that others were smoking marijuana, Washington's Judge Halleck underscored his determination "to show these long-haired ne'er-do-wells" that society will not tolerate their conduct" (*Washington Post*, May 21, 1967).

The incidents of arrest and the exuberance with which the laws are discriminately enforced are justified, although not explained, by the magnifying judgment of "danger." At a meeting of agents from 74 police departments in Connecticut and New York, Westchester County Sheriff John E. Hoy, "in a dramatic stage whisper," said, "It is a frightening situation, my friends . . . marijuana is creeping up on us."

One assistant district attorney stated that "the problem is staggering." A county executive agreed that "the use of marijuana is vicious," while a school superintendent argued that "marijuana is a plague-like disease, slowly but surely strangling our young people." Harvard freshmen were warned against the "social influences" that surround drugs and one chief of police attributed drug use and social deviance to permissiveness in a slogan which has since become more common (*St. Louis Post-Dispatch*, August 22, 1968).

Bennett Berger has pointed out that the issue of danger is an ideological ploy (*Denver Post*, April 19, 1968): "The real issue of marijuana is ethical and political, touching the 'core of cultural values.'" *The New York Times* of January 11, 1968, reports: "Students and high school and college officials agree that 'drug use has increased sharply since the intensive coverage given to drugs and the Hippies last summer by the mass media.'" It is also supported by other attempts to tie drugs to heresy: *The New York Times* of November 17, 1968, notes a Veterans Administration course for doctors on the Hippies which ties Hippies, drugs, and alienation together and suggests that the search for potential victims might begin in the seventh or eighth grades.

The dynamic relationship between ideology, organization and practice is revealed both in President Johnson's "Message on Crime to Insure Public Safety" (delivered to Congress on February 7, 1968) and in the gradual internationalizing of the persecution. The President recommended "strong new laws," an increase in the number of enforcement agents, and the centralization of federal enforcement machinery. At the same time, the United Nations Economic and Social Council considered a resolution asking that governments "deal effectively with publicity which advocates legalization or tolerance of the nonmedical use of cannabis as a harmless drug." The resolution was consistent with President Johnson's plan to have the Federal Government of the United States "maintain worldwide operations . . . to suppress the trade in illicit narcotics and marijuana." The reasons for the international campaign were clarified by a World Health Organization panel's affirmation of its intent to prevent the use or sale of marijuana because it is "a drug of dependence, producing health and social problems." At the same time that scientific researchers at Harvard and Boston University were exonerating the substance, the penalties increased and the efforts to proscribe it reached international proportions. A number of countries, including Laos and Thailand, have barred Hippies, and Mexico has made it difficult for those with long hair and serious eyes to cross its border.

Disobedience

The assumption that society is held together by formal law and authority implies in principle that the habit of obedience must be reinforced. The details of the Hippie culture are, in relation to the grounded culture, disobedient. From that perspective, too, their values and ideology are also explicitly disobedient. The disobedience goes far beyond the forms of social organization and personal presentation to the conventional systems of healing, dietary practice, and environmental use. There is virtually no system of authority that is not thrown into question. Methodologically, the situationalism of pornography, guerrilla theater, and place conversion is not only profoundly subversive in itself; it turns the grounded culture around. By coating conventional behavioral norms with ridicule and obscenity, by tying radically different meanings to old routines, it challenges our sentiments. By raising the level of our self-consciousness it allows us to become moral in the areas we had allowed to degenerate into habit (apathy or gluttony). When the rock group, the Fugs, sings and dances "Group Grope" or any of their other songs devoted brutally to "love" and "taste," they pin our tender routines to a humiliating obscenity. We can no longer take our behavior and our intentions for granted. The confrontation enables us to disobey or to reconsider or to choose simply by forcing into consciousness the patterns of behavior and belief of which we have become victims. The confrontation is manly because it exposes both sides in an arena of conflict.

When questions are posed in ways that permit us to disengage ourselves from their meaning to our lives, we tolerate the questions as a moderate and decent form of dissent. And we congratulate ourselves for our tolerance. But when people refuse to know their place, and what is worse, our place, and they insist on themselves openly and demand that we re-decide our own lives, we are willing to have them knocked down. Consciousness permits disobedience. As a result, systems threatened from within often begin the work of reassertion by an attack on consciousness and chosen forms of life.

Youth, danger, and disobedience define the heresy in terms that activate the host of agencies that, together, comprise the control conglomerate. Each agency, wrote Trevor-Roper, was ready: "The engine of persecution was set up before its future victims were legally subject to it." The conglomerate has its target. But it is a potential of the social system as much as it is an actor. Trevor-Roper comments further that:

> . . . once we see the persecution of heresy as social intolerance, the intellectual difference between one heresy and another becomes less significant.

And the difference, one might add, between one persecution and another becomes less significant. Someone it does not matter who tells Mr. Blue (in Tom Paxton's song): "What will it take to whip you into line?"

How have I ended here? The article is an analysis of the institutionalization of persecution and the relationship between the control conglomerate which is the advanced form of official persecution and the Hippies as an alternative culture, the target of control. But an analysis must work within a vision if it is to move beyond analysis into action. The tragedy of America may be that it completed the technology of control before it developed compassion and tolerance. It never learned to tolerate history, and now it is finally capable of ending history by ending the change that political sociologists and undergroups understand. The struggle has always gone on in the mind. Only now, for this society, is it going on in the open among people. Only now is it beginning to shape lives rather than simply shaping individuals. Whether it is too late or not will be worked out in the attempts to transcend the one-dimensionality that Marcuse described. That the alternative culture is here seems difficult to doubt. Whether it becomes revolutionary fast enough to supersede an officialdom bent on its destruction may be an important part of the story of America.

As an exercise in over-estimation, this essay proposes a methodological tool for going from analysis to action in areas which are too easily absorbed by a larger picture but which are at the same time too critical to be viewed outside the context of political action.

The analysis suggests several conclusions:

• Control usually transcends itself both in its selection of targets and in its organization.

• At some point in its development, control is readily institutionalized and finally institutional. The control conglomerate represents a new stage in social organization and is an authentic change-inducing force for social systems.

• The hallmark of an advanced system of control (and the key to its beginning) is an ideology that unites otherwise highly differing agencies.

• Persecution and terror go in our society. The Hippies, as a genuine heresy, have engaged official opposition to a growing cultural-social-political tendency. The organization of control has both eliminated countervailing official forces and begun to place all deviance in the category of heresy. This pattern may soon become endemic to the society.

Adolescents as a Minority Group in an Era of Social Change

Eugene B. Brody

Minority Groups and Prejudice

How may a minority group be defined for purposes of social and psychiatric research? A minority ". . . is a set of people who, capable of being distinguished on the basis of some physical or cultural characteristic, are treated collectively as inferior."[1] A member of a minority group is, thus, socially visible, that is, his appearance or behavior permits an observer to categorize him from a distance. He is, furthermore, to the degree that he is perceived as representative of a category, deprived of his status as an individual: The attitude of the onlooker toward the minority group man is apt to be determined less by the latter's personal characteristics than by the former's stereotyped feelings and beliefs about the social category into which he can be placed. In other words, minority group status carries with it the probability of becoming a target for the prejudices of the majority.

What is a prejudice? Allport has described it as ". . . an antipathy based upon a faulty and inflexible generalization. It may be felt or expressed. It may be directed toward a group as a whole or toward an individual because he is a member of a group. . . . The net effect of prejudice . . . is to place the object . . . at some disadvantage not merited by his own conduct."[2]

A prejudice held by majority group members usually influences the behavior of its targets; individual behavior is in part a function of the attitudes and expectations of others, or, as Mead has put it, of the "generalized other."[3] If others expect a person to behave in

Source: *Minority Group Adolescents in the United States,* Eugene B. Brody, ed., pp. 1–16, copyright © 1968, The Williams and Wilkins Company, Baltimore, Maryland.

a hostile or irresponsible or contemptible manner, they tend to evoke this kind of behavior through the cues, verbal and nonverbal, emotional and symbolic, which they transmit to him. This impact of expectations, which may not be fully conscious to the transmitter, has been described as the "self-fulfilling prophecy."[4] The stereotyped attitudes and feelings of the prejudiced onlooker become part of the climate of expectations in which the minority group member responds.

Minority status usually includes a history of more recent arrival on the scene (that is, a shorter period of territorial dominance) than the majority. In some instances, for example, the American Indian, prior territoriality has no prestigeful significance. The superior force of arms or the more complex and effective culture of a conqueror are important, and in the evolution of a culture high prestige goes to the man of the dominant society whose ancestors arrived first. In other instances, for example, the Negro in America, the time of arrival is less significant than status upon arrival. An arrival in the status of slave or chattel carries with it the added factor of obliteration of one's cultural history as it had existed before the onset of slavery. The slave is not an adequate culture bearer. Thus, a society emerging from a group of freed slaves is peculiarly vulnerable to the incorporation of fragmented or distorted aspects of the dominant society which surrounds it. Such a society also exemplifies the reality factors which tend to perpetuate minority status: relative distance from sources of community power, incomplete access to social, educational, and economic opportunities, incomplete participation in the dominant culture, and certain other types of restricted behavior including segregation imposed by the larger society.

These features of the minority combined with low socio-economic status contribute to the maintenance of a significant social distance between members of the minority and of the majority. Without sustained emotionally reciprocal relationships, they have only partial and sometimes distorted information about each other. Such a relative information deficit reinforces the tendency on the part of one group to think in stereotyped terms about the other.[5] The minority, which tends to use the majority as an emulative reference group, may, because of its limited knowledge of majority standards and values, adopt such partial or misunderstood variants of these that their behavior when dealing with emulative reference (majority) group members will be a caricature of what the latter regard as desirable.[6] In this way the prejudiced feelings, attitudes, or beliefs of the majority are reinforced.

The Adolescent as a Minority Group Member

How does the adolescent fit into this scheme? His primary identifying characteristics are those of age. The body and face of pubescence, arbitrarily defined as between ages 13 and 18, are easily recognized. He is also a recent arrival on the territory dominated by his elders. He is relatively powerless from the social and economic standpoint. By virtue of age he is excluded from places in which alcohol is served; he is not franchised; he cannot marry without the consent of his parents; he is, after all, legally defined as a "minor."

These features are present in pre-adolescent children as well. Why are they not, then, similar targets for the restrictive practices of their elders? In fact, they are. Young children are much more restricted in their range of activities than their adolescent older siblings. They do not, however, have the will, the strength, or the social capacity to challenge these restrictions. Their continuing dependency needs reinforce their tendency to maintain in an unchanged fashion a security-receiving relationship with a more powerful, sheltering, nurturing figure. The child's physical and psychological weakness, his lack of mastery of the techniques for independent survival, his absolute need for close contact with a source of security—all contribute to the maintenance of a single social world inhabited both by him and by his parents.

In contrast to the child who requires preservation of a social status quo the adolescent is upwardly mobile. He is moving from the role of conforming, dependent child to that of independent, initiating, coping adult. He and his parents are no longer comfortable sharers of the same social world. In a certain sense he may be compared with the "marginal man" who has one foot in the majority world and one in his own but does not feel completely accepted by or comfortable in either. As Kurt Lewin has put it, the marginal

man by virtue of his transitory condition and ambiguous status suffers from "uncertainty of belongingness."[7]

This lack of certainty about belonging, and the precarious self-
esteem associated with it, appear to account in part for the adolescent's strong need to find others of his own kind. This is a narcissistic object choice to the degree that the people in whom he is
interested mirror his own lack of certainty and his own concern
with his changing bodily, emotional, and social status. Overwhelmed
by the consciousness of his own changing state, and of his difference
from comfortably dependent younger humans as well as from more
stable older ones already fixed into their social niches, the adolescent
looks for reassurance and support to those who resemble him. Together they form a community of individuals with shared anxieties,
preoccupations, and, to some degree, feelings of alienation from the
age grades which precede and follow them. This alienation is reflected in the emergence of their own folk-heroes. It is also reflected
in the compensatory attempt (seen in a variety of minority situations) to form one's own group as a basis for social anchorage and
identity formation. This requires the loyalty to group customs and
intense conformity which is so prominent in the adolescent culture.

The threat of loneliness in the face of the mass of those who do
not understand because they are too young, or because they are too
old and have forgotten, gives rise to an intense need for communication. In the privileged classes of United States society this need is
met in part by the telephone which provides an immediate network
through which an aggregate of adolescents may be transformed into
a social system. This is a means by which, though geographically
separated, they may transmit and receive the information which tells
them that they are not alone and validates their perceptions of
reality.

In the less privileged classes this need is met in part by the formation of gangs or street-corner groups. Communication is also
facilitated by the development of distinctive signals which permit
recognition of a person not only of like age status but with similar
values. Extreme styles in hair and clothing, the faddish embrace
of vigorous dances, and familiarity with current songs are examples
of the communicative cues through which mutual recognition is

possible. In the lower socio-economic groups lack of a stable home base and dependence upon shifting loci for congregation may interfere with the formation of a true community. Under such circumstances, the place in which face to face contact is possible becomes invested with particular significance, and the home becomes proportionately devalued. The other forms of nonverbal communication and identifying displays may also assume added importance.

To the degree to which shared values reflected in shared behavior and the use of shared symbols unify the group of adolescents in the pursuit of common aims; to the degree to which these elements provide a set of guidelines for behavior in a variety of situations; to the degree to which they are socially transmitted from one generation of adolescents to another; and to the degree that they constitute a set of standards, symbols, and values acting in opposition to those of the dominant or adult culture; to that degree the group of adolescents in United States society may be said to be a collectivity with a culture, which is in some ways a contra-culture, of its own.

Adolescence viewed in this manner is not identical with puberty. It is possible, in fact, to conceive of puberty as a physiologically defined period which may be traversed under certain circumstances without the emergence of much characteristic adolescent behavior. The pubescent child, for example, who is part of a large, well-integrated, and extended family, in a society with stable institutionalized age roles and which permits little individual choice in regard to marriage or occupation, would not be expected to experience the throes of upward mobility and marginality. In such a situation he would always "belong" and there would be no threat of status ambiguity or of loneliness. Under such circumstances, one would not expect the emergence of defensive manoeuvers, reflected in a contra-culture, of a type which would elicit particular attitudes in the adult power-holding society.

Evocative Adult Behavior in a Context of Social Change

The foregoing discussion has focused upon the "uncertainty of belongingness," individually and as a group, of people in the age period between childhood and adulthood. Uncertainty of status, however, is not confined to members of this group. It is present, as well, in adults who historically have had the responsibility of assigning role-patterns and functions to less mature members of society. But in the contemporary Western world the adults, who constitute the economic basis of the social system and who manage the agencies of social control, are unsure about how to exercise their own prerogatives. Rapidly increasing population pressures, new technology, vastly improved world-wide communications, and increased social and geographical mobility have destroyed the base of consistently reinforcing experience necessary for the maintenance of value and symbol systems. The jostling of values and behavioral modes, previously nurtured under conditions of relative cultural isolation, has fostered a condition of relative ambiguity and a diminished sense of group-distinctiveness; it has also made it increasingly difficult for individuals to arrive at consensual validation of their beliefs about what is really worthwhile. Societies in the process of accelerating change, especially ". . . if the change is not guided by a set of sharply defined master symbols that tell just what the change is about,"[8] may be, thus, assumed to be less effective than stable groups in the socialization of their young. In these latter, "Cultural prescriptions of a powerful nature define the usual sequence of statuses and roles that individuals are to assume during their life span. . . . Advances . . . occur according to certain schedules which integrate his capabilities with age-graded requirements of the society . . . ."[9] However, in complex and changing societies, geographical and social mobility, the heterogeneity of subcultures, and the rapid social changes which render inadequate much childhood learning place unpredictable role-demands upon the individual. "Discontinuities between what is expected in successive roles is greater . . . subgroups with deviant values emerge which do not prepare the child for performance of the roles expected of him by the larger society . . . ."[10]

Thus, the quality of adolescence as a socio-cultural condition is determined by the changing nature of society and mediated by shifts in adult values and acts. This is superimposed upon an inherently unstable youth-parent figure equilibrium which depends upon a system of mutually transmitted, often inconsistent, signals between pubescents and adults. The adults signal their expectations which encourage increasing independence, but at the same time, they emit contradictory messages which discourage changes in the status quo. The adolescents signal their own needs for recognition and self-esteem and, simultaneously, continue to express, although in disguised fashion, their anxieties and persisting needs for support. Even if the desired support is forthcoming, it is often perceived as unacceptable and triggers hostile or rebellious behavior directed against its source. Any locus of support in the dominant society can be regarded as potentially stifling, inhibiting the movement toward increased freedom. The inferred threat of suppressed mobility and of deprivation of the anticipated freedoms of adult status, as well as the anxiety of identity confusion, motivate a range of security operations including those manifested in cultural terms.

Adults as a group respond to the defensively motivated contra-culture with fear and anger and the development of a series of false premises and generalizations. These last are couched in terms of the lack of responsibility of the adolescent, his impulsiveness and untrustworthiness, and his laziness and disregard for moral values. In turn these attitudes have their own evocative impact on the adolescent group, which now in the position of a collective minority engages in a series of adaptive manoeuvers which, temporarily successful in dealing with the majority, may actually impede the ultimate capacity of its members to become full participants in the majority culture. Adaptation to the stress of adult pressures may result in the establishment of a time-limited reciprocal relationship in which the adolescent attempts to disprove the prejudicial hypotheses; the unstable equilibrium may be maintained by the adolescent threat to run away or to behave in a still more unacceptable manner (including an outbreak of acute mental illness viewed as a protest, a cry for help, a panic, or a temporary substitution of fantasies for unbearable reality); it may involve a pseudo-passivity, reminiscent of the "Uncle Tomism" of the conforming Negro which hid a deep reservoir of resentment; or it may be achieved through a variety of complementary behaviors which fit the prejudiced beliefs of the adult world. It may happen, then, that adults who have participated in such pseudo-mutual compromise formations are jolted by noncomplementary behavior and respond with emotional disturbance, even though the noncomplementary move is palpably in the direction of greater social usefulness and competence, for example, a social protest movement. In this instance, the disturbance of the adult may be compared to the anxiety of a majority group member when confronted with irrefutable evidence of the irrationality of his prejudices.

In the last case, it is assumed that prejudices are retained because they have certain psychological functions for the individual. Can it also be assumed that anti-adolescent prejudice has such functions? Adults embracing unmodifiable prejudices against such minority groups as Negroes or Jews, for example, have been shown to suffer from inadequate reality testing reflected in the active selection, modification, or scotomization of incoming information which threatens their prejudiced beliefs or attitudes. They also regard incompatible realities which they cannot deny as exceptions to the rule. In other words, their inadequate reality testing, because it has a prejudice-protecting function, suggests a strong psychological need for the prejudice.[11] Much early work suggests that such prejudices are necessary because they provide a readily available target for the displacement or projection of unacceptable wishes. The target, which is selected on the basis of social circumstances, may determine the quality of the prejudiced beliefs. Thus, the Negro slowly rising from the status of uncultured slave, who was permitted neither individual initiative nor a stable marital union, has been considered as lazy, dirty, and sexually amoral. The Jew, on the other hand, with a different background, has been regarded in terms of a different set of stereotypes.

The presence of prejudice is further complicated by a protective societal response which has been termed "cultural exclusion."[12] This refers to the active denial to minority group members of the right of full participation in all aspects of the dominant majority group culture. The consequence of this exclusion is in the minority man's failure to share the values and symbols of the larger society. Cultural exclusion appears to become most intense when, with increasing knowledge and rising expectations, the minority begins to press for more privileges and more participation, and it becomes both a social and an economic threat.

Is it possible that the adolescent group is an especially suitable target in a culture such as that of the contemporary United States?

Why should yet another target be necessary in the presence of the generally serviceable ones already present? Is the adolescent group used as a target only by those in search of a scapegoat? Or is there something about contemporary adolescence that evokes prejudiced behavior?

First of all, the adolescent group which is not educated beyond high school poses, yearly, a recurrent strain on a labor market increasingly glutted with nonusables because of the automation of industry and the demands for more adequate basic education even at the lowest occupational echelons. The adolescent also symbolizes the threat of youth to displace the aged in the seats of power and influence. More than the child, he symbolizes the threat of the son to overthrow the father. Certainly, with his new interest in exploring his own body and those of others and his new consciousness of physical strength and attractiveness, he becomes a suitable target for the displaced wishes and fears of those concerned with their own conflictful aggression and sexuality. And his heterogeneity as a group, his constantly shifting status as an individual, may make him an ambiguous figure vulnerable to the distorted perceptions of the problem-ridden adult. In a society in flux, then, the adolescent may be particularly useful as a figure around which emotion-laden problem-solving fantasies may be woven.

Clearly, this state of affairs is maximized in a highly developed society which contains large pockets of culturally disadvantaged people whose birthrate exceeds that of the majority and whose adolescent children, inadequately socialized, present themselves in increasing numbers at the gates of welfare agencies. It is maximized in a society in which the middle-aged and elderly have no cultural guarantees of dignity and economic security, so that they are vulnerable to the economic and narcissistic threats of those who are younger and ambitious. It is maximized in a society in which institutional behavior patterns are decreasingly significant as guides and in which, therefore, people of all ages are increasingly forced to make decisions which in the past were automatically accomplished on a cultural basis.

A number of other consequences may logically be expected to flow from this type of social order. It might be expected to produce in its adults a high degree of anxiety about status, security, and the acceptable expression of needs and wishes. Such status-centered anxiety is often dealt with by the development of security-giving systems of prejudiced feelings and beliefs. Under such circumstances there is a constant search for targets, and, for adults, the collectivity of adolescents provides a uniquely suitable target.

Socialization During Adolescence

For pre-adults, impaired role-implementation at the hands of mature members of the society could interfere with the role-cognitions which should be developing in anticipation of future statuses. It also forces greater dependence upon peers for the joint formulation of systems of values and behavioral codes. Value construction for this group does not proceed via the formulation of verbal abstractions but follows from action, success at which defines status. As adult society becomes less dependable as a source of status and values, the adolescent is under increasing pressure to act and to create a social position for himself in his group of peers. The type of action may be delinquent. More typically, however, it involves sports, dancing, and other socializing activities, and the search for a partner of the opposite sex.[13] The need for status achievement through action becomes especially important since the youth is now ". . . a member of a group which both transcends the family and in which he is not in the strongly institutionalized position of being a member of the inferior generation class. It is the first major step toward defining himself as clearly independent of the authority and help of the parental generation." In addition to forming an identification with the sub-society of his age peers, the adolescent normally does the same with three other types of collectivity:

". . . (1) the school, which is the prototype of the organization dedicated to the achievement of a specified goal through disciplined performance; (2) the peer-association, the prototype of collective organization to satisfy and adjust mutual interests; and (3) the newly emerging cross-sex dyad, the prototype of the sole adult relation in which erotic factors are allowed an overt part. . . . These identifications form the main basis in personality structure on which adult role-participations are built. Through at least one further major step of generalization of value-level, participation in the youth culture leads to participation in the values of the society as a whole. Participation in the school leads to the adult occupational role, with its responsibility for independent choice of vocation, a productive contribution, and self-support. The peer-association identification leads to roles of cooperative memberships in a variety of associations, of which the role of citizen in a democratic society is perhaps the most important. Finally the dating pattern of adolescence leads to marriage and to the assumption of parental responsibilities."[14]

This quotation from Talcott Parsons emphasizes the continuity from the objects of identification in childhood to the role and collectivity structure of the adult society. This underlying, though partial and fragmented continuity, despite the surface evidence of a separate, discontinuous youth-culture, suggests the place of minority group status in social evolution. The process of growth and upward mobility seems to require a stage of separation from the original group and a period of development of special capacities before assimilation into the new and dominant group.

The significance of social change as a factor determining the problems of adults and the message transmitted by them to adolescents was discussed earlier. In terms of the youth themselves, "ties to class and family, to local community and region become more flexible and hence often 'expendable' as more choices become available." The process by which the erotic component of sex relations, for example, ". . . has become differentiated, allowing much greater freedom in this area, is closely related to the differentiation of function and the structural isolation of the nuclear family. . . . Since much of the newer freedom is illegitimate in relation to the older standards . . . it is very difficult to draw lines between the areas of new freedom in process of being legitimated and the types which are sufficiently dysfunctional . . . so that the probability is they will be controlled or even suppressed. The adolescent in our society is faced with difficult problems of choice and evaluation in areas such as this, because an adequate codification of the norms governing many of these newly emancipated areas has not yet been developed." In complex societies ". . . the impact on youth of the general process of social differentiation makes for greater differences between their position and that of children, on the one hand, and that of adults, on the other, than is true in less differentiated societies. Compared to our own past or to most other societies, there is a more pronounced, and . . . an increasingly long segregation of the younger groups, centered above all on the system of formal education."[15]

The increasingly prolonged dependency and segregation for educational purposes required by progressive societal differentiation create conditions similar to those experienced by minority group adults expressing new goals and aspirations. Effective information transmission implants new wishes for status, autonomy, and consumer goods in individuals who possess neither the social techniques, the money, nor the power to obtain them. The impossibility of desired achievement may have varied results: hyper-ambitiousness occasionally coupled with a degree of deviousness in attaining particular sub-goals; impulsive aggressiveness; hopelessness and resignation associated with an overwhelming awareness of social and economic powerlessness, resulting in abandonment of the leading social value of achievement; self-narcotization through the use of drugs or alcohol as a means of simultaneously denying the unacceptable aspects of adult (majority) society and facilitating the emergence of substitute fantasy gratifications; the embrace of "radical" political or social beliefs associated with membership in a group of like-minded people, etc.

These alternatives present a spectrum of more or less pathological efforts at problem solving. They omit the more adaptive and less symptomatic course which involves the acceptance of adult values and goals and requires long-term effort toward their achievement with the attainment of a series of symbolic sub-goals, for example, graduation from high school or college, on the way. A universally reported characteristic of adolescents which has classically been attributed to problems stemming from newly active sexual and aggressive drives is a concern with meaningfulness, an attempt to find coherence in a disorderly universe. It seems more plausible to attribute this concern to the inevitable inability of the younger generation to utilize the standards of the older to cover all exigencies. In an era of rapid change, such concern would be expected to be intense.

Dependency and segregation are not confined to those adolescents who continue in the societally required channel of socialization through high school. They may be even more onerous for those whose capacities have been outpaced by the accelerating demands for competence and responsibility. This group of high school "drop-outs," or those, primarily of lower class, who continue as nominal students while learning little in the anonymity of huge urban schools, are subject to progressive alienation from the sources of dominant society power. For them, the pathological solutions are often the most available, especially when they offer an added increment of pleasure in a world promising little aside from the immediate and from bodily-linked gratification. Within the context of the age-segregated social group the utilization of asocial or anti-social techniques of anxiety-reduction or need-gratification tends to be mutually reinforced, and the influence of restraining parents or other agencies of social control is diminished.

A comparable set of consequences within the middle-class group may flow from parental uncertainty about standards and the use of discipline. This forces the adolescents to look to each other in order to develop their own social codes and values, that is, ideas about what is worthwhile, what is condemned, and what is rewarded. As Parsons[16] has stated, the "continual reorganization of the normative system" characteristic of an era of change results in "important elements of indeterminacy in the structure of expectations." Under these circumstances the adolescent must deal both with an outright lack of guidance where it is needed and with conflicting adult expectations which cannot simultaneously be fulfilled. The conflicting expectations generated by a society in change are added to the conflicting expectations and messages inherent in the usual parent-adolescent structure. The resultant paralysis, panic, or maladaptive solution exhibited by the vulnerable adolescent is reminiscent of the behavioral consequences of the conflicting parental messages which have been labelled as the "double-bind."[17]

One little discussed aspect of modern society permitting the development of an adolescent culture is its affluence. The minority aspects of adolescent life would not be so prominent if people in this age range were needed as part of the labor force, that is, if they were immediately integrated into the adult work system. Those pubescent youths who are in the labor force, are married, or are in the armed forces are chronologically but, in Bernard's words,[18] not ". . . culturally, teen-agers. They are neophytes in the adult culture. . . . Teen-age culture is essentially the culture of leisure class." Bernard made the point that since adolescents of the lower socio-economic classes are more apt to take jobs, enter the military services, or get married early, they disappear into the adult world, so that those who remain are disproportionately from the higher socio-economic background. It is these latter who constitute the teen-age market for clothes, cars, record players, and cosmetics. In a manner akin in some respects to that of the minority group person striving for recognition, acceptance, and personal status they engage in the cult of conspicuous consumption. Again, like the minority group person this consumption may result in appearance or behavior almost like a caricature of those with high status in the adult world. Similarly, a major preoccupation is how to be attractive in order to be popular. This, of course, is not confined to middle-class youth and Bernard's statement did not take into account the teen-age culture of the less affluent with similar wishes but without the financial means to readily gratify them. For these adolescents, hard-won wages may also be rapidly spent to acquire the current symbols of status.

The inferred underlying fantasy that one is unlovable or inferior is the same as that which appears to motivate much striving behavior and concern with the opinions of peers in adult members of certain minority groups. Feelings of unlovability or of diminished self-esteem are reinforced by contact with members of the majority. They seem, however, to be displaced onto the peer or normative reference group, and it is in relation to each other that adolescents or adult minority group members strive for popularity and status.

REFERENCES

1. Raymond W. Mack, *Race, Class and Power* (New York: American Book Co., 1963), p. 2.

2. Gordon W. Allport, *The Nature of Prejudice* (Reading, Mass.: Addison-Wesley, 1954).
3. George Herbert Mead, *Mind, Self and Society* (Chicago: University of Chicago Press, 1934).
4. Robert K. Merton, "The Self-Fulfilling Prophecy," *Antioch Review*, 8 (1948), pp. 193–210.
5. Orville G. Brim, "Socialization Through the Life Cycle," in Orville G. Brim and Stanton Wheeler, eds., *Socialization After Childhood* (New York: John Wiley, 1966), pp. 18–30.
6. Robert K. Merton, *Social Theory and Social Structure* (Glencoe, Ill.: Free Press of Glencoe, 1957).
7. Kurt Lewin, *Resolving Social Conflicts* (New York: Harper, 1948).
8. Talcott Parsons, "Youth in the Context of American Society," in *Daedalus*, 91:1 (1962), reprinted in Parsons, *Social Structure and Personality* (New York: Free Press, 1964), p. 158.
9. Brim, *op. cit.*
10. *Ibid.*
11. Eugene B. Brody, "Psychiatry and Prejudice," in S. Arieti, ed., *American Handbook of Psychiatry* (New York: Basic Books, 1966), 3, pp. 629–42.
12. Eugene B. Brody, "Cultural Exclusion, Character and Illness," *American Journal of Psychiatry*, 122 (1966), pp. 852–58.
13. R. Helanko, "Sports and Socialization," in N. J. Smelser and W. T. Smelser, eds., *Personality and Social Systems* (New York: John Wiley, 1963), pp. 238–54.
14. Talcott Parsons, "Social Structure and the Development of Personality: Freud's Contribution to the Integration of Psychology and Sociology," *Psychiatry*, 21 (1954), reprinted in Parsons, *op. cit.*, quotation from pp. 106–7.
15. Parsons, "Youth in the Context of American Society," *op. cit.*, pp. 170–72.
16. *Ibid.*, p. 171.
17. G. Bateson, D. Jackson, T. Haley and T. Weakland, "Toward a Theory of Schizophrenia," *Behavioral Science*, 1 (1956), pp. 251–64.
18. J. Bernard, "Teen-Age Culture: An Overview," *The Annals of American Academy of Political and Social Science*, 338 (1961), p. 2.

The Aged as a Quasi-Minority Group

Milton L. Barron

Employers, whether public or private, whether in Nicaragua, New York, or New Zealand, are generally not eager to hire older workers. Nowhere in the world do employers generally equate the plus-factors of age, such as experience, judgment, know-how, with the energy, adaptability, growth prospects of younger job seekers.

In seeking a job, the older person finds himself at a disadvantage vis-à-vis the younger person, whether he be in the Orient or the West, whether in a statist economy or free enterprise economy or mixed economy, whether he be in a full-employment or a labor shortage environment.

There is no evidence available that indicates that anywhere in the world employers generally are free from prejudice against the hiring of older workers. On the other hand, clear and unmistakable evidence exists that even in areas of labor shortage, employers are reluctant to hire older workers.

The intensity of the reluctance to hire older workers varies from country to country and within countries from region to region, from time to time. Variations in intensity may be cyclical, depending in part on the ups and downs of labor supply in relation to labor demand; it may be due to such mechanistic factors as societal-sponsored propaganda campaigns; it may be due to variations in the degree of industrialization, or to basic cultural conditions.

We learn of the move in Belgium to reduce the age of retirement from 65 to 60 in order to take oldsters out of the labor market, of Iran's work permits for the elderly designed to control their entry into the labor force, and of Italian labor unions' drive against older workers to aid young people seeking jobs.

Source: *The Aging American: An Introduction to Social Gerontology and Geriatrics,* copyright © 1961 by Thomas Y. Crowell Company, New York, and reprinted by permission of publisher and author. This chapter first appeared as "Minority Group Characteristics of the Aged in American Society," in *Journal of Gerontology,* 8 (October 1953), pp. 477–82.

We see, too, significant patterns of social action aiming to improve the older person's position in the labor market in some countries, such as Holland, where a joint government-union-employer educational campaign attempts to widen job opportunities for senior citizens; or England, where pension bonuses are offered for continuation at work past normal retirement age; or France, where dismissals are subject to strict governmental control; Canada, where specialized counselling and placement service is made available to older job seekers; the United States, where special counselling and placement efforts in the public employment service offices are just beginning, where a few states have attempted by law to ban discrimination against older workers, and where voluntary group action by overage job seekers has helped combat discrimination.[1]

For the most part, sociological research on problems of aging has been vigorous in gathering facts but weak in arranging facts abstractly into theoretical frameworks. In this chapter we will develop the possibility of studying and analyzing the aged in American society as an emerging quasi-minority group. We will attempt to demonstrate that both the social psychology of older people at work and retired from it and to a large extent their whole situation in urban industrial life resemble those of the ethnic groups we usually call minorities. To regard the aged thus as an emerging quasi-minority group may well enlarge our understanding of the problems of aging and the aged and hasten their resolution.[2]

A fundamental question, of course, is whether it is sociologically valid to consider the aged a quasi-minority rather than a genuine minority. Why, we may ask, should they be confined conceptually to the quasi-minority level? Are they not, like authentic minorities, stereotyped by other groups (in this case, the younger age groups), and do they not suffer from subordination, prejudice, and discrimination? Is it not true that they demonstrate such typical minority group feelings as hypersensitivity, self-hatred, and defensiveness in reacting to their distinctive trait, old age?

Some scholars[3] say emphatically that minority and majority characteristics and experiences are not confined solely to ethnic groups. They argue, for instance, that most of the essential defining aspects of majority-minority group interaction apply as readily to women in our society in their social relations with men as to intergroup relations between American Negroes and whites.[4] Therefore, they claim, it is unwarranted to think of minorities and majorities exclusively in terms of racial, religious, and nationality groups.

In criticizing this argument, however, we may say it is not enough to show that women and the aged share the traditional minorities' experiences of subordination and exclusion from equal participation in those opportunities American society theoretically extends to all its members. Unlike the traditional minorities, neither women nor the aged are socially organized as independently functioning subgroups in American society. On the contrary, they live as individuals within the very families of the alleged majorities, so that we cannot accurately say they are engaged in intergroup relations in the full sense of that term. Hence, our preference for the quasi-minority over the minority concept certainly seems justified in the case of the aged as well as in that of women.

We should make another basic distinction between the aged as a quasi-minority on the one hand, and as members of interest or pressure groups on the other. Like the membership of other minorities, quasi-minorities, and even majorities, some of the aged have organized themselves into pressure groups, the most conspicuous of which are the Townsend and McLain movements. Pressure groups are seldom identical with the larger groups from which they are derived, although as they contend for influence, directing their pressure at whatever centers of power may exist, governmental and otherwise, they seek to represent those larger groups.

Majority Attitudes and Behavior Toward the Aged

We can easily discern prejudice, stereotyping, and discriminatory behavior against the aged by the majority group of younger adults. One student of the American labor force has even asserted that older workers are the group in the labor market most vulnerable to discrimination. "Many persons," says Bancroft, "can live out their working lives untouched directly by the factors that adversely affect the employment of women, of Negroes, of the foreign-born, or other minority groups, but none can escape the effects of age—as it influences both his own employment and that of someone to whom he is closely related."[5]

1. Fears the Aged Are a Menace

We find an extreme yet useful illustration of majority fears of the threat and menace posed by the aged quasi-minority in the following statement:

> The new class war between the young and the old will manifest itself in several ways. First, there will be heavy pension taxes that may eventually absorb more than one-fourth of the income of both workers and employers. This new class war may progress so far that we will see workers and employers standing shoulder to shoulder against the hard-driven politicians who promise our senior citizens impossible pensions and encourage the older worker to exploit the younger worker, the older farmer to exploit the younger farmer, the older businessman to exploit the younger businessman, the older professional man to exploit the younger professional man. . . . Let us remember that these pension leaders will soon have the votes. Karl Marx and others have taught us that mass movements are rarely rational: they spring from broad social changes. These basic changes in the population pattern started recently and slowly; the resulting mass movement has not yet matured. Townsendism may be as important in the next fifty years as were the doctrines of Karl Marx during the last half century.
>
> May I put the proposition quite bluntly? "Cradle to the grave" is a scheme whereby those close to the grave would fasten themselves on the pay-checks of those closer to the cradle, and ride piggyback (or piggy-bank) to the grave. Has our aging population condemned us or entitled us to an age-conscious future rather than a class-conscious future? Will the increased voting power of older people be used to exploit youth to such an extent that a revolt of youth will become inevitable? Should the state constitution be amended to provide a maximum voting age?[6]

The aged have so far provoked relatively few public statements as hostile or fearful as this. Fear of the aged by younger adults is today still subdued, and the majority acts much less drastically than suggested in the quotation above. This fact is illustrated by the following statement of an oil company defending its practice of compulsory retirement and rationalizing its program of preretirement counseling:

> All of the working population over sixty-five, and to a lesser degree those who have passed the forty-five-year mark, are conscious of the idea of compulsory retirement. They are aware of the difficulty in obtaining employment and are doubly concerned about their uncertain future. If a sizable portion of this group were to band together, the weight of their combined support would be the most powerful political force the country has ever known. . . .
>
> There is another possibility inherent in this problem, however. Conservatism and age are companions. Thus it is possible that the peak of political support for radical changes in our government's economic system has been reached. Preservation of property rights and individual security are of more personal importance to the elder citizen than experimental radicalism. If industry can convince the aging industrial population that it is doing something concrete about their uncertain future, socialistic remedies might well wither for lack of support.
>
> This situation also holds the possibility of unfavorable repercussions for industry. Consider the community aspects. If a man is retired from business and goes into the community feeling that he is no longer useful to himself, to industry or to anyone else, his degeneration tends to be rapid. . . . A defeated, apathetic attitude on the part of retired individuals soon permeates the community and it is not very long before members of the community point to the company from which Jones was retired with such statements as "They certainly killed poor Jones retiring him like that." The cumulative adverse effect of such reaction is obvious.
>
> This company feels that retirement is something earned by faithful service, a form of "graduation" into a new phase of life rather than a "casting out" process. Retirement should be the opportunity for the employee to enjoy the fruits of his labors in freedom, leisure and relaxation as well as an opportunity to serve himself, his family and his community in ways not open to him during his working career.
>
> In seeking to help its employees approach retirement in this way, the company feels that individual counselling and help are basic prerequisites. . . . Thus the concept developed of a seminar or dis-

cussion-type approach, wherein a group of employees approaching retirement is offered the opportunity to gather and explore some of the problems and requirements of a successful retirement.[7]

2. *Employers' Rationalizations for Discrimination*

Many of the reasons employers give for discriminating against older workers in hiring and retirement policies involve the same process of stereotyping that is an integral part of prejudice against ethnic minorities. Pigeonholing, premature generalizations, and unwarranted economy of thought are found in the reasons given for arbitrary retirement and the reluctance to hire older workers. For example, a survey of 94 employment agencies in New York City in 1952 uncovered the unsubstantiated belief held by these agencies that the older job-seeker is "his own worst enemy," destroying his chances for employment by such alleged personality deviations as "talking too much, being hard to please, too set in his ways, and lacking poise and grooming."[8]

Before considering the reasoning of employers, we should note that the advice of insurance companies to employers underlies many of such discriminatory policies. Insurance companies warn employers that to hire men over forty-five years of age and women over forty, or to retain employees beyond sixty-five, would require the companies to request payment of higher premiums for workmen's compensation and such other forms of insurance carried by the employing firm as disability and accident insurance. Another underlying factor is the development of pension plans. If a company is committed to paying a pension at a fixed age, such as sixty-five, it will probably refrain from hiring people fifty or fifty-five years of age. If it hires these people, the company must then set aside enough money to pay them pensions comparable to those going to employees whose service in the company has extended over a greater number of years.

Aside from the arguments that younger workers need to be given a chance to advance into better jobs and that "the organization needs new blood," there are eight reasons given by employers for retiring older workers and refusing to hire them. They are as follows:

1. Older workers are less productive. But such facts as are available do not bear this out. Surveys generally show that the quantity

and quality of work by older workers are equal to or superior to those of younger employees.

2. They are frequently absent. Yet a 1956 survey by the United States Labor Department showed that older workers had an attendance record 20 per cent better than that of younger workers.

3. They are involved in more accidents. Yet the same survey by the Labor Department showed that workers forty-five years of age and over had 2.5 per cent fewer disabling injuries and 25 per cent fewer nondisabling injuries than those under forty-five.

4. They do not stay on the payroll long enough to justify hiring expenses. Yet studies show that separation rates for older workers are much lower than for younger employees.

5. It is too costly to provide them with adequate pensions. But this is an easy generalization that is rarely based on a careful scrutiny of the company pension plan to see just what the impact of hiring the worker will be. It often depends on the type of plan.

6. Older workers cause major increases in employee group insurance costs. But here again the costs all depend on the nature of the plan.

7. They do not have needed job skills. However, on the contrary, the facts show that the older worker is likely to possess more skills, training, and know-how than younger job hunters.

8. They are inflexible and unimaginative and have trouble getting along with younger workers. It is hard to imagine a generalization more susceptible to contradiction by the individual case than this one. The practical experience of many companies indicates that this factor is seriously overrated.

That discrimination based on such reasoning as we have described decreases during time of war further argues the propriety of classifying the aged as a quasi-minority. It is a widely held theory that whenever there are serious external threats to a nation's military security, internal social distinctions are reduced, and discrimination against minorities is held in some abeyance. How precisely this theory applies to the aged is still uncertain, but there is little doubt that the urgent need for industrial manpower during recent wartime emergencies caused a noticeable relaxation in the otherwise stringent restrictions against the hiring or retention not only of ethnic minorities, but of older workers and women as well.

Minority-Group Reactions of the Aged

To be properly categorized as a quasi-minority group, the aged, especially older workers, should exhibit typical minority-group reactions. These include such things as marked self-consciousness, sensitivity, and defensiveness about their social and cultural traits, accompanied by self-hatred. Williams asserts that militant forms of these reactions are most likely when the group's position is rapidly improving, or when the position is rapidly deteriorating, especially following a period of improvement.[9] Young has suggested the hypothesis that the harder minorities are pressed to earn a living, the more likely they are to be defensive about their minority qualities and traditions.[10] This hypothesis is likely to hold true only when minority persons find it impossible to "pass" and identify with the majority.

The bitterness, resentment, and self-hatred of older workers who experience discrimination in employment and reëmployment are minority group reactions. Consider, for example, the following comment of a Midwesterner:

> I am in my middle fifties and want to state that I regard myself a pretty good person and able to do a good day's work, a veteran of World War I. Some of the punishment I go through from persons twenty years up regarding my age is sickly. Such remarks as "you old S.O.B., you're all washed up" at times makes me want to do some harm. I am the oldest in my department. I help the new employees who lack experience with my knowledge of certain types of work, and after they gain the experience, they give you the brush. One thing I notice when a younger person has authority over an older person, there seldom is any consideration.

A Southerner writes:

> I am a construction man and have handled thousands of men as a general labor foreman. But what's killing off the elderly people is being told "you're too old." The government and the employer are to blame. When a man reaches the age of forty, from then on there is the same tune until sixty-five. Right here in the U.S.A., think of

the millions of men who are willing to work but cannot get work. It rings in their ears, "you're too old."

A Westerner says:

No one, except a man who has worked regularly for thirty or forty years at one kind of work and very suddenly at the age of sixty-five is thrown out of work on one-third his regular pay, can realize or understand the depressive mental effect or the worry brought by the fact that he is old and not wanted in a country he worked so hard to build. Eleven months ago at the age of sixty-six and in good health after forty-eight years of railroad work I was taken out of service. I accepted my annuity, $97.31 per month. By living conservatively the wife and I could get by on $160 per month. I have tried many times to secure work with no success. I would be glad to work. Retirement as it is today is a death sentence, by worry, depressive feeling of being useless and an insufficient annuity. I was compelled to drop my lodge dues. I may drop my insurance. I worry almost continually and sometimes feel that I'd be glad to know that I will not awaken tomorrow to a useless and idle life.

Legislation Against Discrimination

Increasingly, the reaction of American society to majority discrimination against minority groups is to enact legislation intended to punish or deter such behavior. Some states have enacted not only "fair employment practices" laws against ethnic discrimination, but also similar legislation against age discrimination, a course other states show signs of imitating. This fact supports further the propriety of viewing the problems of the aged as occurring in a modified majority-minority group framework.

Until the McGahan-Preller Act became effective in New York State July 1, 1958, there had been three main types of laws against age discrimination enacted previously. One was a ban on discrimination in hiring based on age (Rhode Island and Pennsylvania); a second was a ban on hiring and rehiring based on age (Louisiana, Colorado, and Massachusetts); a third was a ban on discrimination based on age for public employees or civil service applicants only (New York).

Massachusetts and Rhode Island limit coverage of their respective laws to ages forty-five to sixty-five, Pennsylvania to forty-five to sixty-two, Colorado to eighteen to sixty, and Louisiana and New York's laws mentioned no specific ages. Exempted from most of the laws were jobs for which age is a "bona fide occupational qualification."

The best known of all of these early laws was that of Massachusetts, passed by the legislature in 1937. The law included virtually no enforcement provisions, however, with the result that virtually no cases of discrimination were brought before the Massachusetts authorities during the first 13 years of the law's existence. In 1950, however, the state enacted into law a bill that included age in the coverage of its Fair Employment Practices Act protecting ethnic groups that had been in existence since 1946. The agency administering the laws tries to "conciliate and persuade" between the parties involved in the violation or alleged violation. If this fails, a penalty up to $300 for a violation may be exacted. The law also provides that the victim of discrimination may secure from the violator between $100 and $500 in payment for the damage of discrimination. One outgrowth of this law is that the Massachusetts Commission against Discrimination has ruled that pension plans with a compulsory retirement age of less than sixty-five are inoperative and in violation of the state law. In contrast with the early inactivity in law enforcement from 1937 through 1950, the Massachusetts Commission against Discrimination from 1953 through 1958 handled over 300 cases of age discrimination in employment. Not a single case went to the courts, being settled in the traditional pattern of "fair employment practices," namely, by conciliation and negotiation.[11]

The generally mixed experience of both success and failure in banning age discrimination by law, prior to the enactment in New York State in 1958, is best expressed by the following list of pros and cons gathered by the New York State Joint Legislative Committee on Problems of the Aging after examining the happenings in other states:

1. Pros
   a. Removes the sanction of discrimination.
   b. Forces reëxamination of unrealistic personnel policies.
   c. Enables power and prestige of the government to be used to "educate" employers.

      d. Reduces overt symbols of discrimination such as age limitations in help wanted ads and job orders.

      e. Provides an agency before which older workers may air their grievances.

      f. Permits older workers at least to gain access to personnel managers and employment office.

      g. Proclaims a state policy.

  2. Cons

      a. Does not materially affect basic conditions of the labor market, which primarily determine hiring of the forty-plus.

      b. Does not wipe out stereotypes and prejudices about older workers.

      c. Does not result in placement of more older workers in jobs.

      d. Evasion is simple, widespread, and enforcement most difficult.

      e. Does not strike at employer concern with increased costs of pensions, insurance, nor with personnel policies of promotion-from-within.

      f. Falsely raises hopes of older workers.

Undeterred by these mixed findings about age discrimination laws elsewhere, New York State amended its already existing law against ethnic discrimination, effective July 1, 1958, to prohibit employers and unions from discriminating against workers forty-five to sixty-five years of age on the basis of age, and to prohibit "help wanted" advertisements and application forms that discriminate against anyone on the basis of age, unless based on a bona fide occupational qualification.

Enforcement of New York State's law is a responsibility of the State Commission against Discrimination, an agency created in 1945 to enforce laws prohibiting discrimination in employment, public housing, and public accommodations based on race, religion, and national origin. The Commission acts on complaint. A cease and desist order by the Commission is enforceable in the courts, but the Commission attempts to effect conciliation before the proceedings reach the enforcement stage.

The rules of the Commission permit any employer or employment agency to obtain age information for *nondiscriminatory* purposes, such as the gathering of statistics, the preëmployment medical examination, eligibility for OASI disability and retirement benefits, and fringe benefits. Also, consideration may be given to age as a bona fide occupational qualification in circumstances such as the following: where age is a bona fide requisite to job performance, as for a person to model clothes for teen-agers; where age is a bona fide requisite to the provisions of a career system for particular jobs, as for jobs filled by upgrading from lower ranking positions; and where age is a bona fide requisite to an apprentice training or on-the-job training program of long duration.

Evidence of some success in achieving the purposes of the New York State law was clear within a year following its passage. For example, placement of nonagricultural workers forty-five years of age and over by the New York State Employment Service increased from 21 per cent of total placements in the first six months of 1953 to 29 per cent in the corresponding period in 1958 and 30 per cent in 1959. There has been a precipitous drop in age specifications in advertising. During the first year of the law's operation, a total of 148 complaints were filed with the New York State Commission against Discrimination; employers were named as respondents in 73 per cent of the complaints, employment agencies in 17 per cent, and labor unions in 10 per cent. Fifty-four of the 148 complaints had been closed by the end of the first year of the law's operation. Charges of discrimination were sustained in nine cases, dismissed for lack of jurisdiction in 28 cases, dismissed for lack of probable cause in 15 cases, and dropped by complainants in two cases. Clerical workers comprised 38 per cent of the complainants; professional, semiprofessional, and managerial workers, 22 per cent; skilled, semiskilled, and unskilled workers, 27 per cent; service workers, salesmen, sales clerks, 13 per cent.

That age discrimination legislation will continue to be adopted elsewhere is a safe prediction to make. Following the precedent established by such pioneering states as Massachusetts, Rhode Island, Pennsylvania, and New York, age discrimination bills were introduced in the 1959 and 1960 legislatures of Connecticut, Oregon, Maine, Kansas, Michigan, Montana, Wisconsin, California, Washington, Nevada, Texas, South Carolina, Ohio, Minnesota, and in the Congress of the United States.

Summary and Conclusion

We have seen that although the aged in urban industrial society are not an independently functioning subgroup, they do meet many other of the criteria for a minority defined in sociological theory concerning majority-minority group interaction. We have presented evidence that in the outgroup of younger adults they are sometimes looked upon as a threat to the present power structure. Prejudiced attitudes against the aged are common. Stereotyping and the reasoning behind discrimination by younger adults are similar to those applied against ethnic minorities. When employer discrimination against ethnic minorities abates in time of war, it also lessens against older workers. The aged have many of the reactions of a minority group. Lastly, legislation against discrimination has begun to be enacted on behalf of the aged, paralleling that for the protection of ethnic groups.

One may conclude, therefore, that there is considerable justification for employing the theory of the aged as a quasi-minority group in collecting and analyzing data on problems of aging in urban industrial societies.

REFERENCES

1. Albert J. Abrams, "Discrimination in Employment of Older Workers in Various Countries of the World," in *Age Is No Barrier*, New York State Joint Legislative Committee on Problems of the Aging (Legislative Document No. 35, 1952), p. 70.
2. It is possible such a theoretical point of view of the aged may even contribute new insights for the fruitful examination of the traditional minorities.
3. See, for example, E. K. Francis, "Minority Groups—a Revision of Concepts," *British Journal of Sociology*, 2 (1951), pp. 219–30.
4. Helen Mayer Hacker, "Women as a Minority Group," *Social Forces, 30* (1951), pp. 60–69; Gunnar Myrdal, *An American Dilemma* (New York: Harper, 1944), Appendix 5; Bernhard J. Stern, "The Family and Cul-

tural Change," *American Sociological Review*, 4 (1939), pp. 199–208; J. J. Williams, "Patients and Prejudice: Lay Attitudes Toward Women Physicians," *American Journal of Sociology*, 51 (1946), pp. 283–87. Hacker and Myrdal are reprinted in this volume.

5. Gertrude Bancroft, "Older Persons in the Labor Force," *The Annals of American Academy of Political and Social Science*, 279 (1952), pp. 52–61.

6. F. G. Dickinson, "Economic Aspects of the Aging of Our Population," in *Problems of America's Aging Population: A Report on the First Annual Southern Conference on Gerontology* (Gainesville, Fla.: University of Florida Press, 1951), p. 79ff.

7. *Preparation for Retirement*, a brochure published by Esso (Standard Oil Company of New Jersey, New York, 1950).

8. *New York Times*, July 31, 1952.

9. Robin M. Williams, Jr., *The Reduction of Intergroup Tensions* (New York: Social Science Research Council, 1947), Bulletin 57, p. 61.

10. Donald Young, *Research Memorandum on Minority Peoples in the Depression* (New York: Social Science Research Council, 1937), Bulletin 31.

11. K. J. Kelley, "Massachusetts Law Against Age Discrimination in Employment," in *No Time to Grow Old*, New York State Joint Legislative Committee on Problems of the Aging (Legislative Document No. 12, 1951), pp. 173–75; *Good News for Later Life*, New York State Joint Legislative Committee on Problems of the Aging (Legislative Document No. 8, 1958), pp. 23–24; Federal Security Agency, *Aging*, 3 (1953), p. 5.

Disabled and Disadvantaged   4

Although civilization has outgrown the medieval treatment of the physically disabled and the mentally ill, when the blind and the lame, the deaf and the epileptic, were despised, hated, excommunicated, sometimes killed or hidden by parents who were ashamed, and often blamed for the ills that befell the world, maltreatment of these people is hardly a thing of the past. The permanently ill, particularly those with visible ailments and handicaps, or those with mental capacities below the average, continue to be subject to social hostility based on unwarranted fears and superstitions, even when commingled with a modicum of sympathy and pity.

Again, one starts with a view from within, a poignant autobiographical statement from Kriegel, a white man who, one might say, "became a Negro," because he learned as a cripple what it meant to be experienced as an abstraction, rather than as a self, "a true self," an individual human like those who walk without crutches, or see and hear like others, or who have white skins. For Truzzi, the problem of the dwarf is one of extreme visibility; one does not see an individual, one sees a member of a group, malformed, handicapped, hence inferior. For him, some aspects of the relations between dwarfs and normal people suggest a fit with race relations. But perhaps the fewness of dwarfs would be a factor here: the individuals are visible, but the problem is not, because it is possible to go through life avoiding it, or just not meeting it.

The same is not true of physical disability as a general category, with Meyerson claiming 26,000,000 physically disabled Americans, and what with automobiles and wars, the number is not likely to diminish, despite advances in the conquest of poliomyelitis and other diseases. Meyerson sees the analogy with race as having one point of difference: there is nothing in skin color that imposes intrinsic limitations. But the problem is whether these limitations can be handled without creating frustration, damaging self-esteem, and being extended and generalized beyond their logical perimeters.

Barker continues this theme by showing that the physically disadvantaged are in a social position that is underprivileged, ambiguous, and marginal, statements that easily apply to the racially stigmatized.

Stigma extends to the mentally retarded and subnormal, and their intrinsic limitations have often been taken for granted, but Orzack demonstrates that the manner in which such persons are treated or experienced often shapes the range of learning and development. It is the self-fulfilling prophecy, which Dexter develops with his tongue-in-cheek analogy, one which might very well be the best application of this theme outside of the ethnic arena.

Of the work of Gussow and Tracy, little need be added. Stigma is almost synonymous with leprosy. It is difficult to imagine a socially-created status more damaging to self-esteem. Even the word "leper" is frightening to almost all of us; imagine the self-hate that must have been engendered in these unfortunately sick persons by their pariah status. All this seemed quite understandable, even justifiable, when it was believed that leprosy was extremely contagious, ugly, and fatal. Now, it appears that much thinking on this subject was exaggerated, but even had it not been, would this have justified the *hatred*, rather than the treatment, accorded the leper?

Finally, Jordan rejects the minority group thesis, in favor of another, the disadvantaged group. The problem is not to determine which is right and which is wrong, but which is more useful in an understanding of this category of people and their relations with all others in society.

Uncle Tom and Tiny Tim: Some Reflections on the Cripple as Negro

Leonard Kriegel

I find myself suddenly in the world and I
recognize that I have one right alone: that of
demanding human behavior from the other.

Frantz Fanon, *Black Skin, White Masks*

It was Nietzsche who reminded the nineteenth century that man
can only define himself when he recognizes his true relation both to
the *self* and to the *other*. When man accepts the umbilical cord tying
him to society, he does so with the knowledge that he must eventually
destroy it if only to re-tie it more securely. Nietzsche was not alone.
The men who wrote the Old and New Testaments, the Greek poets,
indeed, almost all the saints and apocalyptic madmen who embroider
the history of Western civilization like so many flares in our darkness
—for them, as for Freud, recognition of self is the first step toward
recognition of the other. "I attack only those things against which I
find no allies, against which I stand alone," Nietzsche wrote. If such
sentiments have the uncomfortable ring of a rhetoric that might be
better forgotten today, this is only because the particular kind of
inhumanity to which Nietzsche called attention has become so much
greater, so much more dense and impenetrable, than it was in his
time.

What Nietzsche wrote is especially applicable to the cripple and
to those men and women who inhabit, however partially, the cripple's world. It is noteworthy that, at a time when in virtually every
corner of the globe those who have been invisible to themselves
and to those they once conceived of as masters now stridently demand the right to define meaning and behavior in their own terms,
the cripple is still asked to accept definitions of what he is, and of

Source: *The American Scholar*, 38:3 (Summer 1969), pp. 412–30; copyright © 1969 by the United Chapters of Phi Beta Kappa. Reprinted by permission of the publishers and the author.

what he should be, imposed on him from outside his experience. In the United States alone, spokesmen for the Negro, the Puerto Rican, the Mexican, the Indian have embarked upon an encounter with a society that they believe has enriched itself at their expense, that has categorized them by cataloguing their needs and desires, their hopes and fears, their anguish and courage, even their cowardice. What all such encounters share is the challenge they offer to the very limited idea of humanity that the oppressor society grants its victims. And, however insufficiently, the society does respond in its ability to see its victims anew. Late-night television interviewers vie with one another in the effort to titillate their viewers with "militant" after "militant" who rhetorically massages whatever guilt resides in the collective consciousness of white America with threats to burn Whitey's cities to the ground. It is a game that threatens to erupt into an industry, and the nation eagerly watches while David Susskind battles Allen Burke for the privilege of leading nightly sessions of ritual flagellation—all of them, no doubt, designed to enrich the national psyche.

The cripple is conspicuous by his absence from such programs. And the reason for that absence is not difficult to discover. The cripple is simply not attractive enough, either in his physical presence, which is embarrassing to host and viewers, or in his rhetoric, which simply cannot afford the bombastic luxuriance characteristic of confessional militancy. If a person who has had polio, for example, were to threaten to burn cities to the ground unless the society recognized his needs, he would simply make of himself an object of laughter and ridicule. The very paraphernalia of his existence, his braces and crutches, make such a threat patently ridiculous. (Aware of his own helplessness, he cannot help but be aware, too, that whatever limited human dimensions he has been offered are themselves the product of society's largesse.) Quite simply, he can take it or leave it. (He does not even possess the sense of being actively hated or feared by society, for society is merely made somewhat uncomfortable by his presence.) It treats him as if he were an errant, rather ugly, little schoolboy. The homosexual on public display titillates, the gangster fascinates, the addict touches—all play upon a nation's voyeuristic instincts. The cripple simply embarrasses. Society can see little reason for recognizing his existence at all.

And yet, he asks, why should *he* apologize? My crutches are as visible as a black man's skin, and they form a significant element, probably the most significant element, in the way in which I measure myself against the demands of the world. And the world itself serves as witness to my sufferance. A few years ago, the mayor of New York decided to "crack down" on diplomats, doctors and cripples who possessed what he described as "special parking privileges." I single Mr. Lindsay out here because he is the very same mayor who has acted with a certain degree of sensitivity and courage when dealing with the problems of blacks in the ghettos. He soon rescinded the order preventing cripples from using their parking permits, but one notes with interest his apparent inability to conceive of what such an order would inevitably do. Cripples were instructed to drive to the police station nearest their place of work, leave their cars, and wait until a police vehicle could drive them to their destination. One simply does not have to be Freud to understand that a physical handicap carries with it certain decisive psychological ramifications, chief among them the anxiety-provoking question of whether or not one can make it—economically, socially and sexually —on one's own. Forcing a man who has great difficulty in walking to surrender his car, the source of his mobility, is comparable to calling a black man "boy" in a crowd of white onlookers. The mayor succeeded only in reminding me, and the thousands of other cripples who live in New York, that my fate was in his hands and that he controlled my destiny to an extent I did not wish to believe. He brought me once again face-to-face with what Fanon means when he writes, "Fervor is the weapon of choice of the impotent." Fanon, of course, was writing about being black in a psychologically white world, but the analogy is neither farfetched nor unusual. Uncle Tom and Tiny Tim are brothers under the skin.

About six months after I arrived in the New York State Reconstruction Home in West Haverstraw in 1944, a fellow patient, who had been in the home for more than a year, casually remarked, "They got you by the hump. No matter which way you turn, they got you."

At that time, I was not yet twelve, and I took so bland an overture with all the suspicion and self-righteousness of a Boy Scout who finds himself thrust into the center of a gang war. *I,* for one, knew that I had been born to be saved and I was concerned only with caking the shell of my determination to succeed. I simply was not going to be a *cripple.* (I wouldn't even permit myself to use the word then, not even to think it.) I was determined to do everything I had been told I must do by doctors, nurses, physical therapists, by anybody who seemed to me an authority on "my condition." However mysteriously, I was convinced that the task of restoring nerves to my dead legs lay in obediently listening to my superiors, and I accepted anyone's claim to superiority on the very simple and practical basis that he could walk. If I listened, if I obeyed without questioning, I would someday once again lead "a normal life." The phrase meant living in the way my superiors lived. I could virtually taste those words, and for years afterward I could be sent off into a redemptive beatitude if anybody told me that I was on my way toward leading "a normal life." For the cripple, the first girl kissed, the first money earned, the first restaurant entered alone—all are visible manifestations of redemption, symbolic of "a normal life."

In my ignorance, I did not understand that my fellow patient had simply unfolded what would ultimately seem a truism. He understood something that I could not have admitted to myself, even if I had been brave enough to recognize it. My life was not my own, and it would take immense effort for me ever to control it—even to the extent that anyone not crippled can control his life. Whoever *they* were, they had got me, too. And no matter which way I turned, they would decide, in their collective wisdom, how my fate was to be carved out. Nor was it me as an individual cripple alone whom they had got. I was soon to discover that, in varying degrees, they had my family also. Disease is a sharing, a gray fringe of existence where man, however protesting, remains if not at his most communal, then at his most familial. For the cripple, the message of disability is invariably personal, and he carries with the physical reminder— the eyes that do not see, the limp, the rigid fear of undergoing an epileptic seizure in some strange corner of the universe, the bitter dregs of a mind that he realizes works neither wisely nor too well—

the knowledge that he is, in some remarkably fundamental way, the creator of those who have created him. Perhaps it is not what Wordsworth had in mind, but the cripple knows that the child is father to the man—and to the woman, too—especially when that child's existence is conditioned by the peculiar nature of his handicap. There is no choice. "No matter which way you turn, they got you." The cripple, at least, has the immediacy of his own struggle to overcome. His parents have little more than their obligation to his birth.

The cripple, then, is a social fugitive, a prisoner of expectations molded by a society that he makes uncomfortable by his very presence. For this reason, the most functional analogy for the life he leads is to be found in the Negro. For the black man, now engaged in wresting an identity from a white society apparently intent on mangling its own, has become in America a synonym for that which insists on the capacity of its own being. At the risk of demanding from Black America more than it can yet give itself, let me suggest that here we have both analogy and method. No one can teach the cripple, can serve as so authoritative a model in his quest for identity, as can the black man. I say this in spite of my knowledge that Black America may simply be fed up with serving the society in any manner whatsoever. "To us," writes Fanon, "the man who adores the Negro is as 'sick' as the man who abominates him." It is not the black who must offer explanations. Far more than the cripple, he has been the victim of television interviewers, of scientific sociologists of the soul, of those seemingly innumerable bearers of "truth," those contemporary witch doctors intent on analyzing us all to death. For the cripple, the black man is a model because he is on intimate terms with a terror that does not recognize his existence and is yet distinctly personal. He is in the process of discovering what he is, and he has known for a long time what the society conceives him to be. His very survival guarantees him the role of rebel. What he has been forced to learn is how to live on the outside looking in. Until quite recently, he was not even asked how he liked it. But this has been the essential fact of the black man's existence and it is with this very same fact that the cripple must begin, for he, too, will not be asked how he likes it. He, too, must choose a self that is not the self others insist he accept. Just as Uncle Tom, in order to placate the power of white America, learned to mask his true self until he felt himself in a position of total desperation or rising hope (or some combination of the two), so the cripple has the right, one is tempted to say the responsibility, to use every technique, every subterfuge, every mask, every emotional climate—no matter how false and seemingly put on—to alter the balance in his relation to the world around him.

His first step is obvious. He must accept the fact that his existence is a source of discomfort to others. This is not to say that he is not permitted to live with comfort and security; these, in fact, are the very gifts his society is most willing to grant him. The price he is expected to pay, however, is the same price the black man has been expected to pay, at least until very recently: he must accept his "condition," which implies not that he accept his wound but that he never show more of that wound than society thinks proper. He is incapable of defining what selfhood is. His needs will be met, but not as he might wish to meet them.

I was thirteen when I returned to the city after almost two years of life in a rehabilitation home. A rather valiant attempt to rehabilitate me had been made there. I had been taught a number of interesting ways in which to mount a bus; I had been taught to walk on crutches with the least possible strain on my arms. I was a rather lazy patient who lived in the corridors of his own fantasy, but I cannot deny that a great deal of effort was expended upon me by a number of people who were truly interested in my welfare. Looking back, I can do little but acknowledge this and voice my gratitude.

Unfortunately, those people whose task it was to rehabilitate me had also made certain assumptions about me and the world I was to inhabit after I left the home. The assumption about me was simple: I should be grateful for whatever existence I could scrape together. After all, there had been a time when my life itself had been forfeit and, compared to many of my peers in the ward, I was relatively functional. About the world, the assumption was equally simple— although here, perhaps, less forgivable. Society existed. Whatever it meted out to the cripple, the cripple accepted. The way of the world was not to be challenged.

I did not know what to expect when I arrived back home in the
Bronx, although I sensed that my relationship to others was bound
to be that of an inferior to a superior. But I did not know what form
that inferiority would take. No one had bothered to teach me—no
one had even bothered to mention—the position I would occupy in
the world outside the ward. No one had told me the extent to which
I would find myself an outsider. And no one had told me about the
fear, anguish and hatred that would swirl through my soul as I was
reminded every day that I was a supplicant.

The experience that scars must be lived through before it can be
absorbed. Which is why therapy can only soothe and art can create. The reality remains the thing itself. One can go so far as to
suggest that the very existence of language creates a barrier between
the reality the cripple faces when he returns home and what has
been suggested to him about that reality. Even if those responsible
for rehabilitating me had been more forthright, more honest, it would
have made little difference. Only the situation itself could absorb
my energy and interests, not a description or an explanation of that
situation. Once again, the analogy to the black condition is appropriate: the first time the word *nigger* is hurled at a black child by a
representative of white America becomes his encounter with the
thing itself, the world as it is.

In my own case, I was rather lucky. Looking back, withdrawal
and/or paranoia seem to have been distinct possibilities, neither of
which has been my fate. Perhaps what saved me was that I found
myself too numbed to be shocked. There were two possible outs,
which, in a sense, complemented each other. The first was to fan-
tasize. Both fantasy and dreams are left to the cripple—and there is
a great deal to be said for any possession of one's own. The other
was to compete in the world of the "normals."[1] Obviously, such
competition was bound to be false, but it served to make the fantasies somewhat more real in that it fed my illusions of potency.
I recall one incident in particular, perhaps my most vivid recollection
of the strange sort of humiliation I encountered. I had been arguing—I forget about what—with a friend. Enraged at something he
said, I challenged him to fight. He agreed, but most reluctantly.
Fighting a cripple would not reflect creditably on him in the neigh-

borhood, but, true to the obligations of adolescence, he knew that not to have accepted would be a sign of weakness and sentimentality. His compromise was to insist that we wrestle on the ground. We did, and, naturally, he wound up on top of me until his mother arrived to pull him off. Although brief, the fight itself had been highly satisfying. It enabled me to forget momentarily the fact that I was a cripple. We met if not as equals then at least as combatants on the same battleground. But then I heard his mother's shrill scolding as she escorted him away, "*You* are not to fight with a cripple!" And I knew that, once again, my vulnerability had been seen by all. It had not been a fight between two adolescents. It had been, instead, a fight between a normal and a cripple. I could live with the fight. In fact, until I heard her voice, it supplied me with an illusion of potency I would have cherished. But her words were my reality.

A few months after I returned, I began going twice weekly to the Joint Disease Hospital on Madison Avenue and 124th Street. The fusion of cripple and Negro crystallized in my mind during my forays into that alien country. I like to think the Joint Disease Hospital was in Harlem by design rather than by accident. As I surveyed the dingy streets surrounding it or waited in that antiseptic lobby, I had ample opportunity to observe the life surrounding me. More than half the patients were black. And they seemed uniformly solemn, hostile, nursing a hard-core resistance to all the social workers, doctors and nurses who first-named them. While those in authority were themselves a fairly liberal mixture of black and white, the power they represented went beyond pigmentation. They were flesh-and-blood embodiments of society's virtue and charity; they were ready, willing and, to the extent they were capable, eager to cure the leper of his sores, if for no other reason than that they recognized, as we lepers ourselves recognized, that the world for which they stood as subalterns needed both the leper and his sores. What, after all, are faith, hope, and charity to a man who claims to be civilized, except insofar as they are demonstrable and serve to create individual virtue? One sometimes wonders whether the ultimate epitaph for Western civilization will not be, "I gave."

On my first visit to the Joint Disease Hospital, my mother accompanied me. A new perspective thus unfolded: the victim as victimizer. I already knew what my getting polio had done to her. But as long as I was away from home, her weekly visits did little more than embarrass me. Here, however, her presence was a very tangible confirmation of my guilt. On the long ride from the northeast Bronx to Harlem, she had been extremely nervous. When we arrived at the hospital's outpatient clinic, she seated herself—before the social worker assigned to interview her—with that peculiarly aggressive hesitancy so characteristic of the eastern European immigrant. She had learned that one dealt with those in power with respect, humility and firmness. After the interview, we seated ourselves as conspicuously as possible in the front row of the waiting room. All around us, people were waiting to be called into the inner sanctum, most of them staring glumly at the yellow curtains that guarded each cubicle like a mask for pain. My mother grew increasingly uncomfortable. To be the mother of a cripple, I began to understand, was to be the victim of something one simply could not understand. While I had to wrestle with my knowledge that those whose legs functioned were my superiors, she had to wrestle with her suspicion that she had somehow done something to create her fate. Neither God nor his justice are blind. One received in life what one deserved.

The hospital, the waiting in the lobby, the sullen faces around us, the forbidding presence of doctors and nurses gloved by a silence broken only by their occasional whispers to one another—all depicted a world she was henceforth to inhabit. I myself was relatively at ease. This was more or less the way things had been for two years. For my mother, it was original, a slow-motion film of what lay in wait for her, chipping into whatever sense of security she had been able to muster before we left the apartment. To her credit, she refused to panic. When my name was finally called by the receptionist, she entered the inner sanctum and answered questions with honesty and even with pride in her capacity to endure the intimate disclosure of her suffering. Then a doctor examined me, murmured something about "doing our best," and the ordeal was over. My mother glowed. It was as if she had come through some terrible ordeal, marked but not scarred.

My mother did not need Harlem as I did. She knew enough about endurance, that Faulknerian virtue so apparent in those brittle streets. She came through what was, for her, an ordeal and a humiliation, and she came through far more intact that I would come through. She possessed the endurance of her instincts. And she herself was as alien to this America as anyone walking the streets of Harlem, for the kind of endurance I am speaking about here is as much a matter of geography as it is of culture.

Only by existing does the black man remain black and the cripple remain a cripple. A singular, most unfunny lesson. But the cripple could profit from it. The condition of the Negro is imposed from outside. Obviously, this is not altogether true of the cripple. But while his physical condition is not imposed from outside, the way in which he exists in the world is. His relationship to the community is, by and large, dependent upon the special sufferance the community accords him. And whether he wishes to or not, the cripple must view himself as part of an undefined community within the larger community. But there is no sense of shared relationships or pride. Cripples do not refer to each other as "soul brothers." And regardless of how much he may desire to participate in the larger community, the cripple discovers that he has been offered a particular role that society expects him to play. He is expected to accede to that role's demands. And just as it is considered perfectly legitimate to violate a black man's privacy to bolster assumptions that the non-black world makes, so it is perfectly legitimate to question the cripple about virtually any aspect of his private life. The normal possesses the right to his voyeurism without any obligation to involve himself with its object. He wants the picture drawn for him at the very moment that he refuses to recognize that the subject of his picture is, like him, a human being. "If you prick us, do we not bleed?" asks Shylock of his persecutors. The cripple's paraphrase might well be, "If you wish to see my wound, can you deny me the right to show you my self?" But voyeurism is the normal's form of non-involvement. The experience of being the recipient of unasked-for attention is as common to cripples as it is to blacks. Each is asked to show those aspects of his "condition" that will reinforce the normal's assumption about what the cripple (or black) *feels like,* what he wants, and what he is.

I can remember my neighbors, on my return home, praying for me, inquiring about my health, quoting for my benefit the words

of Christ, St. Francis, Akiba, and F. D. R.[2] I can remember their lecturing me, advising me, escorting me. Drunks voluntarily shared their wisdom with me. Almost everyone *did* things for me—except, of course, to see me. For to have seen me would have entailed recognizing my existence as an individual *me,* that kind of personal encounter that results in a stripping away of stereotype and symbol and a willingness to accept the humanity of the other, at whatever personal cost.

One can object that this view simply distorts the problem of the cripple. It is not the black man and the cripple alone who suffer from invisibility in America. The proliferation of books on alienation and anxiety, the increasing sense of disaffiliation from which our younger people suffer, the seemingly endless number of fads, pseudo-religions, life sciences, and spiritual hobbyhorses that clutter the landscape of life in these United States all testify to this. Ultimately, such an objection contains great validity. But one must first see it within the particular situation in which the cripple exists: The possibilities affording relief to others are not usually open to the cripple. There is no way, of course, to define degrees of alienation and invisibility with any sense of accuracy. But one can suggest that if most persons are only half-visible, then the cripple, like the black man until recently, is wholly invisible. Stereotypes persist long after reality fades away; for us, Uncle Tom still prays on bent knees while Tiny Tim hobbles through the world on huge gushes of sentiment and love. But let us see the world as it is, for the world itself has perfected the ability to see what it wishes to see and only what it wishes to see. Those stolid burghers who lived only a few miles from the death camps in Germany possessed a vague idea of what was taking place within those camps, but they never permitted the vagueness to make itself concrete, to push itself forward onto the individual consciousness.

The community, then, makes certain assumptions about the cripple. Whether verifiable or not, it behaves on the basis of those assumptions. The cripple is judged (as are the members of his family in terms of their relation to him), but the judgments are rendered by those for whom neither the cripple nor his family possess any meaningful reality. His "condition" is an abstraction; he himself is not quite real. Who is going to recognize *me?* asks the cripple. But society has already called into question the very existence of that *me* for it refuses to look at that which makes it uncomfortable. And so it leaves the cripple, doubting his potency, not quite ready to face his primary obligation—to extend understanding to himself, to accept the fact that his problems exist now, here, in this world, that they are problems for which relief must be sought, and that his "condition" is arbitrary but not absolute. Choices, as well as obligations, exist within the boundaries of his possibilities.

To strike out on his own in the face of a society whose smugness seems, at times, conspiratorial is difficult. As an attitude, smugness goes beyond indifference. And it is far more harmful. Smugness is the asset of the untouched, the virtue of the oblivious, and the badge of the unthreatened. It is the denial of the existence of that which threatens one's comfort, the right to judge whatever and whenever the smug believe judgment is called for. Smugness is the constant reminder of the line that exists between those who have not been touched by the world's terror and those who have. Smugness is a denial of the motion of the universe, an assumption that time stands still and that mortality itself can be conquered. The cripple knows better; for him, it is time and motion together that form the dialectic of rage.

What the cripple must face is being pigeonholed by the smug. Once his behavior is assumed from the fact that he is a cripple, it doesn't matter whether he is viewed as holy or damned. Either assumption is made at the expense of his individuality, his ability to say "I." He is expected to behave in such-and-such a way; he is expected to react in the following manner to the following stimulus. And since that which expects such behavior is that which provides the stimulus, his behavior is all too often Pavlovian. He reacts as he is expected to react because he does not really accept the idea that he can react in any other way. Once he accepts, however unconsciously, the images of self that his society presents him, then the guidelines for his behavior are clear-cut and consistent.

This is the black man's conflict, too. And it is exactly here that black militancy has confronted the enmity of white society. White America is probably willing to absorb the black American; what it

may not be willing to do is to permit the black American to absorb himself. Negro anxiety, rage and anger are seen only as threats to the primacy of white America when they probably should be seen as the black man's effort to rid himself of all sorts of imposed definitions of his proper social "role." The black view must be total. Given the experience of having been born black in a white world, it is difficult for the black man to think about his life in terms other than color or race. The totality of his experience gives him no edge. And what he witnesses is forced into the mold of what he has known. I once received an essay from a black student describing Canova's *Perseus Holding the Head of Medusa* in the Metropolitan Museum of Art as a depiction of "the contemporary black crisis." When I questioned what she had seen, I discovered that most of the other black students in the class believed that one had the right, perhaps even the obligation, to see that statue and everything else in terms of "the black crisis."

If one calls this confusion, it is a confusion that the cripple shares. For one thing, the cripple is not sure of just who is and who isn't his enemy; for another, he must distrust the mask of language just as the black man does; for a third, he cannot help but see the world itself as the source of his humiliation. He is "different" at the very moment he desires to be created in another's image. And he must feel shame at the expression of such a desire. If anything, his situation is even more difficult than the black's, at least as far as his ability to find relief is concerned. If the black man's masculinity is mangled, he can still assert it in certain ways. Black actors assuage his hunger for a heroic identity; black athletes help him forget, however temporarily, the mutilation of his being; and a worldwide renascent political movement, convinced that it represents the wave of the future, teaches him that his blackness—the very aspect of his existence that he has been taught to despise—is "beautiful" and is to become the foundation of the new life he will create for himself.

Whether this assessment of his situation is accurate is of no immediate concern, for what we are interested in is its validity as an analogy for the life of the cripple. Black Americans now believe that they possess choices and that they need not live as victims. They

are now engaged in the struggle to force society to accept, or at the least to accommodate itself, to the black conception of how blacks are to live. The cripple's situation is more difficult. If it exists at all, his sense of community with his fellow sufferers is based upon shame rather than pride. Nor is there any political or social movement that will supply him with a sense of solidarity. If anything, it is probably more difficult for the cripple to relate to "his own" than to the normals. Louis Battye, an English novelist born with muscular dystrophy, has graphically expressed how the cripple sees himself not merely as the symbol of what society thinks he is but of what he actually is.

> Somewhere deep inside us is the almost unbearable knowledge that the way the able-bodied world regards us is as much as we have the right to expect. We are not full members of that world, and the vast majority of us can never hope to be. If we think otherwise we are deluding ourselves. Like children and the insane, we inhabit a special sub-world, a world with its own unique set of referents.

Battye also speaks of the cripple's "irrelevance to the real business of living." His observations are acute and courageous. One suspects that most cripples feel this about themselves, although few have the courage to admit it. A cripple must see himself as an anachronism, for virtually everything his culture offers him is designed to reinforce his sense of inferiority, to point out to him that he is tolerated in spite of his stigma and that he had best keep his distance if he wishes society's approval. But Tiny Tim is, with whatever modern variations, still his image. He may insist that Tiny Tim is not his true self. But it frames society's picture of him. It is still the model for his behavior.

Self-hatred, then, must be the legacy he derives from his consciousness of what society thinks of him. With what else can he confront a society that values physical strength and physical beauty? (Regardless of how bizarre that sense of beauty may sometimes seem, it remains outside the cripple's range of possibilities.) If growing old is a threat to modern Americans, how much greater a threat is physical deformity or mental retardation?

And what are the cripple's options? Most of the options traditionally available to the "gifted" or "exceptional" Negro are not available to him, since his restrictions are almost invariably functional and rather severely limit the territory he can stake out as his own. He cannot become a movie idol; he cannot become an athlete; he cannot even become a soldier and risk his life in defense of that which has rejected him. His choices are simply far more limited than are the choices of a black man.

But what he can do is to learn one of the fundamental lessons of American Negro history, a lesson that probably accounts for the growing tension between white and black: He can create his own individual presence out of the very experience of his rejection. The black man in America is an obvious model for him, not because of any inherent Faulknerian virtue but because he has spent three hundred and fifty years learning how to deal with his tormentors. Without romanticizing him, we recognize that he has earned his status. It has made him, at one and the same time, both tougher and more paranoid than white America. And a certain amount of toughness as well, perhaps, as a certain amount of paranoia might serve to change the cripple's own conception of self. There is no formula that can force Tiny Tim to stand on his own two crutches. But the cripple can certainly make a start by refusing the invisibility thrust over him by the culture. He can insist on being seen.

In the folklore of white America, Harlem has long been considered exotic as well as dangerous territory. Perhaps it is both exotic and dangerous. But from 1946 to 1951, the years during which I was an outpatient at the Joint Disease Hospital, it was one of the more comfortable places in New York for me. I do not mean to voice that old ploy about those who themselves suffer being more sympathetic, more receptive to the pain of others (although there is probably a certain limited truth here, too). All I mean is that in Harlem I first became conscious of how I could outmanipulate that in society which was trying to categorize me. It is probably a slum child's earliest lesson, one that he learns even before he sets foot in a school, for it is a lesson that carries with it the structure of his survival. Normals begin to appear not as particularly charitable human beings but rather as individuals able to band together for purposes of mutual self-interest. They possess their environment, and the environment itself (which for the black child and for the cripple is part of the enemy's world) is for them a visible symbol of their success.

The normals are a tangible presence in Harlem, or at least they were during my tenure as an outpatient at the Joint Disease Hospital. The normals are *they*, the people in authority—police for the black child, nurses, doctors and social workers for me. It was in this confrontation with the normals that I first noticed what is now called the Negro's "marginality" to the kind of existence the rest of America is supposed to lead. On the short strolls I took on my crutches through the streets surrounding the hospital, the single fact I constantly confronted was the way in which the non-Harlem world imposed its presence on the community. Individuals walking the streets simply froze in its presence. One was always aware of a potential breaking out, an explosion of amassed raw frustration and distorted energy. I can remember stiffening with tension when a patrol car cruised past. Now it must be remembered that I was white, that I was an adolescent, that I moved with great difficulty on braces and crutches, and that I was probably the last person in Harlem who had anything to fear from the police. But none of this changed the fact that in Harlem a patrol car was simply the most decisive presence of the normals one could conceive of—and whether it was because I felt comfortable in those streets or because the air smelled differently or because the tension that seemed to surround me was part of the very manner, the very life, of the community, I remember stiffening with fear and guilt and anxiety. Had I been a black adolescent with legs that functioned, I probably would have run, assuming my guilt as a corollary of my birth. Just as such a boy was a victim, so I knew that I was already a victim: The truth was that I was already on short-term loan to the needs of the outside world. I could exist as an individual only insofar as I could satisfy those needs. At least, this is what I had absorbed. For anything else, I would have to struggle. And at that time (I was not yet sixteen), I was not only not smart enough to resist but I still had fantasies of leaving the world of the cripple. That, too, was part of the legacy.

To choose hope rather than despair is natural enough. But it had been five years since the embrace of my virus and I still could not bring myself to admit that my condition was permanent.

The cripple's struggle to call himself *I,* which is, I take it, what we mean by a struggle for identity, is always with him. He can be challenged in his illusions of sufficiency by the most haphazard event. I used to drop into a drugstore across the street from the Joint Disease Hospital while I waited for the car that was to take me back to the Bronx. It was the kind of drugstore one still saw before 1960. Despite its overstuffed dinginess, perhaps even because of it, the drugstore seemed portentously professional. Somehow, its proximity to the hospital gave it a certain dignity. The man who ran its operation was short and heavy, courteous and solicitous. I remember that his hair was thinning and that he smoked cigarettes in a manner that made smoking itself seem an act of defiance. He would occasionally join me as I sat at the counter drinking coffee and, more often than not, he would inform me of what *the Negro* wanted. I have an image of him, smoke blowing through flared nostrils, staring at the door as he spoke. At such times, he seemed oblivious to the presence of black customers and the black counterman alike. "They want to be accepted. They would like the white man to give them a chance to show what they can do." I had heard the words for years and I could even nod in rhythmical agreement. And then one day he added, in a voice as casual and well-intentioned as when he told me what *they* wanted, "Why don't you plan to get yourself a nice store? Like a greeting card store. Or something like that. Where you don't have to work so hard but you could still earn your own living. That's what you should do."

And so I learned that I existed for him as an abstraction, that he saw through me as if I, too, were smoke he was blowing through his nostrils. *The cripple* had been linked to *the Negro.* A new *they* had been born. As a man of the world, who did not need to move beyond abstraction, he assumed that he had every right in the world to decide what *the cripple* or *the Negro* wanted. He knew what I "should do" because he possessed two good legs and I didn't. Not being a cripple makes one expert on *the cripple,* just as not being black makes one an expert on *the Negro.* It was another example of the normal deciding how that which dared not to be normal should live.

In his conclusion to *Black Skin, White Masks,* Fanon discovers that the final myth he must destroy is the myth of a "black world," for such a myth is ultimately dependent upon an equally inhuman "white world." "There are," Fanon insists, "in every part of the world men who search." This seems to me one of the few workable visions one can accept, despite the fact that I know that, for the cripple, even the act of surrendering himself to the ranks of those who search is enveloped by potential disaster. The cripple must recognize this and he must face it. For no matter how limited his functioning in the society of normals may be, there are certain definitive guidelines that he is offered. Once he has accepted being pigeonholed by society, he finds that he is safe as long as he is willing to live within the boundaries of his categorization. To break out of its confines calls for an act of will of which he may already be incapable. Should he choose to resist, he will probably discover that he has inflamed those who see themselves as kind and tolerant. My inability to tell that man to mind his own business was an act of spiritual acquiescence. Had I told him where to get off, I would have undoubtedly been guilty of an unpardonable sin in his eyes. But I would have moved an inch forward toward personal emancipation. Cripples, though, simply do not address normals in such a way. Tiny Tim was still my image of the cripple. And Tiny Tim had always been grateful for the attention conferred upon him by his betters—any kind of attention. My inability to defy that man was more than a reflection of my weakness: It was also the embodiment of his success, the proof of the legitimacy of his assumption. On my next visit to the Joint Disease Hospital, I dropped in once again for another cup of coffee and another quick chat.

And so the task of the cripple is to re-create a self, or rather to create a true self, one dependent upon neither fantasy nor false objectivity. To define one's own limitations is as close as one can come to meaningful independence. Not to serve is an act of courage in this world, but if it leaves one merely with the desire for defiance then it ultimately succumbs to a different form of madness. The black man who rejects "white culture" must inevitably reject his own humanity, for if all he can see in Bach or Einstein is skin color then he has become what his tormentors have made of him. The only true union remains with those "who search." For the cripple, too, there are no others. To embrace one's braces and crutches would be an act of the grotesque; but to permit one's humanity to be defined by others because of those braces and crutches is even more grotesque. Even in Dachau and Buchenwald, the human existed. It was left to the searchers to find it.

REFERENCES

1. I have taken this term from Erving Goffman's remarkably stimulating little book, *Stigma: Notes on the Management of Spoiled Identity* (Englewood Cliffs, N.J.: Prentice-Hall, 1963). I would like to acknowledge also what is an obvious debt to Norman Mailer's *The White Negro,* which, like so much of Mailer's work, forces the reader to confront himself. And I should add here that David Riesman was kind enough to read this essay and to ask me the kind of questions that I needed to be asked.
2. Roosevelt's ability to "beat" polio was for me, as well as for most of the boys in the ward with me, what Kenneth Burke speaks of as a "symbolic action." Burke, of course, is dealing with literary criticism and his categories are derived from the study of literature and are all verbal. But an icon living within the boundaries of one's memory may serve a similar function to that which Burke had in mind.

Lilliputians in Gulliver's Land: The Social Role of the Dwarf
Marcello Truzzi

Although the folklore and mythology of the dwarf[1] have been of great interest to those in the literary and artistic realms,[2] social science has shown only a minimum of interest in this very specialized social role. There have been historical surveys of a general variety,[3] some biographical studies of individual dwarfs of eminence,[4] and there

Source: *Sociology and Everyday Life,* Marcello Truzzi, ed., copyright © 1968. Reprinted by permission of Prentice-Hall, Inc., Englewood Cliffs, N.J., and the author.

is a reasonable literature dealing with medical cases;[5] but a review of the literature dealing with these persons has revealed only one investigation into this corner of humanity by a psychologist,[6] and the closest approximation to a sociological or social psychological investigation is a somewhat sensationalistic but nonetheless valuable journalistic report.[7]

Despite the paucity of work on the social psychological dimensions of dwarfism, there has been some attention given by social psychologists to the more general interpersonal relationship characterized as *stigma*,[8] and many of the special aspects of these persons' social interactions can be subsumed under the broader rubric of deviance and minority group studies.[9] It is only within such a broader analytic framework, in fact, that any scientifically fruitful results—aside from the value of systematic description—can be obtained. For although the social lives of these small people are fascinating in their departures from conventional life histories, their great value lies in the unique conditions of variable characteristics which they offer to any future theoretical scheme enjoined to explain human behavior. For example, cursory examination of the cross-cultural literature on instances of very small persons (both real and mythological) in a society dominated by persons of normal size would seem to indicate important restrictions of social roles as well as common forms of social types.[10] It is these kinds of generalizations which might be disclosed through intensive study of these groups, and even a lack of such generalizations would be an important factor in the shaping of any future theory of social relations such as that envisioned by Goffman around concepts such as stigma.[11] Let us begin, therefore, with a review of the findings about small stature as a factor in social relations.

Although studies have been conducted on relating height to psychological characteristics such as IQ, with some slight correlations being found,[12] the range of heights in these studies did not include those of dwarf dimensions, and it is doubtful that the slight generalizations made there can be extended to include these very small persons. In fact, such positive correlations as have been found between physical size and social activity and aggressiveness, and with noncriminality, and the negative relation to popularity,[13] might very well be strongly reversed in regard to persons of dwarf dimensions. And the inconsistent and weak correlations found between height and personality inventory scores might be greatly strengthened in the special cases of dwarfs, due to the narrower role restrictions with which they must cope.[14]

Before a more detailed examination of the social conditions of the dwarf can be attempted, it will be necessary to clarify some of the distinctions in *types of dwarfs*. The general term *dwarf* is used in this paper to refer to persons under four feet six inches in height. This definition is not a medical one[15] but refers to the social labeling which occurs among dwarfs themselves and among persons having professional dealings with them in their role as dwarf.[16] The term dwarf is used, therefore, to include *all* persons under this height whether normally proportioned or not. The term is also used here in its usual social meaning to exclude hereditary or racial forms of dwarfism such as the African pigmy. It seems likely that some structural similarities can be found between dwarf-normal and pigmy-normal interaction patterns; but the special problems in the socialization of the dwarf by normal-sized parents are important variable characteristics which sharply differentiate the life cycle of the dwarf from the pigmy. Thus, the dwarf's own initial primary group (his family) is already part of the normal-sized world into which he must emerge as an adult.

Although there are many medical typologies of dwarfs, our concern will not be with many of these subtle distinctions. Instead, our concern here will be only with the usually perceived categories of dwarfism—that is, the socially distinguished categories. Although the biological differences present might have importance for fully understanding the behavioral components of the dwarf's world, the definition of the situation perceived by normals interacting with dwarfs is almost completely unaffected by such subtleties of medical taxonomy; and it would appear that they make little difference to the dwarfs themselves. Thus, in terms of most role relations, it makes little difference, for example, if a dwarf is a result of rickets or chondrodystrophy.

The two categories of dwarfism that will concern us here are: (1) the proportioned dwarf, or *midget,* usually the result of a dysfunction of the pituitary gland; and (2) the disproportioned dwarf, or what is sometimes termed the *true dwarf*, usually the result of achondroplasia, a dysfunction of the thyroid gland. Within each of these major categories, the social problems of each being quite different, there are many sub-categories including those of mental level, sexual potency, etc.; but our concern will be centered around those whose deviation from normalcy is *primarily* that of height. Therefore, we shall begin our examination of this group with a discussion of the proportioned dwarf, or midget.

The Midget

Data on midgets which are presented here are based largely upon the literature described above and upon a series of interviews conducted with a well-known impresario and agent for midgets[17] and several of the midgets in his employ. Other material is based upon contact with midgets had by this investigator in the circus milieu over a period of many years.

It has been estimated that midgets, who are a great deal more rare than disproportioned dwarfs, constitute about one-millionth of the earth's population.[18] Thus, there are approximately 3,000 midgets in the world. Though this estimate is based on the status of medicine in 1934, science has made only small inroads into the treatment of this growth infirmity,[19] and the reported decreases of midgets in show business[20] are probably due to the development of new social roles now open to midgets rather than any startling decrease in their frequency.

Contrary to some folklore, midgets would appear to be evenly distributed in their births throughout the globe. Their survival into adulthood, however, has depended upon their potential "fit" into the cultural roles available to them in their societies. These roles have historically been known to include those of the shaman, king, artisan, soldier, entertainer, scholar, painter, and revolutionary; there have even been midget deities.[21] Most of these historically noteworthy midgets, however, have been rather exceptional persons in somewhat specialized circumstances (for example, the sons or protégés of nobility) which have made it possible for them to escape what were probably the unhappy and certainly the unrecorded lives of most of their fellows. As late as 1934, most professions were closed to midgets,[22] thus forcing many of them to seek employment in exhibitionism through the theater, carnivals, and circuses. Even in 1934, however, there were numerous midgets reportedly employed as watch and clock makers and gold and jewelry workers, largely due to the excellent adaptation of their hands to such intricate tasks; and several other midgets were reported to have had employment in more common occupations including shopkeeping, restaurant ownership, clerking, selling, real estate, brokerage, and even architecture.[23] But these midgets were definitely viewed as exceptional by other midgets, the majority of whom had gone into exhibitionism.[24] And even those outside the theatrical world still often capitalized on their attraction as midgets in their various other businesses. Today, the situation has greatly changed. Few midgets are now on exhibition,[25] but this has been the function of factors other than the acceptance of midgets as fully equal human beings, one of these additional considerations being a decline in public interest in seeing such human anomalies.[26]

The Life History of the Midget

Before any discussion can be undertaken of the typical midget, it must be first pointed out that there are actually four varieties of midget, and these are differentiated by those socially involved with any large number of midgets.[27] First, there is the *true midget,* a normal born child whose body growth stops at any time from infancy to the immediate pre-adolescent years. These midgets constitute the vast majority of the earth's midget population, and are adults in most particulars except for their size.

A second variety of midget is the *primordial midget* whose dwarfism exists from birth. These midgets develop perfectly normally except for height, like the true midget; but since their growth does not abruptly stop in childhood as does that of the true midget, they (1) are not initially brought up as normal children, (2) are naturally the smallest of the midget population (for example, Miss Adele Ber of Yonkers, New York, was only one foot six inches tall, probably the world's smallest person), and (3) have closed bone ends and therefore never continue to grow as do most other types of midgets who sometimes even grow at amazing rates in their thirties.

A third variety of midget is the *infantile midget* who is intellectually normal but has not developed into sexual maturity either in physical appearance (facial hair for the male, breast and hip development for the female) or in erotic desire.

A fourth type is the *hyper-metabolic midget* whose bodily rate is about one and one-half times that of the average person's. This kind of midget is very vigorous and usually lives only about thirty years, unlike most other midgets, who sometimes even live into their eighties and nineties. In fact, many midgets believe that midget longevity is greater than that for normal-sized persons, largely because most midgets take excellent care of their health (this being enhanced by the fact that many leisure patterns like the neighborhood bar are closed to them).

A possible fifth kind of midget is the *feeble-minded midget,* one who fails to develop in mental level as well as in stature. This type, who is not common, shall not concern us here since his major disability is his mental rather than his physical deficiency.

The Initial Realization

The age of onset, as we have noted, can vary a great deal, but it would appear that the most frequent ages are from three to five. The usual pattern of parental response is to assume that the child is late in his growth, that he is merely physically backward. An exception to this pattern occurs when the child has a midget brother or sister already, a not uncommon occurrence, or in the rare case of a midget's own offspring being a midget. In these latter cases, the parent may be expectant of such a possibility and notice it sooner. Parental reactions to the recognition of their child's malady vary a great deal. It often takes an extreme form of either violence or shielding over-protection. The intelligent parent usually consults medical help, whereas the less educated have all too often viewed the affliction as an instrument of God's wrath against themselves and have tried to hide the fact of their abnormal child, frequently pretending that he is younger, removing him from the school, and going to a strange community.

The greatest shock, however, is that experienced by the child upon his learning of his affliction. Many midgets never fully recover from this experience.[28] Since the child is quite young (usually about nine or ten) when he experiences this fateful revelation, its full implications are usually not immediate; and there is often a hopeful disbelief and an expectancy that growth may still come. It is not uncommon for those who seek medical advice, and normally fail to receive any benefit, to turn to quacks.[29]

Before we can understand the nature of the life careers adopted by the midget, some description must be made of the special problems of his condition, aside from the psychic difficulties.

The Material Problems of the Midget

The most important material problem of the midget is the oversized nature of most of the socially produced items that he needs in his daily life. Whether it be the massive bathtub (in which some midgets have been said to drown), the impossibility of obtaining the appropriate ready-made clothes (children's clothes are very limited as a substitute because of differences in the adult's physical shape and his style of fashion—even shoes must be especially made at a cost of about fifty dollars a pair), the necessity of making mechanical adjustments on an automobile before it can be driven (raising the seat level and the operation pedals), or merely the everyday little nuisances such as the too highly placed elevator buttons or telephone in the pay station, the midget finds himself constantly confronted with the symbols of his smallness. And the life of a midget is an expensive as well as a frustrating one. The simple fact is that most midgets simply cannot afford to take many everyday jobs (even where they are open to them), jobs which can provide them with some preservation of their self-picture as a normal human being but not enough pay to meet their many special expenses. Aside from the need for custom-made clothes (which most midgets have learned to partly circumvent by becoming experts with a needle and thread), another basic problem is food. Midgets eat as much as or more than normal-sized persons, but usually must do so in smaller quantities at one time; thus, many eat four or five times a day instead of the usual two or three times. This creates some waste even at home, and is much worse for the midget who eats in commercial establishments. Pride almost always precludes the ordering of a child's-size portion; and this means even greater waste and expense. This is one of the main reasons for the great attraction for midgets of the world of exhibitionism; for despite its cost to the psyche, it often has meant remarkable financial rewards, as well as other compensations to be discussed below.

The Personality of the Midget

As might be expected, the typical midget has developed under a socialization process which is highly hazardous to his ego development. In his investigations, Wilkins applied the Thurstone *Personality Schedule (Clark revision)* to thirty midgets. He found that:

> All but two of these scores indicate . . . some degree—marked or mild—of maladjustment . . . [and] the extreme deviation upon the personality scale showed, beyond peradventure, lack of personality growth which makes social adjustment difficult for most midgets and impossible for many.[30]

As might be expected, such a physical maladjustment often produces strong overcompensatory characteristics. Bodin and Hershey baldly stated in their 1934 work (which included many nonexhibiting midgets) that:

> Midgets, to survive decently in an oversized world, must be egotists.
> When they have finally equipped themselves to survive in what will always be an alien world, they frequently emerge as insufferable egotists.[31]

This overcompensation, however, is centered about their concern with the normal-sized world's recognition of their status as *adult, fellow human beings*. That is, there seems to be not so much a blown-up self-picture (such as that which characterizes some conceited persons), but rather, an overuse made of what Goffman has termed *disidentifiers,* that is:

. . . a sign that tends—in fact or hope—to break up an otherwise coherent picture but in this case a positive direction desired by the actor, not so much establishing a new claim as throwing severe doubt on the validity of the virtual one.[32]

This disidentification centers about their demonstrating that they are

1. *adults* and not children, and
2. *fellow human beings*, and not some sort of freak.

Their insistence that they be treated as adults often involves the invoking of numerous disidentifiers such as hats, canes, cigars, and facial hair by the men; high fashions and elaborate makeup and hairdo by the women; and more formal attire for both sexes than normal-sized persons might generally wear. This defensiveness about being confused with children sometimes has its disadvantages. We have already mentioned the usual refusal to order a child's portion, despite the desire for a limited quantity of food. But this is only one of the many cases where pride precludes the buying of children's things, for example, such limited clothing as might in fact prove adaptable is often scorned. This hatred for treatment as though they were children is evident in many actions which are usually taken by normals to indicate extreme arrogance. This can prove rather embarrassing to one who first meets midgets, since many of our actions toward small persons are habitually those we would extend toward children, for example, the offering of one's hand when crossing the street, or other forms of help offered quite unmaliciously by normal-sized adults. Too, this drive for the recognition of full adulthood sometimes results in the midget male's showing a certain degree of bravado, or boasting about sexual activities, especially with normal-sized women.

The importance of disidentification by the midget from the world of what are often termed freaks or monsters is a second major motivation in the midget's dealings with normal-sized persons. Like most minority groups, midgets have accepted the dominant group as their reference point in the creation of their values. Thus, the midget does not refer to himself as a dwarf at any time. This term is strictly restricted by him to those disproportioned small persons who, to him as well as to most normals, appear somewhat aesthetically grotesque. Thus, midgets see themselves as merely *small persons.* This is well evidenced in their conversations, and in the name given their organization of the Small Men's Association at the Los Angeles County Fair in 1927. Calling a midget a dwarf is considered an insult by most midgets. It seems to be largely because of this fact that midgets seldom have much to do with dwarfs or the professions of dwarfs. Thus, midgets are very seldom found in circuses as clowns, as professional wrestlers, or in other jobs which often falsely advertise themselves as "midget" exhibitions but in fact include only the disproportioned dwarf. On the other hand, many dwarfs prefer to be referred to as midgets even though they are not technically such.

It is in conjunction with this motive to stress his fellow-humanity that the midget in show business has found some conflict. For the midget in show business has classically been asked to present somewhat of a caricature to his audience, a "minstrelization"[33] or clown role of the happy and talented little man mixed with that of the precocious child. Midgets have always resented this role, and have tried to stress their talents as singers, dancers, and musicians. But the audience has always responded to these performers—many of whom are truly exceptional in their professional abilities—as midgets first and performers only second. It is this conflict which has probably done most to drive the midget from show business. And as more midgets have found greater personal freedom and satisfaction in new social roles, there has developed a negative reaction by many midgets against show business in general and against midgets who have turned to it, much in the manner of many Negro Americans' rejection of those Negroes who gave white Americans a stereotyped image of their race and culture.[34]

Sexual and Marital Patterns

No elaborate survey having been conducted on the sexual activities of midgets, our information about such behaviors must remain somewhat clouded. Two main sources of obfuscation other than the paucity of materials exist:

1. the tendency of some midgets to elaborate upon their sexual exploits because of their symbolic value as proof of their adulthood, and

2. lack of knowledge of whether many midgets from whom information has been obtained are, in fact, true, primordial, or infantile midgets.

As we have noted, the infantile midget has no sexual development; but this impotency is something which is usually hidden and is sometimes covered by elaborate fictions. Bodin and Hershey found in their extensive interviews that the true midget male's sexual potency develops only in his late teens or early twenties. This late onset only adds to his maturational problems, and his early learning of the covering process:

> The midget has arrived at the age of puberty, but does not stand on the threshold of maturity, as do his friends. Their smutty stories, their girl-ogling, their growing preoccupation with things of the flesh are foreign to him. He patterns after them in outward behavior, but has no valid reason for doing so. These pubescent boys, so soon to be initiated into the ritual of sex, act and talk instinctively; the midget, with his sexual awakening still a half dozen or more years in the future, apes them to save face.[35]

This kind of artificial role playing is thus begun early, and makes it difficult to objectively ascertain much from the midget male's later tales of conquest.

Bodin and Hershey also reported that impotency comes early to the midget male, usually present by the age of fifty.[36] This fact also makes objective information difficult to obtain in lieu of the exceptional value placed on masculinity as a symbol of adulthood for the midget.

Midget women also develop late, seldom reaching menstruation before nineteen or twenty. But this probably creates few comparable problems for the female. Her great conflict has classically been the fear of pregnancy, for the child would have to be removed by Caesarian section. Although many of the midgets that Bodin and Hershey surveyed led complete sexual lives, they also found that many females had chosen celibacy at the time of their 1934 interviews because of the dangers involved in a pregnancy. With modern advances in medicine and contraception, however, it is unlikely that this latter pattern is common today. And even in these 1934 cases, there is some lack of clarity as to the possibility that these celibate women might have been infantile midgets.

In their 1934 interviews, which surveyed 233 midgets in the United States, Bodin and Hershey found that only slightly over 22 per cent of the midget population married at all, that 56 per cent of these married other midgets, the remaining 44 per cent marrying normal-sized persons.[37] Fifty-nine per cent of all the marriages were childless with fruitfulness greatest in marriages between midgets and normals (70 per cent), with a great decrease in fruitfulness in marriages between midgets (just under 11 per cent). Marriages of midget women to normal males were slightly less fertile than those of midget males and normal women; but this difference was not significant, and can probably be explained by the pregnancy fear of the female midget. Despite these very crude statistics presented by Bodin and Hershey to show relatively small fertility between midgets, history has reported tremendous variations in these patterns. Thus, to cite an extreme and probably exaggerated case, in the eighteenth century Judith Skinner (two feet two inches tall) reputedly gave her husband Robert (two feet one inch tall) fourteen normal-sized healthy children over a twenty-three year period, all of whom survived to adulthood.

Although the reason for marriage by midgets varies with their idiosyncratic personalities, the range of which should not be underestimated, some common patterns can be found here, as in most matings. Probably the most interesting pattern, however, is that of the normal-midget intermarriage. Here it would probably be wise to sharply differentiate whether the midget member was male or female. In the case of the male midget, as we have already noted, there is some desire on his part to prove to normal-sized males that he can engage in relations with normal-sized females on a basis equal to their own. It also must be remembered that the majority of a midget's daily contacts are with normal-sized persons, and not other midgets.

Midgets cannot usually live in an insulated world of their own, nor do they usually so desire. In fact, many of the ideas held of the midget living in an apartment or house with his furniture and other personal objects scaled down to his size are purely mythological, often part of the spiel fed to the gullible public by the men who have exhibited midgets in such bogus surroundings. The midget, like most of us, has internalized the basic values and aesthetic judgments of his general culture, and this includes the usual notions of feminine beauty. Thus, a midget is no less impressed by the strains of a popular song with its ideal of the girl as "five foot two, eyes of blue . . ." just because he is a mere two foot eight.

It is probably true that strong maternal feelings are a component to be found in the normal-sized woman who marries a midget male. Interviews with midget males, many of whom have sexual careers rivaling that of Don Juan, indicate that a strong force in their favor is the curiosity of many normal-sized women. However, it seems unlikely that such curiosity is an important factor in bringing about intermarriage.

The midget female probably presents a different pattern of intermarriage. A diminutive size for a wife and mother is somewhat more expected than it is for a husband and father, and although a woman of midget proportions is exceeding the expectation, she is nonetheless in line with the expected direction. The midget male, on the other hand, has actually reversed the expected pattern in the family, and must cope with the many conflicts his size presents in symbolically limiting and even denying his masculinity. The midget female has no such problems. There is no direct conflict between her size and her role as wife and mother.

Although divorce is not unknown in midget marriages, whether they be between midgets or between midgets and normals, no figures are available. Like the reasons for the original marriage, there are a multitude of causes. But it is likely that, in the case of intermarriages, there is not always a clear understanding by the midget of the difficulties inherent in his assimilation.

Frequently midgets so marry, in part, at least in the belief that union with one of the "big people" will convince the world of their normality and thus gain its tolerance. Quite the reverse is true. Such matings invariably magnify the midget's incongruity and further arouse the onlookers' curiosity as to the sexual experience involved in such alliances.[38]

Finally, a word might be mentioned regarding sexual deviation among midgets. Information on this point is, as one might expect, almost nonexistent. There are numerous cases which have been reported of midget females who have been employed in prostitution, posing in some cases as children for the Humbert Humberts' jaded appetites. As for other deviations, they are probably rare, in light of the exaggerated response of the midget to otherwise attain all the symbols of normality. This would be especially true of male homosexuality, which would be blatantly in conflict with the ultramasculine projection of most midget males; and this is confirmed by the lack of any such cases reported by Bodin and Hershey's 233 informants.[39] Cross-cultural materials may provide some exceptions, of course; but in Western society, as the old joke goes, the midget has quite enough trouble by just being a midget.

The Disproportioned Dwarf

The disproportioned dwarf presents us with quite different problems than the midget; for other than medical (usually physiological) investigations, we have very little knowledge about these people's lives. The disproportioned dwarf can take many forms and his malformation can be the result of many conditions, including chondrodystrophy, cretinism, rickets, Silfverkiöld-Murguios disease, gargoylism, phocomelia, Kashin-Beck's disease, multiple cartilaginous exostoses and chondromata, as well as other rarer causes.[40] By far the most common of these forms of dwarfism, however, is chondrodystrophic dwarfism; and it is only with this form of disproportionate dwarfism that we shall be dealing in this paper.

The chondrodystrophic man is what many persons think of as the *true dwarf,* the dwarf often pictured in Norse mythology. He has a normal-sized torso and head but small arms and legs. This disproportion gives many persons the false impression that his head is actually larger than it should be. This disorder appears to be hereditary, and is actually present from birth. There are also some minor characteristics often present such as bowleggedness and a typical head shape.[41]

Although an organization for dwarfs called Little People of America Incorporated was founded in 1957,[42] and although this organization has mostly chondrodystrophic persons as members[43] (thus making a control data source for research on dwarfs now possible), little objective data are currently available on the social problems of the dwarf in the United States.

The findings of Mørch's excellent 1941 survey of all the 86 living chondrodystrophic persons in Denmark, however, are probably generalized in most ways to the chondrodystrophic population elsewhere, since it is quite well established that their frequency is unaffected by parents' race, geography, or class structure.[44] According to Mørch's findings, chondrodystrophics number one person per 44,000.[45] Thus, there are about 65,000 present in the world today, and about 4,450 in the United States.

Although chondrodystrophic persons are encumbered by their low stature, this problem is at least equaled by their disproportioned appearance, especially in the case of the female, since beauty is normally an important variable in the life of a woman. This lack of physical beauty is an important factor for the social adjustment of the chondrodystrophic person; and it is probably this factor which is reflected in the marital figures given by Mørch. Only about one third of the Danish chondrodystrophic men were married, and only one chondrodystrophic woman, she to a chondrodystrophic man.[46] In the Danish cases this has led to illegitimate pregnancies among these women, a situation similar to that reported as being present in the United States.[47]

In regard to the occupational roles, Mørch found that of the thirty-nine men, there were twenty-one artisans, three tradesmen, four office clerks, one musician, one circus clown, one souffleur, and eight unskilled laborers. Among the thirty-eight women, there were nine seamstresses, one married woman, one owner of an embroidery shop, one teacher of housekeeping, one music student, one farm owner, one music hall performer, two housemaids, and seventeen untrained women.[48] Although the occupational pattern is probably quite similar in the United States, insofar as women are less trained than the men, the situation is otherwise probably quite specific to Denmark and other socialist countries which provide special aid and training for these people. Thus, the picture may well be less bright in the United States, where training is not provided by the government.

Finally, it should be noted that Mørch found his chondrodystrophic persons of normal mental development; and, although they experience great psychological stresses, he found that "The great majority of them have a pleasant, well-balanced disposition of a quite normal emotional nature.[49] However, he also states:

> As is to be expected in patients with such a marked degree of malformation, one will sometimes meet with suspicion, hypersensitiveness to offense—real or imaginary—and aversion to society.[50]

Conclusion

In our examination of the dwarf, we have found that these persons must encounter a variety of problems. The midget represents the true variable condition of stature diminished to the point of having serious interpersonal consequences. The chondrodystrophic dwarf, on the other hand, presents us with a case of this condition plus the presence of a malformation whose grotesque qualities also have their influence.

Although the data are very limited, the compounding of deviant characteristics in the chondrodystrophic person (both his stature and aesthetic appearance) creates much greater problems for him than for the midget. Though both show normal intelligence and ability, both have found social roles and occupations closed to them, and both find their physical stature creating conflict in some of the social roles they can successfully maintain; but the midget seems to have generally found his conflict somewhat smaller. Of the female members of these minority groups, the midget woman, too, has found a great deal less conflict, for she may still retain beauty despite her lack of normal height; thus, marriage is usually available to her, even if she might not choose to take it.

The dwarf presents a unique case for social science investigation. As we have seen, the dwarf undergoes a socialization process which, because of the many roles closed to him, probably represents a greater uniformity than that undergone by most normal-sized persons. What are the implications of this social tightening? From what little we know, this uniformity should have its counterpart in the personality structures of dwarfs. One would also predict, in lieu of their limited access to the achievement of life goals,[51] that dwarfs should be highly anomic. Investigation of this and many similar personality questions awaits our collection of more information.

The dwarf clearly fits the criteria set for definition of a minority group,[52] yet the importance of this group, as well as other nonethnic categories of persons that would fit the definition, has been seriously neglected. It might also be mentioned, in this regard, that, although dwarfs are not a race of people, this has sometimes been thought of them by the general population; thus, some cases of dwarf-normal interactions might fit under the sociological category (if such it can be called) of race relations. However, the point being made here is that these persons, and the reactions of normals to them, constitute important sources for the testing of some of our propositions about minority groups developed elsewhere. Thus, some of our notions about prejudice, as for example in Frank R. Westie's normative theory,[53] would include the commonly held attitude toward the dwarf as one who is an inferior person fitted only for limited roles, but would find this case a difficult theoretical fit. For it is quite possible that the prejudice against the small person has a quite different etiology than that which we find against Negroes or ethnic groups. Thus, Westie's theory states that:

> Individuals are prejudiced because they are raised in societies which have prejudice as a facet of the normative system of their culture. Prejudice is built into the culture in the form of normative precepts—that is, notions of "ought to be"—which define the ways in which members of the group ought to behave in relation to the members of selected outgroups.[54]

It seems likely, however, that the false generalizations held about the dwarf are not directly learned—how many people have ever actually been told the proper behavior toward a dwarf?—but may be the result of something more basic in man's predisposition, for example, a sense of dominance over the small (superiority), and a repugnance toward the malformed (negative affect). In any case, we have no right to assume a simple fit for our theories of prejudice developed in other areas when we attempt to apply them to the case of dwarfism. Though this writer believes that it is probably true that we deal here with the same kind of prejudice found elsewhere, this has simply not been established. Empirical questions are thus posed which need to be answered; for it is not impossible that, for example, persons scoring high on the F scale (authoritarianism) might in fact be less prejudiced toward dwarfs.

The remarkable thing is not that we know so little about dwarfs themselves—although this is certainly regrettable—but that we know so little about attitudes toward them. Clearly, prejudice exists, role expectations are limited, and strong affective reactions can be elicited; but the domain is unmapped. Almost every culture has special roles for the very small person; but the similarities in these social typings have never been investigated.

Social science must broaden its focus to include investigations of groups such as the dwarf. For if it fails to examine the whole of man in all his forms, including his less common ones, its theoretical development will be parochial; and it will fail to analytically encompass but a corner of social life.

REFERENCES

1. The term dwarf is used here in the nonmedical sense referring to any adult person whose height is so low as to socially entail perceptible drawbacks in the form of reduced strength and striking appearance. There appears to be some cross-cultural difference in the demarcation of such heights.

    As regards the definition a number of figures . . . have been stated as limits of dwarfism. . . . The most rational procedure, however, would be to reckon from the mean figure of a large normal material, using the standard deviation as a measure since the conception of dwarfism must be a function of the normal height. It goes without saying that a dwarf is of another height among Lapps than among Swedes or Anglo-Saxons. (Paul Horstmann, "Dwarfism: A Clinical Investigation," *Acta Endocrinologica*, Supplement 5 [Copenhagen: Einar Munksgaard, 1949].)

2. For example, concerning literary criticism and history, see Joseph Ritson, "On Pigmies," in his *Fairy Tales, Legends and Romances Illustrating*

Shakespeare and Other Early Writers (London: Frank and William Kerslake, 1875); or Vernon J. Harward, *The Dwarfs of Arthurian Romance and Celtic Tradition* (London: E. J. Brill, 1958). With respect to the visual arts, see Erika Tietze-Conrat, *Dwarfs and Jesters in Art*, trans. Elizabeth Osborn (London: Phaidon Press Ltd., 1957).

There has also been some utilization of dwarfs in fiction, often for symbolic purposes: for example, Walter De La Mare, *Memoirs of a Midget* (New York: Alfred A. Knopf, Inc., 1922); Aldous Huxley, *Chrome Yellow* (New York: George H. Doran, 1922); or Carson McCullers, *The Ballad of the Sad Cafe* (Boston: Houghton Mifflin, 1951).

It is noteworthy that the social roles in which the dwarf has been cast have been expanded in recent years—a trend well reflected in the literary treatments—from what Orrin Klapp has called the role of the *deformed fool* to what today can also often include heroic and villainous roles. See Orrin Klapp, *Heroes, Villains and Fools* (Englewood Cliffs, N.J.: Prentice-Hall, 1962), p. 80.

3. Edward J. Wood, *Giants and Dwarfs* (London: Richard Bentley, 1868); C. J. S. Thompson, *The Mystery and Lore of Monsters* (London: Williams and Norgate, 1930); and Eduard Garnior, *Les Nains et les Géants* (Paris: Hachette, 1884).

4. For example, Alice Curtis Desmond, *Barnum Presents General Tom Thumb* (New York: Crowell-Collier & Macmillan, 1954). The closest approximation to an autobiography of a dwarf that this reviewer has been able to unearth is that of Henry Viscardi, Jr., *A Man's Stature* (New York: John Day, 1952), but Viscardi's affliction was limited to his legs and therefore makes him rather untypical.

5. For example, Horstmann, *op. cit.*, reference 1; Ernst Trier Mørch, *Chondrodystrophic Dwarfs in Denmark* (Copenhagen: Einar Munksgaard, 1941); Hans Grebe, *Chondrodysplasie* (Rome: Edizione dell' Instituto Gregorio Mendel, 1955); and P. G. Seckel, *Bird-Headed Dwarfs* (Springfield, Ill.: Charles C. Thomas, 1960). The Horstmann study is especially valuable since it includes a variety of dwarf types as well as a large number of cases (74).

6. Walter L. Wilkins, "Pituitary Dwarfism and Intelligence," *Journal of General Psychology, 18* (1938), pp. 305–17.

7. Walter Bodin and Burnet Hershey, *It's a Small World* (New York: Coward-McCann, 1934).

8. Erving Goffman, *Stigma: Notes on the Management of Spoiled Identity* (Englewood Cliffs, N. J.: Prentice-Hall, 1963); and John Cumming and Elaine Cumming, "On the Social Psychology of Stigma," paper read at the Annual Meeting of the American Sociological Society (Washington, D.C., 1962), mimeographed. Whereas Goffman centers attention upon stigma as a discrediting attribute (see pp. 1–3), the Cummings treat stigma as the actual loss of social competence (see pp. 1–3). Goffman's definition stems from his more general approach, and we shall follow his usage.

9. Cf. Howard S. Becker, *Outsiders* (New York: Free Press, 1963); and E. M. Lemert, *Social Pathology* (New York: McGraw-Hill, 1951).

10. For example, the characteristics of the mythical Mehehune of Polynesia bear remarkable resemblances to the leprechauns of Ireland, as well as to

other fictional small people of Oceania. See Katherine Luomala, "The Mehehune of Polynesia and Other Mythical Little People of Oceania," *B. P. Bishop Museum Bulletin,* 203 (Honolulu: Bernice P. Bishop Museum, 1951), pp. 68–69.

11. Cf. Goffman, *op. cit.,* pp. 126–47.

12. Cf. J. A. Harris, *et al., The Measurement of Man* (Minneapolis: University of Minnesota Press, 1930), pp. 140–49; or Roger G. Barker, B. A. Wright, and M. R. Genick, *Adjustment to Physical Handicap and Illness: A Survey of the Social Psychology of Physique and Disability* (New York: Social Science Research Council, 1946), Bulletin 55, pp. 13–15, 19–21.

13. Studies cited in *ibid.,* p. 14.

14. This would seem to be indicated in the study by Wilkins, *op. cit.,* reference 6, pp. 314–15.

15. A variety of medical classifications exist, some of which can be found in Horstmann, *op. cit.,* reference 1, pp. 10–12.

16. This demarcation at four feet six inches would appear to be very widespread; it is consistent in the writing on the subject by nonphysicians as well as in the interview data I have obtained.

17. The entrepreneur, Mr. Nate Eagle, has had business and personal dealings with literally hundreds of midgets and has had charge of many troops of midgets, one group including 187 midgets. His role is essentially very similar to that of the late Leo Singer, the international impresario for midgets from about 1910–1935. Both men have acted in many important buffer roles and functions for the midget community. Re Singer's role in midget history, see: Bodin and Hershey, *op. cit.,* reference 7, pp. 281–97. For information on Mr. Eagle, see: Robert Lewis Taylor, "Profile: Talker," *The New Yorker,* 34 (April 19 and 26, 1958), pp. 47f and 39f.

18. Bodin and Hershey, *op. cit.,* reference 7, p. 41.

19. For example, see Horstmann, *op. cit.,* reference 1, pp. 55–67. A difficult problem in this area—and one not mentioned in the physicians' works we have cited—is the lack of controls in the treatment studies, since dwarfs have often been known to suddenly grow several inches without any treatment at all.

20. See "Goodbye, Tom Thumb," *Time,* 79 (May 18, 1962), p. 53; or John Lentz, "Passing of the Side Show," *Today's Health,* 49 (March, 1964), pp. 48–51.

21. An excellent brief review of midgets in history can be found in Bodin and Hershey, *op. cit.,* reference 7, pp. 189–207.

22. *Ibid.,* p. 90.

23. *Ibid.*

24. This would seem to be borne out by inference from the fact that over half the midgets in Mr. Eagle's troop of 187 midgets were United States born (and this excludes other midget troops in the country which were smaller and therefore less able to afford the importation of foreign midgets), and our estimation that there should only have been about 150 or less midgets born in the United States who were present in this country in the late 1940's. This is also corroborated by Bodin and Hershey's placing the 1934 population of foreign- and native-born midgets in the United States at no more than 300. See Bodin and Hershey, *op. cit.,* reference 7, p. 263.

25. See reference 20.
26. This is part of the larger industrial change which has brought with it the decline of the "rube mentality." For a lengthier discussion of the topic, cf. Marcello Truzzi, "The Decline of the American Circus: The Shrinkage of an Institution."
27. This classification incorporates the three types of midgets mentioned by Bodin and Hershey, *op. cit.*, reference 7, p. 46, as well as those derived from interviews with midgets themselves. It should be mentioned that Bodin and Hershey unfortunately seem to have in some cases made false generalizations to all midgets from some of these specific types.
28. As Goffman well put it: "The painfulness . . . of sudden stigmatization can come not from an individual's confusion about his identity, but from his knowing too well what he has become," Goffman, *op. cit.*, reference 8, pp. 132–33.
29. No statistics are available on midgets' consultations with quacks; but Mørch found that 43 per cent of all cases of chondrodystrophic dwarfism in Denmark had consulted quacks. See Mørch, *op. cit.*, reference 5, p. 111. The number of consultations by midgets is probably less since their disorder is somewhat easier to live with.
30. Wilkins, *op. cit.*, reference 6, pp. 314–15.
31. Bodin and Hershey, *op. cit.*, reference 7, p. 162.
32. Goffman, *op. cit.*, reference 8, p. 44.
33. See *ibid.*, pp. 109–10. The term "minstrelization" comes from A. Broyard, "Portrait of the Inauthentic Negro," *Commentary*, 10 (1950), pp. 59–60.
34. It is interesting that this attitude towards "minstrelization" is still quite new among midgets, and a reaction against this "deminstrelization" or role inversion has not yet been exhibited, except possibly among the ranks of current show business midgets. Show business midgets, however, have an odd form of midget pride since it is also valuable for a midget—given that he must be small all his life—to be as small as possible. Thus, many midgets who relied upon exhibitionism as their livelihood lived in fear that they might (as did some midgets) grow into that intermediary height where they were minimally valuable as midgets but not normal sized either. Thus, one could achieve a strange sort of vested interest in being one of the smallest midgets.
35. Bodin and Hershey, *op. cit.*, reference 7, p. 87. Because of the *visibility* of his stigma, the midget cannot pass as a normal sized person, as can persons with some other kinds of stigma. His stature is very evident to anyone; and this perceptibility of his stigma is present even on the telephone since the voice of most midgets is quite shrill and distinctive compared to the normal adult. The midget is therefore forced to concentrate on minimizing the *obtrusiveness* of his stigma (see Goffman, *op. cit.*, reference 8, pp. 48–51, for an excellent discussion of the nuances of visibility). He therefore learns many *covering techniques* which he can use to reduce tension and normalize interaction (see *ibid.*, pp. 102–4, for a fuller discussion of the covering process).
36. Bodin and Hershey, *op. cit.*, reference 7, p. 101.
37. These and other percentages given in their survey can be found in *ibid.*, pp. 148–50.

204 ■ *Disabled and Disadvantaged*

38. *Ibid.*, p. 151.
39. *Ibid.*, p. 107.
40. See Mørch, *op. cit.*, reference 5, pp. 57–77.
41. A full description can be found in *ibid.*, pp. 28–38.
42. This group held its seventh national convention in Philadelphia in 1965. An investigation of this group is currently being made, but this author must thus far rely on limited information from its newsletters, personal correspondence with its president, and a highly popularized article: Alvin Adams, "The Little People—A Tiny Minority with Big Problems," *Ebony*, 20 (October, 1965), pp. 104–13. It is noted in this article that less than 1 per cent of this organization's members (some 700 according to information from personal correspondence with its president) earn their living in show business (p. 110). This presents some question about the representativeness of this membership. Although these little people strongly reject show business as "minstrelization," informant dwarfs in show business were asked about this new organization and gave it a somewhat negative description as a club for maladjusted dwarfs. Thus, the show business role, which usually places a dwarf in the company of other dwarfs—unlike many other jobs, which isolate the dwarf—often functions to give him a therapeutic milieu within the limits allowed by the show business role.
43. Unfortunately, there is no breakdown of its over 700 members by dwarf type. It might be noted that this organization sets its membership height maximum at four feet ten inches, unlike the four feet six inches we have set in this discussion.
44. Mørch, *op. cit.*, reference 5, pp. 103–11, 122.
45. *Ibid.*, p. 101.
46. *Ibid.*, p. 46.
47. See Adams, *op. cit.*, reference 42, p. 113.
48. Mørch, *op. cit.*, reference 5, p. 56.
49. *Ibid.*, p. 55.
50. *Ibid.*
51. See Dorothy L. Meier and Wendell Bell, "Anomie and Differential Access to the Achievement of Life Goals," *American Sociological Review*, 24 (April, 1959), pp. 189–202.
52. Cf. Louis Wirth, "The Problem of Minority Groups," in Ralph Linton, ed., *The Science of Man in the World Crisis* (New York: Columbia University Press, 1945), pp. 347–72.
53. Frank R. Westie, "Race and Ethnic Relations," in Robert E. L. Faris, ed., *Handbook of Modern Sociology* (Chicago: Rand McNally, 1964), pp. 581–603.
54. *Ibid.*, pp. 583–84.

Physical Disability as a Social Psychological Problem
Lee Meyerson

There is general agreement in the literature on physical disability that the major problems of the handicapped are not physical but social and psychological. However, while speculative theories, folklore, and opinion are plentiful in this field, scientific research in the social psychological aspects of disability has been meager; and theories having operational and conceptual clarity with which to order and explain commonly observed behavioral phenomena have been lacking. It is easy to find medical, educational, sociological, vocational, and mental hygiene discussions of the problem,[1] but only recently have attempts been made to treat variations in physique systematically and to integrate this problem more adequately into the established field of social psychology. . . .[2]

The 26,000,000 physically handicapped individuals in our population and the 350,000 civilians who join the ranks of this group yearly indicate that an atypical physique constitutes a social problem of vast magnitude. If physique, as Allport[3] has pointed out, is one of the three principal raw materials of personality, it is obvious that disability is also a psychological problem. If normal variations in physique such as being strong or weak, tall or short, handsome or ugly, are important factors in personality formation, clearly, the pathological variations known as physical disability are likely to be even more potent.

Social Classification by Physique

Number and clinical significance together, nevertheless, would not create a social psychological problem. The problem arises from the fact that physique, like age, sex, and race, is one of the criteria for social classification.

Source: *The Journal of Social Issues, 4:4,* pp. 6–10; copyright © 1948 by The Society for the Psychological Study of Social Issues. Reprinted by permission of the publisher.

The movies and comics, for example, learned early that one of the easiest ways to characterize an adult as a villain was to cripple him. On a more sophisticated level, *Time* magazine, which cuts thousands of words from each issue, recognizes the significance attached to physique by consistently printing the physical characteristics of persons in the news.[4] In professional publications, it is difficult to find a clinical report that does not describe physique, and findings that "Physical attractiveness seems to be the basic determinant, not only of campus success, but also of the self-conception which these youngsters derive of themselves through social interaction,"[5] are not uncommon.

The attitude of society toward atypical physique has varied from the Greek view of "A sound mind in a sound body" with its negative implication of crooked body, crooked mind, crooked personality, to the widely held "over-compensation" theory which states that the adjustment process necessary to come to terms with life after severe illness or physical misfortune makes a person superior and capable of achievements that otherwise might have been far beyond his grasp.

Similar variation is found in religious doctrine, from the Old Testament conception of disability as punishment for sin to the New Testament view of salvation through suffering.

We have not resolved this conflict. In World War I, Americans were asked to believe that the withered arm of the Kaiser was responsible for the quest for power that led to war, and Goebbels, the late Propaganda Minister of Germany, was repeatedly "explained" in terms of his club foot. On the other hand, Edison has been "explained" in terms of his deafness and Franklin Roosevelt, it is said, became great through polio.

The sources of these attitudes and their behavioral correlates present interesting problems which we cannot consider here. It seems clear, however, that physical disability may have positive, negative or neutral meanings, and it is with these meanings that we shall be concerned.

What is a physical disability? There is evidence in this issue [*J. Soc. Issues*] that we cannot make very much progress in understanding the problem if we consider it only from a physical standpoint. A physical disability is not necessarily something that is physically imposed, recognized as physically caused, or manifested physically or psychologically; nor is it a malformation or malfunction.[6] *A physical disability is simply a variation in physique upon which, ordinarily, we place a highly negative value.* The potency or power of a given variation in physique to affect the behavior of a man who lives in a coal mining town may differ from its potency for a woman who lives in Hollywood. The variations in physique called physical disabilities, however, consistently carry negative values.

We can consider these negative values in three ways: (1) as negative values imposed by society, (2) as negative values imposed by the person upon himself, and (3) as negative values imposed by the atypical physique.

1. The negative values imposed by society, even for minor variations, are obvious. The newspapers and magazines are full of advertisements on how to became taller (by wearing special shoes), slimmer (by diet, drugs, and mechanical apparatus), or more feminine (thru hormones or curious articles of clothing causing "inflation"). For more extreme deviations, society tends to impose positive restrictions. A child with impaired vision, hearing, ambulation or certain chronic diseases, in many states, is not permitted to attend the regular schools, but is either exempt from compulsory attendance laws or must attend classes that are specially set aside for him. Moreover, ordinarily, he may be taught only by teachers who are physically normal. When he grows up, he may not serve in his nation's armed forces; and his difficulty in finding employment is so great that each year we must conduct a "National Employ the Handicapped Week" so that even relatively small numbers of persons like him may enjoy the right to work.[7] Social distance in more personal areas is equally great. In one study of 50 college students[8] 65 per cent said they would not marry, and 50 per cent would not even date a person of the opposite sex who had an amputated leg. In the same group, 85 per cent would not marry and 72 per cent would not date a deaf person. The existence of such low tolerance for differences indicates strongly that the problem of adjustment to disability is not simply a problem for the disabled themselves but is equally a problem for physically normal individuals.

2. The negative values imposed by the atypical person upon himself appear to stem, in part, from the regard in which he is held by his culture. As Lewin[9] has pointed out, "Minority groups tend to accept the implicit judgment of those who have status even where the judgment is directed against themselves." This is as true of the disabled minority as it is of racial and cultural minorities. Self-devaluation is intensified, moreover, by the fact that the great bulk of this minority group originally had majority status and held the majority judgment, so that they devalue themselves with their own previously formed attitudes. Where these attitudes persist, the physical handicap tends to become an emotional handicap and the atypical person is not simply handicapped in some areas, but becomes "handicapped all over."

3. The negative values of the disability itself may be conceived to arise from inability to reach simple, universally achieved goals. The deaf person does not feel inferior because he cannot appreciate good music, but because he cannot communicate easily. The blind person does not experience failure because pictorial art is missing from his life, but because he has great difficulty in the simple task, hardly attended to by the majority, of moving from one place to another. Since communication and locomotion are usually daily, inescapable needs, the blind person and the deaf person tend to have failure piled upon failure until aspiration in these areas is lowered to more realistic levels and adjustment occurs, or the thought "I failed n-times" becomes "I am a failure," and a variety of socially unacceptable behaviors may result. A similar analysis could be made for other types of disability.

In this respect, disability varies somewhat from the usual minority situation. There is nothing in skin color, religion or sex that imposes intrinsic limitations. A Negro's color doesn't affect his intellectual ability; a woman refused a job in an occupation populated by men can externalize her frustration. The barriers to the desired goal are conceivably permeable. On the other hand, there is an intrinsic limitation in a severe disability. There is often internalized failure as well as externalized frustration. New mechanical aids and operations may, in the future, make the disability barrier permeable for some, but it should be recognized that the barrier in disability tends to surround the person rather than the goals.

The negative values that arise because a disabled person is really inferior in some areas is not strictly a social-psychological problem. It becomes so because the disabled person, in order to reach a goal, often must ask for help or tolerance. In doing this he is forced to expose personal areas of his life space and accept from others the lower status, dependence, sympathy, pity, and curiosity that acceptance of help often implies.[10]

Implications

That all but one of the negative values of disability have their sources in social psychological situations carries two important implications:

1. The problem of adjustment to physical disability is, in large part, a problem in creating favorable social-psychological situations.

2. The problem of adjustment to physical disability is as much or more a problem of the nonhandicapped majority as it is of the disabled minority.

REFERENCES

1. Recent scientific journals that have devoted an entire issue to the problem of disability include: *The Nervous Child,* 7 (1948); *Review of Educational Research,* 17 (1947); and *The Annals of The American Academy of Political and Social Science,* 239 (1945). The issue of *Journal of Social Issues,* 4 (1948), in which this article first appeared, is the first to be concerned with psychological aspects.
2. R. G. Barker, Beatrice A. Wright, and Mollie Gonick, *Adjustment to Physical Handicap and Illness* (New York: Social Science Research Council, Bulletin 55, 1946); also Tamara Dembo, Gloria Laudieu, and Beatrice A. Wright, *Social Psychological Rehabilitation of the Physically Handicapped,* Office of the Surgeon General, War Department, 1948 (mimeographed).
3. Gordon Allport, *Personality* (New York: Henry Holt, 1937).
4. The following is typical: "Dr. Wong is not physically impressive: He is under 5 feet and weighs 90-odd pounds, and his homely face is scarred from an auto smash-up. . . ." *Time* (June 7, 1948).
5. S. D. Loomis and A. W. Green, "The Pattern of Mental Conflict in a Typical State University," *Journal of Abnormal and Social Psychology,* 42 (1947), p. 344.

6. For example, a person who loses his memory for recent events as a result of lobotomy is not considered physically handicapped; the "cause" of a disability may vary from "sorcery" to "God wanted it"; and variations considered malformations in our culture may be highly valued in others, for example, elongation of the neck cultivated by some primitive societies.

7. Such discrimination is exercised even against war veterans with "honorable" disabilities. There is evidence that this is not due to inability to perform efficient, productive work, but rather to the resistance of persons whose physiques are normal to admit atypical persons to social participation. There appears to be a negative halo effect by which disability in one area spreads to include all areas. The president of the Blinded War Veterans once remarked: "It is easy to be a well-adjusted blind person so far as society is concerned. All that is necessary is, (1) to be able to blow one's own nose without assistance, and (2) to refrain from showing suicidal tendencies in public." The "inspirational" literature that appears in Sunday supplements and popular magazines appears to confirm this view.

8. L. Meyerson, unpublished research. On general inquiries like this, as in superficial acquaintance, physically normal persons tend to see only a disability rather than a person with a disability. This stereotyping appears to be what semanticists call a "signal reaction."

9. Kurt Lewin, "Action Research and Minority Problems," *Journal of Social Issues*, 2 (1946), p. 44.

10. Help may have positive values also. For a detailed analysis, see Gloria Laudieu, Eugenia Hanfmann, and Tamara Dembo, "Evaluation of Help by the Injured," *Journal of Abnormal and Social Psychology*, 42 (1947), pp. 169–92.

The Social Psychology of Physical Disability

Roger G. Barker

The effects of atypical physique[1] upon behavior and personality have held the interest of men since earliest times. In fact, a continuing controversy has surrounded this issue. For example, Francis Bacon stated that deformed persons are commonly vengeful and ill tempered, returning in like coin the evil which nature has visited upon them. Robert Burton declared, on the other hand, that although deformities and imperfections of body torture many men,

Source: *The Journal of Social Issues*, 4:4, pp. 28–38; copyright © 1948 by The Society for the Psychological Study of Social Issues. Reprinted by permission of the publisher.

they should be comforted by the fact that these imperfections of the body do not blemish the personality, but rather improve it. Scientific studies of differences in behavior, beginning with those of Francis Galton, have dealt systematically with this problem. Despite this long history of lay and scientific interest, we still have only a meager understanding of the psychological effects of physical disability. This is shown by a recent survey of relevant publications.[2] However, a number of tentative generalizations may be made regarding what is known:

1. Physically disabled persons more frequently than physically normal persons exhibit behavior which is commonly termed maladjusted. In almost every study, however, 35 per cent to 45 per cent of the disabled subjects are reported to be as well or better adjusted than the average nondisabled person.

2. The kinds of maladjusted behavior exhibited by physically disabled people are not peculiar to them; they are similar to those shown by nondisabled people. However, there is some evidence that withdrawing, timid, self-conscious behavior is more frequent in these people, although the opposite sorts of behavior are by no means infrequent.

3. There is no evidence of a relationship between kind of physical disability and kind of behavioral maladjustment; within a wide range of physical disabilities, the behavioral resultants do not differ. However, it is possible that disabilities requiring a very special way of living or unique treatment over a long period of time give rise to unique adjustments on the part of the patient; this may be true, for example, of tuberculosis.

4. It is probably true that persons with a long history of physical disability are more likely to exhibit behavior maladjustment than those with a short history of disability.

5. Severely disabled persons appear to have more frequent and more severe adjustment problems than persons with milder handicaps.

If comparative data on the behavior of physically handicapped and normal persons are limited, explanations of the trends discovered are even more so. The efforts which have been made to account for the differences noted are pitched at two levels. On the one hand physical defect has a unique, personal, and often deep, unconscious significance for the disabled person. A number of writers have considered this in terms of such ideas as distortion of the body image, castration fears, inferiority attitudes, and self hostility. We may call this the clinical problem of physical disability. Such explanations suffer at the present time from the absence of data relevant to the hypotheses used, and from primitive concepts lacking conceptual and operational clarity. Here is undoubtedly a field that is ripe for harvesting by theoretically and technically prepared investigators.

In addition to its clinical significance, physical defect has social significances common to broad segments of a population, for physique is one of the grounds upon which class and caste distinctions are based. The person with a physique which has a well-established social meaning is placed in a prescribed social-psychological situation in addition to that which depends upon the very private and personal significance of his defect. Sex, race, and maturity differences have well-established meanings which have been systematically studied in many cultures. Physical normality constitutes another, similar basis for social distinction which has received less systematic attention. We may call this the social-psychological problem of physical disability. It is with this problem that we shall largely be concerned here.

The Physically Disabled Child

In attempting to describe the social-psychological position of physically disabled persons in American culture, it is necessary to distinguish between children and adults, for their situations are quite different. In fact, with children the problem is largely on the clinical level, for, as with race and sex distinctions, the full force of the cultural restraints and coercions associated with physique is not felt until adulthood. To provide some completeness to the picture, we shall sketch some common, general factors in the child's situation, even though these are largely of a clinical nature. Let us take the case of the seriously disabled child. By virtue of the fact of being different and requiring an unusual amount of help and attention he is inevitably a person of unusual importance. This may help to satisfy his needs for social status and self esteem while he is very young. However, in our culture, physically defective children can be a great burden in time and money and in the social disapproval the parent receives from his social group. Two unfortunate reactions to this by the parent frequently occur sooner or later. The parent may feel guilty, resentful, or socially stigmatized for having produced a defective child, and this may cause him to push the child aside. Or, the parent may, either from genuine sympathy or from reaction to his own guilt, do everything in his power to recompense the child for his misfortunes. Both of these reactions are unfortunate for they frustrate the child's ego and social status needs.

If the parents of a disabled child are likely to have feelings of resentment and guilt, the child is likely to have them also. The parent often tends to blame himself for the tragedy that has befallen his child. The child tends to blame himself and his parents. To the young child, the parents are supreme. They are the givers and the takers away. It is almost inevitable that a child should in some degree hold his parents responsible for the evils that befall him. However, such thoughts about a supreme, all-powerful person cannot often be openly expressed. They are, apparently, usually partially retained and partially repressed. To the extent that they are not repressed, hostility of the child for the parent results; to the extent that they are repressed, anxiety and guilt will be the outcome. Self hostility, guilt, and anxiety may also arise from half-repressed self-blame. Here, then, are constellations of factors which may very easily be the basis for behavior difficulties.

Physically disabled children are probably deprived more frequently than physically normal children of the very important adjustive function of play. By play, children are aided in safely exploring the real world and their own emotions and ideas. It is unfortunately probably true that interference with normal play behavior is frequent in the case of physically disabled children.

It is important to recognize, however, that these unfortunate conditions by no means always occur. Some parents are able to accept defective children for what they are, neither rejecting them nor compulsively protecting them. Some physically disabled children have excellent play opportunities. Finally, it must be realized that all children, whether defective or not, can make difficult transitions and meet difficult problems successfully.

As the world of the child expands beyond the limits of the family, two factors begin to operate, one advantageous and one disadvantageous. The disadvantageous factor is this: Depending upon his degree of disability the ordinary accomplishments of life are difficult for him. He is often required to strive with great effort and frequently with intense emotionality to perform even routine actions such as climbing stairs or saying a sentence. He is thus almost inevitably placed under great pressure, and he reacts to this pressure as anyone does: with tension and anxiety. On the other hand, because he is disabled, less is likely to be expected of him by society. To this extent he is in an easier situation than physically normal individuals. There is great variation in how these factors balance in different individuals, but there is a tendency on the part of parents of disabled children to push them to accomplish in nonmotor activities, especially in intellectual activities. This is regrettable since most disabled children do not have extraordinary ability in nonmotor lines and such pressure only serves to add another source of tension to those already operating.

The Physically Disabled Adult

When the child becomes an adult, he faces, in addition to the particular local conditions existing within his family and clique group, a rather well-structured and stable larger social status position which has, in varying degrees, the following characteristics:

1. it is underprivileged;
2. it is ambiguous and marginal;
3. it involves new, unknown social conditions.

Let us consider each of these aspects separately.

Underprivileged Social Position

Physically disabled persons cannot participate in many activities which physically normal people value highly. Thus, the employment opportunities open to disabled persons are sharply limited, and where opportunities do exist, the higher levels are severely restricted. Likewise, the social and recreational activities in which disabled persons are able to engage are limited. In these respects the physically disabled person is in a position not unlike that of the Negro, the Jew, and other underprivileged racial and religious minorities; he is a member of an underprivileged minority. In one important respect, however, his position is different. The reason for the limitation upon the freedom of the physically handicapped person is partly due to formal and informal social ostracism on the part of the dominant majority. For example, many employers as a matter of policy establish physical fitness standards for all employees irrespective of whether a particular job can be effectively handled by a physically disabled person. Many physically normal individuals avoid contact with physically disabled persons as much as possible. There is strong evidence that in spite of favorable public attitudes, the basic, often unconscious attitudes of most physically normal persons are hostile or subordinating toward physically disabled persons. This shows in a variety of ways; for example, the jokes referring to disabled persons are more often of a malicious or ridiculing nature than jokes about nondisabled persons. This is social ostracism of the sort experienced by racial and religious underprivileged minorities.

On the other hand the minority position of the physically disabled person is partly due to limitations on freedom of activity imposed by his own physique. In this, his position differs from that of the racial and religious minority member. The racial and religious minority member can truly place the source of his limited freedom upon the behavior of the dominant majority; he does not have to blame himself for his frustrations. The physically disabled person, on the other hand, cannot completely transfer the cause of his frustrations to another. The fact which the physically disabled individual has to face is that in some respects he is an inferior person. The reality situation of the racial and religious group member, on the other hand, involves only social rejection.

A final difference between the minority situation of physically disabled people and most other underprivileged groups lies in the fact that the disabled person is usually in no sense a member of a real sociological or psychological group deriving from his physique. He is an individual with a minority position which is usually not shared with other similar individuals. Even the Jew or the Negro who lives in a community in which he is the only member of his group may be psychologically a member of the larger group, sharing in its aspirations, accepting its values and participating in its activities. This is hardly ever possible for the disabled person. He is almost inevitably an isolated individual who must meet the limitations which his underprivileged status imposes without the possibility of group support.

Marginal Status

In many spheres of activity, physically disabled people have, as we have just indicated, an underprivileged minority status; however, they are not a caste which do not participate in activities of the dominant majority or share its satisfactions. The physically disabled are analogous to a sociological class inasmuch as some physically disabled persons are able to enter the ranks of, and become accepted as, normal persons, and many of them share common activities and satisfactions with their normal contemporaries. In other words, the demarcation between physical normality and disability is not definite; the distinction between what a particular disabled person can and cannot do is uncertain. This means that most physically disabled persons have a marginal status between the physically normal and the physically helpless.

In this respect, the position of the disabled person is similar to that of the adolescent who has a similar marginal position between the freedom and privileges of the adult in our culture and the restrictions and limitations of the child. We should expect, therefore, to find many points of similarity in the behavior of adolescents and physically disabled persons. Indeed, we find this to be the case. Marginal status involves conflict and uncertainty in both cases. The disabled applicant for a job cannot know in advance whether he will be accepted for his "normal" attributes and admitted to the privileges and prerogatives of a self-respecting wage earner or whether he will be rejected and forced into the less privileged and satisfying position of an inferior person. The same is true of the adolescent. In a particular case, the adolescent may be accepted as a man or he may be forced to assume the role of a child.

Uncertainty of status for the disabled person obtains over a wide range of social interactions in addition to that of employment. The blind, the ill, the deaf, the crippled can never be sure what the attitude of a new acquaintance will be, whether it will be rejective or accepting, until the contact has been made. This is exactly the position of the adolescent, the light-skinned Negro, the second generation immigrant, the socially mobile person and the woman who has entered a predominantly masculine occupation.

Very often the dual requirements of such overlapping minority and majority positions lead to conflicting behavior tendencies. For example, in his role as a child, the appropriate behavior for an adolescent may be lively activity and expressiveness; in his role as an adult, however, he may be expected to exhibit sedentary behavior and self-control. Such different behaviors cannot be carried out simultaneously. While such overlapping situations persist, conflict with resulting inhibition or vacillation of behavior and with heightened tension and emotionality is inevitable. Such marginal positions cannot usually be maintained for long periods of time and the person who is caught in such a conflict will usually make an effort to escape into one or the other of the overlapping situations. Hence, the frequent clannishness of many first generation immigrants and the one-hundred-per-cent Americanism and rejection of all old country standards of second generation immigrants. Similarly, there is the crude exaggeration of upper-class symbols by the nouveau riche and the intolerant rejection of upper-class mores by "unsuccessful" mobile persons. The exaggerated masculinity and femininity of some adolescent-aged children appears to be a similar reaction.

These same adjustment mechanisms are exhibited by the physically disabled. Some reject their disabled status with extreme vigorousness, and escape into the status of a normal person by deprecating their disabilities, by refusing any identification with similarly disabled persons and sometimes by failing to consciously recognize the existence of an obvious defect. This is the case with many hard-of-hearing persons who refuse to wear hearing aids or even to admit that they have hearing difficulties, and of lame persons who punish themselves unmercifully by participating in physical activities entirely beyond their capacities. On the other hand there are disabled persons who retreat into their disabled status, even exaggerating the extent of their disabilities and refusing to admit the possibility of normal behavior. The disabled "realist" who attempts to accommodate himself to the actuality of his marginal social-psychological situation frequently finds himself in an impossible situation where planning and consistent behavior are impossible. His situation is not unlike that of the light-skinned colored individual who must make his choice between accepting himself as a Negro or entering the social-psychological world of the white. He cannot live in accordance with the "realities" of the situation, behaving as a Negro when the external situation so dictates and as a white when the situation requires it. This is usually impossible for the physically disabled person also.

New Situations

An attribute of the marginal social position of many disabled people is the relative frequency with which they have to cope with unknown, new psychological situations. A new psychological situation is one in which the sequence of activities necessary to achieve a particular end is unknown. This is usually the case, for example, for a person in a dark room or in a new community; he may know what he wants to accomplish but he does not know the required directions. The marginal person lives along a boundary; he knows something about the privileged situation beyond, but he can only partially enter it; he does not know the situation completely. Thus, the adolescent boy knows something about how men behave but there are large and important areas where he can know only the goals of behavior in a very general way and very little about the means. The same is true of the socially mobile person who wants to achieve the privileged satisfactions of the upper-class person. In a new psychological situation, one inevitably makes errors, often socially or physically painful errors; his behavior is inconsistent and vacillating; he is in conflict. When the new situation involves central needs, the errors, the vacillation, and the conflict can be very severe.

Physically disabled people inevitably live on a social-psychological frontier where some of the chief satisfactions of life are to be found in the unknown region beyond the frontier. Thus the man with an artificial leg is under pressure to try to ride a bicycle in order to achieve the approval of his girl friend. The man with a heart impairment can never be sure that a particular activity is within his capacity. The deaf person may or may not be able to read the lips of the prospective employer whom he is interviewing. Physically normal persons on the other hand have, by the time of adulthood, explored much more of the world which confronts them. It is, in fact, difficult to place a physically normal adult in a new psychological situation. However, for the blind man every time he ventures from his house he is confronted with such new situations. For the deaf or hard-of-hearing man every social gathering is a new psychological situation. For the cripple the daily round of activities inevitably presents him with a series of new situations.

Mental and Social Hygiene

Although the underprivileged minority status of the physically disabled person and the marginal and new psychological situations which confront him do not by any means fully define his psychological position, they do describe a very important aspect of it. We may consider, therefore, the implications of these aspects of his situation for the mental and social hygiene of physical disability. Basically, the problem is one of reducing minority status, marginality and psychological newness. We may consider each of these in turn.

Underprivileged Status

We have pointed out that the underprivileged status of the physically disabled person is due, on the one hand, to his own physical defects and, on the other hand, to the negative attitudes of the normal majority with whom he must live.

The relative ineffectiveness of the physically disabled person arising from his physical deficiencies is a fact of his situation which he must face. No amount of optimistic talk can remove the fact that, other things being equal, a physically disabled person is relatively ineffective in a social world devised for physically normal persons. Much has been written about the productivity of physically disabled persons when placed in the right job, and of the advantages provided by modern mass production industry in adapting men with limited and specialized abilities to specialized production processes. It is true, for example, that a man with defective legs may be able to operate a sewing machine just as well as a man with normal legs. Nevertheless, it is also true that such a man is relatively inflexible; he could not, for example, shift to the operating of two automatic machines, if such were developed, moving back and forth between them. In an emergency such as a fire, such a man might be a distinct hazard to others. Furthermore, he would usually require special arrangements of machines and of means of egress and exit. One cannot expect industry whose function is production for profit to assume such a present or potential liability if other workers who do not present this liability are available. This means that if the disabled person is to be the economic equal of his nondisabled competitors he must excel them in some productive respect. If he is only the equal of his physically normal competitor, he will justifiably lose out. It is true that there are a few occupations in which such physical deviants as dwarfs and deaf men actually have an advantage over physically normal persons; however, these cases are so infrequent as to be of little social consequence. One advantage of physically disabled workers which has been noted by some employers is a greater reliability, a greater docility, and higher motivation than physically normal employees. This, when it occurs, appears to be a product of the insecurity and anxiety which these people experience and it hardly appears to be a socially desirable form of exploitation.

One proposal for spreading the burden of the handicapped is that of requiring all industries and professions to include within their staffs their proportional share of the physically disabled. Such a policy would, in effect, guarantee a man the right to work up to the limits of his capacity even though he be physically handicapped. This might, by making it unnecessary for him to depend upon the good will of a particular employer and by providing him with specified social rights, reduce his underprivileged position. Such a policy would not be unlike the war-time fair employment practices legislation and, indeed, it might be included in such an enactment.

Another route for reduction of underprivileged status would seem to be self-employment. Here the disabled person carries the burden, real and potential, of his productive handicaps. In such a case, he escapes in some degree from the socially inferior position of being dependent upon the good will of another or of being excluded from employment. It is true that self-employment opportunities usually involve less specialized activities than are available in large industry; nonetheless the psychological advantages to self-employment would appear to be very great. As a matter of fact, some advantages of specialization can be secured in industries where only disabled persons are used as employees. There is a rather widespread opposition to such "segregation," but the basis for this opposition is not clear. From the social psychological viewpoint, industrial groupings of disabled persons would appear to have many advantages through allowing the physically disabled to escape from their dependent, underprivileged position by assuming some of the burdens of their social ineffectiveness.

The minority status of the physically disabled which is due to the negative attitudes of the physically normal majority constitutes an entirely different problem. It would seem to be in almost all respects similar to the problem of racial and religious underprivileged minorities, although it may well be that the source of the negative attitude toward the physically disabled is even deeper and less rational. We cannot go into the problems of education, clinical psychology, propaganda, learning, and politics which are involved here. When and as these problems are solved with respect to these underprivileged minorities, the solutions may be applied to the physically handicapped also.

One point in this connection which may have particular applicability to the physically disabled minority concerns the relative advantages and disadvantages of urban as opposed to village life. There are some indications from studies of social perception that judgments of casual acquaintances are based upon surface indications, such as physical appearance and dress, but that with further acquaintance perception comes to disregard such surface indications and to be determined by personality characteristics. This means that an individual who is a physical deviant encounters upon first acquaintance only attitudes which relate to physical disability. Amongst his intimate associates, however, he will be judged upon the basis of his behavior independent of his physical defects. For this reason it is probably true that the physically disabled person in an urban area who necessarily has to come in contact with large numbers of strangers and casual acquaintances must cope with more stereotyped behavior relating to his handicap than the similarly disabled person who lives in a community where he is known on deeper levels to practically all members of the community. At any rate, this would appear to be a matter worthy of investigation.

A less basically theoretical, but nonetheless important, factor relevant to the matter of community size concerns ease of locomotion. An important source of frustrations for many disabled persons lies in the difficulty of locomotion. Any arrangements which decrease the difficulties with which he is able to get from place to place are usually extremely freeing to him. Large cities where the geography is complicated, the distances great, and where transportation involves subways, busses, street-cars, transfers, steps, crowds, and wide streets with heavy traffic are bound to present great difficulties to many kinds of disabled people. On the other hand, small towns where all of these characteristics are likely to be almost totally absent present correspondingly favorable conditions of life.

Marginal and New Situations

The reduction of marginality and newness appears to be a more hopeful possibility in the mental and social hygiene of disabled people than the reduction of their underprivileged minority status. However, it is a much less general problem since the degree of marginality varies so strikingly with the nature of the physical defect. Defects which are not obvious such as deafness, cardiac defects, and tuberculosis, involve a much greater degree of marginality than those which are immediately apparent. Furthermore, defects which are stabilized involve less marginality than those which continually fluctuate in their severity. Nevertheless, a number of general points may be made.

In the case of invisible injuries certain visible signs may be used to define the person's condition for others, for example, a hearing aid, a white cane, etc. It is much more important, however, to help the disabled person to define the limits of his world of free actions; that is, to make a clear dividing line between the activities which are open to him and those which are closed. Here counseling and psychotherapy can be a great benefit. In the first place, there is the problem of getting the disabled to give up impossible hopes; under the pressure of very central needs, disabled persons are prone to cling to unrealistic behavioral aspirations long after these have become impossible. Procedures by means of which the disabled person is enabled to accept the fact that the world in which he lives presents serious restrictions and frustrations is the first step. After this, the problem becomes one of defining with as much exactitude as possible the limits of freedom which the particular person enjoys. This must be done with respect to all areas: vocational, physical, social, intellectual, etc. The disabled person must know what he is up against. This involves knowing the areas in which opportunities lie as well as those from which he is excluded. The problem of getting a disabled person to accept his disabilities and live within his limitations is by no means an easy one. It does not mean that an attitude of resignation and acceptance of meager goals is necessary. This should be avoided by all means. For almost every disabled person, there are richly satisfying goal hierarchies which he can pursue and within which he can achieve great and lasting satisfactions.

Some aspects of the social-psychological situation of physically handicapped persons in American culture are clear. Their underprivileged and marginal position, with consequent frustration and conflict, make the incidence of maladjustment understandable. Their isolation, and the fact that their underprivileged position is rooted in their own inferiority as well as in the prejudice of others, make frequent intrapunitive and withdrawing adjustments understandable, also. Amelioration of the social-psychological position of the physically disabled appears possible in some degree by providing legal safeguards to employment and to suitable education. However, such provisions cannot remove all the restrictions upon the physically deviant in a world constructed for the physically normal. The ultimate adjustment must involve changes in the value systems of the physically disabled person.

REFERENCES

1. The terms physique, physical disability, and physical deviation are here used to refer to the peripheral physique; we are not concerned with the central mechanism of behavior. We are concerned, rather, with the effects of physical defects which limit freedom of physical and social movement; for example, with the effects of blindness, deafness, crippling, cardiac impairment, tuberculosis, cosmetic defect, etc., upon behavior. We are not concerned with the problem of constitutional type or with psychosomatic problems.
2. R. G. Barker, Beatrice A. Wright, and Mollie R. Gonick, *Adjustment to Physical Handicap and Illness* (New York: Social Science Research Council, 1946), Bulletin 55.

Social Changes, Minorities, and the Mentally Retarded

Louis H. Orzack

In a democratic society, the individual has the freedom to move where he wishes, to marry as he desires, to work at whatever occupation he selects, to worship when and where he prefers, to vote as he believes, to become educated to his capacity, and to live where he wills. These are common privileges that reflect our historic concern for the individual.

Yet, a large number of Americans are prevented by the force of prejudice and by the stigma that has enveloped them from the enjoyment of these specific freedoms. Their role in society has been a confining one, in that restrictions block their full participation in the many activities that other citizens take for granted.

The purpose of this brief article is to examine the changing place in American society of the mentally retarded and of minority groups in American society. Its aim is to examine, with the help of formal knowledge derived from the behavioral and social science of sociol-

Source: *Mental Retardation,* 7:5 (October 1969), pp. 2–6, a publication of the American Association of Mental Deficiency. Reprinted by permission from *Mental Retardation.*

ogy, the position of the mentally retarded, and to attempt both to explain the complex cultural and societal origins of that position and to speculate about the possible position of these mentally retarded in the future. References to other minorities will also be made.

The mentally retarded may be thought of as a minority group, much like a religious or racial minority. Wirth's criteria for a minority group include (1) treatment of physical or cultural characteristics as distinctive, (2) consequent differential and unequal treatment, (3) consideration of oneself as the object of collective discrimination, and (4) the presence of a corresponding dominant group with higher social status and greater privileges. Loss of esteem, hatred, violence, isolation, spatial segregation, restricted educational and occupational opportunities, insecurity, limited property rights, loss of rights to vote and hold public office, lack of access to technology, and the sharing of an attenuated culture, are among the manifestations of minority status that seem applicable to the retarded.[1]

In certain respects, however, the retarded and groups usually conceived to be minorities may be quite different. Wirth's third criterion, consideration of oneself as the object of collective discrimination, gives pause to the treatment of the retarded as a minority. Edgerton reports for the mildly retarded he studied that "one of the major concerns of the released retardate is the avoidance of any public association with other retardates. This kind of association could be highly discrediting." Rejection of the stigma of retardation through attempts to deny one's experience at an institution, to pass in the society of normals, and to avoid the label of retardation, plus reliance on benefactors who provide both help and a shield, are common.[2,3]

Structural substitutes for self-awareness have had to develop. Spokesmen and caretakers drawn from among parents, helping professionals and employees of hospitals, asylums, schools, and clinics, have often spoken for and about the retarded and some indeed have joined in pressure groups to attack discrimination against the retarded.[4]

Until recent years, at least, the retarded did not have any articulate spokesmen or interest groups who were concerned about their place in society. Even now, their cause is backed mainly by those involved by family ties and has not been absorbed into the ideology of any of the politically prominent reform and change oriented segments of society.

Historically speaking, society did make some provision for at least some of the retarded, through the establishment of institutions where they could be confined. These institutions existed to protect the retarded from the ravages, the wear and tear of a highly competitive society, and in a sense, to withdraw from society, to place within an asylum, those who could not otherwise be cared for or who were rejected by society.

The drive for achieved success, the mobility of our population, the decline in size and in significance of the family, the rise of the city, and of the factory, office and school, were all accompanied by the belief that the individual was on his own. The network of attachments that individuals had with other persons became more extensive. Any person now met in his adult lifetime a great many strangers who oftentimes evaluated and judged him, and made decisions important for his life and his career, on the basis of little information. Teachers, government officials, policemen, selective service personnel, gas station attendants, bus drivers, movie ushers, appliance salesmen, office receptionists, and a host of others, react in their various jobs and other roles on the basis of words and glances and the examination of the written record of past performance.

Physical labor came to be less of an important necessity for work, to be replaced by the manipulation of others through language and the exchange and transfer of papers and other written records. With this has come the rise of impersonality as a necessary standard way of reacting to other people. Rules, procedures, identification cards, application forms, eligibilities, credit and other applications, welfare and social security records, are the common currency of daily life in community, in industry, and in government.

These features of social relationships are fundamental to our understanding of the opportunities or lack of opportunities for the mentally retarded. For, in a fundamental sense, the role of the retarded is a social role that is based on the evaluations and attitudes of others and of the retarded themselves. To understand that role, one must accept the premise that social and cultural conditions fully define that role just as they determine and condition the role of other persons and groups.

Our social system is a system of institutions, a word used here in the special technical sense of sociology. This means that it is made up of sets or systems of interrelated roles that are accompanied by values, beliefs, and attitudes. Each person at birth is placed by society in selected roles. He is defined as an infant, a son or daughter, a member of a family, a resident of a neighborhood, of a city or town, of a state. He is nurtured, protected, challenged, and advanced, so that in time he is introduced to the idea that other social roles are open to him. He learns of the school, of the larger community around his neighborhood, of religious organizations, of means of entertainment, and of leisure and ultimately of the world of work. He may be encouraged to make friends and to enter into exchange relationships in the business world, as customer and as job seeker or job holder.

In this evolving world of greater complexity, impersonality, and achievement, doors to many roles increasingly come to be opened or shut not merely by the individual himself, but by individuals who serve as gatekeepers. Our world is composed of organizations. It is both challenging and perilous, for the speed or slowness with which people advance is determined in large measure by persons other than themselves. In one sense, all the individual can do is to offer himself before those doors that previous door openings permit him to confront.

This is clearly a society of uneven opportunity with restrictions and limitations of access for all within it. In this kind of world, the retarded comes to be judged as a total person—and to be judged wanting. But, why is that judgment made?

One answer to this is that the gatekeepers in our society, those who control or at least influence the pace and direction of our movement into roles in different institutions, necessarily make judgments based on partial knowledge of people. This is vital for the effective operation of achievement-based institutions. The information on an application blank, the scores on an achievement test, the entries in a selective service form, the personal items provided in a civil service Form 57, are both achievement oriented and highly selected. The forms themselves obviously *exclude* much information about individuals that may be important and significant to the individuals but will be of no importance and no significance to the organization itself. The readers of such forms make decisions based on the limited data they provide.

Another answer to the question as to why the negative judgment about the retarded is made is that this is a society oriented generally toward achievement and oriented specifically to certain types of achievements. Prominence may be attained by performance in intellectual, artistic, physical, political, or occupational endeavors.

Such narrowly functional judgments are also affected by the evaluations that are part of our general culture. The mentally retarded are not the cultural heroes of our generation or of past generations; nor are they a group of individuals who are highly visible as a group to society. The mentally retarded include many individuals who look, act, and think in patterns that fall within the range of variations that most people consider to be normal. The element of high visibility that has been said to differentiate Negroes or blacks, for example, from whites, is certainly not striking for very many of the retarded. Historically, our culture does not contain the set of deeply ingrained, widely shared, and intensely felt prejudices toward the retarded as are exhibited toward minority group members.

Yet, discrimination against both exists. A close protectiveness characterized the response of families and neighbors to the presence of the retarded. The mentally retarded person would be kept at home and shielded from outsiders. The object of fun and ridicule, he would find that the family gathered around, so to speak, and withdrew him from those situations that were threatening. The alternative pattern sanctioned for the nonretarded was one of exposure and of challenge. Rebuffed, the normal individual would be thrown back into competition by his family and exposed to trials and tribulation of achievement. In contrast, the retarded individual would be kept away by those individuals who sought to protect him from those opportunities in which he could test himself for the roles that society increasingly has considered important.

Discrimination against the retarded may well have often unified the family in self-protection and in the effort to reduce shame felt because a youngster was "peculiar." The limitations of a family member could and did, however, have consequences often unfavorable for family stability, for the experiencing of retardation in a group member is felt by all the others in the family. Instability in role, when it occurred, could affect everyone in the social unit.

Discrimination against minority group members could infringe on all because of color, but would in contrast initially and uniquely hit the father with the most strategically damaging consequences. The breadwinning role component of the father who is black is drastically weakened, he tends to withdraw, and often leaves and abandons the family. The child survives but often without a good balance of role models and mentors. The structure may survive but with a female head and with tenuous role ties.[5]

The psychological cost of continued rejection was and is, of course, a high cost, felt not only by the individual but also felt by his family. The pressure was and is tremendous, and obviously has at times taken the most cruel forms of overt prejudice and discrimination that ridicule, taunting, and rebuff embody. The categorical judgment that an individual is defective, deficient, subnormal, or more simply, different, and thus undesirable and unworthy, is horrendous.

Given this pattern, what have been the effects? What were and are the decisions made in society about the roles of the socially handicapped? A major feature of the response of society to the prejudice and discrimination with the retarded was the emergence of the specialized hospitals, schools, colonies, and treatment centers, and special education programs. These were sanctioned by the humanitarian element in American culture, but their evolution must also be understood in terms of the kinds and types of financial and professional resources that have been allocated to them. Such allocations are affected by social priorities. One of those priorities meant that programs for the retarded were geographically and functionally isolated. The basis for making decisions about care, treatment, custody, and rehabilitation moved into a different and a difficult calculus. This calculus reflected the stress on achievement and reward. With isolated locations, residential institutions could manage more or less well when their programs were primarily along lines of residual treatment and care. In time, these centers suffered because of their isolation and because of their lack of prominence in general public thinking. Any defects in programming would not readily be known to the general public. Shortages and inadequacies of resources, improprieties in treatment and in care, were not marked by public outcry. The public, indeed, turned its energies to other, more appealing, or more intriguing concerns, such as higher and ever higher education, travel, social security and social welfare, occupational advancement, and personal health.[6]

For minority group individuals, enforced withdrawal to isolated institutions has not been a common mode. Blacks have however been permitted to drop out from school and to remain isolated from the general community. Segregated residential ghettoes in the North have inadequate housing, schools, health services, and recreational opportunities, and few high prestige or well-paying jobs available to them; a more dispersed residential distribution but even less adequate schools and jobs have been the pattern in the South.[7, 8]

For the retarded, environmental restrictions, limitations on movement of the person, and unusual or deviant opportunities in the family, in the neighborhood and the school for language learning shape the environment as experienced, limit his range, and reduce the individual's confidence in his own ability to control the environment.[9]

What arouses public attention? Why the current dramatic interest in the retarded? Why have hopelessness and despair been joined by optimism and energy? Have there been changes in American culture, changes in American institutions?

First, of course, one must take account of the amassing of effort represented in the formation of the National Association for Retarded Children, Inc. and the manifold activities that its formation has permitted. This clearly includes its service as an effective agency of pressure for improvement and extension of services for the retarded. Here also the interest of the late President Kennedy is also vital.

Such efforts, in combination with the newer programs of the United States government, as well as state and local government, have struck at the fatalistic assumptions of apathy, neglect, disinterest, despair, and shame. Definitions of what can be done for and with the retarded have changed in ways that would have only been viewed as remarkable and visionary but a generation ago.

Second, however, it must be said that these current efforts toward amelioration of the previous patterns of negativism and neglect are not altogether novel or innovating. Great optimism for the retarded existed in the era of Jacksonian reform to be replaced by more modest and individualized claims in more recent times.[10] As short a time ago as 1933, the distinguished American sociologist, Dr. Howard W. Odum[11] of the University of North Carolina, serving as a member of the President's Research Committee on Social Trends, could write that "present ideals and trends" for the "mentally handicapped" include "individual treatment, nonrestraint and occupational therapy," "a state program of colony or cottage plan with therapeutic occupation," "purpose curative as far as possible" in contrast with "custody (as) the sole purpose of institutions," "scientific attitude and treatment of the mental defective," "search for cause and effect by public institutions and research through clinics and other means," "graded division in colony system," "special vocational training or occupational therapy for defectives," "discovery through routine examination, reports, state censuses, etc.," and "tendency toward scientific process of home finding placement and supervision." Debate, Odum observed, concerning the "relative value and function of the institution versus the home" was "continual" in the last decades before 1900.

These were of course described then as ideals still to be realized. These ideals are still in process of realization. What this thirty-five year old formulation shows is that a process of interaction between cultural ideals, cultural patterns, and organizational realities continues. Indeed, that accommodation is a marked feature and characteristic of American society. As one sociologist states it, ". . . the United States constitutes something close to a crucial experiment as to the consequences of sociocultural diversity in modern mass society."[12]

Williams notes also that our system is "relatively favorable to social change," that our culture is marked by an "orientation away from traditionalism and toward adaptability and ingenuity in meeting new situations."

In this sense, then, one may say that the newer and developing views of treatment, rehabilitation, and community programs for the mentally retarded fall well within the main stream of American culture and structure. What does seem to be new is rather the added attention that the retarded are receiving from powerful agencies, some recently developed, of social change and social welfare. Formerly, a largely neglected group, of concern primarily to parents or relatives and to institution personnel, and to small numbers of scientists, the retarded have come more into the view of the community at large. The mark of this is public attention and concern shown in part by the increase in budgets for public and private agencies, the development of university programs for research, and for education and training of specialists whose work impinges on the retarded, and the effort that is being made for the retarded to break down discriminatory barriers that restrict or prevent entry of numbers of the retarded into a number of socially sanctioned roles.

This effort covers the gamut of American society. Provision of public educational facilities is a case in point. Special classes and the opportunity, where appropriate, to move from special classes back into the regular school track show this. Maintenance of the retarded in the community or the return to the community through halfway houses and day care centers are also part of the pattern. The concern with the development of newer educational techniques especially designed for the retarded must also be mentioned. Job training programs, and the broader use of the retarded in the world of work, may show as well how provision for the retarded can effectively move toward removal of the stigma associated with the older term of "deficiency."

One knows that there are limits to the participation of the retarded in the spectrum of roles available to our citizens. However, definitions of limits may and do change rapidly, as can be seen with the shifts in the freedoms enjoyed in our society by women, by religious minorities, by nationality and race groupings, and by the old. Furthermore, it is indeed highly questionable as to whether any categorical limits should be applied universally to members of as variegated a group as "mentally retarded." Mental capabilities, social adjustment potentials, and personal aspirations need be assessed as carefully and as tolerantly for this group as for any other group that has been in the shadows of prejudice and discrimination. Equal opportunity to advance to the limits set by capabilities and by preferences can appropriately be made available to the retarded.

These efforts toward social and cultural change that impinge on the role of the retarded require special attention and a vigorous thrust. This results, it seems, because the theme of equal opportunity is obviously but one strand in the American system. Other strands that complicate the process include the strong emphasis on achievement through personal effort, competitiveness for grades in the school system and for promotions and greater salary, and other benefits in the world of work, and the pervasive preoccupation with idealized standards of beauty and personal appearance. On the other hand, antipathy toward discrimination that is categorical touches on the humanitarian identification with the underdog that has supported and sanctioned many recent improvements in the social position of depressed groups.

The social system that functions to bring rewards of income and prestige to some, that opens doors to some through achievement and group membership, also holds back its rewards and throws up barriers to some. While Dr. Martin Luther King could call for freedom for blacks, the cry for the retarded is for their humanity. "Free at last" may be echoed by "humanity at last" but for each the promised land remains in the distance and appears to move further away as one approaches it.

Discrimination in schools and in jobs affects the retarded and the minority group member. Stigmatization in the arena of personal relationships exists for each. Cultural definitions that the individual is inadequate, that he does not fit into expectations, affect the black and the retarded.

Our imperfect world of complex organizations, of segmented roles, patterns careers for individuals and manipulates the recognition they are given and the rewards they receive. The systems operate in part to convert minority group membership into retardation, through inadequate schooling, overcrowding, understaffing, and antiquity of school plants.

Rescue efforts exist but are inadequate. In Massachusetts, for example, the recent state-wide survey of mental retardation facilities and resources shows the Boston areas of Roxbury where Negro or black concentrations exist to be among the high need sections in the state. It takes no subtlety of argument to support the belief that inadequate allotments of city, state and federal aid to schools, recreation agencies, playgrounds, workshops, clinics, hospitals, and other community facilities help generate retardation or what passes for it.

Nor is it surprising to learn that special education and child guidance or mental health programs sometimes help the inadequate teacher through separation of anyone who is a learning challenge from the classroom.

The mentally retarded have often been stigmatized through socially enforced patterns of physical exclusion from the social roles that exist in rich supply in our society. Although not seemingly a general target for hostility or aggression, the retarded have been a neglected group; as a result, treatment and care have been minimally supported. Teachers, doctors, special educators, social workers, rehabilitation counselors, psychologists, nurses, and others often find more glamorous, exciting, rewarding, and prestigious careers elsewhere, with retardation services perhaps just a stopping point. For some, work with the handicapped is depressing, quickly therefore to be left behind. A recent effort, undertaken by the writer, to recruit college students anxious for summer employment and manifestly eager to volunteer for service in community projects especially in urban ghetto areas resulted in but one student of a group of thirty-five who expressed willingness to work as an orderly or attendant in a state school for the retarded. The salary was within the range of current compensation for summer jobs but the work itself was not considered either interesting or appealing.

Such patterns are likely to change, but only as persistent limitations of resources of personnel, facilities, and scientific knowledge in the medical and behavioral sciences can be overcome. As this happens, fuller participation by at least some of the mentally retarded in the varied social roles of the community at large can also be expected.

It is critical at this point in history that the discriminatory barriers to jobs, to education, to health and housing that block role access for minorities, black as well as others, be eliminated as they help create functional retardation for many. The resulting double stigma has lasting effects throughout the lifetimes of individuals and the disturbing histories of our cities. Multiplied efforts in ghetto areas by specialists in rehabilitation, special education, social welfare, health services, vocational training, employment, job counseling, and higher learning must now occur and are but a minimum response to the problems of the times with which we must all cope.

REFERENCES

1. Louis Wirth, "The Problem of Minority Groups," in Ralph Linton, ed., *The Science of Man in the World Crisis* (New York: Columbia University Press, 1945), p. 347.
2. Robert B. Edgerton, *The Cloak of Competence: Stigma in the Lives of the Mentally Retarded* (Berkeley: University of California Press, 1967).
3. Erving Goffman, *Stigma: Notes on the Management of Spoiled Identity* (Englewood Cliffs, N.J.: Prentice-Hall, 1963).
4. Louis H. Orzack, John T. Cassell, Benoit Charland, and Harry Halliday, *The Pursuit of Change: Experiences of a Parents' Association During a Five Year Development Period* (Bridgeport, Conn.: Kennedy Center, 1969).
5. Daniel P. Moynihan, *The Negro Family: The Case for National Action* (Washington: U.S. Department of Labor, Office of Policy Planning and Research, 1965).
6. Wolf Wolfensberger, "The Origin and Nature of Our Institutional Models," in Robert B. Kugel and Wolf Wolfensberger, eds., *Changing Patterns in Residential Services for the Mentally Retarded* (Washington: President's Committee on Mental Retardation, 1969).
7. Whitney M. Young, Jr., "Poverty, Intelligence and Life in the Inner City," *Mental Retardation,* 7 (April, 1969), pp. 24–29.
8. Helen Marie Lund and Melvin E. Kaufman, "The Matrifocal Family and Its Relationship to Mental Retardation," *Journal of Mental Subnormality,* 14, Pt. 2, 27 (December, 1968), pp. 80–83.
9. Lewis Anthony Dexter, *The Tyranny of Schooling: An Inquiry into the Problem of "Stupidity"* (New York: Basic Books, 1964).
10. Berenice M. Fisher, "Claims and Credibility: A Discussion of Occupational Identity and the Agent-Client Relationship," *Social Problems,* 16 (Spring, 1969), pp. 423–33.
11. Howard W. Odum, "Public Welfare Activities," in President's Research Committee on Social Trends, *Recent Social Trends in the United States* (New York: McGraw-Hill, 1933).
12. Robin Williams, *American Society* (New York: Knopf, 1960).

Clumsiness and Stupidity: An Analogy

Lewis Anthony Dexter

Even in our own society, those who are clumsy and awkward suffer many of the disadvantages of the stupid. Yet our society places far less emphasis on physical grace than some other societies do. One of the disadvantages which the clumsy and the stupid share is this: Other people are likely to regard clumsiness and/or stupidity as the most significant fact about the individual.

In many aspects of life, of course, stupidity is actually *un*important, just as clumsiness is unimportant in others. The tendency on the part of the average man to regard stupidity or clumsiness as very central facts arises out of his feeling that stupidity or clumsiness represent and demonstrate incompetence in a whole series of fields. But just as a stupid person can be a good waiter, a good cook, or a good nursemaid, so a clumsy person, inept perhaps as a dancer, may be superior in gentling nervous horses for bridling or in doing a workmanlike job with tools, or even in playing pick-up sticks.

The stupid and the clumsy resemble one another also in that their childhood is likely to involve, more often than is true of most people, bumping—literally or figuratively—against things they do not control and cannot understand. The picture they receive of themselves in relation to the world is of a place that bumps them harshly without much reason. To be sure, all children experience this to some degree, and, of course, stupid or clumsy children in any society would probably experience it more than normal children in that same society. But in our society, our emphasis upon normal performance, upon speed of performance, upon neatness of activity, makes such difficulties for clumsy or stupid children greater.

The similarity between the stupid and the clumsy is indicated by two terms which are applicable almost equally to either group: "slow" and "awkward."

Source: *The Tyranny of Schooling*, Chapter 7, pp. 121–32, copyright © 1964 by Basic Books, Inc., Publishers, New York, and the author.

Nevertheless in our society the weight of rejection pressed upon the stupid is probably much greater than that upon the clumsy, because we put so much emphasis upon academic intellect as a virtue. But there is enough sensitiveness about clumsiness so that the parallel will be obvious to many people. It therefore occurred to me that it might be interesting to see what would happen in a society which systematically placed the same emphasis upon avoiding clumsiness as this society (through schooling) puts upon avoiding stupidity.

Students of education will remember the insightful and penetrating discussion of *The Saber-Tooth Curriculum* by Abner Peddiwell.[1] Peddiwell described a society where once upon a time the major effort had been focused upon fighting saber-tooth tigers. Naturally, the educational system was organized to teach children to fight saber-tooths and to lend glory and honor unto successful saber-tooth fighters. Peddiwell traces what happened after saber-tooths ceased to be a serious menace. What happened was that fighting saber-tooths continued to be the central emphasis of the classical curriculum in that society, just as learning Latin and logic was until recently the core of education in our society. And when progressive education, learning by doing, became popular in Peddiwell's Saber-Tooth Society, the children were trained on a few mangy old saber-tooths who had been captured in a desert.

Over the mountains from Saber-Tooth Society I, there was another society which, in the early days, was also greatly plagued by saber-tooths. In the course of time, as the Great Ice Sheet receded, saber-tooth tigers disappeared also, and the countryside actually became tropical. Nevertheless, the educational system in Saber-Tooth II had been set up to deal with the saber-tooths and with an icy countryside; and so it remained.

But, in Saber-Tooth II, the educational system, (1) instead of being developed by priests as in Saber-Tooth I, was developed by hunters *and their wives*; and (2) saber-tooth hunters could marry no one except *retired temple dancers*. Accordingly, in Saber-Tooth II, the emphasis in educational training from the very earliest days was on the movements used in hunting the saber-tooth. There was a strict and graceful pattern which every child was supposed to learn. As the saber-tooth disappeared, the descendants of the old hunters and their wives became dissatisfied with the rather simple movements of attack and evasion which originally constituted the hunt for the saber-tooth. This primitive technique, they said, was all right in its way, but an advanced society, faced with new problems and new needs, should have a more elaborate ritual training for its youngsters. Teachers in Saber-Tooth II therefore concentrated on the *generalizable* skills underlying the movements of their hunting ancestors. "Transfer of training" became their motto. To catch the great cats, their predecessors had of course of necessity to be able to move quickly and gracefully; to assure silence in stalking the tigers to their forest lairs, every moment had to be controlled; to set traps which would deceive the shrewd beasts and hold them safely demanded great dexterity—and the temple dancers, the wives of the hunter-teachers, had introduced into the educational system pretty little dances of challenge and of triumph.

But the old hunters would have probably fainted with astonishment could they have risen from their graves and seen the complex grace with which advanced students in Saber-Tooth II portrayed the movements designed to stalk and kill the wary tiger. And whether the old hunters could ever have brought themselves to understand the Ph.D. degrees which were given in Saber-Tooth II's great universities is uncertain. For example, in 1935, a Ph.D. magna cum laude was granted to a young woman for ritual skill in dancing out the correct movements to use when meeting a six-legged saber-tooth tiger on the top of a modern skyscraper, and having no instruments of hunting except a penknife.

Nevertheless, however the old hunters might have felt about it, every adolescent on completing high school probably knew more about hunting the saber-tooth—more, that is, about the theory of the muscular movements involved in hunting the saber-tooth—than any old hunter ever dreamed of. And, as the Plato of Saber-Tooth II stressed repeatedly, in a world in which "every little movement has a meaning all its own," the purpose of learning to hunt saber-tooths is *not* to hunt saber-tooths, but rather to learn the appropriate essential movements for hunting saber-tooths. In recent years, the great saber-tooth educational system has proliferated and developed all sorts of variations; the spaceshoot scientists of the Saber-Tooth II system are particularly eager to have their children well educated, and at one of the suburban public schools crowded with the children of such scientists, there is great pride because the seventh-graders have developed a rhythm for attacking space whales, borrowed from the saber-tooth tiger hunt. (A recent issue of *Movement*, the most establishment-minded of the mass magazines in the society, explains how any school system can, with a little inspiration, encourage its children in such skills.)

About twenty years ago, as a result of the wartime prosperity which came to neutral Saber-Tooth II, a remarkable growth in true democracy took place. Formerly, education had been pretty much reserved to a small upper-class group and to a few especially talented or fortunate individuals. But by 1947, it was required that every child in Saber-Tooth II complete high school; and not long afterwards one-fourth of all high school graduates actually entered the university.

In consequence, there was a great change in the attitude of clerks, plumbers, street cleaners, waiters, and other such tradesmen. Formerly, they had been content to do a job (Frances Trollope who visited Saber-Tooth II in the 1830s after her stay in Cincinnati, speaks with genuine praise of the efficiency of Saber-Tooth II tradesmen and servants). But the younger generation of tradesmen and servants have learned to do their jobs in an educated way; that means, for instance, that the garbage collectors in Saber-Tooth II spend a great deal of effort in using the appropriate ritual movement from the Saber-Tooth Hunt, as generalized in the latest educational code, when they pick up trash cans. And it is most inspiring to see tailors sewing on a button or plumbers fixing a tap with the appropriate educated movement.

For the last several years Saber-Tooth II has devoted a great deal of emphasis to foreign aid programs. It has stressed that Saber-Tooth II's successful neutrality during World War II was a direct consequence of the graceful Saber-Tooth II educational system, for it taught her rulers then (and now) how to move aright, as compared with clumsy Europeans and Americans.

Much of this foreign aid program has consisted of explaining to foreigners the benefits of the Saber-Tooth II system of educational movement. One unfortunate episode, however, nearly led to a breaking of diplomatic relations between Saber-Tooth II and Pakistan. A Pakistani official discovered a few thousand saber-tooth tigers in the mountains of this country; since these constitute an actual danger to villagers, he arranged with a delegation of Saber-Tooth II educators to join with some visiting British sportsmen in hunting the beasts. Oddly enough, when the hunt actually took place, the British sportsmen did all the killing; and Saber-Tooth II cut off its foreign aid program to Pakistan when Pakistanis laughed at the explanation that Saber-Tooth education is in any case intellectual and spiritual, rather than practical.

But just as there are stupid people in our society who clutter up the educational system, so in the educational system of Saber-Tooth II, there are people who simply cannot learn. In our society we use terms like "morons" or "dummies" for the people who can't learn; and we notice their "low intelligence quotient (IQ)." In Saber-Tooth II, the equivalent phrases are "gracelesses" and "gawkies," and their psychologists ordinarily use a "GQ" which actually means "Grace Quotient," but which is generally thought to mean "Gawkiness Quotient." (A good deal of effort has been devoted by Saber-Tooth II students of Freud to demonstrating that inherent gawkiness, so-called, is generally due to some kind of compulsion neurosis.)

However, under the famous legal rule which bars persons who are too graceless from inheriting certain types of property, gawkiness is defined in the country's legal system as "inherent lack of grace," and the pathological point of gawkiness is said to be reached when a person is unable to differentiate several different muscular movements of the eyelid. In the old days, gawkies used to be put into some menial trade. A boy then could be a good enough waiter or agricultural laborer, a girl a good enough servant or cook, gawky or not. But now that democracy has entered education and that the educational system has come to be influenced by modern psychologists who emphasize its general values, it is expected that everyone should be graceful.

A most interesting symposium occurred three or four years ago when a group of Harvard professors met with a group of Saber-Tooth U. faculty members to discuss: "High School Graduates and Their Future." The Harvard professors, repeatedly, wailed: "What can we do about all these stupid people flooding out of high school?" While the Saber-Tooth savants complained: "Our schools turn out only gawkies."

Special classes and remedial institutions have accordingly been established on a rather large scale for gawkies and clumsies. In consequence, many a country lad and lass, who a century ago would hardly have known if he or she were clumsy or no, lives a life of quiet humiliation and of fear of being sent off to the "clumsy hatch," as these institutions are called.

It should be pointed out that an inordinately high degree of grace is necessary for success in the professions and business in Saber-Tooth II. For instance, their system of writing demands of the use of very fragile brushes; mid-hand muscles must be moved while fingers are completely relaxed. It is argued that this is exactly the kind of skill necessary, under certain circumstances, in approaching a saber-tooth quietly from the rear and stabbing him in the back. And business transactions are confirmed by slight movements of scalp muscles, almost unobservable to Europeans. Now, the school system of course teaches such writing—and advanced commercial courses place a great deal of emphasis on the appropriate movements of the scalp.

And in sheer matters of good manners, gawkies constantly offend too. For instance, the appropriate greeting from a college freshman to a professor involves a rather elaborate sequence of ear-wiggling and nose-twitching, which gawkies never do master properly. Accordingly, every well-trained Saber-Tooth IIian finds it upsetting to have a gawky around him, in a situation where a superior should be greeted properly.

And so, more and more, a high or at least normal grace quotient is being required for employment. The landlords of the big skyscrapers in Saber-Tooth II, for instance, recently decided to require a normal Grace Quotient for all cleaning women in their employ. A distinguished Saber-Toothian psychologist, Seever O. J. Nedyk, showed that by standard indices of cleanliness, buildings cleaned by women with a Grace Quotient 5 points or more below normal were just as clean as those cleaned by women with a normal or superior Grace Quotient. Her findings were presented to the National Association on Clumsiness; but in the upshot the President of that Association felt compelled to insist that Nedyk's findings were her own because they created so much shock and excitement.

REFERENCE

1. Harold Benjamin [pseud.], *The Saber-Tooth Curriculum* (New York: McGraw-Hill, 1939).

Status, Ideology, and Adaptation to Stigmatized Illness: A Study of Leprosy

Zachary Gussow
and George S. Tracy

The social and psychological components of stigma have been the subject of a series of recent essays by Erving Goffman, beginning with his interest in "impression management."[1] By "impression management" he means the efforts made by people to create desired images about themselves in the face of the inescapable fact that whether a person wishes or not, his actions yield expressions about himself. Impression management is a way to "control the conduct of others, especially their responsive treatment" by controlling what they see and hear.[2] In a later work, Goffman focuses on persons characterized by stigma, or "undesired differentness," of which he identifies three general types: (1) physical disfigurement; (2) aberrations of character and/or personality; and (3) social categorizations such as race, nation, and religion.[3] Since stigma may be visible or invisible, known about or not, impression management yields two sub-types: (1) the management of social information about self, and (2) the management of tension in interpersonal encounters. The management of information is the main task of "discreditable" indi-

Source: *Human Organization,* 17 (1968), pp. 316–25. Reprinted by permission of publisher and authors.

viduals possessing a deeply discrediting attribute which may not be known or immediately perceivable to those present. The management of tension is the main task of the "discredited"—stigmatized individuals who can assume that their differentness is either already known or is immediately evident.

"The central feature of the stigmatized individual's situation in life . . . [lies in efforts to achieve] what is often, if vaguely, called 'acceptance' " by normals.[4] We are told that all the stigmatized can ever hope for is a "phantom acceptance" which provides the base for a "phantom normalcy."[5] Much of Goffman's thesis thus postulates an array of "protective" and "defensive" management strategies used by stigmatized individuals in easing interaction with normals, saving situations from embarrassing tensions, withholding information, "passing," "covering," working out "lines" and "codes" of conduct and, in general, trying to cope with mortifying situations in the overwhelming task of salvaging and retaining personal dignity despite some undesired and deeply discrediting attribute which, it would seem, nobody is ever completely willing to overlook or forget.

The stigmatized are involved in a basic dilemma or self-contradiction. Not only are they denied real acceptance but, more importantly, they confirm the evaluation of their condition and remain stigmatized in their own eyes. Goffman's people are both *other-* and *self-* stigmatized and forever doomed. The basis for this dilemma or self-contradiction lies in the fact that those stigmatized are apparently firmly welded to the same identity norms as normals, the very norms that disqualify them. They may ultimately believe that the norms should not be used to their disadvantage. Nevertheless they concur with the norms and therefore view themselves as failures.

The theory as stated offers no possibility of any serious attempt by stigmatized individuals to destigmatize themselves. None seem to engage in efforts to disavow the norms that impute discreditability to them. None apparently try to substitute other norms and standards that might allow them to view their "stigma" as a simple and not especially discredited difference rather than a failing. Nor does there seem to be much chance to move from a discredited to a less discredited or to an accepted deviant status. Surely there are other feasible modes of adaptation. One is the development of stigma theories by the stigmatized—that is, ideologies to counter the ones that discredit them, theories that would explain or legitimize their social condition, that would attempt to disavow their imputed inferiority and danger and expose the real and alleged fallacies involved in the dominant perspective.

Perhaps the reason Goffman gives so little attention to this line of thought is because he deals mainly with single individuals in brief encounters with normals, usually in "unfocused gatherings."[6] He seems less concerned with patients' efforts toward destigmatization in more permanent groupings, especially in social settings where they live together in more or less continuous interaction, where they are able to develop their own subculture, norms, and ideology, and where they possess some measure of control over penetrating dissonant and discrediting views from without.

It is precisely these circumstances under which a *group* of "stigmatized" evolve their own stigma theory that interest us here. We are concerned with the meaning of this more or less consciously constructed perspective to their lives and its function in facilitating a linkage with the wider society. To this end, we conceptualize the *career patient status* as a mode of adaptation to chronic stigmatizing conditions and elucidate its ideological base in a stigma theory.

The argument is developed in terms of problems faced and strategies employed by leprosy patients at the USPHS Hospital, Carville, Louisiana, in their efforts to delineate a viable social and psychological explanation for the widespread prejudice toward leprosy patients. The ideology and strategy presented below serve to provide patients with a means of attenuating self-stigma and altering other-stigma. From a description of this particular system of adjustment it is possible to suggest in the final section some general characteristics of the career patient status and the conditions contributing to its development.

General Background and Methodology

Leprosy has been little studied sociologically as either disease or stigma in the United States and is scarcely known to the American public. Prior to 1961, when the senior author first undertook to study the illness and the hospital-colony at Carville, Louisiana,[7] there had been only a few local psychological and epidemiological studies[8] and no general sociological or social psychological research.

The USPHS Hospital at Carville is the only leprosarium in the continental United States. It was established in 1894 as the Louisiana Home for Lepers and came under PHS jurisdiction in 1921. The resident patient population at Carville is relatively stable at slightly more than 300. In addition to the Carville hospital, there are at present four PHS leprosy out-patient clinics: one each in New Orleans; San Francisco; San Pedro, California; and Staten Island, New York. At San Francisco, the largest leprosy out-patient clinic, 166 cases of leprosy were seen between the years 1960 and 1967.[9] The total number of cases of leprosy in the United States is simply not known. The standardized estimate of 2,000 to 2,500 has been used for some time, but experienced workers in the field believe this is somewhat low and variously estimate the number at approximately two or three times the supposed figure. On a worldwide basis the prevalence is estimated at anywhere from 12 to 16 million cases.

In the present study, over 100 patients, Carville residents plus New Orleans and San Francisco out-patients, were interviewed intensively in interviews that ranged from one hour to, in some cases, over twelve hours, with the average between two and three hours. The patients interviewed for this study equal about one-third of the stable Carville in-patient population and approximately four per cent of the estimated leprosy cases in the United States. In addition to patient interviews, the study included patient group discussions, individual psychotherapy sessions, interviews with Carville staff members, recordings of staff meetings, and participant observation of hospital and colony life.

Some Medical and Behavioral Characteristics of the Disease

Leprosy is a chronic communicable disease of the skin, eyes, internal organs, peripheral nerves, and mucous membranes. It can produce severe physical handicaps and disfigurement, especially when untreated. There are also a number of significant uncertain-

ties regarding basic epidemiological questions of etiology, susceptibility, contagion, resistance, treatment, and societal reactions which
limit treatment and rehabilitation. Five of these are especially relevant here.

1. The mode of transmission is not thoroughly understood. Prolonged and intensive skin-to-skin contact with an active case is
believed necessary for infection to take place. However, respiratory
transmission has not been completely ruled out nor has the role of
insect vectors. The idea that genetic factors may play a crucial role,
particularly with respect to susceptibility, is becoming increasingly
popular. The incubation period is prolonged and undetermined,
apparently anywhere from a few months to many years.[10]

2. The mycobacterium (*Mycobacterium leprae*) thought to be
responsible has not been successfully cultivated *in vitro*. The disease
resists experimental transmission in humans, leaving doubt about the
identified organism, in addition to raising questions about the relationship of host to organism.[11]

3. Success of treatment is also uncertain. Medical authorities are
reluctant to use the term "cure." Current drugs such as the sulfones
introduced in the early 1940's are more effective in general than
earlier drugs but are useless with some patients and induce strong
reactions in others. As a result, individuals do not know and cannot
readily learn what disabilities may occur, or how long they may remain a potential communicable risk.[12]

4. Leprosy, in the United States, at least, is rarely suspected as a
likely diagnosis. Even today diagnosis based on a clinical examination alone, without the aid of a biopsy, is difficult. The disease is
therefore frequently mistaken for other conditions, and patients
may be treated for long periods for the wrong disease.[13]

5. The legal status of patients is also unclear. Aliens are usually
constrained to seek treatment at Carville or face the possibility of
deportation. State laws applying to U.S. citizens are varied and differentially enforced.[14] Criteria for "discharge" from Carville vary
with disease classification, clinical judgment, rehabilitation potential,
and assessment of patients' responsibleness. Indefinite out-patient
treatment may be advised.

Additional insight into the nature of leprosy is provided by Olaf Skinsnes, a pathologist who recently constructed a hypothetical disease expressing the ultimate in physical disablement and in eliciting extreme negative social and emotional responses. This hypothetical disease would: (1) be externally manifest; (2) be progressively crippling and deforming; (3) be nonfatal and chronic, running an unusually long course; (4) have an insidious onset; (5) have a fairly high endemicity, but not be epidemic; (6) be associated with low standards of living; (7) appear to be incurable; and (8) as a masterstroke, it would have a long incubation period.[15] This illness would expose the individual to long and protracted experience with pain, suffering and deformity, as well as social ostracism. Death alone would not be the frightening element; the major threat would be bodily deterioration and assault on the body-ego. Skinsnes notes the resemblance of leprosy to his hypothetical disease and concludes that "it appears reasonable to postulate that it is this complex and its uniqueness which is responsible for the unique social reactions to leprosy."[16]

The popular view of leprosy of course portrays the disease in just such black terms. The very name evokes an image of a maximally ravaged, untreated victim. In addition to its depiction in fiction and film, this view is typically found in the fantasies and expectations of newly diagnosed patients. Like others in the general population, they usually possess little real information about the disease and have had little or no previous contact with persons known to have it. In fantasy and expectation leprosy is considered "highly" contagious, horribly deforming, extremely painful, and eventually fatal. The stereotypic belief is widely held that toes, ears, noses, and other bodily appendages literally fall off. Many individuals also think of it as a legendary disease or one associated only with tropical "jungle" life, and are astonished to learn that leprosy actually exists in industrial nations.

Perhaps best epitomizing the bleakness of the popular view is the fact that it excludes the idea of amelioration. New patients anticipate being banished "for life." Importantly, they rarely have to be told or have to learn from experience the advisability of concealing their disease. Even when they know little about leprosy or profess never even to have heard the name they invariably realize its stigma and begin to develop strategies for keeping this information from others. However, the notion of "high" contagion is usually strong. New patients are apt to take precautionary measures far in excess of anything suggested by medical authorities. The urgency with which some of them consent to immediate hospitalization even when there is no compelling medical or public health pressure in that direction further indicates their perception of the situation as "extreme" and requiring immediate treatment or confinement.

The popular or "folk" view of leprosy seems to represent two levels of experience. In terms of deformity, pain, and societal reactions, though not in terms of contagion or fatality, the image comes close to describing actual leprosy in untreated cases of advanced deterioration, though not what it must be nor is in all or most cases. At another level the "folk" view represents a fantasy of the worst that can happen to one's body—*a fantasy of total maximal illness*.[17] In fantasy the two darkest fates are to "lose one's mind" as in lunacy or to "lose one's body" as in leprosy. Both involve a loss of self, either psychic identity or body image. Given the unique combination of disease characteristics and the associated medical and social limitations and uncertainties, it is readily apparent that neither the fantasy of leprosy as total maximal physical illness nor extreme cases of the real disease is conducive to an optimistic or hopeful outlook for patients.

Leprosy as an Identity Crisis

Diagnosis of leprosy, with or without concomitant hospitalization, signals a sudden, radical, undesired, and unanticipated transformation of the patient's life program. Many activities and relationships formerly engaged in must be modified or given up. The situation is further compounded by the chronicity of the disease and the need for continued prophylactic actions to prevent exacerbation of symptoms. The disease becomes the nucleus around which the patient's life program is transformed. The disease also sets boundaries which, for many patients, impose a severe truncation of their normal status and role activities. In this complex, self- and other-stigmatization are but two facets contributing to a major identity crisis.[18]

A further complication in the crisis comes with the patient's realization that (1) while he has a serious condition (serious either as disease or stigma or both), he has not changed as a person, yet (2) society would now regard him as totally different. The patient fears that his condition will engender not only a discontinuity between his past and previously expected future, but also will create an incongruity between his self-identity and his social identity. As long as he can conceal his condition, he can, within limits, engage normally in behavior open to him on the basis of a social identity in which others do not know of his stigma. But once the condition is known, the patient is faced with the problem of "building a world," to use Goffman's phrase. He has to learn what from the past must be discarded and what is salvageable, which past activities and roles will facilitate adaptation, which will not, and what new behaviors need to be added.

Patients handle the discontinuity and dissonance between self and social identities in a variety of ways, and the kind and quality of their adjustment can be expected to vary according to their relation to others who hold different views about leprosy. In Goffman's treatment of single stigmatized individuals interacting with normals in everyday encounters, the penetrating social norms remain continually in effect. Under these circumstances it is difficult for the stigmatized person to see himself differently than others see him for he continues to live, work, and play in social contexts that affirm the conventional standards.

We are concerned here, however, with situations in which the stigmatized develop and implement an ideology counter to the dominant one that stigmatizes them. They formulate a theory of their own to account for their predicament, to de-discredit themselves, to challenge the norms that disadvantage them and supplant these with others that provide a base for reducing or removing self-stigma and other-stigma. The most significant element for this to take place, it would seem, is a mutually reenforcing collectivity of like-stigmatized people, a subculture capable of maintaining effective immunity from the dominant code. Such collectivities may be of the urban homosexual variety or the rash of "hippie" movements which, although located physically within the larger society, nevertheless manage to set themselves apart, reenforcing each other's actions while setting some degree of social, emotional, and cognitive distance between themselves and their critics.

Another such collectivity is that formed by the leprosy patients at the USPHS Hospital in Carville. Originally (in its pre-sulfone days) an asylum, it is now a "quasi-open residential treatment community,"[19] with a well-developed patient culture which has evolved a distinctive and coherent stigma theory of its own in isolation from the mainstream of American social routines.

The Patients' Theory of Stigma

A diagnosis of leprosy, followed by hospitalization or out-patient treatment, introduces the new patient to the known medical facts and to many of the misconceptions and uncertainties related to the disease. It is a common fact of our observation that new patients hold expectations which compare leprosy with Biblical notions and include the fantasy of "total maximal physical illness." Early in the introduction to their new career, patients learn that Biblical references and contemporary leprosy are associated only in historical myth and misconception. This aspect of the stigma theory attempts to de-mythologize leprosy by emphasizing the historical, social, and medical errors and confusions which surround it. The theory further argues that leprosy as now known is wholly undeserving of the social prejudice it arouses and elaborates the view that society's negative image arises not from the medical and physiological facts but from faulty Bible exegesis based at best on poorly substantiated historical evidence and reasoning. Scientific and medical data are adduced to show that leprosy historically has been mistakenly identified with a wide variety of other skin and nerve conditions and that for centuries it has been a general catch-all category for any number of horrible aspects of innumerable and unexplained deforming illnesses that have afflicted mankind.

The theory also attempts to deal with contagion. Since there are a number of medical and scientific uncertainties relating to contagion, the theory understandably encounters certain difficulties. Much is made of leprosy as a "mildly contagious" disease, but the epidemiology is uncertain; and the question is commonly raised that if it is only "mildly" contagious, how come so many people have it? At Carville it is routine to relate that in nearly three-quarters of a century of operation only one employee ever contracted the disease and this man, it is pointedly added, was reared in the leprosy endemic area of Southern Louisiana. At times, the theory goes further and declares that in some regions leprosy may be considered a "noncommunicable" disease.

In line with the theory, serious proposals are advanced by patients and leprosy workers alike to change the name of the illness to Hansen's Disease. The term "leper" in particular, but also the term "leprosy," is considered opprobrious and inappropriate except in the ancient, Biblical context. The present-day condition is termed "Hansen's Disease" or "so-called leprosy" in order to clarify the distinction between present reality and past symbol and myth.

The stigma, or perhaps more correctly, the destigmatizing theory, is advanced in various ways. Almost without exception it plays a part in all printed or verbal presentations to the public by patients or their representatives. It appears in its most explicit form in the pages of *The Star*, a bi-monthly journal published by the patients and distributed internationally. The theory is less a "line" in Goffman's sense than an ideological position. Unlike "codes" or "lines," it does not emphasize or elaborate rules of conduct by which the stigmatized should guide themselves in their relations with normals so much as it provides a "world view." As ideology the theory is a highly formal explanation of the stigmatic nature of their illness which permits patients to minimize the notion that they are severely afflicted and also provides them with readily available and, to them, provable evidence that society has wrongly labeled them.

The theory is thus a nativistic effort to redefine the disease and remove it from its hitherto eminent position as the idealized maximal horrible illness. It also importantly supplies some measure of hope, optimism, and certainty through the suggestion that the social and psychological problems patients face are due substantially to society's defective view of the disease. The basic assumption is that ostracism and rejection will appreciably diminish and perhaps even totally disappear when social misconceptions are corrected. In this respect, the USPHS Hospital itself actively functions as a disseminator of the stigma theory by encouraging visitors through an established routine of tours, seminars, and planned programs utilizing local groups and the mass media. An average of 13,000 visitors annually tour the hospital.

Since the new patient usually had a somewhat nihilistic view of leprosy before his own socialization into the world of patients, the position that society is wrong about the disease is one he can convincingly endorse. Psychologically, the theory functions to drain energy, and very often hostility, away from physical and medical aspects of the disease that are realistically distressing, about which little is presently known, and for which little or nothing can be done. Instead, the theory focuses attention on a punitive and misunderstanding society whose views, it contends, can be altered if sufficient effort is made to bring the "real" facts before the public and if the public makes an honest effort to replace their erroneous views with the idea that leprosy is "just like any other illness."

The theory understandably heavily emphasizes a social and historical perspective rather than the medical and physiological aspects of the disease since it is an attempt to introduce a measure of certainty and optimism into an area of experience that is for many markedly uncertain, and for some considerably less than hopeful. There is, however, a germ of truth in the theory. Leprosy is not of course, except in extreme conditions, the ultimate disease it is fantasied to be; nor is it the Biblical "disease."

Although incomplete as a social or historical explanation for the prejudices encountered, the theory has important value for patient adaptation and de-discreditation. Psychologically, leprosy patients typically exhibit a sense of total rejection by society and initially even by themselves. Interestingly, this sense of initial self-rejection sometimes offers the patient an opportunity to work out, or at least, work on intrapsychic conflicts that may have antedated the illness. For some patients with a premorbid, diffuse self-identity, leprosy may ultimately have an integrating effect. For regardless of the discrediting nature of the disease, as an identity mark it cannot but impress upon the individual an acute awareness that if he did not know who he was before, there can be no question as to who he is now. In not wishing to accept this "who he is now" which might result in considerable apathy and hopelessness, the stigma theory provides patients with an available rationale for reevaluating their discredited status and, additionally, for engaging in ego-satisfying and socially syntonic assertive actions.

The following selection from a patient interview illustrates the way elements of the stigma theory may be used to explain the non-specialness of leprosy and to account for public prejudice:

> This patient has been at Carville for 15 years and is now married to another patient. She reports the disease has never given her much trouble. Her bacteriological status is close to negative at this time. She believes both cancer and heart disease are worse illnesses than leprosy. Yet, to this day, "my family don't know about my having this disease. My brothers and sisters they just know I'm sick and in a hospital, that's all."
>
> *Interviewer:* What do you think there is about leprosy that makes people afraid of it?
>
> *Patient:* Actually, because they don't know anything about it. When you say leprosy everybody gets so scared. It's so contagious they think, and it has always been in the Bible that it was so contagious that they naturally connect the two and think you had better get away from it.
>
> *Interviewer:* How realistically afraid of the disease do you think people should be?
>
> *Patient:* Well, I don't think they should be afraid of it no more than you would be afraid of tuberculosis. You're not afraid to go out there among people with tuberculosis. The name itself makes people afraid because they don't know anything about it. But, I don't think people would be afraid if they knew more about it.

Compare the above with the way this same patient reports her feelings and views on first learning she had leprosy, and note the connection in her mind between leprosy as the fantasy of maximal illness and leprosy as a real disease:

> *Interviewer:* Had you ever heard the name leprosy before you were diagnosed?
>
> *Patient:* No, I never heard it before not even though my sister was sick with it. In fact, she was never diagnosed for leprosy. The doc-

tors could never find out what was wrong with her. They learned it at the time when she died. But I never connected the word until they told me about it. It was a big shock.

Interviewer: How did you feel when they told you that you had leprosy?

Patient: It was just unbelievable. I never did think that I could have something like this disease. I didn't know it existed either. I thought maybe in India or perhaps out there in the jungles, but then I never thought about it.

Interviewer: Why do you think you were so shocked when you didn't know anything about the disease or never heard the name before?

Patient: Just like I say, the name. You measure it with something out of the Bible and imagine that's what it is. I think everybody who has had this disease experiences the same thing when they are told. They think it is impossible. What kind of a disease is it when we don't know anything about it?

Interviewer: What did you think was going to happen to you after being told you had leprosy?

Patient: Well, at that time when they told me I had to come over here I thought I had come to the end of the world. I had never been out of [another state] all my life and when they told me I had to come all the way to Louisiana I thought I would probably go and never come back again, that I'd die or something. Those were my thoughts, that I'd probably die out here somewheres.

Most patients, as the patient cited above, elect to conceal their leprosy identity from society. Many take up permanent residence at the hospital where they live, work, and sometimes marry. They protect themselves by "colonizing." (They maintain the notion of society's ignorance and misconceptions about leprosy as a means of reconciling their own lowered self-esteem.) Through exposure to and socialization by other patients they incorporate the stigma theory into their own world view. Each patient, however, utilizes the theory in whatever way his own psychodynamics and life situation permits and/or requires.

The Theory as Legitimation for Career Patient Status

A number of patients, apparently independently of severity or visibility of symptoms, reveal their condition to society in quite open ways. In the interest of altering the public image of leprosy, which they hold as bearing the major responsibility for their discredited status and predicament in life, these patients assume the stance of educators bringing specialized information about leprosy to the public. Such *career patients* engage in a number of activities which are legitimized through the elements of the stigma theory and carry the approval of the majority of other patients.

The following case history, abstracted from extensive interviews with one such patient, illustrates some of the ways attitudes toward leprosy are reformulated and basic problems of revealing and educating are handled by those who are career patients.

> The patient has been a fairly regular Carville resident since his first admission more than five years ago. He has a more benign and less contagious form of the disease. He has no visible symptoms and the disease seems dormant at present. The patient is below middle age and his general health is good. His present wife—they married since his admission to Carville—is a Carville patient with a severe form of the disease and requires continuous medical care. Both live together at the hospital, visiting outside for varying periods. He works sporadically both at Carville and at various jobs outside. He does not use an alias.
>
> The patient's view of the disease has been modified considerably since his diagnosis. At that time he believed leprosy to be highly contagious, extremely painful, even fatal, and that he would soon lose various body parts—nose, ears, toes, etc. He continuously tested for signs of atrophy and also experienced depressive moods including rumination about suicide. He carefully concealed knowledge of his disease from others, passing his symptoms off as due to a nonstigmatized condition. He was upset when the Carville staff did not endorse his fantasy for total and immediate confinement. Now he believes leprosy is a minimal disease, especially when treatment is begun early. He ranks cancer, heart disease, tuberculosis, arthritis, and rheumatism as worse than leprosy. He views genetic suscepti-

bility as a prime factor in contagion. Now he never denies having leprosy and pointedly informs others of his true condition.

This patient is an active "educator" of the public and keeps himself informed about leprosy. He frequently talks to various groups as a leprosy patient and appears on television and radio. He is committed to generating more public interest in the disease and welcomes all questions and opportunities to discuss it. He acknowledges the existence of public fear, has personally experienced it, and feels that continuous efforts are necessary to overcome intractable public disinterest and fear. In order to correct erroneous public views and minimize the contagion factor, he paradoxically cites prevalence figures higher than those usually given by medical authorities.

Selective disclosing of information about leprosy is acknowledged by this patient: "There are many ways of telling people." When addressing the public, he sidesteps questions about and minimizes the problems of deformity to avoid reinforcing existing fantasies and misconceptions. In talking to Carville visitors, he feels the matter of deformity can be placed in perspective by pointing to the many patients who are not disfigured and by relating deformity to inadequacy of the older drugs, to the "oldtimers," and to those whose treatment was begun late. He links the maximal illness fantasy of leprosy and the stigma to the teachings of the churches and to writers and film makers who continue to hold erroneous ideas.

The patient cites his own experiences and marked shift in viewpoint as an example of the "conversion" anticipated in the public once an interest in and an understanding of the disease is created. He believes he has avoided developing a discredited self-identity through his education activities and the opportunities they have provided him in disclosing his leprosy identity. Concealers, he notes, have denied themselves this opportunity; their fear of exposure has altered their self-conception to that of an "outsider."

At present he is working outside Carville where his employer and his co-employees know all about him. He would not have it otherwise, he says. Informally he reveals his identity in almost all appropriate situations with only minor reservations.

In functioning as educational specialists the relationship of such patients to society undergoes an important shift. For some it furnishes them with a clear identity perhaps for the first time in their lives, providing them with altruistic service roles which, considering the fact the majority of patients at Carville are lower-class and rural, would not ordinarily be open to them. Some write articles and books, speak on the radio, appear on television or before community groups of various types both out in the community and on patient-panels to Carville visitors. Two prominent examples of career patients are Gertrude Hornbostel and Joey Guerrero, whose brief biographies appear in Stanley Stein's book *Alone No Longer*.[20] Stein himself is probably the most prominent current career patient. All who reveal themselves are potential educators. However, the decision to reveal is usually made only after much thought and weighing of consequences. Only when the patient believes he can cope with the reactions he anticipates is he likely to decide on this alternative.

Some career patients, like the one cited in the above case history, bear little evidence of their condition. This may seem logical insofar as such patients present the best case for leprosy in face-to-face encounters with the public, serving as examples to contradict the "erroneous" public view of the disease and lending credence to the patients' special stigma theory of leprosy. At the same time, there is a paradox in that these individuals are the very ones who could most easily "pass" and thereby minimize social rejection. That they do not choose this path is a comment on the fact that stigma may provide the basis for a total self-conception.

An important limitation of the patient educator relates to the kind and amount of information he may freely impart to the public. His function decrees he present leprosy in a favorable light. To emphasize the medical and social uncertainties or elaborate on the pathological picture of the disease might intensify reactions rather than temper them. The picture of the disease he presents must be carefully designed not to alarm. Thus, in the case history above, the patient mentioned "there are many ways of telling people" and many ways of dealing with difficult and embarrassing questions about deformity. The management of information has its own pitfalls, however. To reveal too much may be self-defeating. At the same time what is presented cannot be so out of tune with reality that it is dismissed as an obvious effort to paint an overly optimistic picture. The situation is especially precarious in view of public ideas of the disease as "extreme." Emphasis is thus placed on correcting errors and misconceptions rather than on fully elaborating all the factual details of leprosy. By no means is this position accepted by all. Dr. Skinsnes, for example, opposes changing the designation of the illness to Hansen's Disease and argues that "lasting returns from efforts to change society's unreasoning dread of leprosy will come from dissemination of facts regarding the true nature of the disease together with information about the hope now found in available effective treatment."[21]

Career patients, when not engaged in public education activities outside of Carville, require a place to which they may retreat. Refuge is most readily available at the hospital itself. Individuals who have attempted to maintain the dual statuses of career patient and private patient in outside communities often, though not always, experience severe role conflicts. While "accepted" as public educators about leprosy, they find that this limited acceptance does not always qualify them for general social acceptance. Patient educators on tour often find it expedient to use an alias so that adverse publicity will not precede or follow them when they wish to settle down.

There are probably few individuals who can permanently tolerate feeling discredited without making efforts to alleviate or restructure their definition of self. Insofar as the career patient status is viable, it assists in this task. From discredited concealers whose safety lies in hiding their identity, such individuals take on a new and laudable, though somewhat marginal, position as educational specialists. Their self-esteem and social prestige are elevated. Their actions receive the approval of the hospital and others within the leprosy community and ultimately may be deemed worthy by society in general. Many patients are thus motivated to energetic and outgoing lives, and the public attitudes to which they address themselves are undoubtedly moved toward some increasing understanding and tolerance. However, it must be pointed out that *at the present time this status appears to be the only legitimate one the leprosy patient has available to him for life in open society.*

Further Perspective on Stigma Theories and Career Patients

Though the destigmatizing ideology and the concept of career patient have been elaborated here in relation to leprosy, such statuses and ideologies are not limited to this illness alone. In mental illness, also, there is a stigma theory operating. Cumming and Cumming note that

> . . . [one] mechanism is redefinition of the situation so that the 'public' is held to be ignorant and prejudiced about those who must go to mental hospitals. In this mechanism, only the initiated know that such people are not crazy at all, but only temporarily ill, or in need of a rest.[22]

The entire mental health movement is in a sense directed toward attenuating the stigma of mental health illness and reducing the public's horror of it. Such ideologies are present also in a number of other conditions, although in a more diffuse form. In alcoholism, for example, there is an attempt to shift public belief in "weakness of character" as a main component to a more acceptable emotional illness model. Similarly, urban homosexuals are active and vocal in their attempts to alter public views and stereotypes.

We offer the generalization that stigma theories tend to develop and achieve a more articulate, coherent, and viable form to the extent that four conditions obtain: (1) there is a basic inadequacy of the existing social model to deal with the many and complex dimensions of the total problem; (2) persons involved in the stigmatized condition are engaged in close and sufficiently prolonged interaction so that a subculture, with ideology and norms, may develop; (3) the stigmatized are sufficiently free of daily encroachment on their lives by dissonant public views; and (4) there are a few (or at least one thoroughly dedicated) of the "discredited" able to enunciate and disseminate a coherent "stigma theory" and willing to risk the concomitant exposure. These few can then, as "career patients," legitimately use the theory for their own adaptation and, more significantly, to effect a transformation in society's attitudes toward their deviant groups.

REFERENCES

1. Erving Goffman, *The Presentation of Self in Everyday Life* (Garden City, N.Y.: Doubleday Anchor, 1959).
2. *Ibid.,* p. 3.

3. Erving Goffman, *Stigma: Notes on the Management of Spoiled Identity* (Englewood Cliffs, N.J.: Prentice-Hall, 1963), pp. 1–5.
4. *Ibid.*, p. 8.
5. *Ibid.*, p. 122.
6. Barney G. Glaser and A. L. Strauss, "Awareness Contexts and Social Interaction," *American Sociological Review, 29* (October 1964), p. 675, have noted that Goffman deals mainly with "persons who are either relatively unknown to each other or respectively withhold significant aspects of their private lives from each other," and point out that "his discussions of impression management might have been very different had he studied neighborhood blocks, small towns, or families where participants are relatively well known to each other."
7. For an early report on the larger project of which this is a part, see Zachary Gussow, "Behavioral Research in Chronic Disease: A Study of Leprosy," *Journal of Chronic Diseases, 17* (1964), pp. 179–89; also, Zachary Gussow and G. S. Tracy, "Strategies in the Management of Stigma: Concealing and Revealing by Leprosy Patients in the United States," 1965 (mimeographed).
8. See especially, Natividad Dimaya, "An Analytical Study of the Self-Concept of Hospital Patients with Hansen's Disease," unpublished doctoral dissertation, Wayne State University, School of Social Welfare, Detroit, 1963; Harold R. Belknap and W. G. Haynes, "A Genetic Analysis of Families in Which Leprosy Occurs," unpublished M.D. thesis, Tulane University School of Medicine, New Orleans, 1960; Paul Lowinger, "Leprosy and Psychosis," *American Journal of Psychiatry, 116* (July 1959), pp. 32–37; Edgar Johnwick, "A Reply to Lowinger's Article on Leprosy and Psychosis," *International Journal of Leprosy, 29* (January-March 1961), pp. 110–11.
9. Paul Fasal, E. Fasal, and L. Levy, "Leprosy Prophylaxis," *Journal of the American Medical Association, 199* (March 20, 1967), p. 905.
10. L. F. Badger, "Epidemiology," in Robert G. Cochrane and T. F. Davey, eds., *Leprosy in Theory and Practice* (Baltimore, Md.: Williams and Wilkins, 1964), Chapter 6; also, "Syllabus of Lecture Notes," 4th and 5th Seminar on Leprosy in Collaboration with American Leprosy Missions, Inc., USPHS Hospital, Carville, Louisiana, 1963, 1964 (mimeographed).
11. Charles M. Carpenter and J. N. Miller, "The Bacteriology of Leprosy," in Cochrane and Davey, *op. cit.*, Chapter 2; also, "Syllabus of Lecture Notes," *op. cit.*
12. S. R. M. Bushby, "Chemotherapy," in Cochrane and Davey, *op. cit.*, Chapter 20; also, "Syllabus of Lecture Notes," *op. cit.*
13. Annual Reports, USPHS Hospital, Carville, Louisiana, 1960, 1961, (mimeographed).
14. James A. Doull, "Laws and Regulations Relating to Leprosy in the United States of America," *International Journal of Leprosy, 18* (April-June 1950), pp. 145–54; also, Annual Reports, USPHS Hospital, *op. cit.*
15. Olaf K. Skinsnes, "Leprosy Rationale," American Leprosy Missions, Inc., December 1964, New York, N. Y., pp. 13–15; also, John R. Trautman, E. B. Johnwick, O. W. Hasselblad, and C. I. Crowther, "Social and Edu-

cational Aspects of Leprosy in the Continental United States," *Military Medicine, 130* (September 1965), pp. 927–29.

16. Skinsnes, *loc. cit.*, p. 15.
17. We are indebted to Edward H. Knight, M.D., for the articulation of this concept. The concept of "total maximal illness" and an early formulation of the "stigma theory" of leprosy appeared initially in Zachary Gussow, E. H. Knight, and M. F. Miller, "Stigma-Theory and the Genesis of the Patient-Professional: Patient Adaptation to Leprosy," paper presented at the 131st Annual Meeting, American Psychiatric Association, New York, 1964 (mimeographed).
18. We are using the term self-identity in the same sense as Erikson has used "identity"—"that is, as a well-organized ego acting in an appropriate environment with a sense of confidence in the persistence of both itself and the environment." [Quoted from J. and E. Cumming, *Ego and Milieu* (New York: Atherton Press, 1966), p. 42]. When the identity is threatened or drastically changed, a crisis ensues which forces the individual to reevaluate himself, the world about him, or both (Cumming and Cumming, Chapter 3).
19. Dorothy S. Nichols, "The Function of Patient Employment in the Rehabilitation of the Leprosy Patient," unpublished M.A. thesis, Department of Sociology, Louisiana State University, 1966, p. 109.
20. Stanley Stein, *Alone No Longer* (New York: Funk and Wagnalls, 1963), pp. 247–59.
21. Skinsnes, *op. cit.*, p. 16.
22. John Cumming and E. Cumming, "On the Stigma of Mental Illness," *Community Mental Health Journal, 1* (1965), p. 1.

FURTHER REFERENCES ON LEPROSY

James A. Ebner, "Community Knowledge and Attitudes About Leprosy: A Social-Psychological Study of the Degree of Stigmatization of a Chronic Disease," unpublished M. A. thesis, Department of Sociology, Louisiana State University, 1968.

James A. Ebner, George S. Tracy, and Zachary Gussow, "Public Views of Three Chronic Illnesses: A Comparative Study with Special Reference to Leprosy" (mimeographed).

Zachary Gussow and George S. Tracy, "An Exploratory Analysis of Patient Adaptation in Two Stigmatizing and Chronic Illnesses: The Case of Schizophrenia and Leprosy," paper presented at the 2nd Annual Scientific Session, National Association for Mental Health, 1966 (mimeographed).

Zachary Gussow and George S. Tracy, "Stigma and the Leprosy Phenomenon: The Social History of a Disease in the Nineteenth and Twentieth Centuries," *Bulletin of History of Medicine* (in press).

Zachary Gussow and George S. Tracy, "Disability, Disfigurement, and Stigma: A Brief Overview," Leonard Wood Memorial Conference Series (in press).

Zachary Gussow and George S. Tracy, "The Social Anthropology of a Disease: The Study and the Institutionalization of a Myth" (mimeographed).

S. Lee Spray, "The Organizational Management of Uncertainty in a Chronic Illness Community: The Leprosarium," paper read at Annual Meeting of the Pacific Sociological Association, San Diego, March 1965 (mimeographed).

George S. Tracy, Zachary Gussow, and C. A. Moseley, "Hospitalization Patterns of Leprosy Patients: A Study of Four Admission Cohorts of the USPHS Hospital, Carville, La., 1934–67" (mimeographed).

The Disadvantaged Group: A Concept Applicable to the Physically Handicapped

Sidney Jordan

Logically, definitions aim to lay bare the principal features of structure of a concept, partly in order to make it definite, to delimit it from other concepts, and partly in order to make possible a systematic exploration of the subject matter with which it deals. A real definition may always serve as the premise, or part of the premise, of a logical inquiry concerning a subject matter.

Morris R. Cohen and Ernest Nagel,
An Introduction to Logic and Scientific Method[1]

The goal of the definition or conceptualization appears to have little applicability when political and social factors are involved. The concept of "disadvantaged group" is an example. When this paper was written, the author was not aware of any other use of the term in print. The term, as the following essay demonstrates, was employed to designate a group with a number of characteristics that, based upon a physiological abnormality, led to social and psychological reactions within the individual and from external sources. This group, it was felt, had little similarity to minority groups, even though they were equated in the literature. The concept appeared applicable for two

Source: *The Journal of Psychology*, 55 (1963), pp. 313–22. Reprinted, with additional material, by permission of the author.

reasons: it described the characteristics of a population that governmental and private agencies were attempting to rehabilitate so that these people could become self-sustaining; it also held that the conceptualization served a heuristic purpose and supplied a conceptual model to aid in potential research. The concept of "disadvantaged group," therefore, was a social-psychological attempt to deal logically and scientifically with a real problem.

Conjectures derived from experience, when given conceptual form, may appear to be particularly applicable to the subject matter, but extraneous factors become a part of, and blur, the basis for the concept. Federally aided bureaus of vocational rehabilitation extended their services to include the emotionally, socially, and culturally disadvantaged. The employment of the term has, therefore, become so extensive that if "disadvantaged group" is to be considered a negative term, what is the implication of the term that is now finding its way into the literature, the "nondisadvantaged"? This term is not only a double negative but what does it imply—that the group so designated is not disadvantaged in any way and is, therefore, fortunate, or that the group members are "disadvantaged" because they are not disadvantaged? For a term to have meaning, it must have limitations, and a signifying capability that will enable the individual using the term to know what he means and the listener to do the same. On a scientific level, the implications of a concept should foster research by suggesting not only the variables to be tested but the limitations. For example, if the researcher is more selective in the population employed, he avoids the problem of having a heterogeneous population where a homogeneous one is desired, as well as the confusion in what might be otherwise meaningful, statistically significant results. Another example of the confusion is found on the operational level. If all the groups that are disadvantaged are similar in varied but specific areas, as defined by the term, then why should the goals of the agencies be to rehabilitate the physically handicapped, habilitate the socially handicapped, and acculturate the culturally handicapped? Considering the complexities encountered, the author can only emphasize that the discussion that follows is concerned primarily with the physically handicapped.

A prevalent practice in the literature concerning the physically handicapped is to compare them with minority groups.[2-7] One such example is the following quote from Rusalem:

> In discussing Lewin's statement that minority groups tend to accept the implicit judgment of those who have status even where the judgment is directed against themselves, Meyerson points out, "This is true of the disabled minority as it is of the racial and cultural minorities." By implication, then, one may transfer some findings from one area to another.[8]

It is not unusual for apparently similar concepts to be grouped together. This grouping can lead to the generalization of research findings from one group to another that appears similar. The application of concepts from one group to another can: (a) implement a reevaluation of previous data and theory; or (b) lead to confusion wherein the original concept becomes so fluid that it is no longer useful.

The question here is whether it is profitable to regard the disabled[9] as a minority group. There appears to be adequate basis for regarding the disabled under separate concepts from those applicable to minority groups. Development of a concept specifically applicable to the physically handicapped may further practical and heuristic ends. The purpose of this paper is to develop such a concept. The term disadvantaged group designates the characteristic of this concept.

Characteristics of Disadvantaged Group

The disadvantaged group is herein defined as that group composed of individuals marked in their sociocultural affiliations, socioeconomic, or professional trade activities, because of a particular, discernible physiological defect.

The one trait (that is, blindness, deafness, etc.) that the members of the disadvantaged group have in common influences the psychological and social orientations of its members, and is the means by which they are identified. As defined, the concept is applicable on the following levels:

Not Self-Perpetuating

A disadvantaged group is not self-perpetuating. The disability around which the group is built may occur at birth or adventitiously, but it is never perpetuated by the group as an ethic. Limited by their disability from full participation or acceptance within their primary group, the physically handicapped find that their joining a disadvantaged group is socially reinforced. The disadvantaged group's orientation, in turn, almost assures acceptance, and offers the physically handicapped person an opportunity to attain status and other role relationships otherwise denied him.

The minority group, on the other hand, perpetuates its values and norms through the family unit. Homogeneity is fostered and multi-leveled association with dissimilar groups is not condoned. Unlike a minority group, the very nature of a disadvantaged group demands that it rely upon outside sources to foster group cohesion and attain group goals.

Misunderstood Social Reactions

The social reactions experienced by members of a disadvantaged group stem from two basic factors: (a) the lack of comprehensibility by an individual not possessing the trait to understand the consequences and limitations of the disability; and (b) the handicapping character of the physical defect is thought to diffuse throughout the total personality and behavior of the individual, so that he can be both classified and identified by this one discernible fact.

Using the standards of their own group's affiliations to act as guides, the dominant group can interpret, or misinterpret, minority group activities. The differences claimed serve a number of purposes, such as proof of the dominant group's superiority, a focus for the projection of unacceptable wishes, and a means of perpetuating social distance, etc. The same standards do not apply to the physically handicapped. To know what it is like to have a sense is not an adequate guide for interpreting what it is like to lack a sense modality. Unable to fully understand the limitations imposed, or the attainments possible, the nonhandicapped rely upon stereotypes of the particular physical handicap to characterize the individual or the group.

The stereotypes, which vary to some degree for each physical handicap,[2, 3, 6, 10-14] reflect and reinforce culturally derived attitudes. Whether it is the belief that the lack of a sense modality forces the person to live in a void, or that any attainment by a physically handi-capped person is to be considered miraculous, the reaction displayed is to the handicap, and not to the individual.

Imposed Psychological Distance

Members of a disadvantaged group must cope with a psychological distance that is imposed upon them, and which they do not directly foster. Factors that indicate that the psychological distance is im-posed are: (a) the obvious emotional overtones of the behaviors displayed by the nonhandicapped to the physically handicapped; and (b) the desire that the disabled be isolated "for their own good."

The inability to know what it is like to lack a sense modality does not totally explain the psychological reactions experienced by the disadvantaged in their dealings with the nonhandicapped. Physically handicapped persons become accustomed to experiencing excessively emotional reactions in most of the situations where interaction be-tween the handicapped and nonhandicapped takes place.[3, 6, 10, 11, 15, 16] Overcoming this reaction demands that the physically handicapped person become known as an individual in spite of his disability. The opportunity to do this is limited by social factors that limit the degree and type of interaction possible, and the personalities of both persons. The most overt means of maintaining psychological distance and avoiding interpersonal contact is through segregation. While a study done by Lukoff and Whiteman is specifically concerned with attitudes toward the blind, one of their findings is applicable to this discussion. They state:

> There is a positive relationship between tendencies to feel pity for blind people on the one hand, and the tendency to espouse com-munity "segregation" for the blind on the other. Our data show that this is not due to "pitiers" seeing the blind as inferior, but to the fact that those that pity the blind feel that it is right that they should be given special protection and help, which is represented at the community level by a "segregated" service, and recreational pat-tern. Thus, espousal of segregation for blind persons has quite different meaning than espousal for ethnic groups.[17]

The segregation of minority or ethnic groups takes different forms and serves different purposes than the segregation of the physically handicapped. The segregation of a minority group is enforced by external pressures and the desire of the group itself. By limiting the interaction of the group's members with others, the minority group can maintain a homogeneity and perpetuate its values and norms. Time, however, the influence of educating the young in schools oriented toward majority group standards, and the rewards offered for conforming to the majority group's social demands, lead to breakdowns in minority group affiliations and values. The disadvantaged, on the other hand, are not segregated because of their minority, or ethnic group backgrounds, and they do not desire the psychological distance imposed. It is the implications of the handicap, as interpreted by the nonhandicapped, that preclude the acceptance of the individual and limit his ability to interact.

Outside Help Sanctioned

Behaviors designed to "help the physically handicapped" are positively sanctioned. Antipathetic attitudes, on the other hand, are not sanctioned, and when displayed, produce negative reactions toward the source from the nonhandicapped. This orientation limits interpersonal relations with the disabled in two ways: (a) it limits the testing out of what is right and wrong behavior toward a disabled person for fear of negative reactions from the nonhandicapped environment; and (b) culturally prescribed sanctions tend to preclude behaviors that would produce a release of tension and enable physically handicapped persons to fully participate in nonhandicapped group structures.

The nonhandicapped person, when dealing with the physically handicapped, must cope with limitations (a) and (b) listed above. Because of these limitations it is easier to rely upon preconceived notions of what the disabled are thought to be like, than to test the suppositions' veracity at the price of misunderstanding or scorn. Social stereotypes and the "definition" of the limitations caused by the disability become the basis for an "objective appraisal" of the handicapped individual. The objective appraisal, in turn, becomes the basis for a number of prescribed behavior patterns in interpersonal situations. These behavior patterns take the form of an over-concern about, and a compulsive need to immediately satisfy the disabled person's wants, and the avoidance of any discussion or activity in which he cannot knowingly participate, or would be at a disadvantage, if he should participate. The handicapped person's companion, if available, is often relied upon to help structure the situation. While directing the conversation to the mediary, the wants, personality characteristics, and likes of the disabled person can be discussed as if he or she were not there. The psychological distance that is maintained by these behavior patterns is not recognized, and if brought to the nonhandicapped person's attention, would be rationalized, and not thought of as unaccepting.

The overt expression of negative attitudes toward members of a minority group, on the other hand, is socially acceptable by many of the groups making up the majority. Negative attitudes about minority groups facilitate their being used as scapegoats, and are employed as the basis for manipulating the group's members economically and socially, with no misgivings. Their "peculiarities" allow joking about them in a flippant fashion, or paying them at different wage scales than members of the majority group. As long as a minority group member holds a subservient position, interpersonal relations are readily attained and are easily maintained. Confidences and jocularities, the imputation of moral freedoms, physiological capabilities, or innate shrewdness, are rendered freely, or are encouraged. Obviously, none of these attitudes would be allowed free expression in dealing with members of disadvantaged groups.

Dependence Upon External Agents

The lack, or restricted use, of a sense modality causes the individual to be unable to function in some areas and fosters a dependency upon external agents to help compensate for the limitations imposed. The societal desire to help the physically handicapped takes two forms: (a) the unorganized and mostly individual attempts to help a specific disabled person in a specific situation; and (b) the institutional attitudes, as reflected in legal statutes and service agencies, where organized attempts are made to help the physically handicapped as members of a disadvantaged group. The societal characteristic of both reactions can be a source of secondary gain for the physically handicapped.

When dealing with a disabled person on an individual level, the desire to be the outside agent helping him serves an objective and socially espoused purpose. The degree and type of help usually given, however, is indicative of the confusion felt by not knowing how to act toward, or what is desired by, the handicapped person. Examples of the excessive reactions, more than occasionally displayed, usually are seen when a cripple attempts to carry a parcel, and it is taken away from him without asking, in spite of, or in ignorance of, his wishes or capabilities. For a blind person to find his destination by himself is considered impossible or miraculous. He, therefore, is to be helped to his destination, whether he wants the help or not. Hearing aids improve the audition of persons with impaired hearing. Therefore, if the person doesn't have a hearing aid, get him one. The fact that there is no attempt made to understand the physically handicapped person as an individual, with feelings and judgments of his own, is strongly evident. The help is thrust upon him. Whether he wants or can use what is being offered is virtually a secondary concern.

Examples of institutionalized attitudes are evident on the national, state, and community levels. They include the division of welfare categories, so that recipients of Aid to the Blind, and Aid to the Disabled, receive built-in considerations because of their handicap. Special tax-supported agencies are maintained to educate, train, and rehabilitate group members. A number of disabled groups receive special tax considerations and differentiated treatment in the courts.[10]

Private agencies act as a direct means by which specific physically handicapped groups can be helped. These agencies collect funds by focusing the attention of the giver on one or more of the limitations caused by the disability, and upon rehabilitation. They do not distribute funds as governmental agencies do. Their centers of interest may extend from the offering of the educational or diagnostic facilities that may prevent an incipient loss from becoming severe, to the supplying of specific compensatory aids, counseling, or recreational services, and the maintenance of sheltered workshops for those already disabled.

The handicapped individual can experience a degree of secondary gain by manipulating the institutionalized and individual help thrust upon him. If properly utilized, the individual need not assert himself, or achieve, in competition with nonhandicapped persons, in order to survive. He need not work, but if he desires to work, a number of prescribed jobs are set aside for him. If the disabled individual is involved in a social disturbance, the blame is either put onto others, or is attributed to the handicap, not to the individual as an individual. Minor breaks in social mores are either overlooked, or if punished, receive differential treatment from the law.

The secondary gains allowed members of a minority group take different and less compensatory form than those provided members of disadvantaged groups. As long as the individual maintains his identification with the minority group, he knows what is behaviorally expected and tolerated. The group affords him social and recreational releases, wherein he can attain a level of status not possible in reactions with the majority group. The group also acts as a buffer against inadequacy, by attributing failure to the prejudices of the majority group. Confirmation of the prejudicial attitudes is found in the limited job offerings for minority group members, and the differential and negative treatment received from judicial and law enforcement agencies.

External Definition of Adjustment

It is not the physically handicapped person who defines whether he is socially or psychologically adjusted. The judgment is made of him by the nonhandicapped, or representatives of agencies, whose policy is structured by the social-psychological interpretations of what disadvantaged group members are supposed to be like. The reaction of handicapped persons to these interpretations extends along a continuum. At one end is the individual who submits to the "imputation of inferiority"[18] associated with his disability, and accepts the segregation and secondary gains afforded. This individual is assured a subsistence as a welfare recipient, or earns his livelihood in a number of prescribed areas, or in a sheltered placement. While these jobs pay comparatively little, they present the physically handicapped person with an opportunity to attain a higher status, or a significant role within a structured environment. Individuals at this end of the continuum have adjusted, in the societal sense.

On the other end of the continuum is the physically handicapped individual who does not accept the psycho-social implications of his disability. Desiring to test his capabilities as an equal in a competitive setting, he relies upon the devices designed to help him compensate for his disability, and tries to deny his dependency upon others. He does not employ, to any marked degree, the secondary gains allowed him, and overtly refuses to conform to majority expectations. The individual aspiring to this goal is not considered to have adjusted to his physical handicap in the psycho-social sense.

While the handicapped person may desire to be accepted as an equal in a competitive setting, he is rarely given the opportunity to do so. Factors beyond the individual's control effectively limit his getting a job equal to his skills or training in a setting not oriented to his particular disability. Among the obstructions are the attitudes of management, and the antipathy of the nonhandicapped workers with whom the disabled worker would be employed.[19] If the disabled person is given an opportunity to work as an equal in an integrated setting, he becomes a competitive force, and the attitudes that usually define his status and role do not prove applicable. The behavior that would permit a change in attitudes and expectations is limited by the handicapped worker's physical impairment, and the able-bodied workers' inability to accept as equal, or as supervisor, a person who cannot deny his dependency upon others, and outside devices, to perform the same tasks that the nonhandicapped can do without guides. During times of employment crisis, the nonphysically handicapped worker tends to feel threatened by the adequate performance of those he perceives as inferior. He attributes his own deficiencies to the difficulties caused by working with a disabled person. Management, relying upon their own culturally engendered, preconceived notions, frequently take the position that disabled workers demand special considerations, and costs, and impair the morale and performance of other workers. This opinion is maintained despite objective criteria as to the adequacy of performance and production by the physically handicapped.

Just as the sources of conflict differ for the minority group and disadvantaged group members, there are differences in the social interpretations of the individual's adjustments to being a member of either group. Unlike the disadvantaged, minority group affiliation is not constantly reinforced by the majority. While many members of the majority may desire that the minority group member know and keep his place, subtle and coercive factors, such as interpersonal contact, education, the mass media, legal pressures, and the desire for economic or occupational advancement, foster identification with the dominant group's values and orientations. The same factors that lead to the identification with the dominant group thwart the minority group's attempts to segregate itself, in order to maintain its own ethic.

Should the minority group member continue to adhere to his group's values, there is still a degree of tacit acceptance in a competitive setting, as long as the competition is open, and follows the rules set down by the dominant group. Acceptance in employment or political situations does not imply acceptability on a social level. The inability to socialize with members of a dominant group can be a major source of frustration for a minority group member.

The minority group can be perceived as a group in transition. While constantly being influenced by subtle and coercive factors to assimilate, it is also able to assert itself in a competitive setting. A disadvantaged group, on the other hand, finds itself in a "social limbo."[20] Segregation is enforced and attempted assimilation is frustrated, making it difficult to function as an effective social influence.

Summary and Conclusion

With the ever-increasing number of studies of the physically handicapped, there is a need for a rigorous examination of basic premises and conceptualizations. One widely employed premise is the equation of physically handicapped and minority groups. It is held that adherence to this premise leads to conceptual confusion, and impedes heuristic goals, for the facts derived from the study of the physically handicapped are nonidentical with, or are contrary to, the findings of studies of minority groups. This paper is an attempt to develop a concept that is specifically applicable to the physically handicapped. The phrase used to designate the concept is Disadvantaged Group. To demonstrate the dissimilarities of minority and disadvantaged groups, comparisons were drawn on six inferences, derived from the basic premise underlying the proposed concept.

REFERENCES

1. Morris R. Cohen and Ernest Nagel, *An Introduction to Logic and Scientific Method* (New York: Harcourt, Brace, Jovanovich, 1934), pp. 231–32.
2. R. G. Barker, "The Social Psychology of Physical Disability," *Journal of Social Issues, 4* (1948), pp. 28–38.
3. H. Chevigny and S. Braverman, *The Adjustment of the Blind* (New Haven: Yale University Press, 1950).
4. P. H. Mussen and R. G. Barker, "Attitudes Toward Cripples," *Journal of Abnormal and Social Psychology, 39* (1933), pp. 351–55.
5. L. Meyerson, "Physical Disability as a Social Psychological Problem," *Journal of Social Issues, 4* (1948), pp. 2–10.
6. H. Rusalem, "The Environmental Supports of Public Attitudes Toward the Blind," *New Outlook for the Blind, 44* (1950), pp. 277–88.
7. B. A. Wright, *Physical Disability—A Psychological Approach* (New York: Harper, 1960).
8. Rusalem, *op. cit.*
9. The terms disability and physically handicapped are not synonymous as employed in this paper. The distinction, derived from K. W. Hamilton: "A disability is a condition of impairment, physical or mental, having an objective aspect that can usually be detected by a physician. . . . A handicap is the cumulative result of the obstacles which disability interposes between the individual and his maximum functional level." K. W. Hamilton, *Counseling the Handicapped in the Rehabilitation Process* (New York: Ronald Press, 1950).
10. R. G. Barker, B. A. Wright, L. Meyerson, and M. R. Gonick, *Adjustment to Physical Handicap and Illness: A Survey of the Social Psychology of Physique and Disability* (New York: Social Science Research Council, 1953, Bulletin 55).
11. A. G. Gowman, *The War Blind in American Social Structure* (New York: American Foundation for the Blind, 1957).
12. H. H. Kessler, *Rehabilitation of the Physically Handicapped* (New York: Columbia University Press, 1947).
13. E. S. Levine, *The Psychology of Deafness* (New York: Columbia University Press, 1960).
14. I. F. Lukoff and M. Whiteman, "Attitudes Toward Blindness," *New Outlook for the Blind, 55* (1961), pp. 39–44.
15. H. Best, *Deafness and the Deaf in the United States* (New York: Macmillan, 1943).
16. T. J. Carroll, *Blindness: What It Is, What It Does, and How to Live with It* (Boston: Little, Brown, 1961).
17. Lukoff and Whiteman, *op. cit.*, p. 42.

18. The phrase, derived from Chevigny and Braverman, *op. cit.*, is employed by the authors specifically for the blind. It is employed in this context because it is applicable to all disadvantaged groups, as defined.
19. E. W. Noland and E. W. Bakke, *Workers Wanted: A Study of Employers' Hiring Policies, Preferences and Practices in New Haven and Charlotte* (New York: Harper, 1949).
20. A. G. Gowman, *op. cit.*, employs this phrase to describe the psychosocial reactions experienced by the blind. It is held that the phrase is also applicable to other disadvantaged groups.

Transgressors and Enforcers

5

The minority group has generally been seen not only in terms of racial, religious, and other ethnics, but as an ascribed status, or at least an involuntary one. That people can voluntarily enter into the ranks of a group with minority status, or minority treatment at the hands of others, would seem to be sufficiently unlike the condition of the racial minorities so as not to warrant further investigation. For the two types of minorities would differ in one major respect: responsibility for their own status.

For the ex-convicts, this responsibility has with it the inescapability of one's biography. No matter how much one may have been capable of becoming or not becoming a convict (and presumably, before that, a criminal), one is devoid of any capability of escape from being an *ex*-convict. Kuehn here examines this group, one which has "paid its debt to society," yet which continues to be subject to collective discrimination and punishment. While visibility is low for the public, the strangers, it is high for employers in this era of security checks, questionnaires, social security numbers, and other identifications. Only recently, in this era of protest, have ex-convicts started to organize, make demands, and break through the impasse created by a stigma for which they do not deny responsibility.

One turns to Howard, and finds another group in conflict with large portions of society, the radical right; and the thesis that he develops might very well be delineated, albeit with some changes, for the radical left as well. More than any other group looked at thus far, this one is not only voluntary in membership and entirely escapable, but self-righteous. Its viewpoint is that the group is correct and others are wrong. If one were to examine nudists as a minority, one might see them as self-righteous, but they would not be rejecting the many millions who choose to reject them. One might say that nudists would only reject the rejectors' rejection of them. For Howard, the radical right is another manifestation of social inequality, but it is social inequality voluntarily assumed and, in the view of many sociologists and social thinkers, properly imposed.

Finally, Goldstein examines the police as a minority, and one comes face to face with an anomalous situation in the sociology of intergroup relations: the in-power rather than the out-of-power minority.

Ex-Convicts Conceptualized as a Minority Group

William C. Kuehn

In a survey of the literature of sociology, and particularly in the field of criminology, there appears to be a significant void in the area of after-care of convicted criminals. This void centers around the problem of what befalls these people after their sentences have been completed.

In abstracto, when a person is tried and convicted for a crime, he is sentenced by the court to a specified period of time to be served either in an institution or under the auspices of a probation service. Upon completion of this sentence, the person is released to society—by the philosophy of the court as a rehabilitated, free man.

However, the facts seem to indicate that the released inmate, or "ex-convict," is hardly free to enjoy equal opportunities with the dominant, free society. He is actually not an *ex*-convict, but still very much a prisoner of society. This paper will demonstrate to what extent he is not free—economically, politically, and socially.

Utilizing the concept of the minority group, an attempt will be made to arrive at a more complete understanding of the problems faced by ex-convicts. The analysis will begin by trying to arrive at an acceptable definition of exactly what a minority group consists of. Then, information will be presented to ascertain if ex-convicts fall within the parameters of the definition. Going beyond the definition itself, it seems necessary to discover what type of minority group, if any, ex-convicts comprise. For this purpose, Louis Wirth's typology,[1] which delineates four types of minority groups, will be utilized.

There appear to be two definitions as to the characteristics of a minority group which are currently used by sociologists in their analysis of minority group problems and intergroup relations. These are the definitions of Wirth[2] and Wagley and Harris.[3] Wirth feels that "a minority group is any group of people who, because of their physical or cultural characteristics, are singled out from the others in the society in which they live for differential and unequal treatment, and who therefore regard themselves as objects of collective discrimination."

Wagley and Harris delimit five characteristics which they feel define the concept. These characteristics have been consolidated by Williams[4] into a statement of definition: "Minorities . . . are any culturally or physically distinctive and self-conscious social aggregates, with hereditary membership and a high degree of endogamy, which are subject to political or economic or social discrimination by a dominant segment of an environing political society."

The obvious difference between the two is found in the more restricting parameters of the Wagley and Harris definition which assumes hereditary membership along with a high degree of endogamy. Vander Zanden, however, in discussing the Wagley and Harris assumption of the hereditary nature of minority group status, suggests that it is not *always* involuntary or inherited. In his words: "*Generally* a person does not become a member . . . voluntarily; he or she is born into it."[5]

Membership can come to a person later in life as a result of a change in his position either socially or ecologically. Thus a person is able to convert from one religion to another to escape (or acquire) minority group status. Also, a person who is persecuted in one country or region, due to his minority religion or ethnic characteristics, may sometimes escape this situation by relocating to an area where his particular group maintains a majority status. In this respect, a Jew living in the United Arab Republic could move to Israel to escape his minority position. He has been a Jew all his life, but the very fact of his removal from one country to another was sufficient to rid him of his membership in a minority group.

It appears, then, upon closer inspection that the hereditary characteristic suggested by Wagley and Harris is of limited utility. Wirth's definition seems to be the more lucid of the two and is the one which will be used in this paper.

Inherent in Wirth's definition are two aspects of minority groups which must be considered—the objective and the subjective. The objective aspect which must be satisfied in order that a particular social aggregate be classified as a minority group is that of discrimination against it, and it is not difficult to document the discrimination suffered by most minorities. It is evident and well known in housing, employment, and education. In some cases it may be protected by law, in other cases it may be blatantly illegal.[6]

It is more difficult to document the subjective aspect of minority groups—the consciousness of discrimination attributable to the members due solely to their membership in the particular group. This is partly the result of a lack of a measuring instrument which could detect this consciousness in persons belonging to minority groups,[7] but mainly attributable to the absence of a literature on this topic. Perhaps the best which can be done at this time is to offer some examples of this phenomenon.

Also, aside from conforming to the objective and subjective characteristics of the definition, it is necessary that the group fit somewhere within Wirth's typology in which he outlines four types of minority groups delineated by "the major goals toward which the ideas, the sentiments, and the actions of minority groups are directed."[8]

Until recently, minority group status was confined to nationality, religious, and other groups which, because of their particular features, were prevented from enjoying equal opportunity with the dominant society. However, this concept has been expanded recently by Hacker[9] and de Beauvoir,[10] Cory,[11] and Friedenberg[12] to include women, homosexuals, and adolescents, respectively.

Let us begin by seeing to what extent ex-convicts fit the objective aspect of Wirth's definition. There seems to be no lack of information to verify the fact that they are discriminated against. The fact that a person has been incarcerated for a crime, which official ideology would say has been paid for and which would further claim that the criminal has been changed into a law-abiding citizen, invokes an immediate negative response from those he contacts upon entry into free society. For example, Martin[13] attempted to ascertain how much men were punished by society after the official punishment decided by the courts had been completed. He looked particularly at the effects of imprisonment on relationships with family and friends, on employment, and on the assistance given by the social service agencies to the ex-convicts. While these preliminary findings do not cite specific statistics, they do indicate beyond any doubt that the offender suffers much more than the official punishment, particularly if he is of higher status and achievement.[14]

Reinhardt,[15] in discussing the unique disadvantages that confront the ex-convict upon his release, suggests that, unlike the mental patient and the alcoholic, he is not encouraged to band together for mutual support, but is strongly urged to forget his past, his friends and acquaintances. In some cases this is even demanded by law.

Although seemingly undetected in society, the ex-convict becomes "visible" whenever an account of one's past life is necessary. If he applies for a loan, a mortgage to buy a house, a job, or a license to drive a motor vehicle or to carry a firearm, investigation will reveal that he has been convicted and incarcerated for a crime. Sometimes he tries to fill in the time he has been incarcerated with spurious employment which he hopes will fool his prospective employer. Other times he is compelled to be honest by his parole officer or by his reputation which might be known from the publicity surrounding his crime and trial.[16] If he is honest, the road to employment will be rough. Many jobs which fall into the category of unskilled labor, which is frequently all that the ex-convict can perform, require that he hold a driver's license or be bonded. But if the man was convicted of a crime involving the use of a motor vehicle, he is usually barred from holding a license for the rest of his life. Others are not able to obtain licenses due to restrictions placed on them by minimum waiting periods between release from prison and application for a license.

Probably the most severe problem facing the ex-convict in relation to employment revolves around the necessity to be bonded which is all but impossible for the ex-convict to obtain.[17] One response to this problem is Bonabond, Inc., which was set up in Washington, D.C., to bond ex-convicts who came to them for individual bonds. It was funded through anti-poverty funds and the bonding arrangements were handled by a private insurance company upon recommendation of the staffers—who were ex-convicts themselves. After almost two years of operation there had been no claims made against their bonds.[18]

But discrimination in employment is not limited to bonding and licensing practices alone. It transcends this reality and is found in the attitudes and practices of most employers. Schwartz and Skolnick found that the noncriminal applicant was offered a job nine times more often than the applicant with a criminal record.[19]

Job discrimination is not the only problem facing the ex-convict, for his civil rights are also heavily eroded. In 1960 the Federal Probation Officers Association conducted a survey of various state and federal practices relating to the civil rights lost by virtue of conviction for crimes. They found that in forty-five states persons convicted of a felony lost their right to vote, in forty-one states the right to hold public office was denied, and in twenty-one states eligibility for jury service was also denied. In seven states these forfeited rights were restored automatically upon expiration of sentence, but in the vast majority of states these rights could only be restored by the issuance of a pardon by the governor or the pardon board.[20]

Many municipalities have criminal registration laws which make it necessary for a released convict to register with the police in order to travel through or live in the particular area covered by the ordinance. Yet, when the ex-convict so registers, despite police disclaimers, he is generally harassed by them whenever a crime of the type the individual committed years past occurs in their jurisdiction.[21] A further abridgment of the right of freedom of movement is seen in the case of persons who have been convicted of narcotics violations. These people must register with Customs officials when entering or leaving the country.[22]

The result is a situation where one continues to be observed and followed, not only by the authorities but by the record of his past deeds. In his study at the Nebraska State Penitentiary, Reinhardt found that what prisoners wanted most upon release was to be left alone and not treated like criminals.[23] However, as the evidence indicates, he is treated like a criminal for a long period of time after his release—even until his death.

Thus there are blatant as well as subtle discriminations which are suffered by the ex-convict. They affect almost all of his constitutional rights which are guaranteed to other members of society—the right to vote, to hold public office, to have freedom of movement, to bear arms, and to gain employment regardless of his former type of servitude. In some cases this discrimination is established and perpetuated by law; in other cases the legal dimension is lacking. In any case, it is evident that the ex-convict is singled out from society and becomes the target of collective discrimination due solely to the fact that he has been convicted of a crime at some point in his life. He, therefore, certainly fits the minority group model with respect to the objective aspect of Wirth's definition.

It is more difficult to demonstrate how a minority group member fits the subjective characteristic, that is, the awareness he has of discrimination against him. It, however, becomes manifest in his response to the imposition of the objective aspect of his status. If discriminated against, it does not take long for him to realize what is transpiring.

When released from prison, the ex-convict desires to strip his memory of the time he spent behind bars and of the type of life that he led which resulted in his incarceration. However, he finds it difficult if not impossible to accomplish this end due to the constant discrimination which he suffers and which reminds him that he is "different." He, perhaps more than almost any other member of society, needs every possible encouragement and opportunity if he is to adjust properly to a normal life in society. Yet, he is discriminated against as much as, if not more than, other "traditional" minority groups, thus making him constantly and increasingly aware of his lower status.

The vast majority of ex-convicts greatly resent the discrimination against them and find it unjustified. They see society as being hypocritical in its treatment of them. It is evident to them that they have been incarcerated for offenses which society conditioned them to commit and which many persons other than themselves have committed but for which they have not been apprehended or convicted.[24] This negative feeling is frequently observed in the released offender who harbors resentment toward the society which he is reentering. Another hypocrisy of society is evidenced in the gap between the ideal and the real confidence which it has in its courts. Society gives the power to judge criminals to the courts, and the courts give the correctional institutions the duty of reforming their charges. However, after seeing that the sentence is carried out by the justly appointed authorities, society seems to say, "We want more. We do not trust our courts or correctional authorities. We think the criminal should get a life sentence—whether it be served in prison or within society."

The ex-convict is aware of this attitude, and after attempting to convince society to give him another chance—only to be rebuffed—he frequently reveals his frustrations by going back to the only life he is able to pursue, crime.[25] This frustration and its ultimate effects are seen dramatically in an interview with an English career criminal. When asked to describe himself in one word, the man replied, "A criminal. That's what I am, I never think of myself in any other way."[26]

Also, in demonstrating that the ex-convict fits the subjective aspect of Wirth's definition, it should be pointed out that one of two reactions frequently takes place in the mind of an ex-convict. He may perceive himself to be a criminal with a sense of pride in his fast, exciting life, or he may look at his career and life with disgust. In any case, the ex-convict is aware of the fact that he is different. He has been indoctrinated with this idea for the duration of his incarceration and after his release. Knowing that he is perceived to be different, and, as a result of this, is treated differently, the ex-convict appears to fit the subjective characteristic of the minority group definition.

It is essential that a group conform in both its objective and its subjective aspects if it is to be labeled a minority group. Moreover, and equally important, the group must fit somewhere within Wirth's four-part typology. These types are delineated by the goal orientation of the group. They are not static types, but are in a state of change— change which is initiated either by the dominant or the minority group. The initial change on the part of one group brings about reactive behavior on the part of the other. As Marden and Meyer observe, "Changes in either dominant or minority behavior will bring about reactive behavior, favorable or unfavorable in the other group, and this affects the pattern of relationships."[27]

Also, these types are not mutually exclusive. As with all minority groups, there are those who feel one way and react accordingly, and others who feel and react in another manner. It is possible, but not mandatory, that more than one type—even all four—will be manifest by a particular minority group at one time. Let us examine the typology.

Wirth's first type of group is the pluralistic minority "which seeks toleration for its differences on the part of the dominant group," as well as economic and political equality.[28] But toleration of a minority, with its different patterns of life and thought, requires that the dominant group be secure in its position of dominance and that it feel no immediate threat from the minority. Also, it must be presupposed that coexistence is possible in that society for groups with radically divergent cultural or subcultural patterns.

The second type of minority group, the assimilationist, "craves the fullest opportunity for participation in the life of the larger society with a view to uncoerced incorporation in that society. It seeks to lose itself in the larger whole by opening up to its members the greatest possibilities for their individual self-development."[29]

Wirth sees the typical development of a minority group as starting with the pluralistic type and then moving toward the assimilationist position. After the assimilationist stage is reached, the group may go one of three ways. If it becomes assimilated at this point, it will have disappeared and no longer exist as a minority. However, if assimilation fails, a minority group takes on the characteristics of either a secessionist or a militant type. The former type is not interested in assimilation with the dominant society. Rather its interests lie in seceding from it and setting up a society which is in line with its way of life. By contrast, the militant type rejects the goals of all three other types, attempts to overthrow the existing dominant group and to become the new dominant group.[30]

Some ex-convicts, although they are few in number, fit the pluralistic model in that they are willing to accept their position of social subjugation in society. Although they seek economic and political equality with the dominant, they are content to remain in social isolation from it.

Most ex-convicts, however, seem to fall into the second type of group, the assimilationist. This point of view is evidenced in the ex-convict's desire not to be treated like a criminal upon release from prison. He seeks economic, political and social freedom of opportunity—opportunity which he has probably never enjoyed even prior to his incarceration. He has paid his debt to society and wishes that society would realize this and treat him as a man with a "clear slate."

In working toward this goal of complete assimilation in society, ex-convicts have found that society offers little or no help, and that the most expedient means for attaining their goals lies in the area of self-help movements. Following the models of black people in

America,[31] alcoholics and narcotics addicts,[32] ex-convicts banded together to organize self-help groups specifically designed to alleviate
their problems in and with society. Some of these groups began
within the walls of prisons and spread outward; others began in
society and worked their way into the prison setting.

The major obstacle facing such groups is the tradition in American
corrections and parole work that a discharged prisoner, on parole, is
forbidden from associating with known criminals. So even though
some authorities favor the concept of such groups, the law comes
between theory and practice. Perhaps the most eloquent plea for the
use of ex-convicts in the rehabilitation of criminals comes from
Cressey. He feels that the most valuable contribution made by such
groups comes from "the requirement that the reformee perform the
role of the reformer."[33]

There may be some question as to what reformation has to do with
the escape from minority group status, but it should be obvious, as
has been borne out in the case of other types of minority groups, that
the only way the ex-convict can rid himself of his status will be first
to rid himself of his involvement in crime. Starting with this realization, the self-help group begins in the area of personal reformation
and then works its way from a pluralistic orientation to that of the
assimilationist. There are many of these self-help groups of ex-
convicts in existence in this country, Canada, and abroad too numerous to mention at this time.[34] What seems important to glean
from this fact is that ex-convicts want to be left alone or solve their
own problems, and are not immediately willing to be assimilated into
society until they feel that they are ready. But when this time comes,
they become a solidly assimilationist type minority group.

Thus, ex-convicts are representative to a limited extent of the
pluralistic type of minority, and to a greater extent of the assimilationist type. The third type of minority group, the secessionist, is
revealed in many career or professional criminals, who remain apart
from society, its norms and values. They find little worth in living
"straight" lives, either because society will not let them or because
society's values have been poorly transmitted to them.[35] Related to
this type of minority group is the criminal subculture which, although living within society, maintains its own values, beliefs, and

ways of doing things.[36] To use the terminology of Merton,[37] such people are more retreatist, however, than recessionist in Wirth's sense of that word.

The militant type of minority group seems least characteristic of the ex-convict. Because of his position in society, he finds it impossible to lash out against society with any degree of success. He knows how society treats those who violate its laws—be they just or unjust. Some might argue that the criminal is, in fact, lashing out against society for the discrimination and unequal opportunities which it has dealt to him. According to criminological theory, this may be the cause of his crime. However, with the exception of the person involved in organized crime, he is acting alone or in a very small group. He is not involved with a "community" of other members of the minority group in his actions. The benefits of the particular crime go to the individual perpetrator, not to the group as a whole. Therefore, although individual criminals may be looked at as militants attacking society for the lack of justice which it gives, ex-convicts as a group cannot be so classified.

In conclusion, then, it appears that ex-convicts fit the minority group definition of Wirth, as well as exemplifying the orientations which he sees as characteristic of such groups, even if they do not fall into all four of his categories.

The implications of this are important. By applying the minority group concept to ex-convicts, one may more accurately observe and predict what is causing fluctuations in and, particularly, rising crime rates. Existing minority group theory can be applied to the study of the ex-convict and his relation to crime and society.

With the civil rights of other minority groups being given much attention and some action today, it would be wise to consider the application of these same rights to ex-convicts. Only when such is done can crime in our society drop significantly.

REFERENCES

1. Louis Wirth, "The Problem of Minority Groups," in Ralph Linton, ed., *The Science of Man in the World Crisis* (New York: Columbia University Press, 1945), pp. 347–72.

2. *Ibid.*
3. Charles Wagley and Marvin Harris, *Minorities in the New World*, 2nd ed. (New York: Columbia University Press, 1964), pp. 4–11.
4. Robin M. Williams, Jr., *Strangers Next Door* (Englewood Cliffs, N.J.: Prentice-Hall, 1964), p. 304.
5. James W. Vander Zanden, *American Minority Relations*, 2nd ed. (New York: Ronald Press, 1966), p. 12. (Emphasis not in original.)
6. For example, public school segregation is illegal, but de facto school segregation escapes the limits of our present laws.
7. Helen Mayer Hacker, "Women as a Minority Group," *Social Forces, 30* (1951), p. 61; reprinted in this volume.
8. Wirth, *op. cit.*, p. 347.
9. Hacker, *op. cit.*, pp. 60–69.
10. Simone de Beauvoir, *The Second Sex* (New York: Knopf, 1968), pp. xii–xxix.
11. Donald Webster Cory, *The Homosexual in America* (New York: Greenberg, 1951), Chapter 1, "The Unrecognized Minority."
12. Edgar Z. Friedenberg, "The Image of the Adolescent Minority," in *The Dignity of Youth and Other Atavisms* (Boston: Beacon Press, 1965); reprinted in this volume.
13. J. P. Martin, "Sociological Aspects of Conviction," *Advancement of Science, 21* (1964), pp. 12–16.
14. *Ibid.*, p. 14.
15. James M. Reinhardt, "The Discharged Prisoner and the Community," *Federal Probation, 21* (1957), pp. 47–51.
16. Facts revealed through many conversations and interviews with inmates and ex-convicts during study conducted by the author in Boston, Spring 1968.
17. There are two kinds of bonding arrangements between the employer and the bonding company. The first is where the employer receives a "blanket coverage" for all of his employees; the second provides for the separate and individual bonding of each employee. See: Arthur Lykke, "Attitude of Bonding Companies Toward Probationers and Parolees," *Federal Probation, 21* (1957), pp. 36–38.
18. "Helping Cons Go Straight," *Time* (September 22, 1967).
19. A field experiment conducted with employers of unskilled workers. See Richard Schwartz and Jerome Skolnick, "Two Studies of Legal Stigma," in Howard Becker, ed., *The Other Side* (New York: Free Press, 1964).
20. Reed Cozart, "The Benefits of Executive Clemency," *Federal Probation, 32* (1968), p. 33.
21. A. M. Kirkpatrick, "The Human Problems of Prison After-Care," *Federal Probation, 21* (1957), pp. 19–28.
22. Cozart, *op. cit.*, p. 33.
23. Reinhardt, *op. cit.*, p. 49.
24. Donald R. Taft and Ralph W. England, Jr., *Criminology*, 4th ed. (New York: Macmillan, 1964), pp. 271–79.
25. This fact is borne out by recidivism figures. See, for example: John Edgar Hoover, *Crime in the United States: Uniform Crime Reports* (Washington, D.C., 1968), pp. 34–44.

26. Tony Parker and Robert Allerton, "On Being a Criminal," in Charles McCaghy, James Skipper, and Mark Lefton, eds., *In Their Own Behalf: Voices from the Margin* (New York: Appleton-Century-Crofts, 1968), p. 178.
27. Charles F. Marden and Gladys Meyer, *Minorities in American Society,* 2nd ed. (New York: American Book Co., 1962), p. 51.
28. Wirth, *op. cit.,* p. 354.
29. *Ibid.,* pp. 357–58.
30. *Ibid.,* pp. 361–63.
31. See Stokely Carmichael and Charles V. Hamilton, *Black Power: The Politics of Liberation in America* (New York: Random House, 1967).
32. See Edward Sagarin, *Odd Man In: Societies of Deviants in America* (Chicago: Quadrangle Books, 1969).
33. Donald R. Cressey, "Social Psychological Foundations for Using Criminals in the Rehabilitation of Criminals," *Journal of Research in Crime and Delinquency,* 2 (1965), p. 56.
34. For a review of the phenomenon of self-help groups of convicts and ex-convicts, see William C. Kuehn, "The Concept of Self-Help Groups Among Criminals," *Criminologica,* 7 (May, 1969), pp. 20–25; also Edward Sagarin, *op. cit.,* Chapter 7.
35. See, for example, Edwin H. Sutherland, *The Professional Thief* (Chicago: University of Chicago Press, 1936).
36. For probably the most thorough treatment of the concept of subcultures of criminals and criminal types, see Marvin E. Wolfgang and Franco Ferracuti, *The Subculture of Violence* (London: Tavistock, 1967).
37. Robert K. Merton, *Social Theory and Social Structure* (New York: Free Press, 1957), pp. 153–55.

The Radical Right as a Minority Group

John Howard

There is a growing body of literature in which the concept of minority group is employed to understand the problems and status of women, youth, the aged, the physically handicapped, and various other categories of persons. This literature suggests that concepts and models originally developed in the study of racial and ethnic categories may have analytic utility when applied to populations not ordinarily thought of as minority groups. This article is addressed to the question of whether the radical right can be usefully conceptualized as a minority group.

My conclusions can be briefly summed up as follow:

1. In a structural sense the radical right is not a minority group as the concept is conventionally understood.

2. The perspective of many persons on the far right is similar, however, to that of members of a minority group. In terms of political attitudes and values many manifest what Hofstadter has labelled "the paranoid style."[1]

3. The perspective of the right derives from certain persistent strains and tensions in the American system and is important in that occasionally it breaks through to broadly mark the course of political events.

4. The persistence of the strains and tensions which generate the paranoid style can be better understood if one departs from the broadly conventional conceptualization of minority group and employs what might be termed a radical conception of the minority group phenomenon.

The Radical Right

The right can be identified in terms of certain organizations and/or in terms of a given constellation of attitudes. The former is more important as it determines the impact of rightist organizations on the society. If these organizations speak for broad masses of people, if they reflect widely shared beliefs and attitudes, then obviously they become something more than sectarian curiosities, the object of contempt and amusement.

Here I shall briefly identify the major constituencies of rightist organizations and the broad constellation of beliefs to which they subscribe.

The Hard Right and the Soft Right

Several students have attempted to identify the organizations on the right. The task is made difficult by the fact that a number are sweaty, transient affairs consisting of hardly more than one zealot and a packet of letterhead stationery. Among the more tenacious right-wing organizations are the Christian Crusade, the John Birch Society, and the Ku Klux Klan. Borrowing from the terminology of the right, one can refer to the members of these organizations as hard-core and the constituencies to which they appeal as being fellow-travelers or softs. These three organizations differ from each other in orientation, but the spectrum they represent comes close to embracing the range of thought found on the right. Their constituencies overlap, but nevertheless there are differences in the profile of the typical member. In discussing these organizations one can both survey the range of radical right thinking and describe the characteristics of members and supporters.

The three broad orientations found among these organizations are Christian fundamentalism (the Christian Crusade), anti-Communism (the John Birch Society), and racism (the Ku Klux Klan).[2] There is a high degree of overlap in their doctrines; they differ with regard to emphasis.

The Christian Crusade was founded by the Reverend Billy James Hargis, a graduate of Ozark Bible College. The Crusade is centered in Tulsa, Oklahoma and sponsors speaking tours, radio programs, and special schools.

Hargis articulates a straightforward kind of fundamentalism.

> Never did the founding fathers of America intend that our government become which denies God. Never did they intend for our government to "shield" our children from the saving knowledge of God's truth by banning the Bible and prayer from the public schools. The first great American president, George Washington, made it clear that it is impossible to govern the world without the Bible.[3]

The Christianity of Hargis rests on the belief that the mission of the church is to save souls, not correct social ills. He identifies as communist in inspiration those actions of clerics which are ecumenical in intent or which spring from the social gospel.

Hargis' strength seems to be in the Southwest and the South. His radio program is carried by stations in those areas more so than by stations in the East. His appeal seems to be to the small town and rural white Anglo-Saxon Protestant.

The John Birch Society deals primarily in fear of communism. It intensifies that fear, then presents its own program for combatting the communist beast. Its anti-communism is expressed mainly via

militant nationalism in terms of foreign affairs and opposition domestically to policies intended to improve the lot of have-not groups such
as blacks and the poor.[4]

The supporters of the Society tend to be more affluent than those
of the Christian Crusade and they are more likely to live in urban
areas. A California poll of attitudes toward the Birch Society suggested that the profile of the average person with a positive attitude
was as follows: Male, traditionally Republican, Protestant, either
some college or a college graduate, medium to high economic level,
a business man, professional, or retired.[5] "Its sociological profile,"
observed Hofstadter, "is that of a group enjoying a strong social
position, mainly well-to-do and educated beyond the average, but
manifesting a degree of prejudice and social tension not customarily
found among the affluent and the educated."[6] John Sheerin has
suggested a similar profile:

> It is true that the movement has its roots in fundamentalist, rural
> Protestants, especially among people of some affluence. Among its
> leaders are Edgar C. Bundy, an ordained minister of the Southern
> Baptist Church; (and) Carl McIntire, a "defrocked" Presbyterian
> minister from Collingswood, New Jersey.[7]

The Ku Klux Klan must by now be regarded as an old American
institution, part of our national heritage. It has experienced several
reincarnations but in each of its lives has traded principally in racism.
On the whole its members and vocal supporters seem to be inferior in
socioeconomic status to those of the Birch society and less staid and
respectable than the Christian Crusade followers. In the nature of
things it is not easy to get reliable data on the Klan, but Vander
Zanden managed to obtain information on 153 Klansmen. They
held such jobs as gas station attendant, grocery store clerk, truck
driver, garage mechanic, machinist, and carpenter.[8] Chalmers indicated that whereas in parts of the South the White Citizens Councils
drew businessmen, bankers, and lawyers, the more openly and vio-
lently racist Klan recruited "mechanics, farmers, and storekeepers."[9]

There are hundreds of right-wing organizations. These three
represent three major orientations: religious fundamentalism, anti-
communism expressed as strong nationalism and opposition to domes-

tic social welfare programs, and racism. No one knows how many members these organizations have, but that is not wholly to the point. The number of supporters is much greater than the number of members. There seem to be three overlapping constituencies. The interests of these constituencies are not always wholly consistent (Birchers, for example, are probably more conservative on economic questions than are the less affluent members and supporters of the Klan). Consequently, there is often bitter strife between organizations on the right.

A fourth group might be added to the constituencies of the right: the urban, working poor, the white worker earning $5,000 to $10,000 a year. This individual finds himself in a continual economic bind; he sees many of the values and institutions which he was taught to revere attacked and ridiculed. He is against the putative agents of destruction: niggers, peace creeps, weirdoes, eggheads, commies, politicians, students, dope fiends, sex perverts, and anyone else whom he does not understand or whose difference makes him uncomfortable. George Wallace probably drew the bulk of his support in the North from among the white working poor.

In summary, something which might be termed "right-wing sentiment" probably characterizes much of the population. The extreme conservative radio commentator, Paul Harvey, articulated a perspective found among many persons on the right.

> I am a displaced person though I never left my homeland. I am a native-born American. I never left my country. It left me.

There is the sense in that statement of viewing oneself as a member of a minority group, a stranger in the land.

The Minority Group Concept and the Radical Right

To ask whether the radical right is a minority group is to ask any or all of three questions:

1. Can the theoretical models commonly employed to account for the existence of negative attitudes about racial and ethnic groups be used to explain popular views on the radical right?

2. Is the radical right exposed to some form of discrimination which flows from and is explainable by their collective political identity?

3. Does the radical right show a collective perspective similar to that of ethnic or racial minorities?

There are at least three theoretical approaches widely employed to account for negative attitudes toward minority groups: the frustration-aggression-displacement theory, the repression-projection theory, and what for want of a better term can be called "interest" theories. None of these accounts for popular views toward the radical right. Briefly, the frustration-aggression-displacement approach suggests that racial and ethnic hostility is a consequence of displacing upon these groups the anger arising from sources of which one is unaware or over which one has no control. The right is not an object of popular contumely, in large part, because many people are unaware of its existence. The general public does not view given constellations of attitudes as being rightist in nature. Most people are unaware of the existence of right-wing organizations. The John Birch Society is the best known conservative organization, yet a Gallup poll of February, 1962, taken on a national sample, indicated that 7 persons out of 10 had either never heard of the Society or had no opinion about it.[10]

The repression-projection process has been discussed in terms of such things as the sexual overtones in the anti-Negro stereotype, the sexually repressed individual presumably being able to have his psychological cake and eat it too by indulging in all sorts of fantasies about Negro sexuality while feeling indignant at the reality he supposes his fantasies represent. Clearly there is no analog of this as regards the image of the right. To the extent that a stereotype does exist, it is one of amused contempt ("the little old lady in tennis shoes") rather than intense fear and hatred.

The interest group approach suggests that racism is a device which allows certain groups to secure and rationalize unfair privileges. Thus, allegedly, management uses it to drive a wedge between white and black workers, white workers use it to keep blacks in the lowest paying and dirtiest jobs or out of work altogether. Again, clearly this model is not applicable in terms of the radical right.

As regards the second question, there is no evidence that rightists collectively experience discrimination. Unlike Jews and blacks they do not have an historically formed collective identity based, in large part, on having been the victims of severe and pervasive discrimination. Shibutani and Kwan suggest that "a minority group consists of people of low standing—people who receive unequal treatment and who therefore come to regard themselves as objects of discrimination."[11] In these terms, the radical right is not a minority group.

In terms of the third question, the radical right does in many striking ways reveal a perspective similar to that of minority groups. Minority groups commonly develop a certain view of the world. There is a tendency toward obsessive concern with the characteristics which define one's status, to see it as mediating every interaction. There is a tendency to view all of the persons not a member of one's group as hostile and to feel that one's compatriots are peculiarly prone to "selling out." There is what might be termed a "collective ego." In other words, any triumph or failure of a member of the group is felt to have meaning for the status and future of the entire group.

The perspective of racial, ethnic, and religious minorities is grounded in reality. They really have historically been the victims of discrimination and prejudice. The collective ego develops as a response to the tendency of nonmembers of the group to assign collective blame or virtue.

The persecutions visited upon the radical right are less visible to the dispassionate observer. It is not so much that the right is persecuted but that it believes that it is. There are certain key elements in the world view of the minority group member: a sense of being blameless and possibly even praiseworthy, and a belief that others not only do not recognize one's virtue but are actively engaged in malicious actions. There is a sense then that the members of the group must band together, that they must "all hang together or hang separately."

These elements are prominently displayed in the thinking of the radical right. The radio commentator, Paul Harvey, communicated the sense of being innocent yet put upon:

> Youngster, let me tell you what it was like in the Old Country. We had fun in the Old Country . . . we didn't concentrate on learnin' the tricks of the trade; we learned the trade.
> . . . religion and education were all so mixed up together when I was a boy you couldn't tell where one left off and the other began. Patriotism was taught in every school class every day. Our national heroes were honored, almost revered.
> In the Old Country.
> . . . Folks who worked harder were rewarded for it, so everybody worked harder.
> We had no card-carrying Communists; we had Cross-carrying Christians . . . in the Old Country. We told dialect jokes and everybody laughed, because all of us were "mostly something else," in the Old Country. It isn't there anymore.[12]

The sense of moral virtue of most rightists comes from perceiving themselves as the guardians of an older and finer ethic. Ezra Taft Benson, Secretary of Agriculture during both Eisenhower administrations, and later a vocal spokesman for various right-wing organizations, articulated this:

> I wonder what our founding fathers would do and say about America today if they were here. . . . They would be concerned with the growing alarming growth of a something-for-nothing philosophy, a failure of people to stand on their own feet. They would find some bad examples by unscrupulous politicians and by delinquent parents, and possibly a weakening of religious training, and the substitution therefore of a faith-destroying materialism.[13]

There is an obsessive quality to the minority group world view. The black sees all his dealings with people as mediated by color. He is sensitive to the least nuances from others. If the media do not portray blacks, he is angry; if they do, he questions the sincerity of media executives and the "honesty" of the way blacks are portrayed. There is literally no phase of existence which cannot be filtered through colored lenses. Likewise, the hard core rightist tends to be obsessive in his thinking. Issues which are ordinarily not deemed political are interpreted by him in terms of the need to maintain vigilance against communists, liberals, and other enemies. Thus there is a rich literature on the dangers of mental health programs, for example, Kenneth Goff's *Facts on Mental Health,* Tom Sullivan's *Mental Health,* Martin Gross' *The Brain Watchers,* and Lewis Alesen's *Mental Robots.* Virtually every political or economic issue is interpreted in terms of the evil manipulations of communists. Thus the gold crisis was "explained" in Major George Racey Jordan's *The Gold Swindle,* the income tax in Frank Chodorov's *Income Tax: Root of All Evil,* student discontent in E. Merrill Root's *Brainwashing in the High Schools.* Rightists see themselves as living in a world in which evil people have power, a world in which the things they believe in are under attack and the goods they possess not securely theirs. The Birch Society observed in 1965:

Medicare: ". . . the principal object of 'medicare' is to destroy the independence and integrity of American physicians . . . ."

The economic situation: "The conspiracy can produce a total economic collapse any time that it decides to pull the chain."

The Federal Government: "Communist domination of many of the departments of the Federal Government is too obvious to require much comment."[14]

The world view of the rightist is not unlike that of the member of a minority group. There is the same obsessive quality, political and social values taking the place of race or ethnicity in pervading every situation, in ordering reality, and in ranking people. There is the same sense that one's vital interests are threatened, that one's enemies are in control of the situation. There is something of the same sense of being outnumbered and often beleaguered.

Is it correct to call the radical right "sick"? Would it be correct to refer to them as paranoid in a clinical sense? I think not. Just as the world view of the black or Jew or Puerto Rican or woman has some basis in reality, in a certain kind of way, that of the radical right does also.

American Social Structure and the Radical Right

A value system such as that in the United States, which suggests that every man has a chance to be upwardly mobile and that talent and ambition are required for such mobility, also suggests that those who are not mobile are quite possibly lacking in talent and ambition. Robert Lane's discussion of the attitudes of a selected group of adults in an Atlantic seaboard community which he called "Eastport" dealt, in part, with this perspective. There was in the community ". . . a tendency to believe that men in high places deserve the power and honor and responsibility; otherwise they wouldn't be there . . . those who are unsuccessful are . . . thought to have failed, in considerable part, because of 'playing the ponies,' drink, laziness, or shiftlessness."[15]

The Psychological Meaning of Status in American Society

If an individual has internalized this value system, then there is a linking of class position and conception of self. This link exists not only subjectively for the individual but also for others in the society as they view him. There is a tacitly assumed link between the slot an individual occupies in the stratification system and the kind of person he must be. Hence, the first question one asks in this society if one wants to learn about another is, "What does he do for a living?" The answer is assumed to give a rough indication of status, and from this inferences are made about the other characteristics an individual must have.[16]

For those with high status in an open society there are certain psychological gratifications in that there can be some sense of possessing the culturally approved characteristics. The potential for a positive self-conception is greater given that the possession of a high status position is assumed tacitly or explicitly to be the consequence of possessing certain approved personality characteristics. For those with a low status within the open society there are certain psychological pressures: A tacit or explicit assumption of their position is that they are personally inadequate. The literature on mobility suggests that downwardly mobile persons resist identifying with the class into which they have fallen while the upwardly mobile become, in some respects, over-identifiers with the class into which they have moved. It can be reasonably inferred that the sense of personal adequacy generated by the former and of personal self-worth derived from the latter account for this. Within the open society it becomes psychologically important for those with position to attempt to conserve it, and equally important for those without position to seek, by whatever means, to achieve it.

The Extrinsic Meaning of Status in American Society

In a closed society one cannot, in the nature of things, expect more—more in the way of material rewards, more in the way of positive feedback from others. Rewards are differentially distributed in this kind of open society as they are in the closed society, but in this society the individual without position is always aware of the possibility of getting more, and those with position of the possibility of getting less. Put somewhat differently, it is simply more comfortable to have position,[17] but the ethic of openness implies to the individual that he has no immutable claim to comfort for himself or his progeny. Again within the society those with rewards are faced with the task of seeking by various ways and means to conserve them, those without of seeking to gain them.

Implicit in this discussion is the assumption that the individual seeks to conserve or enhance his status position. This is the key assumption in terms of the theoretical position being taken here. In the above discussion the attempt was made to indicate why an individual in an open society seeks to conserve or enhance his status position.

A society can distribute rewards to its members because of their position along either achieved or ascribed dimensions. The open society, of course, explicitly emphasizes the former, while reward distribution in closed societies is based on the latter. Both play a role in every society and it is a matter of the relative weighting attached to each. This means that some people in the open society because of their ranking on both dimensions may be able to invoke claims to status, while others because of their ranking along both dimensions may be unable to invoke claims to status. Yet other people may be able to invoke such claims because of their ranking on one dimension or the other. It is possible, then, to classify people in terms of the following four categories: (1) high ascription, high achievement, (2) high ascription, low achievement, (3) low ascription, high achievement, and (4) low ascription, low achievement.*

Persons in different categories have a different complex of experiences and are exposed to different kinds of pressures, or, to put it another way, the kinds of threats they perceive are a consequence of the place they happen to occupy in the social matrix. As a result of these status-linked threats a perspective is created for those in each category which makes the ideology of particular kinds of deviant political organizations meaningful. Categories (1) and (2) seem to yield a perspective supportive of rightist organizations.

High Ascription, High Achievement

Those high on both of these dimensions in the United States have traditionally been the middle, upper-middle, and upper class, white, Anglo-Saxon Protestants. This group subdivides into an eastern urban and urbane wing and a midwestern, southern, and western, small-town, more provincial wing.[18] These groups differ in several ways. The eastern segment tends toward the more intellectual Protestant denominations—Congregationalism, Episcopalianism, Unitarianism—the midwestern element toward denominations with a more literal interpretation of scripture and a less ecumenical outlook. The midwestern group tends toward a greater puritanism, that is, prohibition on the use of alcohol, concern with "smut," rejection of "foreign" ideas.

Threats, insofar as this group is concerned, relate both to pressures within the open society to widen the channels for upward mobility, thus facing the group with a whole host of new competitors for the rewards of the society, and to measures which in promoting universalistic principles undermine their ascriptive-based claims to status. For a period during the 1960s this group was in precipitate cultural

---

* In this paper only two of the categories are dealt with. Persons in the other two tend to be left radical in their orientation. This is discussed in John Howard, "The Social Basis of Political Deviance," a paper delivered at the meetings of the Western Political Science Association, March, 1965.

decline. Their styles, values, and privileges were eroding. They saw an Irish Catholic assume the presidency, a Negro senator, Negro city councilmen in many municipalities, and Jews in a variety of higher level government posts.[19] They saw the civil rights movement undercut their claims along the ascribed dimension. Hofstadter has enlarged on their sense of being expropriated:

> These people, whose stocks were once far more unequivocally dominant in America than they are today, feel that their ancestors made and settled and fought for this country. They have a certain sense of proprietorship in it. . . . These people have a considerable claim to status which they celebrate by membership in such organizations as the D.A.R. and the S.A.R. . . . although very often quite well-to-do, they feel that they have been pushed out of their rightful place in American life, even out of their neighborhoods. Most of them have been traditionally Republican by family inheritance, and they have felt themselves edged aside by the immigrants, the trade unions, and the urban machines in the last thirty years.[20]

In terms of conserving status one would then expect the persons in this category to react to moves toward further openness in the society by accentuating the importance of the ascribed dimension and by attacking those measures which broaden the channels for mobility from below.

The kinds of deviant political organizations which draw their membership largely from persons in this category do show these two characteristics in terms of goals and ideology.

The John Birch Society probably draws the bulk of its support from persons in this category as does the Christian Crusade and many of the other older, more stable right-wing organizations.

The Birch program, involving as it does attacks upon trade unions, the civil rights movement, welfare measures, civil liberties organizations, etc., can be seen as an advocacy of measures which would have the effect of introducing greater closure into the society, thus conserving the status of persons in this group.[21] The Birch conception of Americanism seems to be synonymous with a set of attitudes and policy positions which would have the consequence of making unassailable the status and cultural style largely of the fundamentalist having small-town oriented, "old Americans" in the high-high category.

High Ascription, Low Achievement

Those in this category have traditionally been working class or poor whites in the South and Southwest who have enjoyed higher status in terms of ascription than Negroes, Mexicans, or other racial minorities. A tendency toward greater conservatism in this group than one would expect in terms of their class position can possibly be explained in the following way: To the extent that public policies intended to open channels for upward mobility also involve supporting the principle of universalism, thus bringing into question the legitimacy of basing claims to status upon ascription, persons in this category will be opposed to them. Widening channels for mobility might or might not benefit them, while undermining the ascribed basis for their status definitely would not benefit them. Thus, virtually in probability terms conserving status is better served by opposing any measure which introduces universalism even if that measure also promises to widen the channels for upward mobility.

As was indicated, Klansmen tend to be persons whose only unequivocal claim to status is along the ascribed dimension. In these terms, in the faces of moves to open further the society they gravitated to a deviant political organization accentuating the importance of the one dimension along which they did unequivocally have high status.

The perspective of the right has some basis in reality, then. The radical right is not a minority group in the conventional sense. Its members manifest the perspective of a minority group which feels itself persecuted because their fears about the erosion of caste and class status and privilege have some foundation in reality. Greater equity in the society means that they will lose a privileged position. Although the style may be paranoid, the people are not paranoid in a clinical sense.

The conventional conceptualization of minority group only partially encompasses the radical right. An alternative conceptualization of the minority group phenomenon, which would embrace the right as well as youth, women, racial and ethnic minorities and other persons to whom the category is conventionally related, is needed.

Toward a Radical Conception of Minority Group

"When they speak of social stratification, sociologists are referring to the ranking of categories of people, not the ranking of individuals. Some persons live in comfort while others endure deprivation, not because of their . . . personal qualities, but because of their social status."[22]

Minority groups, as conventionally conceived of, are found in certain kinds of stratified societies. The minority group is disadvantaged as regards political power, access to material resources, and the opportunity to acquire wealth and power. The disadvantaged position of the minority group is rationalized and justified by privileged persons in terms of the alleged negative aspects of certain ascribed characteristics of the minority group, for example, "women are too emotional to make good executives," "students are too young and immature to be able to set their own social codes," "blacks are too dumb to be promoted· to skilled jobs."

Let us take a member of the working poor, a 28-year-old, semiskilled, white worker with a wife and two children, making $8,000 a year. Let us say that when the wife works part time, the family income goes up to $10,000 a year. Let us say that this worker is anti-black and that he opposes the civil rights movement, feeling the blacks are getting the treatment they deserve at the hands of the traditionally hostile segments of the society.

This worker is better off than many blacks, but relative to the executives of the plant for which he works he is more disadvantaged than blacks relative to him. A large body of research has indicated that the distribution of wealth is greatly skewed in the United States.[23] A small number of people are very wealthy but the great majority of wage earners are only a paycheck or two away from disaster. Most do not realize this, but it is as true of the college professor as it is of the factory hand.

The white worker, with his constant worry over time payments and his chronic shortage of funds near the end of the week, is far from affluent. He is better off than the black but he is not particularly well off. This is true of the small entrepreneur, of the salesman, of the small farmer, of the elderly retired, and of the others who make up the legions of the radical right.

As regards per capita share of the wealth, the white worker and minor entrepreneur are probably much closer to blacks than they are to the top executives in the 100 largest firms in the country.

The children of the white worker enjoy better mobility possibilities than the children of the black worker. The former enjoy the opportunity to get the same or possibly a slightly better job than their father had. But again, what they are getting is not likely to substantially provide security or even well-being.

The persistence of tax loopholes and various kinds of subsidies and allowances indicates that corporate elites have enough power to bring about the creation of laws beneficial only to themselves and are able to deflect efforts to alter these laws.

Finally, the mythology subscribed to by much of the public, the ideology of the common man, has the consequence of rationalizing and justifying the interests of economic and political elites while not really serving the interests of nonelites. In other words, if the common man moralizes downward and resents "welfare chiselers" but does not direct anger upward at corporate thieves who may have picked his pocket infinitely more, this serves the interest of corporate figures but not the common man. Much of the public mythology about success being a result of "working hard" and "getting ahead on your own" has the consequence of undermining social welfare policies which might in fact provide sounder structural supports for mobility and a decent standard of living. Conventionally members of minority groups are deemed to suffer a low estate because of certain innate failings. In a similar fashion, the worker or small businessman falling on hard times is likely to be deemed to have "lacked the stuff" to make a go of it.

In short, the position being taken here is that there are elites and then there are the masses, and vis-à-vis elites everyone is a member of a minority group. Some know it and some do not. The typical Bircher thinks he is in a privileged position. But in focusing on the alleged threat from below of the nonwhite rather than the political and financial advantages of those above him, he saves himself a fraction in terms of status advantage rather than a more substantial sum.

If credence is given to the notion of a power elite, then everyone is a member of a minority group vis-à-vis that elite. Some are privileged members of the minority group (as the black bourgeoisie is among blacks in terms of the more conventional conceptualization), but in a larger sense all are *dis*privileged.

In terms of the conventional conception of minority group, supporters of the radical right fit only marginally; in terms of the radical conception suggested here, of course, they are a minority group.

In this radical definition of minority group, a number of questions arise: How does it articulate with the concept of class? Does it obscure important distinctions such as the difference between disprivilege based on ascription and disprivilege based on other factors? These are important questions which require extended answers. At this point I would simply suggest that it might be fruitful to make "minority group" the most inclusive concept in terms of stratification.

If this approach is useful then, of course, both you and I are minority group members. We may differ only in perception of what we are.

REFERENCES

1. See Richard Hofstadter, *The Paranoid Style in American Politics and Other Essays* (New York: Knopf, 1964).
2. Other organizations in each category include the following: Christian fundamentalist—the American Action Council, Inc.; anti-Communist—Alerted Americans, America First, The Christian Anti-Communist Crusade, and We, The People; racist—Association of Southern Defenders, National Segregation Party, National States Rights Party, Patriots of North Carolina, Sons of Confederate Veterans, and White Citizens of America.
3. Billy James Hargis, *Communist America: Must It Be?* (Tulsa, Okla.: Christian Crusade, 1960), pp. 32–33.
4. For an articulation of the views of the Society's founder, see Robert Welch, *The Blue Book of the John Birch Society,* published by the Society, Belmont, Mass.
5. Seymour Martin Lipset, "Three Decades of the Radical Right," in Daniel Bell, ed., *The Radical Right* (New York: Doubleday, 1964), pp. 422–25.
6. Hofstadter, *op. cit.,* p. 71.

7. John B. Sheerin, "Catholic Right Wing Extremists," *Catholic World* (March, 1962), p. 325.
8. James W. Vander Zanden, *Race Relations in Transition* (New York: Random House, 1965), pp. 41–43.
9. David Chalmers, *Hooded Americanism: The First Century of the Ku Klux Klan, 1865–1965* (Garden City, N.Y.: Doubleday, 1965), p. 345.
10. Lipset, *op. cit.*, p. 422.
11. Tamotsu Shibutani and Kian M. Kwan, *Ethnic Stratification* (New York: Macmillan, 1965), p. 35.
12. Paul Harvey, "Why Not Return to the Old Country," *Human Events* (September, 1963).
13. Ezra Taft Benson, *The Red Carpet* (Salt Lake City: Bookcraft, 1962), pp. 239–40.
14. William F. Buckley, Jr., "The Birch Society, August 1965," *National Review* (October 19, 1965), pp. 916–18.
15. Robert Lane, "The Lower Classes Deserve No Better Than They Get," in Robert E. Will and Harold O. Vatter, eds., *Poverty in Affluence* (New York: Harcourt, Brace and World, 1965), p. 68. Hence, also the widespread belief that those on welfare are the unworthy poor.
16. In a closed society, one might ask, "What family?" "What lineage?" "What clan?" What the individual is assumed to be is a consequence of the category into which he was born.
17. This is hardly debatable. Greater income and job security mean a better chance to clothe oneself adequately, to eat properly, to live in a comfortable dwelling, to send one's children to summer camp, etc.
18. For a discussion of variations in degree of intellectualization in Protestant denominations, see H. Richard Niebuhr's *The Social Sources of Denominationalism* (New York: Meridian Books, 1960). For a discussion of the religious styles of particular regions, see John Dollard's *Caste and Class in a Southern Town* (New York: Doubleday, 1957), August Hollingshead, *Elmtown's Youth* (New York: Science Editions, 1961), and W. Lloyd Warner, *Yankee City* (New Haven: Yale University Press, 1963).
19. One interesting indicant of the decline of this group is the change in practice with regard to finding names for movie stars. Prior to the 1950s, most movie stars had Anglo-Saxon names, the principal exceptions being those who were obviously foreigners. Presumably, changing names which had an ethnic identity resulted from the fact that white, Anglo-Saxon Protestant identity was the cultural ideal. Thus, Jules Garfinkle became John Garfield, Bernard Schwartz became Tony Curtis, David Kaminsky became Danny Kay, and Jerome Levitch became Jerry Lewis. In the last decade, however, Marilyn Novak was changed only to Kim Novak, the ethnic last name being retained, while neither Annette Funicello nor Anthony Franciosa changed their names.
20. Hofstadter, *op. cit.*, pp. 54–55.
21. An implication of the position being taken here is that anti-Communism, as such, is not an explanation for Birchism. Rather, the Birchers identify the things they do not happen to like with a currently very unpopular movement as a result of a not uncommon human tendency to identify whatever happens to be inimical to personal interests with something

widely regarded as evil. Analogously, an individual reared in a puritanical home might have certain guilt feelings about sex and a consequent tendency toward reaction formation expressed in fighting "smut." He might argue his case on religious grounds, coming genuinely to feel that girlie magazines were not simply personally upsetting but an actual violation of "God's law."

22. Shibutani and Kwan, *op. cit.*, p. 29.
23. For a comprehensive treatment of the subject, see Ferdinand Lundberg, *The Rich and the Super-Rich* (New York: Lyle Stuart, 1968).

Crisis in Blue: The Police as a Minority Group

Jeffrey Goldstein

I am seated in a small auditorium of a New York City elementary school. It is located in a Puerto Rican ghetto. Surrounding me sit one hundred and fifty fourth grade pupils grouped as follows: 83 per cent are Puerto Rican, 15 per cent Negro, 2 per cent white and others. Projected upon a large white screen is a color slide of two men standing in unison, dressed identically.

A deep voice questions: "And what are these men called?"

Hands are raised. "Cops," replies one child in an obviously serious tone.

"Fuzz," chides another, while a third shouts, "The Man." The young audience remains still. Eyes fix dramatically upon the Police Department's guest speaker, and Jewish teachers appear to be nervous.

The above is merely a trivial incident. Yet with close scrutiny and contrived inquisitiveness, many socially relevant questions can be asked. One such question arising from the above is: Are the police, by virtue of the badge and uniform they wear and the relationship they bear to others in the society, members of a minority group, comparable in many ways to racial, ethnic, religious, and national minorities? In other words, does the police subgroup fit into a methodologically sound sociological framework that may be applicable to the discussion of all minority groups?

Before discussing the circumstances surrounding the police as a collectivity and those characteristics inherent to it, it is essential to establish a reasonable definition and/or framework of the minority group construct that may be used to channel this investigation and to arrive at a useful answer.

That the concept of minority group is not well defined is illustrated by Morton B. King, who writes:

> On my desk are twelve books, published since 1948. The publisher of each hopes I will adopt it as a text for a course called "minority groups." The titles, points of view, and the contents vary widely. The most frequently occurring word is minority, yet the authors use it with different denotative and connotative meanings.[1]

The problem of definition of the minority group concept is not a new one. The arrived at definition is often only workable and salient to its originator. And, as King points out, many groups labeled minorities would not fulfill the requirements offered by certain definitions that supposedly describe the minority group. It is fruitless to discuss a concept, and particularly to see whether a single phenomenon fits into it, without a proper definition. Ideally, it is the goal of social scientists, as it is of all scientists, to establish applicable and universally acceptable definitions so as to avoid the confusions that otherwise must follow.

As Bierstedt points out in *The Social Order*,[2] it is possible to see four types of groups in society. A group may be statistical (a mathematical collectivity, for which many avoid the word group, and prefer such a term as aggregate), societal (often ascribed, not involving face-to-face interaction, as an ethnic group), social (primary, interactive, but unstructured, as a gang or clique), and associational (organizational, structured, rather formal). Inherent in all groups except statistical, in the view of Bierstedt, is a consciousness of kind, a sense of identification of the members with one another. Many of these groups are of course statistical minorities, but they are not minority groups in the sense in which that phrase is being used, if only because the members are not in a subordinate position in society. On the other hand, there are societies in which a numerical majority of the people are in a subordinate or, one might say, a minority status.

Subordinate status seems to be the first key trait of the minority, and this requires the ability of the society (particularly the dominant group) to identify the minority members. "If the members of a society are to exclude some of their fellows from full participation in the culture and define them as a minority, the people who comprise the minority must have some visible characteristic by which they can be identified," state Young and Mack,[3] who bring into play other characteristics of the minority group. These characteristics are: exclusion from full participation in society and a superordinate-subordinate relationship. Exclusion from full participation in society is a characteristic common to all minority groups. An example of this is found in the Negro's difficulty, by virtue of his minority status, to obtain employment, housing, medical care, and other needs available to those not sharing his status. The exclusion is involuntary, and is prescribed by the rest of society. The desire of a minority to enter the full stream of the society becomes irrelevant to the dominant group.

Nevertheless, visible characteristics are not inherent to all minority groups. The Jews, Catholics, and others are barely discernible from the rest of society. Young and Mack reason that visible characteristics must exist in order to enable a dominant group to actively prohibit a minority's entrance into the mainstream of the society. While the prohibitions or discriminations are facilitated by the visibility of the group or its members, this is not unique or even crucial in making discriminatory practices possible. Screening policies of many agencies do not necessarily rely upon visibility of group membership of potential employees. Perhaps a more precise word would be identifiability, with visibility being the most obvious, accurate, and rapid form for making such identification.

"The existence of a minority in society implies the existence of a corresponding dominant group with higher social status and greater privileges," states Gittler.[4] He asserts that the essential approach in understanding the minority group concept must center about the superordinate-subordinate relationship in all minority interaction. "Relationships not groups should be the focus of attention," writes

King.[5] "Our task is then to define a particular type of relationship which may be called (with some reservations) the minority-dominant relationship."

Logic asserts that unequal social power does and must exist in all minority-dominant relationships. Thus, King continues:

> Minority-dominant relationships may be distinguished from other interclass relationships by two main criteria. First, the relationship springs from membership in the kind of categories called groups: real social groups whose members have a definite sense of belonging and well developed we-they feelings. Secondly, the groups are distinguished by real or imaginary (alleged) differences in observable physical traits, in culture, or in both.[6]

The characteristics of the minority relationship that have so far been mentioned are summarized by King:

> Minority-dominant relationships are those which occur within a society between persons who belong to well defined social groups whose members: (a) differ or are thought to differ in culture and/or observable physical characteristics; (b) respond to each other in terms of patterns of culturally defined reciprocal attitudes imputing inherent superiority to members of one group and inherent inferiority to members of another; and (c) have because of membership in the groups unequal access to the sources of institutionalized power and hence to the opportunities and the rewards of society.[7]

Still another approach to defining the minority group is to discern whether the group in question is subject to irrelevant negative generalizations. The term generalization is used to denote a single idiosyncratic trait that is in turn thrust upon the entire group. Illustrating this concept are the following statements: Never trust a Negro, Jews are stingy, women make incompetent motorists, and the like. These irrelevant negative generalizations may very well help to illuminate the ways in which a minority group is perceived and hence treated by the rest of society. Emerging from these generalizations are the actual perceptions and reality of the minority-dominant relationship.

An analysis of the goals of a group will perhaps afford another way to delineate and sharpen the minority group concept. We can assume that the classical minority group reactions to oppression and discrimination are: (a) to assimilate into the society; (b) to "pluralize," that is, to attain equal status without losing separate identity; (c) to secede from the society; and (d) to attempt to take over the dominant position.

Keeping in mind the characteristics of the dominant-minority relationship, as cited by King and to which the negative generalization has been added, one approaches a specific group in society: the police.

Modern law enforcement practices stem from two traditional systems, the Continental and the Anglo-Saxon. The Continental tradition began with the military acting as direct agent of the central authority, functioning primarily as an instrument of despotic monarchs. The police bodies were often branches of the national military, in terms of training, salaries, authority and uniforms. Bruce Smith states: "To this day continental European countries benefit from this tradition not alone in efficiency of law enforcement but also from the fact that career police officers enjoy a social status akin to that of career military personnel."[8]

The Anglo-Saxon police tradition stems from societal attitudes characterized by suspicion and hostility toward central authority, antagonistic toward the idea that national military bodies would be held responsible for safeguarding peace. This tradition, emerging early in the growth of America, stemmed from the Edict of Winchester that suggested the local populace be responsible for the maintenance of order. And by early nineteenth century it was felt by most Americans that the protection of their property and rights could only be successfully done by themselves. Suspicion of the police body perpetuated as the United States grew. "In less dramatic form," according to Taft and England, "the growing cities in the United States similarly put up with crime and disorder, relying upon ineffective day and night watches, private police, and in a few places, militia."[9] The police forces of the late nineteenth century were characterized as inefficient. The prerequisites for this low paying job, at that time, were what Taft and England call "brawn and a taste for violence."[10] The Anglo-Saxon tradition of small areas supplying, maintaining, and organizing their own police force, coupled with citizen suspicions, similarly characterize our present police structure.

Just what are the functions of the police, and particularly the urban or city police system? Leaving the small town and state police in the background, one can begin with the statement of Smith: "To the modern mind the term police connotes a body of civil officers charged with suppressing crimes and public disorders, and regulating the use of the highways. While this popular usage is substantially correct, it fails to recognize the additional and sometimes burdensome regulatory duties which police discharge."[11] These regulatory duties often include various licensings and inspections.

Hoover, as cited by Niederhoffer, states: "Officially, the function of the police organization is: (1) protection of life and property; (2) preservation of the peace; (3) prevention of crime; (4) detection and arrest of violators of law; (5) enforcement of laws and ordinances; (6) safeguarding the rights of individuals."[12] A more radical view, also cited by Niederhoffer, reads: "The police function [is] to support and enforce the interests of the dominant political, social, and economic interests of the town, and only incidentally to enforce the law."[13]

The police function also requires subtle discriminations concerning law enforcement in the community. Essentially, the role of "acting blind" toward certain violations is part of the expectations of the police. Society and the incumbent power structure rarely desire that all laws be enforced all of the time.

Exactly how the public perceives the police and police roles is fundamental to an understanding of the police as a minority group. Regardless of the official positions offered by individual police departments concerning the function of its members, the attitudes of the public toward the force have a reality with greater significance than any formalized or apparent roles written into codes or guidelines. The renowned statement of W. I. Thomas is quite obviously pertinent: "If men define situations as real, they are real in their consequences." As Niederhoffer says, "The policeman is a 'Rorschach' in uniform as he patrols his beat. At one moment [he] is a hero, the next [a] monster."[14] On the one hand, it is society that molds the police reality; on the other it is the police self-perception that forms their own role.

The majority of people in urban society rarely come into contact with the police except in matters of traffic violations and parking rule infractions. "Overzealous traffic enforcement," writes O. W. Wilson, ". . . creates in a community, antagonism toward the police which may interfere with the successful accomplishment of the total police job."[15] Society, or rather that portion of it involved in the capacity of being motorists, will often have hostile reactions toward summonses and tickets issued by the police for an infraction of the rules, and the hostility will therefore be directed toward those issuing these summonses. This hostility is quite apparent when one realizes that a person rarely says that he got a ticket; he is usually given one.

Hence, the circumstances as well as the situation surrounding a police-civilian interaction will determine the societal reaction and concomitantly police behavior. But no aspect of community-police relationships is so fraught with hostility as the charge (or belief) that American society has in recent years seen a great deal of police brutality and unnecessary use of violence on the part of police. A writer in the *New York Times* puts it succinctly when he states: "The level of violence in police behavior tolerated at any given time is very much determined by society."[16] The reactions of the police usually vary with the circumstance and the personality of the officer. Society may react differently to each situation. In 1858, in New York, the police force recruited ten stocky, powerfully built men to round up and rid the city of a band of people described as "vicious criminals." It was reported that these men sought out the lawbreakers, and much to the approval of the public, nearly beat the enemies to death.

Some leaders of the society, some organs of influence with the public, may proselytize or defend police actions, as can be seen in a *Saturday Evening Post* editorial, which stated: "Today it is primarily the lazy or cruel policeman who wants to protect society by indiscriminate violence."[17] Nevertheless, others appear to be vindictive, seeking tight public control over the police departments and public surveillance over police actions. It is to be expected that the New York Patrolmen's Benevolent Association, as spokesman for the police, calls them New York's finest, labelling them as outstanding Americans, but others will dismiss this as self-flattery. Opponents of police speak of them as uneducated, conjecture that they are latent homosexuals, and stereotype them as sadists, all remarks heard in various segments of the intellectual community. Among the ghetto people, they are fuzz, The Man. And so it follows that within various subgroups in the big city, certain attitudes will be shared and expressed, all of which are relevant to a chosen life style.

To some, there is little respect for the occupation of policeman. Queens College students in New York City, for example, ranked the patrolman as seventeenth out of a group of twenty-three occupations. Among the youth and ghetto people, many hold the police in contempt, and see in the uniform a symbol of a society that keeps them in restraint, a society that is oppressive. Among such persons, and in such groups, it is not at all rare that the police are referred to, not merely as the enemy and The Man, but as pigs, motherfuckers, and self-righteous bastards, depending on the group and the level of sophistication. As Paul Woelfe describes: "To people who live in the slums, the police are, naturally, the most spectacular symbol of that society and hence draw the full brunt of disapproval. It is futile to demand respect for the institution [of the police] which in various localities has been exposed as riddled with organized crime."[18]

The media contribute to the formation of attitudes and the shaping of public perceptions of the police. Again, these attitudes are the result of the selective screening of television and newspaper coverage on behalf of members of society that hold their self and group identities as criteria of their opinions and statements. Thus, heavy coverage of head-smashing and club-swinging may be cheered by some, ignored by many, and criticized by others.

Many groups in society (that is, clergy, civil rights leaders, assorted liberals, politicians appealing to ethnic minorities for their support) have sought to establish civilian review boards. From one viewpoint, they were seeking to protect the public against the police; from another, to diminish the suspicion that people have for police, by making the latter accountable. In 1958, the citizens of Philadelphia pressed for such a board, but it proved virtually ineffective. In November 1966, New York City abolished its own board, in a referendum vote about which Niederhoffer writes: "It was not clear whether or not the vote was in favor of the police or was a backlash against minority groups."[19] Quite clearly, in this clash of views on the police, there is only a reflection of a more fundamental clash of interests.

The police reaction to suspicion, hostility, and general anti-police propaganda is similar to that of any minority group. The police force will band together in order to utilize that section of public sentiment which will enhance its situation or the position chosen to be desirable by the police power structure. The police reaction may be characterized by the statement, which they believe applies to themselves, "Damned if you do, damned if you don't." The police may see themselves at odds with many powerful and representative sections in society. They must be lenient and not lenient; violent and nonviolent. The majority of police defend their claim to the tools of the trade. They may feel that they are at war with certain elements of society, and in turn must employ those tactics and devices that are legitimate in war. "The police finds his most pressing problems in his relationship to the public," writes Westley.[20] "His service occupation is unusual in that he must discipline those whom he serves."

In carrying out their role as policemen the members of the force adopt a private language and exclusive group of norms. "The identification with this new group," Niederhoffer states, "is revealed in many facets of behavior and personality. Speech patterns reflect the loss of influence of Academy training."[21]

According to Whitaker, "More often than not isolation is forced on the policeman's family by the local population, though here too there are those who choose it. The fact is that quite apart from professional work, a large number of actions which would normally be private are controlled to some extent by the expectations of workmates and superiors and the public at large."[22]

William A. Westley offers another view of the self-perception of the police: "The police use violence illegally because such usage is seen as just, acceptable, and at times expected by his colleague group and because it constitutes an effective means for solving problems in obtaining self-esteem and status which policemen as police have in common."[23] And Whitaker asserts: "Much of [their] dissatisfaction results from a feeling of low status which in turn sometimes gives rise to violence, verbal or physical."[24] This statement should be read in conjunction with the remark of Reid, not made about police but about ethnic minorities: "What the group does as a minority is done in order to support its feelings of self-regard."[25]

The police subgroup has established a set of written and/or unwritten yet mutually agreed upon norms that govern their behavior. These norms, constituting the expected and accepted behavior among the members of one's group, particularly emphasize the we-group solidarity, as a reaction to their self-perception as victims of prejudice. "Feeling themselves continually and unjustly criticized," writes Westley, "they stand together against all outsiders including those who discipline them. There exists a tradition that no policeman turns another in."[26] They are words that could easily be written about members of an ethnic minority.

The police reaction to the civilian review board illustrates how it may be useful at times to be seen (or at least to project an image that one is seen) as an unjustly treated minority. The claim of the police focused around the appeal, on the one hand, to law and order against criminals and other unmanageable portions of the populace; and on the other, to sympathies of the public against those who harass the police and make his plight such a difficult one in life.

Is the police force a minority group? Intertwined with this question is still another, namely, whether the police-public relationship is one of interclass relations or dominant-minority intergroup relations. King, it will be recalled, used two criteria to differentiate interclass from dominant-minority relationships. First, the latter spring from membership in real groups: real social groups whose members have a definite sense of belonging and well-developed we-they feelings. Such a group has consciousness of kind, and if it does not have heightened social interaction and formal social organization, it has the potential for such. The police certainly meet this criterion: They are a cohesive group, bound together by strong we-they feelings. Due to their occupational status, they are not only police during work hours, but at all times, and have a considerable amount of social interaction among themselves, at work and at other times. Within the police force of almost every medium-sized and large city, some social organization is to be found. With its regulations and rules, the organization is well defined, often developing associational norms that supplement the professional or occupational ones. In short, the police are a real group, and may be considered such in any discussion of dominant-minority relationships.

Secondly, King mentions that these groups must be distinguished by real or alleged differences in physical and/or cultural characteristics. The visibility of the patrolman is apparent: He may easily be spotted in the conspicuous blue, brass-studded uniform and military-type hat. To the practiced eye, plainclothesmen can readily be seen dispersed among crowds, while rookies are seen in their gray uniforms (that is the color in New York and several other cities). Still, some members remain hidden, detected only by a few or on the occasions that they choose to reveal their identities, as in court. But even these members, although not meeting the criterion of visibility sometimes laid down, are part of the group, identifiable through payroll records, self-definition, and definition by those others who are aware of their identities.

Members of dominant and minority groups respond to each other in terms of patterns of culturally defined reciprocal attitudes imputing inherent superiority to members of one group and inherent inferiority to members of another. These culturally defined patterns of reciprocal attitudes are seen in the mutual suspicion, contempt, and hostility with which sections of the public see the police and the latter in turn see themselves as being defined by those sections of the public. Police, like members of ethnic minorities, exploit those attitudes, maintaining that they are without warrant and in conflict with the values and needs of the society. The responses of the police can be characterized as defensive.

Relationships between minority and dominant groups are most often characterized by irrelevant negative generalizations. Uneducated, violent, fuzz, cops with a hand out for a bribe, are just a few of the negative generalizations held by the public. These negative sentiments, whether brought forth by real or imaginary incidents, are generalized rather than allowed to remain particular. The irrelevancy is determined, or said to be, if an idiosyncratic trait, found in one individual, is thrust upon the entire group. Whatever condemnable act may have been performed by a Catholic, Jew, Negro, Puerto Rican, Italian, or policeman, the minority group status becomes apparent when the description takes on the form of a stigmatizing generalization to all those who are in the category. The entire group is labeled because of the act of a member. In the case of the policeman, some people impute the negative quality to police as a group when it is encountered (or even imagined) in a policeman as an individual. All other statuses, as man or person, are forgotten as one is judged as a group member.

Finally, in a minority-dominant situation, the members of the minority group, because of this fact, have unequal access to the sources of institutionalized power, and therefore the opportunities of the members to reap the rewards of the society are limited. The police clearly do not fit into this minority group framework, for they are not the out-of-power or subordinate group. In most respects the police are the dominant group, having unequal access to the sources of institutionalized power. They may carry and discharge firearms within city limits; they may infiltrate into even the most legitimate civil rights organizations with impunity; in the charge of many, they have helped to create riots, for which mild reprimand and little or no punishment is granted; they may break laws in order to enforce them; and they exploit the perception of themselves as a minority in order to obtain legislative action that they desire.

Like other minorities, the police are identifiable when they are not visible, and they are cohesive. They respond to culturally-defined reciprocal attitudes, and they are the recipients of negative generalization. Although dominant in relationships with other groups in the society, they are denounced with the invective usually reserved for the subordinate group. They will accept the minority or even subordinate position when that self-image is useful and politically advantageous. They in turn support the definition of themselves as a minority by calling attention to the negative generalizations cast upon them as a group. It is a manipulation that has become useful since minority groups have gained intellectual respectability, since their cause has been generally accepted as being just, and they have been seen as victims rather than victimizers. The police want to have their cake and eat it, too. They want the advantage of being in the dominant position in society, while taking umbrage as if they were a minority group when they are under attack.

REFERENCES

1. Morton B. King, Jr., "The Minority Course," *American Journal of Sociology* (February, 1956), pp. 80–83.
2. Robert Bierstedt, *The Social Order* (New York: McGraw-Hill, 1963), Chapter 10.
3. Raymond W. Mack and Kimball Young, *Sociology and Social Life* (New York: American Book Co., 4th ed., 1968), p. 189.
4. Joseph B. Gittler, ed., *Understanding Minority Groups* (New York: John Wiley, 1956), pp. 134–35.
5. King, *op. cit.*
6. *Ibid.*
7. *Ibid.*
8. Bruce Smith, Jr., *Police Systems in the United States* (New York: Macmillan, 1960), p. 14.
9. Donald R. Taft and Ralph W. England, Jr., *Criminology* (New York: Macmillan, 1964), pp. 320–21.
10. *Ibid.*
11. Smith, *op. cit.*, p. 15.
12. Arthur Niederhoffer, *Behind the Shield* (Garden City, N.Y.: Doubleday, 1967), p. 11.
13. *Ibid.*, p. 12. The quote cited by Niederhoffer is from the late Joseph Lohman.
14. Niederhoffer, *op. cit.*, p. 1.
15. O. W. Wilson, *Police Administration* (New York: McGraw-Hill, 1950), p. 158.
16. Thomas R. Brooks, "Necessary Force—or Police Brutality?" *New York Times Magazine* (Dec. 5, 1965), p. 60 *et seq.*
17. Editorial, *Saturday Evening Post* (March 13, 1965).
18. Paul Woelfe, "The Policeman and His Public," *America* (November 25, 1960).
19. Niederhoffer, *op. cit.*, p. 2.
20. William A. Westley, "Violence and the Police," *American Journal of Sociology* (July, 1953), pp. 34–41.
21. Niederhoffer, *op. cit.*, pp. 54–55.
22. Ben Whitaker, *The Police* (Baltimore: Penguin Books, 1964), p. 126.
23. Westley, *op. cit.*
24. Whitaker, *op. cit.*, p. 131.
25. Ira de A. Reid, "The American Negro," in Gittler, *op. cit.*
26. Westley, *op. cit.*

Intellectuals and Stereotypes

6

That the language of minorities, the mechanisms by which certain people are thought of as minorities, and the reactions of those people to themselves and to others, can extend to socially advantaged and approved groups is the burden of the two articles by Seeman and Berger. Together, they illustrate how all-pervasive is the minority-group thinking in America, how easily the stereotype becomes a reality, even in areas least expected.

One is reminded, in reading Seeman, of the once frequently employed word, "egghead," with its connotation both of intellectual respect and of pejorative sneer. But just as Kenneth Clark, Gordon Allport, and others emphasized the extent to which minority group members internalized the antipathy and turned hostile attitudes inward toward themselves and other members of their own minority, so Seeman finds as his great surprise, his "unanticipated discovery," the use made by intellectuals of "the language and mechanisms of minority status to describe themselves and their situation."

Finally, there is Berger, who turns to sociologists to analyze the stereotypes to which they have been subject at the hands of humanist intellectuals. Although the article is essentially a contribution to the sociology of sociology, it is here that Berger finds that stereotypes (and hence minorities, by extension), have inherent similarities: Like ethnic stereotypes, Berger points out, fostered by segregation and reinforced by the consequent cultural isolation, intellectual stereotypes likewise are fostered by professional specialization and reinforced by their diverse perspectives.

The Intellectual and the Language of Minorities

Melvin Seeman

I

The signs of deep concern about the contemporary position of the intellectual in America are not hard to find. To be sure, as Merle Curti has stressed in his presidential address to the American Historical Society, anti-intellectualism—in one form or another—has a long history in American life.[1] But in recent years the situation of the intellectual has not resembled the mere continuation of a somewhat consistent and historically routine negativism. The current sense of urgency regarding the definition of the intellectual's role has found expression in a wide variety of places: from *Time* magazine's alarm about the "wide and unhealthy gap" between the American intellectuals and the people, to a series of symposiums which have appeared in the *Journal of Social Issues,* in the book edited by Daniel Bell entitled *The New American Right,* and in the thoughtful British journal, *Encounter.*[2]

Yet, in spite of this volume of words, and the talent of those involved, it is still possible to agree with Milton Gordon's remark that "the man of ideas and the arts has rarely been studied seriously as a social type by professional students of society."[3] Whether, as some have argued, this retreat from self-analysis reflects a basic disorder in the scientific study of man is debatable enough; but the fact is clear that the research techniques which have been applied to nearly everybody else—from the hobo to the business elite—have rarely been applied to ourselves.[4]

This paper is a report on one such study of ourselves, its aim being to determine how intellectuals in the current social climate deal with their identity as intellectuals and, beyond that, to suggest what difference it may make if this identity is handled in different ways.

Source: *American Journal of Sociology,* 64 (July 1958), copyright © 1958 by The University of Chicago Press. Reprinted by permission of publisher and author.

The empirical base for this report was obtained through relatively unstructured interviews (on the average about one hour in length) with all the assistant professors teaching in the humanities and social science departments of a midwestern university.[5] These interviews were not content-analyzed in any statistical sense but were simply examined (as the illustrations in the next section will show) for patterns of response.

The total number of persons interviewed was forty. They came, in the number indicated, from the following departments: Economics (7), English (6), German (2), History (4), Law (1), Mathematics (3), Philosophy (4), Political Science (2), Psychology (4), Romance Languages (3), and Sociology-Anthropology (4). The sample included no one from the physical or biological sciences, from the engineering and applied fields, or from the creative arts; and, when an appropriate level in the staff hierarchy had been selected, there was no further sampling problem. Cooperation was good: of a total of forty-five persons listed in the university directory at the assistant-professor level, only one refused to be interviewed (and four were unavailable because of assignments out of the city).

The procedure in the interview was consistent though not standardized. There was no attempt to get answers to preformed questions. We engaged, rather, in a conversation regarding a letter which outlined a plan for exploring the situation of the intellectual today. The letter was not mailed; it was read by the respondent at the start of the interview and served in this way as a common stimulus object. The body of the letter, which carried my signature, follows:

> There is considerable evidence (though debatable evidence, to be sure) that the role of the intellectual has become increasingly problematic in American life. Such evidence includes: (1) the widespread expression of anti-intellectual attitudes; (2) the increasing pressure for conformity in intellectual work; and (3) the typical isolation of the intellectual in community life. These current trends are presumably matters of considerable moment to university people who are uniquely concerned with the social conditions under which intellectual activity is carried forward.
>
> It seems to me that some effort to assess the problem among our-

selves is in order, and that such an effort might proceed initially by calling together small, informal groups of faculty members to clarify issues and get an exchange of viewpoints. This letter comes as an invitation to you to participate in one of these discussions on the current situation of the intellectual. The discussion would include four or five other persons from the humanities and social sciences, and would take roughly one hour of your time. Since several discussions are planned, I would consider it part of my responsibility to provide you with some type of analytical summary of the sessions held—in effect, a research report.

Let me emphasize that the purpose of these discussions is not to canvass possible lines of action, but to achieve a clarification of issues on matters which are clearly controversial.

Would you indicate whether you wish to be included in the list of discussants by returning this letter to me with the appropriate notation?[6]

After the respondent had read the letter, he was encouraged to comment freely on any aspect of it; then each of the three points listed in the first paragraph of the letter was discussed; and, finally, I raised the question, "Do you classify yourself as an intellectual?"

The latter question raises for us, no less than for the respondents, the matter of definition. As a first approximation, I defined the intellectuals as a group for whom the analysis of ideas in their own right (that is, for no pragmatic end) is a central occupation. The group I chose to interview was taken as a sample of intellectuals, in spite of the fact that some would surely not qualify on more stringent criteria (for example, their degree of dedication to the life of the mind or the quality of their intellectual work). The sample is defensible, however, on the ground that by social definition—whether he or his colleagues prefer it or not—the university professor teaching in the humanities or social sciences is probably the prime case of intellectual endeavor (that is, of nonpragmatic and ideological pursuits). Thus, we are concerned with the self-portrait of those who, by social definition at least, are intellectuals.[7]

II

In a certain sense the chief finding of this study consisted of a "surprise": the unanticipated discovery of the extent to which these intellectuals use the language and mechanisms of minority status to describe themselves and their situation. It may be suggested that this should have been no surprise—that arguments quite consistent with this have been advanced in many places. And to some degree that is true.

In a recent well-publicized paper in *Harper's,* for example, a French writer had this to say:

> It seems to me that the attitude of the American intellectual in comparison with his European counterpart is based on frustration and an inferiority complex. I am continually meeting people who tell me that the intellectual in Europe enjoys a position which, if not happier, is at least more dignified than that of the intellectual in America. . . . Whose fault is this? They go on to tell me that the fault rests with the American people, who have no appreciation for things of the intellect. I wonder whether it is not also in great measure the fault of the American intellectuals themselves.[8]

In a similar vein Riesman and Glazer have commented that "the opinion leaders among the educated classes—the intellectuals and those who take their cues from them—have been silenced more by their own feelings of inadequacy and failure than by direct intimidation."[9] And Marcus Cunliffe, describing the United States intellectual for *Encounter* magazine, concludes: "Altogether, there has been an unfortunate loss of self-respect. Some intellectuals have felt that, wrong about communism, they must be occupationally prone to be wrong about everything."[10]

But the point is that comments of this kind do not constitute evidence; and, indeed, it is possible, if one questions the evidence, to treat such comments themselves as reflections of a kind of minority-style indictment of one's own group (like the Jew who agrees that "we" are too clannish, the intellectual says that "we" are too weak in will). Furthermore, the comments we have cited do not provide a systematic view of the specific forms of minority language which intellectuals employ in discussing themselves. Our empirical task here is to indicate that such minority references are surprising, indeed, in their frequency and to make a start toward a categorization of the forms these references take.[11]

The clearest of these forms may be labeled *the direct acceptance of majority stereotypes*. Like the Negroes who have accepted the whites' definition of color and who choose "light" among themselves, our respondents appear eager to validate the outsider's negative view of them. One need only read these forty protocols to emerge with a collective self-portrait of the soft, snobbish, radical, and eccentric intellectual who is asocial, unreliable, hopelessly academic, and a bit stupid to boot. It is impossible to cite here the evidence for all this; but each of the stereotypes in the previous sentence has a parallel affirmation in the interview material. These affirmations are, to be sure, frequently hedged with restrictions and limitations—we are dealing, after all, with a group of highly trained qualifiers. But the significant thing is that the respondents take this opportunity to affirm the stereotype; and this affirmation is typically set in a context which makes it clear that the stereotype, rather than the qualification, has a competing chance to govern behavior. Let me give some examples:

> If there is anti-intellectualism in our community, I feel frankly we are to blame. If we can't throw off our infernal need for preaching and dictating, they have a right to damn us, and we have no answer but our own human fallibility [C-1].[12]

> It's pretty difficult for the intellectual to mix with people. They feel ill at ease. Many intellectuals are not very approachable; perhaps his training is not complete enough. The intellectual may be more to blame for that than anyone else [C-2].

> My general attitude is that some of the intellectuals are so concerned with academic freedom that it kind of tires me. And, I think, this sometimes adds up to wanting more freedom than anybody else— the kind of freedom to be irresponsible. [And later, when asked whether the letter should include the action alternative, this subject said:] It shouldn't be in there, because basically I think that except in the most long-run sense there is not a thing you can do. Maybe we can breed a new line of professors [C-3].

We could go on here, if space permitted, about "the snobbishness we are all guilty of" and about the "queer birds" who "make a profession of being different" and "don't have sense enough to pour sand out of a boot" (these quotations coming from four different protocols).

This direct acceptance by intellectuals of the negative stereotype regarding intellectuals follows the pattern of the minority "self-hate" which Lewin has described in the case of the anti-Semitic Jew[13] and which has been clearly expressed in Negro color attitudes.[14]

A second, and somewhat less extreme, variety of minority attitude may be labeled *the concern with in-group purification.* This label points to language and behavior which are guided by the idea that the minority's troubles are rooted in the misguided ways of a small fraction among them. The parallel with traditional minorities reads: for the Jews, it is the "bad" Jew—the one who is, indeed, aggressive and loud—who breeds anti-Semitism; and, for the intellectuals, it is the radical, asocial types who are responsible for the group's difficulty. Thus, on the radical issue, one respondent, speaking of his effort to establish a research contact downtown, said:

> I realized we had one or two strikes against us because we were from the university. We had to have people vouch for us. We don't enjoy the best reputation down there; we're blamed for the actions of a few who make radical speeches and seem to overgeneralize [C-4].

Another respondent, speaking of an "extreme liberal" in his college, remarked:

> I've got nothing against it, but the average man might translate this [liberalism] over to our college. In this sense, he does a slight disservice to the college [C-5].

Similarly, on scores other than radicalism there are expressions of the view that the position of the intellectuals turns on the "impure" behavior of the intellectual himself. One respondent, discussing anti-intellectualism in general, remarked that we could lick the problem:

> If we had people getting out and who really did mix, as speakers and members. . . . I've worried about this: would I be willing to be in an organization if I were only a member? We get to be president and vice-president all the time. It doesn't do any good to be in and be officers; in order to get over the thought of us as intellectual snobs, we have to be satisfied to be just members [C-6].

This quotation highlights one interesting result of this concern with the "impure"—and a result which, again, has a clear minority flavor. The intellectual becomes involved in the need to prove that the impurity really is not there (or, at the very least, that the intellectual in question is not one of the "impure" few). We are familiar with the Jewish person who is inordinately careful to demonstrate in his own behavior that Jews as a group are not what the stereotype says; and Anatole Broyard has nicely described the various forms that Negro "inauthenticity" of the same type may take (for example, what he calls "role inversion" is a careful and extreme negation of precisely those qualities embodied in the Negro stereotype—"cool" music and passive behavior, for example, being a negation of the primitive, hot, carefree quality in the Negro stereotype).[15]

The interviews reveal a similar concern with disproving the stereotype. Thus, one respondent, discussing possible action alternatives, commented:

> We could, of course, go out and make talks to various groups— show them that intellectuals really aren't bad guys [C-7].

Another, speaking about the isolation of the intellectual, said:

> Well, in neighborhood isolation, there's a lot of it due to their initial reaction—when they find out you're a professor they slightly withdraw, but, if you continue to make connections, then they find out you're a human being [C-5].

Still another person commented:

> If we mixed more, and became known as people as well as college teachers, maybe it would be better. Frequently, the antipathy to college teachers melts when they meet you personally; though we do have a tendency to carry our classroom personality into other areas [C-8].

A third major category of minority-like response may be titled *the approval of conformity*. In a certain sense, of course, the pattern just described is a specialized form of conformity; for its main aim is to emphasize the conventional as against the divergent aspects of the intellectual's behavior. But the pressure for conformity goes beyond this. It involves the same kind of passive, conservative, and attention-avoiding behavior that Lewin has described as prototypical for minority leaders, his "leaders from the periphery."[16] And, in the long run, this pressure for conformity leads to assimilation—to the very denial of any significant observable differences on which minority status may rest. As far as the more traditional minorities are concerned, the classic Adorno volume on prejudice and personality has put one part of the conformist case as follows:

> Since acceptance of what is like oneself and rejection of what is different is one feature of the prejudiced outlook [that is, of the authoritarian personality], it may be that members of minority groups can in limited situations and for some period of time protect themselves and gain certain advantages by conforming in outward appearance as best they can with the prevailing ways of the dominant group.[17]

As with these minorities, we find that there is considerable commitment to conformity among intellectuals and that this is expressed variously as a need to adjust, to avoid controversy, or to assimilate and deny differences entirely. Thus, one respondent, discussing the conformity question raised in the letter, said:

> On that, I can't say I've experienced it. I'm in a pretty safe field. ... [He then described a book of readings he had collected and said that here was a short passage from a well-known writer which had been taken out before publication.] There's no use stirring up trouble. I don't think it was a lack of courage on my part. We thought—that is, the editor and I—that it was too touchy. It's a very beautiful thing, but we took it out [C-9].

Another individual, discussing the community life of the intellectual, noted that they often do not take an active part and added:

> Part of that is good, in that they are lending the prestige of the university when they do take part, and shouldn't be doing that. I don't want to be written up in the paper as Professor X of university holding a certain opinion. I've deliberately refrained from expressing political opinion [C-5].

Still others appear to argue for conformity by denying that there is a difference to which the notion of "intellectual" points:

> I don't feel any different from my electrican-neighbor [C-10].

> I get a kind of inferiority complex if they call me "professor"; I know that my work with the intellect is on the same level in the eyes of the man in the street as, say, a chain-store manager [C-11].

Or else there is insistence that it is important for the intellectual to assimilate or disguise himself more successfully. Thus, one respondent, speaking of occasions when he makes public addresses, said:

> When I go out and meet these people, I try to fit myself into their realm, into the climate of the various groups [C-12].

Another gave, as part of his recipe for the intellectual's behavior, the directive:

> He should adjust his personality so he can mix in better with the person who isn't an intellectual [C-2].

And one I have quoted before, speaking of the intellectual's isolation in community life, said:

> You must make concessions. I would find it pretty hard to have contacts, for example, in places like Wilder's *Our Town* or Anderson's small Ohio town, but I couldn't accuse the people in the town of being anti-intellectual; it's probably my fault. If you make a certain amount of concession, you will find a way [C-11].

There are other comments which are less clear in their conformist implications—for example, more than faintly guilty remarks to the effect that "my neighbors see me home in the early afternoon and wonder just what it is I do in my job" [C-13]. On the whole, there is considerable evidence in these protocols that the typical minority response of conformity is found in a variety of forms among intellectuals.[18]

The fourth category of response represents the extreme of minority assimilation from the standpoint of the individual, namely, *the denial of group membership*. Like the name-changing Jew and the Negro who "passes," many intellectuals find means to hide or escape their unwelcome identity. An interviewee nicely described this pattern as follows:

> One consequence of anti-intellectualism is for some intellectuals to deny that they are intellectuals. This is a behavioral denial; it's part of the psychological revolution, the adjustment trend. . . . The pressure to be well-adjusted is high, and so he becomes non-intellectual and begins to deny in some respects that he is an intellectual [C-15].

The evidence in the interviews indicates that the retreat from membership is a substantial one and takes many forms. Indeed, one of the real surprises, during the course of these interviews, was the rarity of real acceptance of intellectual status. This nonacceptance is revealed in several ways. First, there is the frequency with which this freely offered remark appears: "Intellectuals, I hate the word!" Second, there are the direct denials to the question, "Do you consider yourself an intellectual?" A complete listing of the protocol responses on this point would reveal a quite consistent, though subtly varied, pattern of maneuvering, all aimed at being counted out—the kind of "Who, me?" response one gets from the obviously guilty.[19] Thus, one respondent said:

> That's a word that always does bother me. I don't think of myself so. It's a self-conscious word that sets us apart from the rest of the population. The only thing that sets us apart, in fact, is that we have gone to school longer than some, and there are doctors who have gone longer, and we don't consider them intellectuals [C-10].

Another said:

> I don't apply it to myself. I never use it myself. It's sort of snobbish [C-17].

And still another:

> I would [use the designation "intellectual"] in the professional sense only. . . . Professionally, I suppose we can't avoid it. Only in the very narrow professional sense, in the sense that we are trying to improve the intellect of students, I suppose it applies. I don't see how a university professor can escape the narrow meaning of the term [C-1].

And, finally, one respondent clearly recognized the social definition of himself yet reflected no eagerness in his personal definition:

> I suppose I would [consider myself an intellectual]. . . . I don't know if I am twenty-four hours a day, but still I suppose my work would be classified or considered as intellectual. . . . I teach the best I can, and certainly I'm classified as an intellectual by the community, my neighbors, and my colleagues [C-9].

A third kind of denial of membership is shown in the efforts that are made to avoid having one's affiliation publicly known. Thus, one respondent said:

> When I'm away from the university, I usually have plenty of dirt under my nails, or I'm getting a harvest. Some of us fool ourselves into believing that the stain of our profession doesn't follow us. I can work with a carpenter for several weeks, and he has no notion I'm a university professor. I take a foolish pride, I suppose, in this [C-1].

Another remarked:

> By training we get so we show contempt for those who overgeneralize, as in the Rotary, and we don't want to be in arguments all the time so we stay away. And how often do we go out of the way to announce that we're college professors. I don't conceal it, but I don't volunteer it. It would change your relation to the group [C-4].

Thus, in one way or another, many of our respondents indicate that they do not cherish their name or identity as intellectuals; and they adopt a language of evasion and anonymity which is minority-like, indeed. Though one may argue that this rejection of the name is not, after all, so terribly important, it seems to me more reasonable, in this case, to see the "naming trouble" as an essential part of the status involved.[20]

The fifth, and last, category of minority-like response can be designated *the fear of group solidarity*. This label indicates behavior whose essential function is similar to the conformist response; namely, behavior calculated to keep the majority's attention off the minority as such. In our intellectuals this typically takes the form of strong resistance to any clearly identifiable group action on the group's problems; the answer lies, rather, in individual goodness. One respondent, in fact, while stating the case against group action, made the minority tie himself:

> The notion of action involves the whole place of the intellectual in society. In addition, direct action puts us in the position of special pleading. It's like a Jew going out and talking about anti-Semitism [C-7].

Another said:

> Individual action seems more feasible. One has to measure one's forces and deploy them properly. . . . If you try to organize a society for X, Y, or Z, and you have the right people on the letterhead, maybe you're O.K.; but otherwise you're considered radical. Many things can be carried out without anybody knowing there is an organization [C-18].

Still another remarked:

> I'm frankly very much afraid of any action that has the label of the organized action of the intellectuals—not afraid of what they might do, but of public reaction. It ought to be unorganized [C-19].

Many of those interviewed seem committed to "having an effect the individual way" and are against "forming an organization that's militant." They wish, in a certain sense, to be (as one respondent [C-20] described himself) "the kind of social actionist who never appears to be one." I am interested here not in asserting that the strategy of organizational effort is a sounder strategy but in noting that the arguments against it frequently reflect a desire—common in other minorities—not to become too visible or too aggressive in one's own interest.

III

Neither the quotations nor the categories above exhaust the minority language in these protocols. Moreover, I have intentionally failed to analyze or report in any fullness the more "positive" remarks on the intellectual's role in society or on the anti-intellectualism within university life itself (as one person put it [C-21]: "the destruction of the intellectual community within the university"). It was, in fact, only after the interviews were almost completed, and the variability in self-definition became ever more striking, that it was clear we might treat intellectual status directly, as one which presents a standard problem in minority adjustment.

I have argued elsewhere that marginalities of this kind provide the opportunity for the development of perspective and creativity—an opportunity whose realization depends upon the adjustment which is made to marginal status.[21] In this earlier study, using the Jews as a case in point, I found that favorable adjustment to marginality was, indeed, associated with what was called "intellectual perspective"; and it now seemed possible to apply the same general logic to this sample of intellectuals.

Certainly many have asserted that there is an inherent alienative potential—an inescapable degree of marginality—in the intellectual role; and the assertion usually follows that the individual's style of adjustment to this marginality affects his performance as an intellectual. The usual view, of course, is that those who are "frozen" by this marginality and who retreat into conformity are less creative as intellectuals. Cunliffe, almost incidentally, makes this tie between mode of adjustment and creativity in advancing his distinction between two types of American intellectuals, whom he calls the *"avant-garde"* and the "clerisy":

> So, if there have been many alienated Western intellectuals since 1800, whom I will label the *avant-garde,* there have also been others, [the "clerisy"] of similar intellectual weight, though as a rule of less creative brilliance, who have remained more or less attached to their society.[22]

The discovery, in the interviews, of so many and so varied responses to this marginal aspect of the intellectual's position suggested the possibility of testing, in a small-scale empirical way, such common assertions about the consequences (or correlates) of the intellectual's adjustment to marginality. The hypothesis to be tested parallels that given in my earlier paper on the Jews as a minority; namely, that those intellectuals who have successfully adjusted to the marginal character of their role—those who, let us say, reveal a minimum of our five minority-style attitudes toward themselves as intellectuals—will be, in turn, the more creative workers in their respective crafts.

For a provisional glimpse of such a test, and to illustrate at the same time one possible utility of the descriptive categories developed in the previous section, I attempted to score the forty protocols for evidence of commitment to, or rejection of, each of the five categories. At the same time, I asked a group of persons in the various departments (in all cases, men of higher academic rank than the individual in question) to judge the professional creativity of those interviewed. Creativity here refers to the ability to make the "given" problematic: the ability to challenge the routines and to provide alternatives to the standardized "right answers" in the respective fields.

Unfortunately, though expectedly, the free-response character of the interviews led to some serious limitations as far as the present more quantitative interest is concerned. For example, on two of the five minority categories (No. 2, "concern with in-group purification," and No. 5, "fear of in-group solidarity") more than one-third of the protocols received a score of 3, which indicated a lack of substantial evidence in the interview; and, in addition, among the remaining two-thirds of the cases, there was a very poor numerical split between "high" versus "low" adjustors on these two categories.

In view of these limitations, I shall not attempt to present what would amount to a complete, but premature, account of the adjustment ratings and creativity judgments.[23] But it is of illustrative interest to note what happened on the three remaining "minority response" categories where a more reasonable split between high versus low adjustment was obtained. "High" adjustment refers to a tendency to reject the use of the minority-like modes of response in self-description; "low" adjustment refers to a tendency to embody the indicated minority-type response. Table 1 reveals what was obtained when individuals who scored 3 (no evidence) on each category were eliminated and when the high and low adjustors were compared on their average creativity. The data in Table 1 are read as follows: For the twelve persons who scored either 4 or 5 on category 1 (that is, whose responses were antithetical to the acceptance of majority stereotypes about the intellectual), the mean creativity

TABLE 1. Mean Creativity Scores and Standard Deviations for Individuals Scored High versus Low on Three Categories of Minority Response to Intellectual Status

Adjust-ment Group	Category 1— Acceptance of Stereotypes			Category 3— Approval of Conformity			Category 4— Denial of Membership		
	N	Mean	S.D.	N	Mean	S.D.	N	Mean	S.D.
High	12	3.27	0.65	16	2.74	0.84	13	2.48	1.02
Low	13	2.54	1.19	15	2.53	1.35	15	2.34	1.06

score was 3.27, with a standard deviation of 0.65. For the thirteen persons who scored low in adjustment on this same category (that is, who revealed a clear tendency to accept negative stereotypes), the mean creativity score was 2.54, with a standard deviation of 1.19.

The differences in creativity between adjustment groups are consistently in the direction of higher ratings for those who do not use the minority-style response to intellectual status. Though the *N*'s are small, and the differences are not uniformly great, the trend is clear, and the difference between adjustment groups for Category 1 is statistically significant.[24]

I do not take this as an unequivocal demonstration of the hypothesis in question. For one thing, there are other variables of considerable relevance (for example, the age of the respondent) that cannot be controlled adequately in a sample of this size; and, in addition, questions remain open about the reliability of the adjustment ratings.[25] But for purposes of illustration the trend revealed in Table 1 is of considerable interest, for it suggests that the minority orientations I have attempted to specify here may be treated (provisionally, at least) not simply as categories of description but as relevant factors in the performance of the intellectual role as such.

It is customary, of course, to conclude by noting the need for further research—in this case, research on the forms and consequences of anti-intellectualism. But there is one crucial thing—to find, as we have, that many intellectuals adopt, without serious efforts to build a reasoned self-portrait, an essentially negative, minority view of themselves and to find, in addition, some plausible ground for believing that this failure in self-conception is not independent of role performance—gives a special cast to the usual call for research. Thus it would seem essential to recognize that this research must include, if we may call it that, an "inward" as well as an "outward" orientation—that is, we must presumably conduct two related research operations: a study of the attitudes that others take toward intellectuals as well as a more intensive study of the intellectuals' attitudes toward themselves. A serious effort along those lines might yield considerably more than the usual research project; it can become an opportunity for self-discovery.

REFERENCES

1. Merle Curti, "Intellectuals and Other People," *American Historical Review, 60* (1955), pp. 259–82.
2. See S. S. Sargent and T. Brameld, eds., "Anti-intellectualism in the United States," *Journal of Social Issues, 2,* No. 3 (1955); D. Bell, ed., *The New American Right* (New York: Criterion Books, 1955); and *Encounter, 4* and 5 (1955).
3. M. Gordon, "Social Class and American Intellectuals," *A.A.U.P. Bulletin, 40* (1955), p. 517.
4. The roster of those who have recently written, more or less directly, on the problem of the intellectual would comprise a list of the contemporary great and near-great in a variety of humanistic and social science fields (not to mention the physical sciences): for example, Schlesinger and Hofstadter in history; Parsons and Riesman in sociology; Tolman and Fromm in psychology. Two well-known older works that embody the spirit of self-study are those by Znaniecki (*The Social Role of the Man of Knowledge*) and Logan Wilson (*The Academic Man*). There have, of course, been many commentaries on the intellectual, especially in the more or less Marxist journals; but I am referring here to the more formally analytic mode of investigation.
5. It seemed wiser, with a limited sample, to hold staff level constant rather than sample all levels of permanent staff. The assistant-professor group was chosen for two reasons: (1) it was large enough to provide suitable frequencies, yet small enough to be manageable without taxing time and finances, and (2) it is, in the institution studied, basically a tenure group like the higher ranks but presumably less involved in official committee work and graduate work and therefore more likely to give the time required for interviewing.
6. The italicized portion of this letter was underlined in the original; but in one-half of the cases a more action-oriented statement was substituted for the underlined portion given here. The two types of letters were randomly alternated in the interviewing program. In the second version, the underlined sentence read: *"Let me emphasize that the purpose of*

these discussions is not only to achieve a clarification of issues on matters which are clearly controversial; but also to canvass suitable lines of action."
In all cases, at the end of the interview, the respondent was asked to comment on what his reaction to the letter would have been if the alternative not presented to him had been used. The variation in letter style is mentioned here for the sake of completeness; it is not directly relevant to the treatment of the interviews reported here. The proposed discussions never took place, owing to both the press of time and a certain lack of enthusiasm—a lack which the remainder of this paper may make more understandable.

7. This assertion, obviously, is an assumption, since the public definition of an intellectual is not a matter of empirical record, so far as I know. One could hold, further, that, if they are not so designated, they should be— that, in the ideal university, the group I have described would be identifiable as intellectuals in the sense of my stated definition. That definition has its difficulties, to be sure. For example, one might ask why an intellectual cannot believe that (or behave as if) ideas are of more than simply aesthetic interest, that ideas have consequences, and that the analysis of them serves a "pragmatic" end. A host of names come to mind of persons who would appear to have indorsed this view and whom we would presumably not wish to dismiss as intellectuals—for example, Marx, Lenin, Jefferson, among others. The best provisional answer to this, I should think, would be that being an intellectual is not the designation for a person but for a role and that many who play the intellectual role, and play it well, are also deeply involved with the course of societal and individual development. One does not need to say, therefore, that Marx was not an intellectual because he was also a revolutionary.

In any event, though this definition does not thoroughly solve matters, it does suggest a line of approach and clarifies, perhaps, the senses in which our sample may or may not be considered as members of the class. To my mind it is much less important to determine whether they are, so to speak, "in" or "out" of the category than it is to recognize that they are candidates in several senses: (1) in public definitions of them; (2) in their personal self-definitions; and (3) in the definition of a university ideal. The issue is nicely captured in Randall Jarrell's fictional *Pictures from an Institution*, where he says of an academic man: "He had never been what intellectuals consider an intellectual, but other people had thought him one, and he had had to suffer the consequences of their mistake" (p. 110).

8. R. L. Bruckberger, "An Assignment for Intellectuals," *Harper's*, 212 (1956), p. 69.

9. D. Riesman and N. Glazer, "Intellectuals and the Discontented Classes," *Partisan Review*, 22 (1955), p. 50.

10. M. Cunliffe, "The Intellectuals: II. The United States," *Encounter*, 20 (1955), p. 31.

11. A word is in order about the meaning of "minority" and the occasion for "surprise." On the latter I am aware of the fact that many occupational groups (and certainly "notorious" ones—for example, policemen, farmers, or traveling salesmen) develop somewhat negative images of themselves. But two special conditions make this case, it seems to me, somewhat dif-

ferent. First, we are dealing with a high status group (note, for example, their generally high placement in the North-Hatt prestige scale); and, second, we are dealing with a group whose very function, in good part, is the objective analysis of society and its products. On these grounds, I would argue that it is not enough to dismiss the problem by saying that all occupations reflect negative self-images or that the problem approach in the stimulus letter occasioned the results obtained. The question is: What occupations have stereotypes about them, in what degree, and how are these stereotypes handled by the incumbents, with what consequences? This is the broader problem to which this paper is addressed.

With regard to "minority": I use it here to designate a group against which categorical discrimination is practiced. A minority, in this view, is determined not by size but by the behavior of being subjected to categorical discrimination. It should be clear, however, that I am not attempting to prove that intellectuals *are* a minority in this sense but that they use the typical language and forms of the classical minority groups in their self-descriptions.

12. The source of each quotation from the interviews is identified by an assigned case number so that the reader may note the spread of the illustrations. Departmental identifications are avoided, though these would be of some interest, to preserve anonymity. There is, I presume, every reason to believe that the frequency and subtlety of minority responses will vary among universities and departments—by region, eminence, and the like. But it also seems reasonable to believe that the bulk of American universities are not substantially different from the one involved here.

13. Kurt Lewin, *Resolving Social Conflicts* (New York: Harper, 1948), pp. 186–200.

14. M. Seeman, "Skin Color Values in Three All-Negro School Classes," *American Sociological Review, 11* (1946), pp. 315–21.

15. Anatole Broyard, "Portrait of the Inauthentic Negro," *Commentary, 10* (1950), pp. 56–64.

16. Lewin, *op. cit.,* p. 196.

17. T. W. Adorno et al., *The Authoritarian Personality* (New York: Harper, 1950), p. 974.

18. Two of the respondents themselves commented on this "trimming of sails" in the university setting. One, for example, after noting an increase in anti-intellectual pressures, said:

> "If you work at the university, you want the outside to be as noncontroversial as possible; to say, 'Look at me, I'm just like anybody else.' This is part of the general line of not hurting the university by getting in the news in negative ways" [C-14].

Another person, in similar vein, remarked:

> "The intellectual is assuming more of the role of the nonintellectual and seeks to be a part of the gang—denies that he's different" [C-15].

19. Even where there is acceptance of the "intellectual" label, there is sometimes a suspicious belligerence about it. One respondent, who vigorously denied the validity of the view embodied in the stimulus letter and felt

that anti-intellectualism was a fictitious problem, said: "You need to live your life as if you were proud of it—talk it up" [C-16].

20. On a similar point Everett Hughes has written in an essay titled "What's in a Name": "Words are weapons. As used by some people the word 'Hebrew,' for example, is a poisoned dart. When a word is so expressively used, we are face to face with no simple matter of social politics, but with part of the social process itself. This is, in part, what Durkheim had in mind in his long discussion of collective symbols and concepts. Words, he pointed out, are not merely something that happens along with the social process, but are its very essence. Naming is certainly part of the social process in inter-ethnic and racial relations" (*Where Peoples Meet* [Glencoe, Ill.: Free Press, 1952], p. 139).

21. M. Seeman, "Intellectual Perspective and Adjustment to Minority Status," *Social Problems*, 3 (1956), pp. 142–53.

22. Cunliffe, *op. cit.*, p. 25.

23. I am indebted to Mrs. Frances Mischel, a graduate student in sociology and anthropology, for the two hundred "minority" ratings (five ratings on each of forty protocols). These ratings were "blind" as far as identification of individuals or specialty fields was concerned. They were done as independently as possible, as far as the five categories are concerned, to minimize "halo." A total of 120 creativity judgments by colleagues were secured; and the evidence suggests that there is substantial agreement among them. Both the adjustment and the creativity ratings were made on five-point scales. For minority adjustment, the scale read as follows: 1—very much evidence of this; 2—some evidence of this; 3—no evidence one way or the other; 4—some evidence of rejection of this mode of response; 5—clear evidence of rejection of this mode. The creativity scale ran simply from 1 ("low in creativity") to 5 ("high in creativity") and was accompanied by a full-page explanation of both the meaning of creativity in this context and the method to be used in making the ratings. It should be clear that the term "adjustment" does not refer to the standard psychological meaning of the term; it designates only whether the respondent reflects or does not reflect the five categories of response described here. Thus, "high adjustment" refers to those who scored either 4 or 5 on the given category; "low" refers to a score of 1 or 2 on the category.

24. A test of the homogeneity of the two variances for the adjustment groups yielded an F ratio which approximated the 0.05 level of significance and raised doubt about the wisdom of pooling the variances for the two groups in computing the t test between the creativity means. The obtained t ratio for the test of Category 1 was 1.841, a figure which is significant at the 0.05 level using a one-tailed test. Neither of the two remaining categories yielded a significant t. The method used to test for homogeneity of variance and for the significance of the difference between means is given in A. Edwards, *Statistical Methods for the Behavioral Sciences* (New York: Rinehart, 1954), pp. 271–74.

25. The question of reliability of ratings may not be a serious problem. The same judge who did the ratings in this case was also used in the previously mentioned study of Jewish adjustment; and in that case the ratings

of two independent judges, completing a task quite similar to the rating
task involved here, were quite reliable (see the paper cited in reference 21
above). I have not deemed it essential for purposes of this illustration to
compute another reliability figure for the judge in question.

Sociology and the Intellectuals:
An Analysis of a Stereotype
Bennett M. Berger

I

For some years, humanist intellectuals have been cultivating a
hostile stereotype of sociology and sociologists. Like other stereotypes, this one has its foundation in fact; like other stereotypes too,
its exaggerations, whether expressed in the language of annihilating
wit or of earnest bludgeoning, call for some serious comment. It is
surprising therefore, that the responses of sociologists have been anything but dispassionate. These responses range all the way from (1)
Daniel Lerner's polemical defense of sociology in his article analyzing the book reviews of *The American Soldier,* to (2) the posture of
tolerant disdain toward the "misguided" stereotype, to (3) a sort of
nervous embrace of the stereotype by sociologists themselves (which
attempts—usually unsuccessfully—to demonstrate that they do *too*
have a sense of humor), often involving a self-parody whose furtive
masochism is almost startling.

There is no real need to document the stereotype with exhaustive
quotations since it is rife enough in intellectual circles for everyone
to have had his own personal experience of it. The overt expression
of the stereotype in print is the exception, and whole articles devoted
to it are rare. The most common vehicle for its expression is the
derisive "remark" and the parenthetical aside. Occasionally, one finds
a curiously ambiguous statement like the following:

> Popular images are rarely entirely wrong; and if the mass media
> and the popular mind today see the social scientist as a man with
> pencil and pad in hand, buttonholing hapless citizens on the street,

Source: *Antioch Review, 17*:3 (September 1957), pp. 275–90. Reprinted by
permission of The Antioch Press.

the error is not in the observation—it is only in seeing the social scientist as the interviewer. . . . Today, no matter what the question
put to the social scientist, he begins his answer by composing a ques-
tionnaire, which he then gets filled out by having an appropriate
number of respondents interviewed. (In an introductory note by
Nathan Glazer to I. L. Perez' "The Interviewer at Work," *Commentary*, February 1953, p. 195.)

One of the interesting things in this statement is the apparent convergence of images held by the "popular mind" with those held by
intellectuals like Glazer. I say "apparent" because intellectuals do
not often share the stereotypes of the popular mind, and the quoted
instance is not one of the exceptions. Glazer does not describe a
popular image in his remarks, but a stereotype held by intellectuals.
Anyone who has done extensive interviewing of the "popular mind"
knows that ordinary people are generally naïvely interested as well
as pleased and flattered to be interviewed by a social scientist; it takes
considerable sophistication to feel disdainful of and superior to the
poised pencil of the interviewer. But in a curiously inverted "proof
by authority" Glazer attributes an image to the popular mind in order
to validate his own.

Using evidence like this demands some reading between the lines.
For example, nowhere in the above quotation does Glazer explicitly
state that the image supposedly held by the popular mind is an invidious one; it is largely a matter of tone, created by key connotative
words like "buttonholing," and "hapless," and "appropriate." Many
expressions of the stereotype are of this hit-and-run kind, and depend for their meaning and effect upon one's being "in" on the
current scapegoatology. For example, the poet and critic Randall
Jarrell explicates a few lines from a Robert Frost poem, then says,
"if you can't feel any of this, you *are* a Convention of Sociologists."
A remark like this would be meaningless to someone not "in" on the
current stereotype; to those who *are* "in," and presumably a good
number of readers are, it is very funny indeed. There are, of course,
more elaborate and heavy-handed assaults, J. P. Marquand's portrait
of W. Lloyd Warner in *Point of No Return* not being the only one.
Still, it is the light touch of people like Auden and Jarrell which
is most effective in spreading the stereotype.

Stereotypes, and hostile stereotypes especially, do injury to the group stereotyped, and it is or ought to be our responsibility to correct them. But stereotypes are not generally exorcised by pretending they do not exist, nor are they dispelled by polemic or a demonstration of innocence. Although founded in fact, stereotypes are non-rational, and flourish in spite of the preponderance of evidence against them. Thus arguing from facts to correct an emotional excrescence is vain. What we want to know are the conditions that have generated the stereotype and permitted it to grow. Knowing these, we can transcend polemic and use our understanding in more effective ways.

II

The stereotype of the sociologist has two dimensions, founded in contradictory beliefs which, in turn, have their source in the structure of the intellectual professions. The image of the sociologist as a pathetically ignorant and pompous bumbler (jargon-ridden, pretentious, and without insight) is based on the conviction that sociology has no special subject matter, and is therefore no science; its technical apparatus and methodological strictures are hence not only presumptuous but futile, and result only in pretentiousness and banality. The image of the sociologist as a Machiavellian manipulator, however, clearly rests on a recognition of the efficacy of scientific, especially statistical, techniques in dealing with a human subject matter. But both of these—the perceived failure as well as the perceived success of sociology—have elicited from the intellectuals a hostile response.

A. The Problem of Subject Matter: The Sociologist as Bumbler

The tendency to specialization in the intellectual professions submits them to pressure to define specifically a subject matter uniquely their own, in order to justify their existence in a profession- and specialty-conscious culture, to establish and preserve their identities with foundations and university administrations, and to demonstrate their utility and their subsequent right to public support. As new specializations develop, and claim professional status, entirely reasonable questions of justification can be raised. What can you do that others not trained in your profession cannot do? What competence has your training conferred on you that is denied to others because of their lack of such training? I take it that the flourishing health of the image of the sociologist as bumbler can in part be attributed to the failure of sociologists to answer these questions satisfactorily. Any discipline which claims as its special subject matter the domain of "social relations" or "social systems" or "society" or any of the other textbook-preface definitions claims not a special subject matter but the whole gamut of human experience, a claim which thousands of scholars and intellectuals are with good reason likely to dispute. Louis Wirth's definition of sociology as the study of that which is true of men by virtue of the fact that they have everywhere and at all times lived a group life strikes the eye as somewhat better, but runs into the difficulty of generally assuming that pretty nearly everything that is true of men is true by virtue of this fact.

It is in part due to this failure to meet the responsibility of defining one's professional competence simply and clearly to interested laymen that sociological "jargon," for example, is met with such resistance and resentment. Laymen react with no such rancor to the technical vocabularies of mathematics, the physical and natural sciences, and engineering because by an act of faith (based, to be sure, on a common-sense understanding of what these disciplines do) they decide that behind the jargon, which they do not understand (because it is a descriptive shorthand, familiarity with which requires special training), lies a *special subject matter amenable to technical treatment* which they *could* understand *if* they took the trouble. Thus the intelligent layman feels no shame or outrage at not being able to understand a technical article in a chemistry journal—or, for that matter, in not understanding the job specifications in a newspaper want ad for engineers. No such toleration is likely toward the technical vocabulary of sociology until it is accepted as a legitimate scientific profession.

That this acceptance is not forthcoming is due partly to the belief of many intellectuals that the technical vocabulary is not a natural concomitant of scientific enterprise, but rather an attempt to disguise the banality of the results of sociological studies: sociologists "belabor the obvious"; they lack insight, and substitute in its place a barrage of carefully "proven" platitudes. Doubtless, some sociologists do, but every intellectual discipline has its share of brilliant people, as well as hacks, and there is no reason to suppose that sociology has more than a normal complement of either. That the hacks are identified as *representative* of sociology is probably due more to judgments regarding the quality of sociological prose rather than to any analysis of the significance of its contents. Certainly, the prose of sociologists may seem clumsy when compared to the efforts of those whose business it is to write well. But whereas the results of scientific endeavor can legitimately be expected to be true and important, one cannot legitimately expect either that science be beautiful or that scientists be literary stylists.

In short, then, the hue and cry about the jargon and turgidity of sociological prose, about the pretentiousness of its methodology and the banality of its preoccupations, is meaningful as criticism only if one assumes that sociology has no special subject matter amenable to technical treatment; if it has not, then it must be judged by the same criteria as general essays on social and cultural topics. But as long as sociologists commit themselves to the traditions of science, and address their work not to a general literate audience, but to a community of their colleagues, these criticisms cannot seem other than beside the point. For the continuing application of aesthetic criteria of judgment to a nonaesthetic pursuit reveals only a refusal to grant to sociology the status of a science.

B. *The Threat of Technique: The Sociologist as Diabolist*

Stereotypes generally contain contradictory elements, and the stereotype of the sociologist is no exception. For along with his alleged gifts for the labored cliché and the clumsy, inept sentence, the sociologist is also credited with the diabolical potential of making puppets out of men, of destroying their individuality with IBM machines, of robbing them of their "individual human dignity," and presiding, finally, over their total mechanization. This image of the sociologist as diabolist rests not on a conviction regarding the failure to define a specific subject matter, but on a fear regarding the success of sociological techniques, particularly statistics, which is seen by some intellectuals as *threatening* in two ways. First, the possibility of a science of society apparently implies the possibility of human behavior being controlled or manipulated by those who know its "causes" or by those with access to this knowledge. This vision, fostered by stimulus-response psychology, nourished by the "sociological perspective," which finds the source of individual behavior in group influences (and thus runs head on into the myth of the autonomous individual), and made fearful by reports of brain washing and by novels like *1984* and *Brave New World,* is perhaps responsible for the peculiar ambivalence felt by some intellectuals toward the very *desirability* of a science of society. Sociology is thus seen as a potential threat to democratic society. Second, and more relevant in the present context, is the fact that the application of the techniques of science to human behavior is perceived as a threat to the viability of the most basic function of intellectuals in the Western tradition: to comment on and to interpret the meaning of contemporary experience.

III

The noun "intellectual" is one of those words which, in spite of lack of consensus regarding their meaning, continue to flourish in common usage. Attempts to define the term, to ask who the intellectuals are or what the intellectuals do, while useful, have seemed to me inconclusive. Certainly some intellectuals are "detached" or "free-floating"; surely a great number are "alienated"; doubtless "neurosis" is widespread among them; "irresponsibility," although currently out of fashion, is nevertheless affirmed by some of them. There is great magic in some of their bows; but, like Philoctetes, they often carry a corresponding wound whose stench forces them to live somewhat marginally. Finally, it is true that they create and transmit cultural values—sometimes. There are, however, two difficulties with these and similar attempts at definition. First, the relation between the key criteria of the definitions and the perspectives of the definers is generally only too transparent. Second, and for my purposes more interesting, is that although the word is part of common usage, the attempts to define it have generally ignored this fact. I propose here first to ask not who the intellectuals are or what they do, but rather who they are *thought* to be—whom do people have in mind when they use the term?—and only then to go on to the other questions.

In this connection, I was present a few years ago at a forum on "The Role of the Intellectual in Modern Society" held at The Museum of Modern Art in New York. The panel members were Granville Hicks, Clement Greenberg, W. H. Auden, and Robert Gorham Davis. Auden spoke last, and at one point in his remarks he looked around at his colleagues on the platform as if to take note of the experts chosen to talk on this topic. Hicks, he said, was a novelist and literary critic; Davis was a literary critic and English professor; Greenberg was an art critic and an editor of *Commentary;* and Auden identified himself as a poet and critic. Had this forum been held in the Middle Ages, he pointed out, we panel members would have been mostly members of the clergy; in the sixteenth and seventeenth centuries, we would have been mostly natural scientists; in the twentieth century, we are mostly literary men. Auden did not attempt to answer the question that he had left implicit, but the question is a very leading one because the contemporary image of the intellectual *is,* I believe, essentially a literary one—and in two senses: he is conceived *as* a literary man, and this conception has been reinforced by the fact that it is literary men who have been most interested in, and who have written most on, the problem of the intellectual.

But it would be a mistake to assume that, because the intellectual is conceived in the image of the literary man, his essential property is that he is an artist or a student of literature. His identification as an intellectual rests not on the aesthetic value of his novels, plays, poems, essays, or literary criticism, but on his assumption, through them, of the role of *commentator on contemporary culture and interpreter of contemporary experience.* But if the intellectuals are those who assume this role, Auden's implicit question still remains: Why, in our time, has it been typically literary men who have assumed the role of the intellectual? It is in attempting to answer this question that the relation between "the intellectuals" and the stereotyping of sociologists will become clear.

In our time literary men have pre-empted the intellectual's role because of (a) their maximal freedom from the parochial demands of technical specialization, (b) their freedom (within their status as literary men) to make large and uncompromising judgments about values, and (c) their maximal freedom from institutional restraints.

A. Specialization

Intellectuals, I have said, are commentators on contemporary culture and interpreters of contemporary experience; they are critics, liberal or conservative, radical or reactionary, of contemporary life. The range of their competence is not circumscribed; it includes nothing less than the entire cultural life of a people. If they are academic men, they may be specialists in various subjects; but their professional specialties do not generally interfere with their being intellectuals. In the humanities, and particularly in literature, a specialty usually consists of *expertise* regarding a given historical period and the figures important to one's discipline who are associated with it: Dr. Johnson and the English literature of the eighteenth century; the significance of Gide in the French literature of the twentieth century; Prince Metternich and the history of Europe after 1815; Kant, Hegel, and German Idealism 1750–1820. Specialties like these do not militate against one's assuming the role of the intellectual, because the traditions of humanistic study encourage the apprehension of cultural wholes; they encourage commentary and interpretation regarding the "backgrounds"—social, cultural, intellectual, spiritual—of the subject matter one is expert about. The humanities—and particularly literature—offer to intellectuals a professional status which impedes little if at all the fulfillment of their function as intellectuals. On the other hand, the commitment of empirical sociology to "scientific method" frequently renders it incompetent to deal with the "big problems," and often instills in sociologists a trained incapacity to say anything they cannot prove.

B. Values

In commenting on contemporary culture and in interpreting contemporary experience, intellectuals are under no seriously sanctioned injunction to be "detached" or "objective." Unlike the sociologist, who functions under the rule of strict separation between facts and values, the intellectual is expected to judge and evaluate, to praise and blame, to win adherents to his point of view and to defend his position against his intellectual enemies. In the context of free debate among intellectuals, the exercise of this function takes the form of polemics; in an academic context, it develops into the phenomenon of "schools of thought." The point is that, whereas in sociology the existence of schools of thought is an embarrassment to everyone (since it is a constant reminder that not enough is *known*—in science, opinion is tolerated only where facts are not available), in the humanities the existence of schools of thought is accepted as normal and proper, because the humanities actively encourage evaluation, the development of point of view, and heterogeneity of interpretation.

C. *Freedom from Institutional Restraints*

Literary men have been able, more than members of other intellectual professions, to resist the tendencies toward the bureaucratization of intellectual life. This has been possible because of the large market for fiction in the United States, and because of the opportunities of selling critical and interpretive articles to the high- and middle-brow magazines, which, in spite of repeated protestations to the contrary, continue to flourish in this country. The ability of free lance writers to support themselves without depending upon a salary from a university or other large organization maximizes their freedom to be critics of contemporary life. Such opportunities are not typically available to sociologists. In addition, major sociological research is increasingly "team" research, while literary and humanistic research in universities is still largely a matter of individual scholarship. Obviously, collective responsibility for a work restrains the commentaries and interpretations of its authors; the individual humanistic scholar, usually responsible only to himself, is free from the restraints imposed by the conditions of collective research.

The purpose of this discussion of the intellectuals has been to highlight the fact that although sociology has arrogated to itself the right to *expertise* regarding society and culture, its commitment to the traditions of science (narrow specialization, objectivity, and team research) militates against sociologists assuming the role of the intellectual. The business of intellectuals has always been the critical discussion and evaluation of the affairs of contemporary men, or, if

I may repeat it once more, to comment on contemporary culture and interpret contemporary experience. When the sociologist arrogates *expertise* regarding the affairs of contemporary men, he is perceived as saying, in effect, that he *knows* more about the affairs of contemporary men than the intellectual does; and once this implication is received into the community of intellectuals, the issue is joined. The fact of this implication becomes one more fact of contemporary experience to which the intellectuals can devote their critical faculties—and with considerable relish, because the implication seems to threaten the basis of their right to the position which, as intellectuals, they hold.

Even those intellectuals with sympathies for the goals of sociology often exhibit a fundamental underestimation of the consequences of its commitment to science. The characteristic plea of these people is an exhortation to "grapple with the *big* problems." Although this advice is without doubt well intentioned, it characteristically underestimates the degree to which the mores of science and the responsibility of foundations and university research institutes can command the type of work sociologists do. I mean by this simply that the sociologist is responsible to the community of social scientists for the *scientific* value of his work, and that university research institutes are sensitive to charges of financing "biased" or "controversial" research (a possibility that is maximized when one deals with the "big problems"). And when the "big problems" *are* grappled with, for example, in books like *The American Soldier* and *The Authoritarian Personality,* or in other types of work like *The Lonely Crowd, White Collar,* and *The Power Elite,* controversy and polemic follow. For the sympathetic intellectual's exhortation to the sociologist to "grapple with the big problems" says, in effect, "don't be a scientist, be a humanist; be an intellectual." This implication is supported by the respectful (if not totally favorable) reception given by intellectuals to the works of Riesman and Mills (least encumbered with the trappings of science), and their utter hostility to works like *The American Soldier,* which fairly bristles with the method of science.

There is one more source of the intellectual's hostility to sociology that I would like to examine, a source that was anticipated by Weber in his lecture on science as a vocation. For if it is true that intellectualization and rationalization, to which science commits itself and of which it is a part, means "that principally there are no mysterious incalculable forces that come into play, but rather that one can, in principle, master all things by calculation," then it is not only true, as Weber said, that "the world is disenchanted," but also true that the social scientist is perceived as challenging that tradition of humanism and art which has subsisted on the view that the world *is* enchanted, and that man is the mystery of mysteries. To the carriers of this tradition, every work of art and every poetic insight constitutes further proof that the world is enchanted, and that the source of man's gift to make art and to have poetic insight is a mystery made more mysterious by each illumination. The power of this tradition should not be underestimated; it is well rooted in the thinking of modern literature, with its antiscientific temper and its faith in the recalcitrance of men to yield up their deepest secrets to the generalizations of science. From Wordsworth's "to dissect is to kill," to Mallarmé's "whatever is sacred, whatever is to remain sacred, must be clothed in mystery," to Cummings' "mysteries alone are significant," the tradition has remained strong. And surely, it must have reached its apotheosis when, before a Harvard audience, Cummings made the following pronouncement:

> I am someone who proudly and humbly affirms that love is the mystery of mysteries, and that nothing measurable matters "a very good God damn": that "an artist, a man, a failure," is no mere whenfully accreting mechanism, but a givingly eternal complexity— neither some soulless and heartless ultrapredatory infra-animal nor any un-understandingly knowing and believing and thinking automaton, but a naturally and miraculously whole human being—a feelingly illimitable individual; whose only happiness is to transcend himself, whose every agony is to grow. (E. E. Cummings, *six nonlectures* [Cambridge: Harvard University Press, 1955], pp. 110–11.)

Intellectuals in this tradition seem to believe that the fulfillment of the goals of social science necessarily means that the creative powers of man will be "explained away," that his freedom will be denied, his "naturalness" mechanized, and his "miraculousness" made formula; that Cummings' "feelingly illimitable individual" will be shown up as a quite limited and determined "social product," whose every mystery and transcendence can be formulated, if not on a pin, then within the framework of some sociological theory. It is no wonder, then, that a vision as fearsome as this can provoke the simultaneous convictions that a science of society is both impossible and evil.

IV

It is no great step from the stereotypes consequent to ethnic and racial diversity to the stereotypes consequent to the diversity of occupational specialization. In those occupations which claim technical, professional status, occupations in which advanced, specialized training is necessary, it is likely that occupational stereotypes should find fertile ground because those on the "outside" have only secondary, derivative "knowledge" of the occupation. It is likely to be even more true of those professions which, like sociology, are so new that the nature of their subject matter is still being discussed by their members, and *still* more true if the new profession, by arrogating to itself a field of study formerly "belonging" to someone else (or to everyone else), raises, either intentionally or unintentionally by implication, invidious questions of relative competence.

Noteworthy in this regard is the fact that the social sciences which have been most active in the "interdisciplinary" tendencies of recent years are sociology, cultural anthropology, and psychology—precisely those disciplines with the most broadly defined subject matter. Each of these claims nothing less, in effect, than the totality of man's nonphysiological behavior as the field of its special competence; and it is no wonder that economics and political science, whose claims are considerably more modest (that is, whose subject matter is relatively clearly and narrowly defined), have not found it strikingly to their interests to participate much in this convergence. For it is no doubt partly a matter of common professional interest as well as a matter of theoretical clarification that is behind this pooling of their intellectual resources by sociologists, anthropologists, and psychologists. The satire (which invokes the extant stereotype) to which social scientists are submitted is of common concern to them, for the public image of the social sciences, largely created by the commentaries of intellectuals on them, is related to the amount of public support that the social sciences receive.

The stereotype of sociology and sociologists is part of a larger configuration which stereotypes social science in general; sociology, however, is the most successfully maligned of the social sciences. This special vulnerability is due largely to its relative lack of the sources of prestige available to the other social sciences. Economics commands a respect consequent to its age, to the generally accepted legitimacy of its subject matter, to its demonstrated usefulness, and to the wide variety of jobs available to people trained in it. Cultural anthropology borrows scientific prestige from physical anthropology and archeology, and gets some of its own as a result of its concern with the esoteric subject matter of primitive peoples. Political science has the prestigious correlates of law, diplomacy, and international relations. Clinical psychology has the towering figure of Freud, an affinity to medicine, and the presence of the almost mythic dimensions of The Psychiatrist. Unlike economics, sociology has no hoary past, and no long line of employers clamoring for access to its skills. Unlike clinical psychology, it has no founding figure generally recognized as seminal in the history of western science; and the tenuousness of the concept of a "sick society" denies to sociology the status of a clinical discipline, and hence the prestige that accrues to The Healer. Unlike political science, it has neither an empirical nor an historical relation to the high concerns of nations, governments, or law; and unlike cultural anthropology, it has neither empirical roots nor an esoteric subject matter. Not only is sociology's subject matter not esoteric, but its traditional concern with such peripheral problems of social life as crime, delinquency, and divorce, and others conventionally classified under the rubric "social disorganization," quite likely tends, as Merton has suggested, to diminish its prestige.

Sociology, then, is *vulnerable* to stereotyping; its position in the contemporary structure of the intellectual professions exposes it to criticism from all sides. In numbers the weakest of the social sciences, it is the bastard son of the humanities, from which it gets its subject matter, and the sciences, from which it gets its methods. Fully acknowledged by neither parent, it finds itself in the role of *upstart*, now utilizing the existing methods of science, now improvising new scientific methods, in an attempt to make the enchanted data of the humanities yield up their mysteries.

Like ethnic stereotypes, which are fostered by segregation and reinforced by the consequent cultural isolation, intellectual stereotypes are fostered by professional specialization and reinforced by the diverse (and sometimes conflicting) perspectives developed in each. The lack of an intellectual perspective that transcends the provincialism generated by the limitations of a specialized perspective makes one susceptible to clichés and stereotypic thinking about related fields of study. In race and interethnic relations, the marginal man has, with his proverbial "one foot in each culture," provided this transcendent perspective. Humanist intellectuals can fulfill this function in intellectual life by addressing their criticisms of sociology *to sociologists,* rather than to their own colleagues; for it is the ironic fact that in writing to his own colleagues about sociology, the humanist intellectual himself tends to use obvious clichés to which his immersion in his own perspective blinds him. The kind of cross-fertilization that might be achieved by having humanist intellectual perspectives critically directed at an *audience of sociologists,* perhaps *in* a sociological journal, might go a long way toward providing this transcendent perspective.

B C D E F G H I J   9 8 7 6 5 4 3 2 1